SOCIAL SECURITY LE
SUPPLEMENT 2

General Editor
Nick Wikeley, M.A. (C.....,

Commentary by
Ian Hooker, LL.B.
Formerly Lecturer in Law, University of Nottingham
Formerly Chairman, Social Security Appeal Tribunals

John Mesher, B.A., B.C.L. (Oxon), LL.M. (Yale)
Retired Judge of the Upper Tribunal
Emeritus Professor of Law, University of Sheffield

Edward Mitchell, LL.B.
Judge of the Upper Tribunal

Mark Rowland, LL.B.
Retired Judge of the Upper Tribunal

Tom Royston, M.A. (Cantab)
Barrister

Christopher Ward, M.A. (Cantab)
Judge of the Upper Tribunal

Nick Wikeley, M.A. (Cantab)
Judge of the Upper Tribunal,
Emeritus Professor of Law, University of Southampton

Consultant Editor
Child Poverty Action Group

SWEET & MAXWELL

THOMSON REUTERS

Published in 2023 by Thomson Reuters,
trading as Sweet & Maxwell.
Registered in England & Wales. Company No. 1679046.
Registered office and address for service: 5 Canada Square, Canary
Wharf, London, E14 5AQ.

For further information on our products and services, visit
http://www.sweetandmaxwell.co.uk.

Typeset by Wright and Round Ltd., Gloucester
Printed and bound by CPI Group (UK) Ltd, Croydon, CR0 4YY

A CIP catalogue record for this book is
available from the British Library.

ISBN (print): 978-0-41411-188-2
ISBN (e-book): 978-0-41411-190-5
ISBN (print and e-book): 978-0-41411-189-9

FSC
www.fsc.org
MIX
Paper | Supporting
responsible forestry
FSC® C013604

PREFACE

This is the Supplement to the 2022/23 edition of *Social Security Legislation*, which was published in September 2022 in four volumes. Part I of this Supplement contains new legislation, presented in the same format as in the main volumes. Parts II, III, IV and V contain the standard updating material—a separate Part for each volume of the main work—which amends the legislative text and key aspects of the commentary, drawing attention to important recent case law, so as to be up to date as at December 5, 2022 (although we have squeezed in some more recent case law developments thanks to the generous understanding of our publishers Sweet & Maxwell). Part VI comprises the cumulative updating material for Volume V, *Income Support and the Legacy Benefits*, which was last published in the 2021/22 edition. Finally, Part VII gives some notice of changes forthcoming between December 2022 and the date to which the main work (2023/24 edition) will be up to date (mid-April 2023) along with the April 2023 benefit rates.

The updating changes in this Supplement include a multitude of amendments to both the primary and secondary legislation governing social security provision. There is detailed analysis of the developing case law on universal credit, now the main means-tested benefit. As ever, the text also covers important developments in the Upper Tribunal jurisprudence relating to the descriptors for personal independence payment (PIP) (appeals for these benefits form the great bulk of social security cases heard by the First-tier Tribunal (Social Entitlement Chamber)). There have in addition been significant changes to devolved social security provision in Scotland, including the introduction of Adult Disability Payments.

As always, we welcome comments from those who use this Supplement. Please address these to the General Editor, Nick Wikeley, c/o School of Law, The University of Southampton, Highfield, Southampton SO17 1BJ (njw@soton.ac.uk).

Ian Hooker
John Mesher
Edward Mitchell
Mark Rowland
Tom Royston
Christopher Ward
Nick Wikeley

February 16, 2023

CONTENTS

USING THE UPDATING MATERIAL IN THIS SUPPLEMENT

The amendments and updating material contained in Parts II–VI of this Supplement are keyed to the page numbers of the relevant main volume of *Social Security Legislation 2022/23*. Where there have been a significant number of changes to a provision, the whole section, subsection, paragraph or regulation, as amended will tend to be reproduced. Other changes may be noted by an instruction to insert or substitute new material or to delete part of the existing text. The date the change takes effect is also noted. Where explanation is needed of the change, or there is updating relating to existing annotations but no change to the legislation, you will also find commentary in this Supplement. The updating material explains new statutory material, takes on board Upper Tribunal or court decisions, or gives prominence to points which now seem to warrant more detailed attention.

For the most part any relevant new legislation since the main volumes were published is contained in Part I, while amendments to existing legislative provisions are contained in Parts II–VI respectively, together with commentary on new case law. This Supplement amends the text of the main volumes of *Social Security Legislation 2022/23* to be up-to-date as at December 5, 2022.

Nick Wikeley
General Editor

PAGES OF MAIN VOLUMES AFFECTED
BY MATERIAL IN THIS SUPPLEMENT

Main volume
page affected

Relevant paragraph
in supplement

VOLUME I

Main volume page affected	Relevant paragraph in supplement
p.101	2.001
p.114	2.002
p.117	2.003
p.236	2.004
p.325	2.005
pp.332–335	2.006
p.337	2.007
p.368	2.008
p.413	2.008A
p.459	2.009
p.470	2.010
p.521	2.011
p.534	2.012
p.562	2.013
pp.573–574	2.014
pp.610–611	2.015
pp.613–614	2.016
pp.657–658	2.017
p.772	2.018
p.775	2.019
p.789	2.020
p.794	2.021
p.865	2.022
p.904	2.023
p.905	2.024
p.908	2.025
p.922	2.026
p.933	2.027
p.935	2.028
p.1128	2.029
pp.1136–1138	2.030
pp.1152–1155	2.031
p.1159	2.032
pp.1205–1207	2.033
p.1221	2.034
p.1240	2.035
p.1256	2.036
p.1290	2.037
p.1303	2.038

VOLUME V

Main volume page affected	Relevant paragraph in supplement
p.1146	6.052
p.1147	6.053
p.1149	6.054
p.1151	6.055
p.1153	6.056
pp.1167–1168	6.057
p.1168	6.058
p.1177	6.059
p.1184	6.060
p.1187	6.061
p.1188	6.062
p.1209	6.063
p.1209	6.064
p.1220	6.065
p.1230	6.066
pp.1238–1239	6.067
p.1250	6.068
p.1260	6.069
p.1302	6.070
pp.1334–1335	6.071
pp.1341–1342	6.072
p.1373	6.073
p.1377	6.074
p.1378	6.075
p.1382	6.076
p.1413	6.077
pp.1431–1432	6.078
pp.1494–1496	6.079
pp.1507–1514	6.080
pp.1525–1532	6.081
p.1540	6.082
p.1542	6.083
p.1544	6.084
p.1546	6.085
pp.1558–1559	6.086
p.1559	6.087
pp.1565–1566	6.088
p.1613	6.089
p.1613	6.090
p.1615	6.091
pp.1663–1664	6.092
pp.1670–1672	6.093
pp.1670–1672	6.094
p.1674	6.095
p.1681	6.096
pp.1681–1683	6.097
p.1732	6.098

TABLE OF ABBREVIATIONS USED IN THIS SERIES

Table of Abbreviations used in this Series

ASPP	Additional Statutory Paternity Pay
A.T.C.	Annotated Tax Cases
Attendance Allowance Regulations	Social Security (Attendance Allowance) Regulations 1991
AWT	All Work Test
BA	Benefits Agency
Benefits Act	Social Security Contributions and Benefits Act 1992
B.H.R.C.	Butterworths Human Rights Cases
B.L.G.R.	Butterworths Local Government Reports
Blue Books	*The Law Relating to Social Security*, Vols 1–11
B.P.I.R.	Bankruptcy and Personal Insolvency Reports
B.T.C.	British Tax Cases
BTEC	Business and Technology Education Council
B.V.C.	British Value Added Tax Reporter
B.W.C.C.	Butterworths Workmen's Compensation Cases
c.	chapter
C	Commissioner's decision
C&BA 1992	Social Security Contributions and Benefits Act 1992
CAA 2001	Capital Allowances Act 2001
CAB	Citizens Advice Bureau
CAO	Chief Adjudication Officer
CB	Child Benefit
CBA 1975	Child Benefit Act 1975
CBJSA	Contribution-Based Jobseeker's Allowance
C.C.L. Rep.	Community Care Law Reports
CCM	HMRC *New Tax Credits Claimant Compliance Manual*
C.E.C.	European Community Cases
CERA	cortical evoked response audiogram
CESA	Contribution-based Employment and Support Allowance
CFS	chronic fatigue syndrome
Ch.	Chancery Division Law Reports; Chapter
Charter	Charter of Fundamental Rights of the European Union
Citizenship Directive	Directive 2004/38/EC of the European Parliament and of the Council of April 29, 2004
CJEC	Court of Justice of the European Communities

CJEU	Court of Justice of the European Union
Claims and Payments Regulations	Social Security (Claims and Payments) Regulations 1987
Claims and Payments Regulations 1979	Social Security (Claims and Payments) Regulations 1979
Claims and Payments Regulations 2013	Universal Credit, Personal Independence Payment, Jobseeker's Allowance and Employment and Support Allowance (Claims and Payments) Regulations 2013
CM	Case Manager
CMA	Chief Medical Adviser
CMEC	Child Maintenance and Enforcement Commission
C.M.L.R.	Common Market Law Reports
C.O.D.	Crown Office Digest
COLL	*Collective Investment Schemes Sourcebook*
Community, The	European Community
Computation of Earnings Regulations	Social Security Benefit (Computation of Earnings) Regulations 1978
Computation of Earnings Regulations 1996	Social Security Benefit (Computation of Earnings) Regulations 1996
Consequential Provisions Act	Social Security (Consequential Provisions) Act 1992
Contributions and Benefits Act	Social Security Contributions and Benefits Act 1992
Contributions Regulations	Social Security (Contributions) Regulations 2001
COPD	chronic obstructive pulmonary disease
CP	Carer Premium; Chamber President
CPAG	Child Poverty Action Group
CPR	Civil Procedure Rules
Cr. App. R.	Criminal Appeal Reports
CRCA 2005	Commissioners for Revenue and Customs Act 2005
Credits Regulations 1974	Social Security (Credits) Regulations 1974
Credits Regulations 1975	Social Security (Credits) Regulations 1975
Crim. L.R.	Criminal Law Review
CRU	Compensation Recovery Unit
CSA 1995	Children (Scotland) Act 1995
CSIH	Inner House of the Court of Session (Scotland)
CSM	Child Support Maintenance
CS(NI)O 1995	Child Support (Northern Ireland) Order 1995
CSOH	Outer House of the Court of Session (Scotland)

CSPSSA 2000	Child Support, Pensions and Social Security Act 2000
CTA	Common Travel Area
CTA 2009	Corporation Tax Act 2009
CTA 2010	Corporation Tax Act 2010
CTB	Council Tax Benefit
CTC	Child Tax Credit
CTC Regulations	Child Tax Credit Regulations 2002
CTF	child trust fund
CTS	Carpal Tunnel Syndrome
DAC	Directive 2011/16/ EU (Directive on administrative co-operation in the field of taxation)
DAT	Disability Appeal Tribunal
dB	decibels
DCA	Department for Constitutional Affairs
DCP	Disabled Child Premium
Decisions and Appeals Regulations 1999	Social Security Contributions (Decisions and Appeals) Regulations 1999
Dependency Regulations	Social Security Benefit (Dependency) Regulations 1977
DfEE	Department for Education and Employment
DHSS	Department of Health and Social Security
Disability Living Allowance Regulations	Social Security (Disability Living Allowance) Regulations
DIY	do it yourself
DLA	Disability Living Allowance
DLA Regs 1991	Social Security (Disability Living Allowance) Regulations 1991
DLAAB	Disability Living Allowance Advisory Board
DLADWAA 1991	Disability Living Allowance and Disability Working Allowance Act 1991
DM	Decision Maker
DMA	Decision-making and Appeals
DMG	*Decision Makers' Guide*
DMP	Delegated Medical Practitioner
DP	Disability Premium
DPT	diffuse pleural thickening
DPTC	Disabled Person's Tax Credit
DRO	Debt Relief Order
DSD	Department for Social Development (Northern Ireland)

DSM IV; DSM-5	Diagnostic and Statistical Manual of Mental Disorders of the American Psychiatric Association
DSS	Department of Social Security
DTI	Department of Trade and Industry
DWA	Disability Working Allowance
DWP	Department for Work and Pensions
DWPMS	Department for Work and Pensions Medical Service
EAA	Extrinsic Allergic Alveolitis
EEA EFTA Separation Agreement	Agreement on arrangements between Iceland, the Principality of Liechtenstein, the Kingdom of Norway and the United Kingdom of Great Britain and Northern Ireland following the withdrawal of the United Kingdom from the European Union, the EEA agreement and other agreements applicable between the United Kingdom and the EEA EFTA States by virtue of the United Kingdom's membership of the European Union
EEA Regulations 2016	Immigration (European Economic Area) Regulations 2016
EAT	Employment Appeal Tribunal
EC	European Community
ECHR	European Convention on Human Rights
ECJ	European Court of Justice
E.C.R.	European Court Reports
ECSC	European Coal and Steel Community
ECSMA	European Convention on Social and Medical Assistance
EEA	European Economic Area
EEC	European Economic Community
EESSI	Electronic Exchange of Social Security Information
E.G.	Estates Gazette
E.G.L.R.	Estates Gazette Law Reports
EHC plan	education, health and care plan
EHIC	European Health Insurance Card
EHRC	European Human Rights Commission
E.H.R.R.	European Human Rights Reports
EL	employers' liability
E.L.R	Education Law Reports
EMA	Education Maintenance Allowance
EMP	Examining Medical Practitioner
Employment and Support Allowance Regulations	Employment and Support Allowance Regulations 2008

EPS	extended period of sickness
Eq. L.R.	Equality Law Reports
ERA	evoked response audiometry
ERA scheme	Employment, Retention and Advancement scheme
ES	Employment Service
ESA	Employment and Support Allowance
ESA Regs 2013	Employment and Support Allowance Regulations 2013
ESA Regulations	Employment and Support Allowance Regulations 2008
ESA WCAt	Employment and Support Allowance Work Capability Assessment
ESC	employer supported childcare
ESE Scheme	Employment, Skills and Enterprise Scheme
ESE Regulations	Jobseeker's Allowance (Employment, Skills and Enterprise Scheme) Regulations 2011
ESES Regulations	Jobseeker's Allowance (Employment, Skills and Enterprise Scheme) Regulations 2011
ETA 1973	Employment and Training Act 1973
ETA(NI) 1950	Employment and Training Act (Northern Ireland) 1950
ETS	European Treaty Series
EU	European Union
Eu.L.R.	European Law Reports
EWCA Civ	Civil Division of the Court of Appeal (England and Wales)
EWHC Admin	Administrative Court, part of the High Court (England and Wales)
FA 1993	Finance Act 1993
FA 1996	Finance Act 1996
FA 2004	Finance Act 2004
Fam. Law	Family Law
FAS	Financial Assistance Scheme
F.C.R.	Family Court Reporter
FEV	forced expiratory volume
FIS	Family Income Supplement
FISMA 2000	Financial Services and Markets Act 2000
F.L.R.	Family Law Reports
FME	further medical evidence
F(No.2)A 2005	Finance (No.2) Act 2005
FOTRA	Free of Tax to Residents Abroad
FRAA	flat rate accrual amount

Table of Abbreviations used in this Series

FRS Act 2004	Fire and Rescue Services Act 2004
FSCS	Financial Services Compensation Scheme
FTT	First-tier Tribunal
General Benefit Regulations 1982	Social Security (General Benefit) Regulations 1982
General Regulations	Statutory Shared Parental Pay (General) Regulations 2014
GMCA	Greater Manchester Combined Authority
GMFRA	Greater Manchester Fire and Rescue Authority
GMP	Guaranteed Minimum Pension
GMWDA	Greater Manchester Waste Disposal Authority
GNVQ	General National Vocational Qualification
GP	General Practitioner
GRA	Gender Recognition Act 2004
GRB	Graduated Retirement Benefit
GRP	Graduated Retirement Pension
HB	Housing Benefit
HB (WSP) R (NI) 2017	Housing Benefit (Welfare Social Payment) Regulations (Northern Ireland) 2017
HBRB	Housing Benefit Review Board
HCA	Homes and Communities Agency
HCD	House of Commons Debates
HCP	healthcare professional
HCV	Hepatitis C virus
Health Service Act	National Health Service Act 2006
Health Service (Wales) Act	National Health Service (Wales) Act 2006
HIV	Human Immunodeficiency Virus
HL	House of Lords
H.L.R.	Housing Law Reports
HMIT	Her Majesty's Inspector of Taxes
HMRC	Her Majesty's Revenue and Customs
HMSO	Her Majesty's Stationery Office
Hospital In-Patients Regulations 1975	Social Security (Hospital In-Patients) Regulations 1975
HP	Health Professional
HPP	Higher Pensioner Premium
HRA 1998	Human Rights Act 1998
H.R.L.R.	Human Rights Law Reports
HRP	Home Responsibilities Protection
HSE	Health and Safety Executive
IAC	Immigration and Asylum Chamber
IAP	Intensive Activity Period

Table of Abbreviations used in this Series

IB	Incapacity Benefit
IB PCA	Incapacity Benefit Personal Capability Assessment
IB Regs	Social Security (Incapacity Benefit) Regulations 1994
IB Regulations	Social Security (Incapacity Benefit) Regulations 1994
IB/IS/SDA	Incapacity Benefits Regime
IBJSA	Income-Based Jobseeker's Allowance
IBS	Irritable Bowel Syndrome
ICA	Invalid Care Allowance
I.C.R.	Industrial Cases Reports
ICTA 1988	Income and Corporation Taxes Act 1988
IFW Regulations	Incapacity for Work (General) Regulations 1995
IH	Inner House of the Court of Session
I.I.	Industrial Injuries
IIAC	Industrial Injuries Advisory Council
IIDB	Industrial Injuries Disablement Benefit
ILO	International Labour Organization
Imm. A.R.	Immigration Appeal Reports
Incapacity for Work Regulations	Social Security (Incapacity for Work) (General) Regulations 1995
Income Support General Regulations	Income Support (General) Regulations 1987
IND	Immigration and Nationality Directorate of the Home Office
I.N.L.R.	Immigration and Nationality Law Reports
I.O.	Insurance Officer
IPPR	Institute of Public Policy Research
IRESA	Income-Related Employment and Support Allowance
I.R.L.R.	Industrial Relations Law Reports
IS	Income Support
IS Regs	Income Support Regulations
IS Regulations	Income Support (General) Regulations 1987
ISA	Individual Savings Account
ISBN	International Standard Book Number
ITA 2007	Income Tax Act 2007
ITEPA 2003	Income Tax, Earnings and Pensions Act 2003
I.T.L. Rep.	International Tax Law Reports
I.T.R.	Industrial Tribunals Reports
ITS	Independent Tribunal Service

ITTOIA 2005	Income Tax (Trading and Other Income) Act 2005
IVB	Invalidity Benefit
IW (General) Regs	Social Security (Incapacity for Work) (General) Regulations 1995
IW (Transitional) Regs	Incapacity for Work (Transitional) Regulations
Jobseeker's Allowance Regulations	Jobseeker's Allowance Regulations 1996
Jobseeker's Regulations 1996	Jobseeker's Allowance Regulations 1996
JSA	Jobseeker's Allowance
JSA 1995	Jobseekers Act 1995
JSA (NI) Regulations	Jobseeker's Allowance (Northern Ireland) Regulations 1996
JSA (Transitional) Regulations	Jobseeker's Allowance (Transitional) Regulations 1996
JSA Regs 1996	Jobseeker's Allowance Regulations 1996
JSA Regs 2013	Jobseeker's Allowance Regulations 2013
JS(NI)O 1995	Jobseekers (Northern Ireland) Order 1995
J.S.S.L.	Journal of Social Security Law
J.S.W.L.	Journal of Social Welfare Law
K.B.	Law Reports, King's Bench
L.& T.R.	Landlord and Tenant Reports
LCW	limited capability for work
LCWA	Limited Capability for Work Assessment
LCWRA	limited capability for work-related activity
LDEDC Act 2009	Local Democracy, Economic Development and Construction Act 2009
LEA	local education authority
LEL	Lower Earnings Limit
LET	low earnings threshold
LGA 2003	Local Government Act 2003
L.G. Rev.	Local Government Review
L.G.L.R.	Local Government Reports
L.J.R.	Law Journal Reports
LRP	liable relative payment
L.S.G.	Law Society Gazette
Luxembourg Court	Court of Justice of the European Union (also referred to as CJEC and ECJ)
MA	Maternity Allowance
MAF	Medical Assessment Framework
Maternity Allowance Regulations	Social Security (Maternity Allowance) Regulations 1987
MDC	Mayoral development corporation
ME	myalgic encephalomyelitis

Medical Evidence Regulations	Social Security (Medical Evidence) Regulations 1976
MEN	Mandatory Employment Notification
Mesher and Wood	*Income Support, the Social Fund and Family Credit: the Legislation* (1996)
M.H.L.R.	Mental Health Law Reports
MHP	mental health problems
MIF	minimum income floor
MIG	minimum income guarantee
Migration Regulations	Employment and Support Allowance (Transitional Provisions, Housing Benefit and Council Tax Benefit (Existing Awards) (No.2) Regulations 2010
MP	Member of Parliament
MRSA	methicillin-resistant Staphylococcus aureus
MS	Medical Services
MWA Regulations	Jobseeker's Allowance (Mandatory Work Activity Scheme) Regulations 2011
MWAS Regulations	Jobseeker's Allowance (Mandatory Work Activity Scheme) Regulations 2011
NCB	National Coal Board
NDPD	Notes on the Diagnosis of Prescribed Diseases
NHS	National Health Service
NI	National Insurance
N.I.	Northern Ireland Law Reports
NICA	Northern Ireland Court of Appeal
NICom	Northern Ireland Commissioner
NICs	National Insurance Contributions
NINO	National Insurance Number
NIRS 2	National Insurance Recording System
N.L.J.	New Law Journal
NMC	Nursing and Midwifery Council
Northern Ireland Contributions and	Social Security Contributions and Benefits
Benefits Act	(Northern Ireland) Act 1992
N.P.C.	New Property Cases
NRCGT	non-resident capital gains tax
NTC Manual	Clerical procedures manual on tax credits
NUM	National Union of Mineworkers
NUS	National Union of Students
OCD	obsessive compulsive disorder
Ogus, Barendt and Wikeley	A. Ogus, E. Barendt and N. Wikeley, *The Law of Social Security* (1995)

Old Cases Act	Industrial Injuries and Diseases (Old Cases) Act 1975
OPB	One Parent Benefit
O.P.L.R.	Occupational Pensions Law Reports
OPSSAT	Office of the President of Social Security Appeal Tribunals
Overlapping Benefits Regulations	Social Security (Overlapping Benefits) Regulations 1975
P	retirement pension case
P. & C.R.	Property and Compensation Reports
para.	paragraph
Pay Regulations	Statutory Paternity Pay and Statutory Adoption Pay (General) Regulations 2002; Statutory Shared Parental Pay (General) Regulations 2014
PAYE	Pay As You Earn
PC	Privy Council
PCA	Personal Capability Assessment
PCC	Police and Crime Commissioner
PD	Practice Direction; prescribed disease
Pens. L.R.	Pensions Law Reports
Pensions Act	Pension Schemes Act 1993
PEP	Personal Equity Plan
Persons Abroad Regulations	Social Security Benefit (Persons Abroad) Regulations 1975
Persons Residing Together Regulations	Social Security Benefit (Persons Residing Together) Regulations 1977
PIE	Period of Interruption of Employment
PILON	pay in lieu of notice
Pilot Scheme Regulations	Universal Credit (Work-Related Requirements) In Work Pilot Scheme and Amendment Regulations 2015
PIP	Personal Independence Payment
P.I.Q.R.	Personal Injuries and Quantum Reports
Polygamous Marriages Regulations	Social Security and Family Allowances (Polygamous Marriages) Regulations 1975
PPF	Pension Protection Fund
Prescribed Diseases Regulations	Social Security (Industrial Injuries) (Prescribed Diseases) Regulations 1985
PSCS	Pension Service Computer System
Pt	Part
PTA	pure tone audiometry
P.T.S.R.	Public and Third Sector Law Reports
PTWR 2000	Part-time Workers (Prevention of Less Favourable Treatment) Regulations 2000
PVS	private and voluntary sectors

Table of Abbreviations used in this Series

Q.B.	Queen's Bench Law Reports
QBD	Queen's Bench Division
QCS Board	Quality Contract Scheme Board
QEF	qualifying earnings factor
QYP	qualifying young person
r.	rule
R	Reported Decision
R.C.	Rules of the Court of Session
REA	Reduced Earnings Allowance
Reciprocal Agreement with Ireland	Convention on Social Security between the Government of the United Kingdom and Northern Ireland and the Government of Ireland
reg.	regulation
RIPA	Regulation of Investigatory Powers Act 2000
RMO	Responsible Medical Officer
rr.	rules
RR	reference rate
RSI	repetitive strain injury
RTI	Real Time Information
R.V.R.	Rating & Valuation Reporter
s.	section
S	Scottish Decision
SAP	Statutory Adoption Pay
SAPOE Regulations	Jobseeker's Allowance (Schemes for Assisting Persons to Obtain Employment) Regulations 2013
SAWS	Seasonal Agricultural Work Scheme
SAYE	Save As You Earn
SB	Supplementary Benefit
SBAT	Supplementary Benefit Appeal Tribunal
SBC	Supplementary Benefits Commission
S.C.	Session Cases
S.C. (H.L.)	Session Cases (House of Lords)
S.C. (P.C.)	Session Cases (Privy Council)
S.C.C.R.	Scottish Criminal Case Reports
S.C.L.R.	Scottish Civil Law Reports
Sch.	Schedule
SDA	Severe Disablement Allowance
SDP	Severe Disability Premium
SEC	Social Entitlement Chamber
SEN	special educational needs
SERPS	State Earnings Related Pension Scheme

ShPP	statutory shared parental pay
ShPP Regulations	Statutory Shared Parental Pay (General) Regulations 2014
SI	Statutory Instrument
SIP	Share Incentive Plan
S.J.	Solicitors Journal
S.J.L.B.	Solicitors Journal Law Brief
SLAN	statement like an award notice
S.L.T.	Scots Law Times
SMP	Statutory Maternity Pay
SMP (General) Regulations 1986	Statutory Maternity Pay (General) Regulations 1986
Social Security Directive	Council Directive 79/7/EEC of 19 December 1978 on the progressive implementation of the principle of equal treatment for men and women in matters of social security
SPC	State Pension Credit
SPC Regulations	State Pension Credit Regulations 2002
SPCA 2002	State Pension Credit Act 2002
SPL Regulations	Shared Parental Leave Regulations 2014
SPP	Statutory Paternity Pay
ss.	sections
SS (No.2) A 1980	Social Security (No.2) Act 1980
SSA 1975	Social Security Act 1975
SSA 1977	Social Security Act 1977
SSA 1978	Social Security Act 1978
SSA 1979	Social Security Act 1979
SSA 1981	Social Security Act 1981
SSA 1986	Social Security Act 1986
SSA 1988	Social Security Act 1988
SSA 1989	Social Security Act 1989
SSA 1990	Social Security Act 1990
SSA 1998	Social Security Act 1998
SSAA 1992	Social Security Administration Act 1992
SSAC	Social Security Advisory Committee
SSAT	Social Security Appeal Tribunal
SSCBA 1992	Social Security Contributions and Benefits Act 1992
SSCB(NI)A 1992	Social Security Contributions and Benefits (Northern Ireland) Act 1992
SSCPA 1992	Social Security (Consequential Provisions) Act 1992
SSD	Secretary of State for Defence

SSHBA 1982	Social Security and Housing Benefits Act 1982
SSHD	Secretary of State for the Home Department
SSI	Scottish Statutory Instrument
SS(MP)A 1977	Social Security (Miscellaneous Provisions) Act 1977
SSP	Statutory Sick Pay
SSP (General) Regulations	Statutory Sick Pay (General) Regulations 1982
SSPA 1975	Social Security Pensions Act 1975
SSPP	statutory shared parental pay
SS(S)A 2018	Social Security (Scotland) Act 2018
SSWP	Secretary of State for Work and Pensions
State Pension Credit Regulations	State Pension Credit Regulations 2002
S.T.C.	Simon's Tax Cases
S.T.C. (S.C.D.)	Simon's Tax Cases: Special Commissioners' Decisions
S.T.I.	Simon's Tax Intelligence
STIB	Short-Term Incapacity Benefit
sub-para.	sub-paragraph
subs.	subsection
Swiss Citizens' Rights Agreement	Agreement between the United Kingdom of Great Britain and Northern Ireland and the Swiss Confederation on citizens' rights following the withdrawal of the United Kingdom from the European Union and the Free Movement of Persons Agreement
T	Tribunal of Commissioners' Decision
T.C.	Tax Cases
TCA 1999	Tax Credits Act 1999
TCA 2002	Tax Credits Act 2002
TCC	Technology and Construction Court
TCEA 2007	Tribunals, Courts and Enforcement Act 2007
TCGA 1992	Taxation of Chargeable Gains Act 2002
TCTM	*Tax Credits Technical Manual*
TEC	Treaty Establishing the European Community
TENS	transcutaneous electrical nerve stimulation
TEU	Treaty on European Union
TFC	tax-free childcare
TFEU	Treaty on the Functioning of the European Union
TIOPA 2010	Taxation (International and Other Provisions) Act 2010

TMA 1970	Taxes Management Act 1970
T.R.	Taxation Reports
Transfer of Functions Act	Social Security Contributions (Transfer of Functions etc.) Act 1999
Tribunal Procedure Rules	Tribunal Procedure (First-tier Tribunal)(Social Entitlement Chamber) Rules 2008
UB	Unemployment Benefit
UC	Universal Credit
UC Regs 2013	Universal Credit Regulations 2013
UCB	Unacceptable Customer Behaviour
UCITS	Undertakings for Collective Investments in Transferable Securities
UKAIT	UK Asylum and Immigration Tribunal
UKBA	UK Border Agency of the Home Office
UKCC	United Kingdom Central Council for Nursing, Midwifery and Health Visiting
UKFTT	United Kingdom First-tier Tribunal Tax Chamber
UKHL	United Kingdom House of Lords
U.K.H.R.R.	United Kingdom Human Rights Reports
UKSC	United Kingdom Supreme Court
UKUT	United Kingdom Upper Tribunal
UN	United Nations
Universal Credit Regulations	Universal Credit Regulations 2013
URL	uniform resource locator
USI Regs	Social Security (Unemployment, Sickness and Invalidity Benefit) Regulations 1983
USI Regulations	Social Security (Unemployment, Sickness and Invalidity Benefit) Regulations 1983
UT	Upper Tribunal
VAT	Value Added Tax
VCM	vinyl chloride monomer
Vol.	Volume
VWF	Vibration White Finger
W	Welsh Decision
WCA	Work Capability Assessment
WCAt	limited capability for work assessment
WFHRAt	Work-Focused Health-Related Assessment
WFI	work-focused interview
WFTC	Working Families Tax Credit
Wikeley, Annotations	N. Wikeley, "Annotations to Jobseekers Act 1995 (c.18)" in *Current Law Statutes Annotated* (1995)
Wikeley, Ogus and Barendt	Wikeley, Ogus and Barendt, *The Law of Social Security* (2002)

Withdrawal Agreement	Agreement on the Withdrawal of the United Kingdom of Great Britain and Northern Ireland from the European Union and the European Atomic Energy Community 2019
W.L.R.	Weekly Law Reports
WLUK	Westlaw UK
Workmen's Compensation Acts	Workmen's Compensation Acts 1925 to 1945
WP	Widow's Pension
WPS	War Pensions Scheme
WRA 2007	Welfare Reform Act 2007
WRA 2009	Welfare Reform Act 2009
WRA 2012	Welfare Reform Act 2012
W-RA Regulations	Employment and Support Allowance (Work-Related Activity) Regulations 2011
WRAAt	Work-Related Activity Assessment
WRPA 1999	Welfare Reform and Pensions Act 1999
WRP(NI)O 1999	Welfare Reform and Pensions (Northern Ireland) Order 1999
WRWA 2016	Welfare Reform and Work Act 2016
WSP (LCP) R (NI) 2016	Welfare Supplementary Payment (Loss of Carer Payments) Regulations (Northern Ireland) 2016
WSP (LDRP) R (NI) 2016	Welfare Supplementary Payment (Loss of Disability-Related Premiums) Regulations (Northern Ireland) 2016
WSPR (NI) 2016	Welfare Supplementary Payment Regulations (Northern Ireland) 2016
WTC	Working Tax Credit
WTC Regulations	Working Tax Credit (Entitlement and Maximum Rate) Regulations 2002

TABLE OF CASES

Table of Cases

TABLE OF SOCIAL SECURITY COMMISSIONERS' DECISIONS

TABLE OF EUROPEAN LEGISLATION

TABLE OF STATUTES

TABLE OF STATUTORY INSTRUMENTS

PART I

NEW LEGISLATION

NEW STATUTES

Part 7ZA of the Courts Act 2003 (inserted by ss.198 and 199 of the Police, Crime, Sentencing and Courts Act 2022 (c.32))

PART 7ZA

TRANSMISSION AND RECORDING OF COURT AND TRIBUNAL PROCEEDINGS

Remote observation and recording

Remote observation and recording of proceedings by direction of a court or tribunal

85A.—(1) This section applies (subject to subsections (12) and (13)) 1.001
to proceedings in any court; and in this section "court" has the same meaning as in the Contempt of Court Act 1981 (see section 19 of that Act).

(2) If the proceedings are specified under subsection (8)(a), the court may direct that images or sounds of the proceedings are to be transmitted electronically for the purpose of enabling persons not taking part in the proceedings to watch or listen to the proceedings.

(3) A direction under subsection (2) may authorise only the following types of transmission—

(a) transmission to designated live-streaming premises, or

(b) transmission to which individuals are given access only having first identified themselves to the court (or to a person acting on behalf of the court).

(4) In subsection (3)(a), "designated live-streaming premises" means premises that are designated by the Lord Chancellor as premises that are made available for members of the public to watch or listen to proceedings in accordance with directions under subsection (2).

(5) A direction under subsection (2) may include further provision about—

(a) the manner of transmission, or

(b) the persons who are to be able to watch or listen to the transmission (including provision making that ability subject to conditions, or aimed at preventing persons who are not meant to watch or listen from being able to do so).

(6) If images or sounds of the proceedings are transmitted electronically (whether under a direction under subsection (2) or any other power), the court may direct that a recording of the transmission is to be

3

made, in the manner specified in the direction, for the purpose of enabling the court to keep a record of the proceedings.

(7) A direction under subsection (2) or (6)—

(a) may relate to the whole, or to part, of the proceedings concerned, and

(b) may be varied or revoked.

(8) The Lord Chancellor may by regulations—

(a) specify proceedings (by reference to their type, the court in which they take place, or any other circumstance) in relation to which directions under subsection (2) may be made;

(b) specify matters of which the court must be satisfied before deciding to make such a direction;

(c) specify matters that the court must take into account when deciding whether, and on what terms, to make such a direction;

(d) require directions under subsection (2) to include certain provision under subsection (5).

(9) Before making regulations under subsection (8), the Lord Chancellor must determine whether the function of giving or withholding concurrence to the regulations would most appropriately be exercised by—

(a) the Lord Chief Justice of England and Wales,

(b) the Senior President of Tribunals, or

(c) both of them.

(10) Regulations under subsection (8) may be made only with the concurrence of the Lord Chief Justice of England and Wales, the Senior President of Tribunals, or both of them, as determined under subsection (9).

(11) Regulations under subsection (8) may make different provision for different purposes.

(12) This section does not apply to proceedings in the Supreme Court.

(13) This section does not apply to proceedings if provision regulating the procedure to be followed in those proceedings could be made by—

(a) an Act of the Scottish Parliament,

(b) an Act of Senedd Cymru (including one passed with the consent of a Minister of the Crown within the meaning of section 158(1) of the Government of Wales Act 2006), or

(c) an Act of the Northern Ireland Assembly passed without the consent of the Secretary of State.

GENERAL NOTE

1.002   This section and s.85B came into force on April 28, 2022 and have superseded provision originally made by s.55 of, and Sch.25 to the Coronavirus Act 2020.

The Remote Observation and Recording (Courts and Tribunals) Regulations 2022 (see below) are made under subs.(8).

The 2020 Act, and temporary Tribunal Procedure Rules made while it was in force, recognised that remote hearings had a practical effect on the general public's ability to observe hearings in accordance with the principle of open justice. The new legislation makes more permanent provision to mitigate that impact. It has not been thought necessary to retain provisions allowing tribunals to direct that a case be heard in private because a public hearing is not practical. Instead, provision is made for allowing people to observe proceedings that are transmitted to them, either to "designated live-streaming premises" or to a more limited audience. Since most tribunal cases will not be transmitted to designated live-streaming premises, it remains the case that, when a tribunal case is heard remotely, it will not usually be possible for members of the public to observe it unless the tribunal is made aware that they wish to do so. The legislation does not expressly require all transmission to be live, so it appears that recordings made under subs.(6) may be transmitted after the event to those who have a good enough reason for wishing to watch, or listen to, the proceedings.

Guidance on the making of directions under subs.(2) has been issued by the Lord Chief Justice and Senior President of Tribunals and is published *at https:// www.judiciary.uk/guidance-and-resources/practice-guidance-on-remote-observation- of-hearings-new-powers/*. Standard operating procedures are being developed, although practice may be expected to vary from jurisdiction to jurisdiction.

Offence of recording or transmission

Offence of recording or transmission in relation to remote proceedings

85B.—(1) It is an offence for a person to make, or attempt to make—   1.003

(a) an unauthorised recording, or

(b) an unauthorised transmission,

of an image or sound within subsection (2) or (3).

(2) An image or sound is within this subsection if it is an image or sound of court proceedings that is being transmitted to the place where the recording or transmission referred to in subsection (1) is made or attempted to be made.

(3) An image or sound is within this subsection if it is an image or sound of a person while that person is remotely attending court proceedings.

(4) A person is remotely attending court proceedings at any time when the person—

(a) is not in the same place as any member of the court, and

(b) is taking part in, watching or listening to the proceedings by way of a transmission.

(5) For the purposes of this section a recording or transmission is "unauthorised" unless it is—

(a) authorised (generally or specifically) by the court in which the proceedings concerned are being conducted, or

(b) authorised (generally or specifically) by the Lord Chancellor.

(6) It is a defence for a person charged with an offence under subsection (1) to prove that, at the time of the actual or attempted recording or transmission, the person—

(a) was not in designated live-streaming premises, and

(b) did not know that the image or sound concerned was of a sort within subsection (2) or (3).

(7) In subsection (6)(a), "designated live-streaming premises" has the meaning given by section 85A(4).

(8) A person guilty of an offence under subsection (1) is liable on summary conviction to a fine not exceeding level 3 on the standard scale.

(9) Conduct that amounts to an offence under subsection (1) is also a contempt of court.

But a person cannot, in respect of the same conduct, be both convicted of the offence and punished for the contempt.

(10) For the purposes of this section it does not matter whether a person making, or attempting to make, a recording or transmission intends the recording or transmission, or anything comprised in it, to be seen or heard by any other person.

(11) This section does not apply to proceedings in the Supreme Court.

(12) This section does not apply to court proceedings if provision regulating the procedure to be followed in those proceedings could be made by—

(a) an Act of the Scottish Parliament,

(b) an Act of Senedd Cymru (including one passed with the consent of a Minister of the Crown within the meaning of section 158(1) of the Government of Wales Act 2006), or

(c) an Act of the Northern Ireland Assembly passed without the consent of the Secretary of State.

(13) In this section—

"court" has the same meaning as in the Contempt of Court Act 1981 (see section 19 of that Act);

"court proceedings" means proceedings in any court;

"recording" means a recording on any medium—

    (a) of a single image, a moving image or any sound, or

    (b) from which a single image, a moving image or any sound may be produced or reproduced;

"transmission" means any transmission by electronic means of a single image, a moving image or any sound (and "transmitted" is to be construed accordingly).

GENERAL NOTE

1.004   See the annotation to s.85A, above.

It should be noted that subs.(9) makes it clear that conduct that would amount to an offence under this section is also a contempt of court that may be punished by a sentence of imprisonment of up to two years or a fine (the maximum amount of which is not limited by statute) or both (see ss.14, 15 and 18(2) of, and para.14 of Sch.4 to, the Contempt of Court Act 1981), as an alternative to a sentence on conviction in criminal proceedings under this section.

Social Security (Additional Payments) Act 2022

(2022 c.38)

An Act to make provision about additional payments to recipients of means-tested benefits, tax credits and disability benefits.

[28th June 2022]

ARRANGEMENT OF SECTIONS

GENERAL NOTE

This Act implements part of the package of measures announced by the 1.005
Chancellor of the Exchequer on May 26, 2022 in response to the increasing cost
of living crisis. The package included (i) an expansion of the Energy Bills
Support Scheme, providing £400 to every household, without repayments; (ii) a
one-off cost of living payment of £300, paid through the Winter Fuel Payment
scheme; (iii) additional funding for the Household Support Fund, administered
by local authorities; (iv) extra support for those on certain means-tested benefits
in the form of a one-off cost of living payment of £650, payable in two instalments; and (v) a further £150 disability cost of living payment paid to those in
receipt of eligible disability benefits. The Act makes provision for the latter two
measures ((iv) and (v)). The Act was introduced in the House of Commons on
June 15, 2022 on a fast-track procedure and received Royal Assent less than a
fortnight later on June 28, 2022.

Means-tested additional payments: main payments

1.—(1) The Secretary of State must secure that— 1.006
  (a) a single payment of £326 is made to any person who has a
      qualifying entitlement to a social security benefit in respect of 25
      May 2022 (the first "qualifying day"), and
  (b) a single payment of £324 is made to any person who has a
      qualifying entitlement to a social security benefit in respect of the
      second qualifying day.
(2) HMRC must secure that—

(a) a single payment of £326 is made to any person who has a qualifying entitlement to child tax credit or working tax credit, but not to a social security benefit, in respect of 25 May 2022, and

(b) a single payment of £324 is made to any person who has a qualifying entitlement to child tax credit or working tax credit, but not to a social security benefit, in respect of the second qualifying day.

(3) The social security benefits are—

(a) universal credit under the Welfare Reform Act 2012 or the Welfare Reform (Northern Ireland) Order 2015 (S.I. 2015/2006 (N.I. 1));

(b) state pension credit under the State Pension Credit Act 2002 or the State Pension Credit Act (Northern Ireland) 2002;

(c) an income-based jobseeker's allowance under the Jobseekers Act 1995 or the Jobseekers (Northern Ireland) Order 1995 (S.I. 1995/2705 (N.I. 15));

(d) an income-related employment and support allowance under Part 1 of the Welfare Reform Act 2007 or Part 1 of the Welfare Reform Act (Northern Ireland) 2007;

(e) income support under section 124 of the Social Security Contributions and Benefits Act 1992 or section 123 of the Social Security Contributions and Benefits (Northern Ireland) Act 1992.

(4) The second qualifying day is such day, not later than 31 October 2022, as may be specified by the Secretary of State in regulations.

(5) Regulations under subsection (4) may specify a day before the regulations come into force.

(6) In this section, and in sections 2 to 4, references to a "person" are to an individual or to a couple (but not to each member of a couple separately).

DEFINITIONS

1.007 "person"—see subs.(6).
"HMRC"—see s.9(1).
"a qualifying day"—see s.9(2).
"the second qualifying day"—see s.9(1).
"social security benefit"—see s.9(1).

GENERAL NOTE

1.008 This section provides for means-tested additional payments to be paid to eligible persons in two tranches. These additional payments are the "main payments" (see the heading to the regulation) to distinguish them from the "disability additional payments" made under s.5. The payments are not mutually exclusive. Subsection (1) deals with payments by the Secretary of State to social security claimants while subs.(2) makes parallel provision for payments by HMRC to recipients of tax credits. The Act does not in terms give all such claimants a direct entitlement to an additional payment (nor does it provide for claims for such payments to be made). Instead, a duty is imposed on the Secretary of State (and HMRC) to make such payments to those claimants who have a "qualifying entitlement", i.e. a right to at least one of the specified means-tested social security benefits or tax credits (see subs.(3) and s.2).

Subs. (1)

This subsection requires the Secretary of State to make two means-tested additional payments of £326 and £324 respectively to an eligible person (but see subs.(6) on what is meant by a "person", which stipulates that a "person" is an individual or a couple but not each member of a couple separately). Eligibility depends on having a "qualifying entitlement" (on which see s.2) to a "social security benefit" (as listed in subs.(3)) in respect of either one or both of two dates, being the "first qualifying day" and the "second qualifying day" in turn. The "first qualifying day" is May 25, 2022 (see subs.(1)(a)) while the "second qualifying day" has since been fixed by regulations as September 25, 2022 (see subs.(4)).

The one-off payment of £650 was split into two payments with two eligibility windows to ensure that people who became claimants of relevant means-tested benefits by autumn 2022 will receive assistance even if they did not qualify for the first instalment earlier in the year. The qualifying days were both announced after they had passed (and so a claimant's eligibility or not was already determined) to limit the risk of fraud. Thus, the first qualifying day was fixed as the day before the cost of living package was announced. The slightly uneven split of the total £650 payment was also an anti-fraud measure.

Subs. (2)

This subsection makes parallel provision to subs.(1) for working tax credit and child tax credit claimants, with the duty to make means-tested additional payments at the two dates being imposed on HMRC. But see also s.4 below.

Subs. (3)

This subsection lists the relevant social security benefits that can generate a "qualifying entitlement" for the purposes of subs.(1). In short, they are universal credit, state pension credit and the means-tested legacy benefits, albeit with the exception of housing benefit. The thinking is that those on means-tested income-replacement benefits are most likely to struggle with the sharply rising cost of living. Claimants who only receive housing benefit have been excluded because of the difficulty (or impossibility) of the DWP and HMRC identifying such individuals, as local authorities deal with housing benefit claims. Some of these individuals may benefit from the discretionary Household Support Fund administered by local authorities. Claimants who qualify only for contributory benefits are likewise excluded. Note that state pension credit is a relevant social security benefit irrespective of whether it comprises the guarantee element or the savings credit or both variants of state pension credit.

Subss. (4) and (5)

The second qualifying day was September 25, 2022 (see Social Security Additional Payments (Second Qualifying Day) Regulations 2022 (SI 2022/1011) reg.2).

9

Qualifying entitlements

1.013   **2.**—(1) A person has a qualifying entitlement to a social security benefit in respect of a qualifying day if—

(a) in respect of universal credit, the person is entitled to a payment of at least 1p in respect of an assessment period ending during the period of one month ending with the qualifying day;

(b) in respect of state pension credit, an income-based jobseeker's allowance, an income-related employment and support allowance or income support, the person is entitled to a payment of at least 1p in respect of any day during the period of one month ending with the qualifying day.

(2) A person has a qualifying entitlement to child tax credit or working tax credit in respect of a qualifying day if—

(a) where the qualifying day is 25 May 2022, the person receives a payment or has an award of the credit in question in the period beginning with 26 April 2022 and ending with 25 May 2022;

(b) where the qualifying day is the second qualifying day, the person receives a payment or has an award of the credit in question in the period of one month ending with the second qualifying day,

and, in either case, the payment or award of the credit in question is of at least £26 or HMRC expects the person to receive total payments or have an award of the credit in question of at least £26 in respect of the tax year 2022-23.

(3) References in this section to a person receiving a payment or having an award do not include payments received or awards made as a result of fraud.

DEFINITIONS

1.014   "HMRC"—see s.9(1).
"a qualifying day"—see s.9(2).
"the second qualifying day"—see s.9(1).
"social security benefit"—see s.9(1).
"tax year 2022-2023"—see s.9(1).

GENERAL NOTE

1.015   This section defines what is meant by a "qualifying entitlement" to a relevant social security benefit (subs.(1)) or tax credit (subs.(2)) by reference to a qualifying day. These definitions reflect the minimum amounts of benefits and tax credits payable—see e.g. Universal Credit Regulations 2013 (SI 2013/376) reg.17 and Tax Credits (Income Thresholds and Determination of Rates) Regulations 2002 (SI 2002/2008) reg.9. Payments received or awards made as a result of fraud do not count for the purposes of a "qualifying entitlement" (subs.(3)).

Subs. (1)

1.016   The definition of a "qualifying entitlement" differs depending on whether universal credit or one of the other social security benefits is involved. This reflects the different structures of universal credit and other benefits respectively. Thus, for universal credit the test is whether "the person is entitled to a payment of at least 1p in respect of an assessment period ending during the period of one month ending with the qualifying day" (subs.(1)(a)). It follows that a claimant with an assessment period running from the 30th of one month to the 29th of the next month would have to have been entitled in the assessment period ending on April 29, 2022. Entitlement in the assessment period ending on May 29, 2022 would not qualify as that assessment period does not end "during the period of one month ending with the qualifying day" (May 25, 2022). This is so even though that assessment period would have covered the great majority of days in the month ending on May 25, 2022. More straightforwardly, claimants of other relevant social security benefits must just have an entitlement of at least 1p in the month preceding the relevant qualifying day (subs.(1)(b)).

Subs. (2)

Tax credit recipients must have had an entitlement in respect of one day in the month before the relevant qualifying day and have a payment or an award for the tax year 2022/23 of at least £26.   **1.017**

Applicable benefits or tax credits

3.—(1) Where a person has a qualifying entitlement to universal credit and to another social security benefit in respect of a qualifying day, the benefit by reference to which the means-tested additional payment in respect of the qualifying day is to be made is universal credit (if the payment is made under section 1(1)).   **1.018**

(2) Where a person has a qualifying entitlement to child tax credit and to working tax credit in respect of a qualifying day, the tax credit by reference to which the means-tested additional payment in respect of the qualifying day is to be paid is child tax credit (if the payment is made under section 1(2)).

<small>DEFINITIONS</small>

"means-tested additional payment"—see s.9(1).   **1.019**
"a qualifying day"—see s.9(2).
"social security benefit"—see s.9(1).

<small>GENERAL NOTE</small>

Claimants may have a qualifying entitlement to both universal credit and another social security benefit in respect of the period of a month ending with the same qualifying day (e.g. where they move from one benefit to universal credit). In such a case the means-tested additional payment is paid by reference to the universal credit entitlement, which takes precedence (subs.(1)). In the same way, where both child tax credit (CTC) and working tax credit (WTC) are in payment, the CTC entitlement takes priority (subs.(2)). So, for example if CTC and WTC are paid to different members of the same couple, the additional payment will be made to the CTC recipient.   **1.020**

Means-tested additional payments: final payments

4.—(1) HMRC must secure that a single payment of £326 is made to any person who—   **1.021**

(a) receives a payment or has an award of child tax credit or working tax credit in respect of the period beginning with 26 April 2022 and ending with 25 May 2022,

(b) is not entitled to a payment under section 1(1)(a) or (2)(a), and

(c) receives total payments or has an award of the credit in question of at least £26 in respect of the tax year 2022-23.

(2) HMRC must secure that a single payment of £324 is made to any person who—

(a) receives a payment or has an award of child tax credit or working tax credit in respect of the period of one month ending with the second qualifying day,

(b) is not entitled to a payment under section 1(1)(b) or (2)(b), and

(c) receives total payments or has an award of the credit in question of at least £26 in respect of the tax year 2022-23.

(3) Where a person is entitled to a payment under this section by reference to child tax credit and working tax credit, the tax credit by reference to which the payment is to be made is child tax credit.

(4) References in this section to a person receiving a payment or having an award do not include payments received or awards made as a result of fraud.

DEFINITIONS

1.022   "HMRC"—see s.9(1).
"the second qualifying day"—see s.9(1).
"tax year 2022-2023"—see s.9(1).

GENERAL NOTE

1.023   This is a fall-back provision for tax credits claimants who did not qualify for an additional payment under s.1(1) or s.1(2) above. It applies to claimants who have an award or payments of tax credits of at least £26 for the 2022/23 tax year and who have an award or payments of CTC or WTC for the month from April 26, 2022 to May 25, 2022. HMRC must pay them the first additional payment if they have not already otherwise received it (subs.(1)). The same principle applies with the necessary modification for the dates involved for the second additional payment (subs.(2)). The second qualifying day was September 25, 2022 (see Social Security Additional Payments (Second Qualifying Day) Regulations 2022 (SI 2022/1011) reg.2). Where both CTC and WTC are in payment, CTC takes precedence as under s.3(2) (see subs.(3)). As with s.2(3), payments made because of fraud do not count (subs.(4)).

Disability additional payments

1.024   **5.**—(1) The Secretary of State must secure that a single payment of £150 (a "disability additional payment") is made to each individual who is entitled to a payment of a disability benefit that is payable in respect of 25 May 2022.

(2) The disability benefits are—

(a) a disability living allowance under section 71 of the Social Security Contributions and Benefits Act 1992 or section 71 of the Social Security Contributions and Benefits (Northern Ireland) Act 1992;

(b) a personal independence payment under the Welfare Reform Act 2012 or Part 5 of the Welfare Reform (Northern Ireland) Order 2015;

(c) an attendance allowance under section 64 of the Social Security Contributions and Benefits Act 1992 or section 64 of the Social Security Contributions and Benefits (Northern Ireland) Act 1992;

(d) a constant attendance allowance under section 104 of the Social Security Contributions and Benefits Act 1992 or section 104 of the Social Security Contributions and Benefits (Northern Ireland) Act 1992;

(e) an adult disability payment under the Disability Assistance for Working Age People (Scotland) Regulations 2022 (S.S.I. 2022/54);

(f) a child disability payment under the Disability Assistance for Children and Young People (Scotland) Regulations 2021 (S.S.I. 2021/174);

(g) an armed forces independence payment under article 24A of the Armed Forces and Reserve Forces (Compensation Scheme) Order 2011 (S.I. 2011/517);

(h) a constant attendance allowance under—

(i) article 14 or 43 of the Personal Injuries (Civilians) Scheme 1983 (S.I. 1983/686);

(ii) article 8 of the Naval, Military and Air Forces etc. (Disablement and Death) Service Pensions Order 2006 (S.I. 2006/606);

(i) a mobility supplement under—

(i) article 25A or 48A of the Personal Injuries (Civilians) Scheme 1983;

(ii) article 20 of the Naval, Military and Air Forces etc. (Disablement and Death) Service Pensions Order 2006.

(3) Where an individual is entitled to a payment of more than one disability benefit that is payable in respect of 25 May 2022, the benefit by reference to which the disability additional payment is to be made is the first benefit in the list in subsection (2) to which the individual is entitled.

DEFINITIONS

"disability additional payment"—see subs.(1) and s.9(1).   1.025
"disability benefit"—see s.9(1).

GENERAL NOTE

The one or two means-tested additional payments may be supplemented by a   1.026
single disability additional payment made under this section, amounting to £150. The Secretary of State must make such payments to claimants who were entitled to a qualifying payment of a prescribed disability benefit in respect of May 25, 2022 (subs.(1)). The relevant disability benefits are those listed in subs.(2). Those listed in subs.(2)(a)–(d) are the responsibility of the DWP or its Northern Ireland equivalent. Those in subs.(2)(e)–(f) are paid by the Scottish government, while the benefits in subs.(g)–(i) are administered by the Secretary

of State for Defence (or on his behalf by the Veterans UK). Given these disparate responsibilities, the Act makes provision for data sharing (see s.7).

Administration of additional payments

1.027   **6.**—(1) For all purposes relating to the administration of an additional payment, any provision applying in relation to a social security benefit, child tax credit, working tax credit or disability benefit by reference to which that payment is made is to apply in relation to that payment as if that payment were a payment or award of the social security benefit, child tax credit, working tax credit or disability benefit in question.

(2) The provision applied by subsection (1)—

(a) includes provision relating to overpayments and recovery, and appeals relating to overpayments and recovery (but not provision relating to appeals or reviews about entitlement to the social security benefit, tax credit or disability benefit in question), and

(b) is subject to any necessary modifications.

(3) Subsection (1) has effect in relation to a payment made in purported compliance with a duty under section 1 or 4 as if that payment were the additional payment which it purported to be.

(4) Subsection (1) (including as it has effect as a result of subsection (3)) is subject to regulations made by the Secretary of State, the Treasury or HMRC under subsection (5).

(5) The Secretary of State, the Treasury or HMRC may by regulations make provision, in relation to additional payments or payments purporting to be additional payments, applying or disapplying, with or without modifications, any provision applying in relation to a social security benefit, child tax credit, working tax credit or a disability benefit.

(6) The regulations may make provision having effect from the day on which this Act comes into force.

DEFINITIONS

1.028   "additional payment"—see s.9(1).
"disability benefit"—see s.9(1).
"HMRC"—see s.9(1).

GENERAL NOTE

1.029   Note that there is no provision in the Act for anyone to make a claim for a means-tested additional payment. As a result, there is also no provision for the Secretary of State to make a decision under s.8(1)(a) of the Social Security Act 1998. In the same way it follows that the usual mechanism of revisions, supersessions and appeals does not apply. Instead, s.1 simply imposes a duty on the Secretary of State and HMRC to make payments to eligible individuals.

Subs. (1)

1.030   This provision applies the relevant administrative provisions relating to the qualifying benefit to the new additional payment. This method has been adopted so that the additional payments can be administered in the same manner and subject to the same rules as those which apply to a claimant's existing benefit entitlement (e.g. by payment to the same bank account as the qualifying benefit).

Subs. (2)

The provision made under subs.(1) includes provision relating to overpayment and benefit recovery procedures. This reflects the fact that different rules govern overpayment and benefit recovery procedures for different social security benefits and tax credits. This does not include provisions relating to appeals or reviews, there being no decision as such on entitlement to an additional payment to be appealed. See further the Tax Credits Act 2002 (Additional Payments Modification and Disapplication) Regulations 2022 (SI 2022/1208).   **1.031**

Cooperation etc between the Secretary of State and HMRC

7.—(1) The Secretary of State and HMRC must cooperate in exercising their functions in relation to additional payments.   **1.032**

(2) Section 3 of the Social Security Act 1998 (use of information) has effect—

  (a) in relation to HMRC as it has effect in relation to the Secretary of State, and

  (b) as if, in subsection (1A), the reference to social security included additional payments.

(3) Section 127 of the Welfare Reform Act 2012 (information-sharing between Secretary of State and HMRC) has effect as if—

  (a) functions of HMRC conferred by or under this Act were HMRC functions within the meaning of that section, and

  (b) functions of the Secretary of State conferred by or under this Act were departmental functions within the meaning of that section.

(4) Section 34 of the Scotland Act 2016 (information-sharing between the Secretary of State and the Scottish Ministers) has effect as if, in subsection (7), the reference to social security in the definition of "social security function" included additional payments.

(5) Subsection (6) applies where—

  (a) the Secretary of State or HMRC make a payment to a person in purported compliance with a duty in section 1 or 4,

  (b) the person was entitled to receive an additional payment of an amount equal to that payment under a different duty in section 1 or 4 ("the applicable duty"), and

  (c) the person does not receive the additional payment to which they are entitled under the applicable duty.

(6) The payment made in purported compliance with a duty in section 1 or 4 is to be treated as if it had been made in accordance with the applicable duty (and, accordingly, the payment is not recoverable on the grounds that it was not made in compliance with a duty in section 1 or 4).

DEFINITIONS

"additional payment"—see s.9(1).   **1.033**
"the applicable duty"—subs.(5)(b).
"HMRC"—see s.9(1).

1.034   This section provides for data-sharing between the DWP, HMRC and the Secretary of State for Defence (given his role in administering the benefits itemised at s.5(2)(g)–(i)) along with the relevant authorities in Northern Ireland and Scotland.

Payments to be disregarded for the purposes of tax and social security

1.035   **8.**—No account is to be taken of an additional payment in considering a person's—
   (a) liability to tax,
   (b) entitlement to benefit under an enactment relating to social security (irrespective of the name or nature of the benefit), or
   (c) entitlement to a tax credit.

DEFINITION

1.036   "additional payment"—see s.9(1).

GENERAL NOTE

1.037   Additional payments under this Act are disregarded for the purposes of liability to income tax (para.(a)) and entitlement to social security benefits (para.(b)) and tax credits (para.(c)). So far as entitlement to social security benefits is concerned, the usual drafting technique to provide for a disregard for such forms of capital or income other than earnings is by way of a regulation (see e.g. Universal Credit Regulations 2013 (SI 2013/376) reg.76) or Schedule (see e.g. Income Support (General) Regulations 1987 (SI 1987/1967) Sch.9). However, the fact that entitlement to additional payments is directly governed by primary legislation has allowed a different and all purposes route to a statutory disregard to be adopted.

Interpretation

1.038   **9.**—(1) In this Act—
   "additional payment" means a means-tested additional payment or a disability additional payment;
   "disability additional payment" has the meaning given by section 5(1);
   "disability benefit" means a benefit listed in section 5(2);
   "HMRC" means the Commissioners for Her Majesty's Revenue and Customs;
   "means-tested additional payment" means a payment under section 1 or 4;
   "the second qualifying day" means the day specified in regulations under section 1(4);
   "social security benefit" means a benefit listed in section 1(3);
   "the tax year 2022-23" means the period beginning with 6 April 2022 and ending with 5 April 2023.
   (2) In this Act—
   (a) references to "a qualifying day" are to—
      (i) 25 May 2022, or
      (ii) the day specified in regulations under section 1(4);

(b) references to child tax credit or working tax credit are to child tax credit or working tax credit under the Tax Credits Act 2002.

Regulations

10.—(1) A power to make regulations under any provision of this Act includes power to make—   1.039
    (a) consequential, supplementary, incidental, transitional or saving provision;
    (b) different provision for different purposes.

(2) Regulations under this Act are to be made by statutory instrument.

(3) A statutory instrument containing regulations under this Act is subject to annulment in pursuance of a resolution of either House of Parliament.

Extent, commencement and short title

11.—(1) This Act extends to England and Wales, Scotland and Northern Ireland.   1.040

(2) This Act comes into force on the day on which it is passed.

(3) This Act may be cited as the Social Security (Additional Payments) Act 2022.

GENERAL NOTE

The Act received Royal Assent on June 28, 2022.   1.041

Social Security (Special Rules for End of Life) Act 2022

(2022 c.42)

An Act to provide for certain social security rules which apply where life expectancy is 6 months or less to apply instead where life expectancy is 12 months or less.

[25th October 2022]

GENERAL NOTE

1.042   This Act will enable people who are thought to be in the final year of their lives to get fast-tracked access to Disability Living Allowance (DLA), Personal Independence Payment (PIP) and Attendance Allowance (AA). When fully in operation, the Act will amend the definition in existing legislation of terminal illness, also referred to as nearing the end of life, which was based on the claimant having 6 months or less to live, replacing it with a 12-month definition. However, at the time of writing s.1 has not yet been brought into force.

Rules to apply where death expected within 12 months

1.043   **1.**—(1) In section 66 of the Social Security Contributions and Benefits Act 1992 (rules for attendance allowance in cases where death can reasonably be expected within 6 months), in subsection (2)(a) (meaning of "terminally ill" in relation to attendance allowance and disability living allowance), for "6" substitute "12".

(2) In section 82 of the Welfare Reform Act 2012 (rules for personal independence payment in cases where death can reasonably be expected within 6 months), in subsection (4) (meaning of "terminally ill"), for "6" substitute "12".

(3) In the Universal Credit, Personal Independence Payment, Jobseeker's Allowance and Employment and Support Allowance (Decisions and Appeals) Regulations 2013 (S.I. 2013/381), in regulation 2, in the definition of "terminally ill", for the words from "expected" to the end substitute "expected within 12 months".

Extent, commencement and short title

1.044   **2.**—(1) This Act extends to England and Wales and Scotland.

(2) Section 1 comes into force on such day or days as the Secretary of State may by regulations made by statutory instrument appoint.

(3) Regulations under subsection (2) may contain such transitional, transitory or saving provision as the Secretary of State considers appropriate.

(4) This section comes into force on the day on which this Act is passed.

(5) This Act may be cited as the Social Security (Special Rules for End of Life) Act 2022.

NEW REGULATIONS

The Statutory Sick Pay (General) (Coronavirus Amendment) Regulations 2022

(SI 2022/380)

The Secretary of State makes the following Regulations in exercise of the powers conferred by sections 151(4) and 175(1), (3), (4) and (5) of the Social Security Contributions and Benefits Act 1992.

In accordance with section 172(1) of the Social Security Administration Act 1992, the Secretary of State has referred the proposals in respect of these Regulations to the Social Security Advisory Committee.

Citation, commencement and extent

1.—(1) These Regulations may be cited as the Statutory Sick Pay (General) (Coronavirus Amendment) Regulations 2022 and come into force on 25th March 2022. **1.045**

(2) These Regulations extend to England and Wales and Scotland.

Amendment of the Statutory Sick Pay (General) Regulations 1982

2.—(1) The Statutory Sick Pay (General) Regulations 1982 are amended as follows. **1.046**

(2) In regulation 2(1)—

(a) in sub-paragraph (a)(iii), after the words "contract of service,", insert "or";

(b) omit sub-paragraphs (c) and (d).

(3) Regulation 2(4) is omitted.

(4) Schedules 1 and 2 are omitted.

GENERAL NOTE

Regulation 2(2), (3) and (4) of these Regulations revoke the provisions within the Statutory Sick Pay (General) Regulations 1982 which deem people to be incapable of work where they are unable to work either due to isolating themselves in such a manner as to prevent infection or contamination with coronavirus, or due to shielding themselves in such a manner as to prevent infection or contamination with coronavirus. **1.047**

The Statutory Sick Pay (Coronavirus) (Suspension of Waiting Days) (Saving Provision) Regulations 2022

(SI 2022/381)

The Secretary of State makes the following Regulations in exercise of the power conferred by section 89(3) of the Coronavirus Act 2020.

Citation, commencement and extent

1.048   **1.**—(1) These Regulations may be cited as the Statutory Sick Pay (Coronavirus) (Suspension of Waiting Days) (Saving Provision) Regulations 2022 and come into force on 25th March 2022.

(2) These Regulations extend to England and Wales and Scotland.

Saving provision related to the suspension of waiting days

1.049   **2.**—(1) Despite the expiry of section 40 of the Coronavirus Act 2020, regulation 2 of the Statutory Sick Pay (Coronavirus) (Suspension of Waiting Days and General Amendment) Regulations 2020 ("the 2020 Regulations") shall continue to have effect, subject to the modifications specified in paragraph (3), as set out in this regulation.

(2) Regulation 2 of the 2020 Regulations shall continue to have effect, subject to the modifications specified in paragraph (3), in relation to a period of incapacity for work which is related to coronavirus where that period of incapacity for work begins on or before 24th March 2022.

(3) The modifications are that regulation 2 of the 2020 Regulations is treated as though the following were omitted—

   (a) the word "or" at the end of paragraph (3)(b)(i) of that regulation; and

   (b) paragraphs (3)(b)(ii) and (4) of that regulation.

(4) In this regulation—

   (a) "period of incapacity for work" has the meaning given by section 152 of the Social Security Contributions and Benefits Act 1992; and

   (b) whether a period of incapacity for work is related to coronavirus is to be determined in accordance with regulation 2(3)(b) of the 2020 Regulations.

GENERAL NOTE

1.050   Section 155(1) of the SSCBA 1992 provides that SSP is not payable for the first three days of a period of incapacity for work. Section 40 of the Coronavirus Act 2020 allowed regulations to disapply SSCBA 1992 s.155(1) where a period of incapacity for work was related to coronavirus. Regulation 2 of the Statutory Sick Pay (Coronavirus) (Suspension of Waiting Days and General Amendment) Regulations 2020 (SI 2020/374), made under that power, enabled SSP to be payable from day 1 of a period of incapacity for work which was related to coronavirus, as opposed to day 4 as would otherwise be the case. However, s.40 of the Coronavirus Act 2020 expired at midnight on March 24, 2022, and as a result the 2020 Regulations also expired. Regulation 2(1) and (2) of SI 2022/381 make saving provision by providing that reg.2 of the 2020 Regulations continues to have effect where a period of incapacity for work commences on or before March 24, 2022. This is subject to the modifications in reg.2(3) which in turn reflect the revocation of the deeming provisions contained in reg.2(1)(c) and (d) and Schs 1 and 2 of the Statutory Sick Pay (General) Regulations 1982.

The Remote Observation and Recording (Courts and Tribunals) Regulations 2022

(SI 2022/705)

Made	*at 10.05 a.m. on 27th June 2022*
Laid before Parliament	*at 5.00 p.m. on 27th June 2022*
Coming into force	*28th June 2022*

The Lord Chancellor, with the concurrence of the Lord Chief Justice and the Senior President of Tribunals as required by section 85A(10) of the Courts Act 2003 (the Lord Chancellor having determined under section 85A(9) of that Act that the function of giving or withholding concurrence would most appropriately be performed by both of them), makes the following Regulations under section 85A(8) and (11) of that Act.

Citation, commencement, interpretation and extent

1.051   **1.**—(1) These Regulations may be cited as the Remote Observation and Recording (Courts and Tribunals) Regulations 2022 and come into force on 28th June 2022.

(2) In these Regulations, "section 85A" means section 85A of the Courts Act 2003.

(3) These Regulations extend to England and Wales, Scotland and Northern Ireland.

Specified proceedings

1.052   **2.** Directions under section 85A(2) may be given in relation to proceedings, of any type and in any court to which section 85A applies, which are—

(a) in public; or

(b) proceedings at which the general public is not entitled to be present but specific categories of person, or specific individuals, who are not taking part in the proceedings are entitled to be present by virtue of provision made by or under any enactment or of being authorised by the court.

Matters of which the court must be satisfied

1.053   **3.** Before making a direction under section 85A(2), the court must be satisfied that—

(a) it would be in the interests of justice to make the direction; and

(b) there is capacity and technological capability to enable transmission, and giving effect to the direction would not create an unreasonable administrative burden.

Matters that the court must take into account

1.054   **4.** Before deciding whether, and on what terms, to make a direction under section 85A(2), the court must take into account—

(a) the need for the administration of justice to be, as far as possible, open and transparent;

(b) the timing of any request or application to the court or tribunal to make a direction, and its impact on the business of the court or tribunal;

(c) the extent to which the technical, human and other resources necessary to facilitate effective remote observation are or can be made available;

(d) any limitation imposed by or under any enactment on the persons who are entitled to be present at the proceedings;

(e) any issues which might arise if persons who are outside the United Kingdom are among those watching or listening to the transmission;

(f) any impact which the making or withholding of such a direction, or the terms of the direction, might have upon—

   (i) the content or quality of the evidence to be put before the court or tribunal;

   (ii) public understanding of the law and the administration of justice;

   (iii) the ability of the public, including the media, to observe and scrutinise the proceedings;

   (iv) the safety and right to privacy of any person involved with the proceedings.

Provision which must be included in a direction

5.—(1) A direction under section 85A(2) made in relation to proceed-   **1.055**
ings specified in regulation 2(b) must include provision which has the effect of—

(a) prohibiting any person other than a person entitled to be present at those proceedings from watching or listening to the transmission; and

(b) requiring any person so entitled to demonstrate, in such manner as specified in the direction, the capacity in which that person is so entitled.

(2) A direction under section 85A(2) made in relation to any proceedings must, except where the direction is for transmission to designated live-streaming premises, include provision which has the effect—

(a) that no person will be able to watch or listen to the transmission without first, when identifying themselves to the court, providing their full name and their email address, unless the court dispenses with this requirement;

(b) of requiring as a condition of continued access that any person given access will during the transmission conduct themselves appropriately and in particular in accordance with any requirements of the direction or instructions of the judge for persons observing the proceedings.

GENERAL NOTE

This regulation reflects s.85A(3) of the 2003 Act, which provides that a   **1.056**
direction under subs.(2) may authorise only transmission to designated live-streaming premises (as defined in subs.(4)) or transmission to which individuals are given access only having first identified themselves to the court (or to a person acting on behalf of the court).

The Childcare (Free of Charge for Working Parents) (England) Regulations 2022

(SI 2022/1134)

The Secretary of State for Education makes these Regulations in exercise of the powers conferred by sections 1(2), (3), (4) and (7), 2(1), (2), (4) and (5) and 4(2) of the Childcare Act 2016.

In accordance with section 2(3) of the Childcare Act 2016, these Regulations are made with the consent of the Treasury.

ARRANGEMENT OF REGULATIONS

Part 1

Preliminary provisions

Part 2

Interpretation

Part 3

Determinations as to qualifying children of working parents

Description of young child

Conditions relating to parent and partner of parent

Part 4

Offences and penalties

Part 5

Reviews and appeals

PART 1

PRELIMINARY PROVISIONS

Citation and commencement

1.057   **1.** These Regulations—
> (a) may be cited as the Childcare (Free of Charge for Working Parents) (England) Regulations 2022, and
> (b) come into force on 1st December 2022.

Extent and application

1.058   **2.** These Regulations—
> (a) extend to England and Wales, and
> (b) apply in relation to England.

Consequential amendments and revocations

1.059   **3.** The Schedule makes consequential amendments and revocations.

26

PART 2

INTERPRETATION

Definitions

4.—(1) In these Regulations—   1.060
"the Act" means the Childcare Act 2016;
"adjusted net income" has the meaning given in section 58 of the
    Income Tax Act 2007;
"care plan" has the meaning given in regulation 5;
"childcare provider" has the meaning given in regulation 6;
"childminder" means an early years childminder within the meaning
    given in section 96(4) of the Childcare Act 2006;
"the Commissioners" means the Commissioners for His Majesty's
    Revenue and Customs;
"declaration" means a declaration under section 1(2)(e) of the Act;
"early years childminder agency" has the meaning given in section
    98(1) of the Childcare Act 2006;
"employee" has the meaning given in regulation 7;
"the First-tier Tribunal" means the tribunal established under section
    3(1) of the Tribunal, Courts and Enforcement Act 2007;
"foster parent" has the meaning given in regulation 8;
"inspection report" means—
    (a) in relation to an early years childminder agency, a report
        under section 51E of the Childcare Act 2006;
    (b) in relation to a childcare provider, a report under any of the
        following—
        (i) section 5 of the Education Act 2005;
        (ii) section 50 of the Childcare Act 2006;
        (iii) section 109 of the Education and Skills Act 2008;
"looked after by a local authority" has the meaning given in regulation
    9;
"partner" has the meaning given in regulation 10;
"relevant tax year" means, in relation to a declaration, the tax year in
    which the declaration is made;
"responsible local authority" means, in relation to a child, the English
    local authority for the area in which the child may be a qualifying
    child of working parents;
"review" means a review under regulation 36;
"Social Security Act" means—
    (a) the Social Security Contributions and Benefits Act 1992,
        or
    (b) the Social Security Contributions and Benefits (Northern
        Ireland) Act 1992;
"tax year" has the meaning given in section 4(2) of the Income Tax
    Act 2007.
(2) The following table—

   (a) sets out the expressions of the Act used in these Regulations, and

   (b) shows where in that Act each of those expressions is defined.

Expression used in these Regulations	Location of definition in the Act
"childcare"	sections 1(9) and 2(8)
"English local authority"	section 2(8)
"parent"	section 1(9)
"qualifying child of working parents"	section 1(2)
"young child"	section 1(9)

Meaning of "care plan"

1.061   **5.** A "care plan" is any of the following—

   (a) a care plan within the meaning given in regulation 2(1) of the Care Planning, Placement and Case Review (England) Regulations 2010;

   (b) arrangements recorded in writing under regulation 3(5) of the Arrangements for Placement of Children (General) Regulations (Northern Ireland) 1996;

   (c) a child's plan prepared under regulation 5 of the Looked After Children (Scotland) Regulations 2009;

   (d) a care and support plan maintained under section 83 of the Social Services and Well-being (Wales) Act 2014.

Meaning of "childcare provider"

1.062   **6.**—(1) A "childcare provider" is an early years provider—

   (a) who is not an excluded provider, and

   (b) to whom section 40 of the Childcare Act 2006 (duty to implement Early Years Foundation Stage) applies.

(2) An excluded provider is any of the following—

   (a) an independent school, other than an Academy school, that does not meet the standards prescribed under section 157(1)(b) of the Education Act 2002 (which relate to the spiritual, moral, social and cultural development of pupils at independent schools);

   (b) an early years provider any English local authority has reasonable grounds to believe—

      (i) does not actively promote the fundamental British values of democracy, the rule of law, individual liberty and mutual respect and tolerance of those with different faiths and beliefs, or

      (ii) promotes as evidence-based views or theories those contrary to established scientific or historical evidence and explanations.

(3) In this regulation—

"Academy school" has the meaning given in section 1A of the Academies Act 2010;

"early years provider" has the meaning given in section 96(3) of the Childcare Act 2006.

Meaning of "employee"

7.—(1) An "employee" is any of the following—　　　　　　　　1.063
(a) a person in employment under a contract of service who is not on unpaid leave;
(b) a person who is the holder of an office (including an elected office);
(c) a person in an engagement to which a relevant Chapter applies;
(d) a person who expects, in relation to a declaration, to be a person mentioned in any of paragraphs (a) to (c) within 31 days of the day on which the person makes the declaration.
(2) In this regulation—
"office" has the meaning given in section 5(3) of the Income Tax (Earnings and Pensions) Act 2003;
"relevant Chapter" means any of Chapters 7 to 10 of Part 2 of the Income Tax (Earnings and Pensions) Act 2003 (which relate to agency workers and workers' services provided through intermediaries or managed service companies).

Meaning of "foster parent"

8.—(1) A "foster parent" is any of the following—　　　　　　　1.064
(a) a person who—
　　(i) is approved as a local authority foster parent in accordance with regulations made by virtue of paragraph 12F of Schedule 2 to the Children Act 1989, and
　　(ii) has a child placed with the person under section 22C(5) of that Act;
(b) a person who—
　　(i) is an authority foster parent within the meaning given in article 27(3) of the Children (Northern Ireland) Order 1995, and
　　(ii) has a child placed with the person under article 27(2)(a) of that Order;
(c) a person who—
　　(i) is a foster carer within the meaning given in regulation 2 of the Looked After Children (Scotland) Regulations 2009, and
　　(ii) has a child placed with the person pursuant to a permanence order under section 80 of the Adoption and Children (Scotland) Act 2007;
(d) a person who—
　　(i) is a local authority foster parent within the meaning given in section 197(1) of the Social Services and Well-being (Wales) Act 2014, and
　　(ii) has a child placed with the person under section 81(5) of that Act.

Meaning of "looked after by a local authority"

1.065   **9.**—(1) A young child is "looked after by a local authority" if the child is any the following—

(a) a child who is looked after by a local authority within the meaning given in section 22(1) of the Children Act 1989;

(b) a child who is looked after by an authority within the meaning given in article 25(1) of the Children (Northern Ireland) Order 1995;

(c) a child who is looked after by a local authority within the meaning given in section 17(6) of the Children (Scotland) Act 1995;

(d) a child who is looked after by a local authority within the meaning given in section 74(1) of the Social Services and Well-being (Wales) Act 2014.

(2) Despite paragraph (1), a young child is not looked after by a local authority during any period the child is—

(a) being looked after by an English local authority for the purposes of providing a brief respite for the person with whom the child normally lives,

(b) placed with a foster parent (see regulation 8), or

(c) placed with any other person pursuant to arrangements made under—

(i) section 22C(2) of the Children Act 1989,

(ii) article 27(2)(a) of the Children (Northern Ireland) Order 1995,

(iii) regulation 8(1) or 11 of the Looked After Children (Scotland) Regulations 2009, or

(iv) section 81(2) of the Social Services and Well-being (Wales) Act 2014.

Meaning of "partner"

1.066   **10.**—(1) A person is a "partner" of another person if—

(a) the person is—

(i) married to, or the civil partner of, the other person, and

(ii) a member of the same household as the other person, or

(b) the person is living together with the other person as if they were a married couple or civil partners.

(2) Despite paragraph (1), a person is not a partner of another person if either person is—

(a) under 16 years of age,

(b) serving a sentence of imprisonment, or

(c) remaining with a third person in a pre-existing relationship of a kind mentioned in paragraph (1).

Meaning of "person in the United Kingdom"

1.067   **11.**—(1) A "person in the United Kingdom" is any of the following—

(a) a person who is—

(i) ordinarily resident in the United Kingdom, and

    (ii) not a person taxed as if they were not so resident by virtue of double taxation arrangements;

(b) a person who is—
    (i) a resident of an EEA State or Switzerland,
    (ii) in paid work in the United Kingdom, and
    (iii) not a person subject to immigration control;

(c) a person who has been granted—
    (i) refugee permission to stay or temporary refugee permission to stay under rule 339QA of the Immigration Rules, or
    (ii) temporary humanitarian permission to stay under rule 339QB of the Immigration Rules;

(d) a person who has been granted, or deemed to have been granted, outside the Immigration Rules—
    (i) discretionary leave to remain, or
    (ii) leave to remain under the destitution domestic violence concession;

(e) a person who—
    (i) has been deported, expelled or otherwise removed by compulsion of law from another country to the United Kingdom, and
    (ii) is not a person subject to immigration control.

(2) In this regulation—

"a person subject to immigration control" has the meaning given in section 115(9) of the Immigration and Asylum Act 1999;

"double taxation arrangements" means arrangements that have effect under section 2(1) of the Taxation (International and Other Provisions) Act 2010;

"the Immigration Rules" means the rules laid before Parliament under section 3(2) of the Immigration Act 1971;

"paid work" means work done for payment or in expectation of payment and does not include being engaged by a charitable or voluntary organisation, or as a volunteer, in circumstances in which the payment received by or due to be paid to the person is in respect of expenses.

When periods begin and end

12. A period of time described in these Regulations in a manner set out in the table is calculated in accordance with the corresponding rule.   **1.068**

If the period is described as—	*then the period—*
beginning with a specified day	includes that specified day.
being within a specified number of days of a specified day	does not include that specified day.
ending before a specified day	does not include that specified day.

PART 3

DETERMINATIONS AS TO QUALIFYING CHILDREN OF WORKING PARENTS

Description of young child

Description of young child

1.069   **13.**—(1) This regulation relates to section 1(2)(c) of the Act.

(2) A young child must be a child who—

(a) has attained the age of three, and

(b) is not looked after by a local authority (see regulation 9).

Conditions relating to parent and partner of parent

Conditions relating to parent

1.070   **14.**—(1) This regulation relates to section 1(2)(d) of the Act.

(2) A parent of a young child must be a parent mentioned in paragraph (3) or (4).

(3) A parent who—

(a) meets the qualifying paid work requirement in regulation 16 or 17,

(b) seeks the childcare, which is available free of charge by virtue of the Act, to enable the parent, or the parent's partner (if any), to work,

(c) does not for the relevant tax year—

(i) expect their adjusted net income to exceed £100,000,

(ii) make a claim under section 809B of the Income Tax Act 2007 (which relates to certain residents not domiciled in the United Kingdom), or

(iii) expect section 809E of Income Tax Act 2007 to apply (which relates to certain residents not domiciled in the United Kingdom), and

(d) if a foster parent of the young child, has confirmation from the responsible local authority that it is satisfied that engaging in paid work other than as a foster parent is consistent with the child's care plan (see regulation 5).

(4) A parent who—

(a) has a partner (see regulation 10), and

(b) is any of the following—

(i) a person with limited capability for work;

(ii) a person with limited capability for work and work-related activity;

(iii) a person entitled to a specified benefit;

(iv) a resident of an EEA State or Switzerland who is, under the law of the EEA State or Switzerland, entitled to a benefit of a kind that is substantially similar to a specified benefit.

(5) In this regulation—

"limited capability for work" has the meaning given in the Universal Credit Regulations;

"limited capability for work and work-related activity" has the meaning given in the Universal Credit Regulations;

"specified benefit" means any of the following—

(a) an award of universal credit under the Universal Credit Regulations that includes the carer element;

(b) carer's allowance under the Social Security Act;

(c) carer's assistance given in accordance with regulations made under section 28 of the Social Security (Scotland) Act 2018 except a young carer grant given under the Carer's Assistance (Young Carer Grants) (Scotland) Regulations 2019;

(d) credits for incapacity for work or limited capability for work under any of the following—

(i) the Social Security (Credits) Regulations 1975;

(ii) the Social Security (Credits) Regulations (Northern Ireland) 1975;

(e) employment and support allowance under any of the following—

(i) the Welfare Reform Act 2007;

(ii) the Welfare Reform Act (Northern Ireland) 2007;

(f) incapacity benefit under the Social Security Act;

(g) long-term incapacity benefit under any of the following—

(i) the Social Security (Incapacity Benefit) (Transitional) Regulations 1995;

(ii) the Social Security (Incapacity Benefit) (Transitional) Regulations (Northern Ireland) 1995;

(h) severe disablement allowance under the Social Security Act; "Universal Credit Regulations" means any of the following—

(i) the Universal Credit Regulations 2013;

(ii) the Universal Credit Regulations (Northern Ireland) 2016.

Conditions relating to partner of parent

15.—(1) This regulation relates to section 1(2)(d) of the Act.   1.071

(2) If a parent of a young child has a partner, the partner must be a person who—

(a) meets the qualifying paid work requirement in regulation 16 or 17,

(b) does not for the relevant tax year—

(i) expect their adjusted net income to exceed £100,000,

(ii) make a claim under section 809B of the Income Tax Act 2007 (which relates to certain residents not domiciled in the United Kingdom), or

   (iii) expect section 809E of Income Tax Act 2007 to apply (which relates to certain residents not domiciled in the United Kingdom),

 (c) in the last year has not been, and does not expect in the next year to be, living away from the parent for more than six months, and

 (d) if a foster parent of the young child, has confirmation from the responsible local authority that it is satisfied that engaging in any paid work other than as a foster parent is consistent with the child's care plan (see regulation 5).

Qualifying paid work requirement: employee

1.072 **16.**—(1) A person who is an employee is in qualifying paid work if the person—

 (a) holds a national insurance number (unless paragraph (2) applies), and

 (b) meets the minimum income requirement in regulation 18 (unless paragraph (3) applies).

(2) Despite paragraph (1)(a), a person is not required to hold a national insurance number if the person is—

 (a) a resident of an EEA State or Switzerland, and

 (b) not an employee in the United Kingdom.

(3) Despite paragraph (1)(b), a person is not required to meet the minimum income requirement during any of the following—

 (a) any period the person is on specified leave other than adoption leave of the kind mentioned in sub-paragraph (b);

 (b) in the case of a person on adoption leave relating to a young child in respect of whom a declaration is being made, the period of 31 days ending before the day on which the person returns to work;

 (c) in the case of a person in an EEA State or Switzerland, any period the person is, under the law of the EEA State or Switzerland, on leave of a kind substantially similar to specified leave.

(4) In this regulation—

"adoption leave" means, in relation to a person, any of the following—

 (a) a period the person is, under an employment rights enactment, absent from work during any of the following—

  (i) an adoption leave period (whether ordinary or additional);

  (ii) a shared parental leave period;

 (b) a period the person is receiving statutory adoption pay under the Social Security Act;

"employment rights enactment" means any of the following—

 (a) the Employment Rights Act 1996;

 (b) the Employment Rights (Northern Ireland) Order 1996;

"national insurance number" means a national insurance number allocated under any of the following—

 (a) the National Insurance Act 1965;

(b) the National Insurance Act (Northern Ireland) 1966;

(c) the Social Security Act 1975;

(d) the Social Security (Northern Ireland) Act 1975;

"specified leave" means, in relation to a person, any of the following—

    (a) a period the person is, under an employment rights enactment, absent from work during any of the following—

        (i) an adoption leave period (whether ordinary or additional);

        (ii) a maternity leave period (whether ordinary or additional);

        (iii) a parental bereavement leave period;

        (iv) a shared parental leave period;

        (v) a statutory parental leave period;

    (b) a period the person is, under the Social Security Act, receiving any of the following—

        (i) state maternity allowance;

        (ii) statutory adoption pay;

        (iii) statutory maternity pay;

        (iv) statutory parental bereavement pay;

        (v) statutory paternity pay;

        (vi) statutory shared parental pay;

        (vii) statutory sick pay.

Qualifying paid work requirement: self-employed person

17.—(1) A person who is a self-employed person is in qualifying paid work if the person—   1.073

    (a) holds a national insurance number (unless paragraph (2) applies), and

    (b) meets the minimum income requirement in regulation 18 (unless paragraph (3) applies).

(2) Despite paragraph (1)(a), a person is not required to hold a national insurance number if the person is—

    (a) a resident of an EEA State or Switzerland, and

    (b) not in self-employment in the United Kingdom.

(3) Despite paragraph (1)(b), a person is not required to meet the minimum income requirement during any of the following—

    (a) any period the person would, if the person were an employee, not be required to meet the minimum income requirement (see regulation 16(3));

    (b) if the person is in a start-up period, the period of 12 months beginning with the day on which the declaration relating to the person is made.

(4) In this regulation, "start-up period" means the period of 12 months—

    (a) beginning with the day on which the person commences self-employment, but

(b) only if the person did not commence self-employment in any trade, profession or vocation in the period of five years ending before that day.

Minimum income requirement

1.074   **18.**—(1) A person meets the minimum income requirement if the amount of income the person expects to earn from qualifying paid work in the relevant period is an amount of income equal to or greater than the product of—

(a) the minimum weekly income, and

(b) the number of weeks in the relevant period.

(2) The person may include the amount of income the person expects to earn as—

(a) an employee,

(b) a self-employed person, or

(c) an employee and a self-employed person.

(3) In this regulation—

"income" means—

    (a) in relation to an employee—

        (i) any earnings within the meaning given in section 62 of the Income Tax (Earnings and Pensions) Act 2003, and

        (ii) any amount treated as earnings under Chapters 7 to 10 of Part 2 of the Income Tax (Earnings and Pensions) Act 2003 (which relate to agency workers and workers' services provided through intermediaries or managed service companies);

    (b) in relation to a self-employed person—

        (i) the amount of non-capital receipts the person expects to derive from a trade, profession or vocation less the amount of non-capital expenses the person expects to incur wholly and exclusively for the purposes of the trade, profession or vocation, or

        (ii) if the person carries on a trade, profession or vocation in a business partnership, the share expected to be allocated to the person of the partnership's non-capital receipts less the share expected to be allocated to that person of the partnership's non-capital expenses incurred wholly and exclusively for the purposes of the trade, profession or vocation;

"minimum weekly income" means, in relation to a person, the product of—

    (a) 16, and

    (b) the hourly rate of the national minimum wage to which the person is entitled to be paid under the National Minimum Wage Act 1998;

"non-capital" means not of a capital nature;

"relevant period" means one of the following—

(a) in the case of income as an employee, the period of three months beginning with the day on which the declaration relating to the employee is made;

(b) in the case of income as a self-employed person, any of the following—

    (i) the period mentioned in paragraph (a);

    (ii) the relevant tax year;

(c) in the case of income as an employee and a self-employed person, the period mentioned in paragraph (a).

Declaration

How to make a declaration

19.—(1) This regulation relates to section 1(2)(e) of the Act.   1.075

(2) A person who makes a declaration in respect of a young child must be—

(a) the parent, or the partner of the parent, with whom the child normally lives, and

(b) a person in the United Kingdom.

(3) The declaration must be made—

(a) to the relevant authority,

(b) in either of the periods mentioned in regulation 20, and

(c) in the form and manner specified under regulation 21 (if any).

(4) In this regulation—

"person in the United Kingdom" has the meaning given in regulation 11;

"relevant authority" means—

(a) in the case of a declaration in respect of a child who is placed with a foster parent, the responsible local authority, or

(b) in the case of any other declaration, the Commissioners.

When a declaration may be made

20. A declaration in respect of a young child may be made—   1.076

(a) in the period of 16 weeks ending before the day on which the child will meet the description in regulation 13 (if known), or

(b) in the period—

    (i) beginning with the day on which the child meets the description in regulation 13, and

    (ii) ending before the day on which the child ceases to satisfy the requirements of section 1(2)(a) or (b) of the Act.

Form and manner of declaration

21.—(1) The Commissioners or the responsible local authority (as the case may be) may specify the form of a declaration and the manner in which it is to be made.   1.077

(2) The specification may (amongst other things)—

(a) require a declaration to include information to—

    (i) identify the person making the declaration (and any partner of that person),

      (ii) identify the young child in respect of whom the declaration is being made, and

      (iii) determine whether the young child is a qualifying child of working parents;

(b) require a declaration to be made by electronic communications;

(c) if a declaration relates to a self-employed person, require a declaration to be accompanied by confirmation, orally or in writing, that the self-employed person has complied with any notice given under section 8(1) of the Taxes Management Act 1970 (which relates to personal returns).

Determination

Determination of qualifying child of working parents: Commissioners

1.078   **22.**—(1) This regulation applies if—

(a) a person makes a declaration to the Commissioners in respect of a young child, and

(b) the Commissioners have not declined to make a determination in respect of the declaration (see regulation 23).

(2) The Commissioners must—

(a) make a determination as to whether the child is a qualifying child of working parents,

(b) notify the person of the determination, and

(c) include in that notification a statement to the effect that the person has—

      (i) a right to apply to the Commissioners for a review of the determination (see regulation 36), and

      (ii) a right to appeal to the First-tier Tribunal against the determination, but only after the Commissioners have considered an application for a review (see regulation 40).

Power to decline to make a determination

1.079   **23.**—(1) This regulation applies if—

(a) two or more persons each make a declaration to the Commissioners in respect of the same young child, and

(b) it appears to the Commissioners that two or more of those persons may meet the requirements in regulation 19(2) (which provides for who can make a declaration).

(2) The Commissioners may, in respect of one or more of the declarations, decline to make a determination as to whether the child is a qualifying child of working parents.

(3) If the Commissioners decline to make a determination, they must—

(a) notify the person who made the declaration, and

(b) include in the notification a statement to the effect that the person has—

      (i) a right to apply to the Commissioners for a review of the decision (see regulation 36), and

(ii) a right to appeal to the First-tier Tribunal against the decision, but only after the Commissioners have considered an application for a review (see regulation 40).

Determination of qualifying child of working parents: responsible local authority

24.—(1) This regulation applies if a person makes a declaration to the responsible local authority in respect of a young child placed with a foster parent.   1.080

(2) The responsible local authority (on behalf of the Commissioners) must—

(a) make a determination as to whether the child is a qualifying child of working parents, and

(b) notify the person of the determination.

Effect of declaration

Period for which declaration has effect

25.—(1) A declaration in respect of a young child has effect for three months beginning with—   1.081

(a) the day on which the young child is determined to be a qualifying child of working parents, or

(b) if the declaration was made in accordance with regulation 20(a) (which provides for anticipatory declarations), the day on which the young child meets the description in regulation 13.

(2) Despite paragraph (1), the Commissioners may, if they consider it appropriate, vary the period for which a declaration has effect—

(a) by no more than two months to align the period with—

(i) any entitlement period relating to the child in respect of whom the declaration was made,

(ii) the period for which any declaration relating to another child has effect, or

(iii) any entitlement period relating to another child, or

(b) by no more than one month for any other reason.

(3) This regulation is subject to regulation 26 (when parallel declaration ceases to have effect).

(4) In this regulation—

"another child" means—

(a) another child of the parent of the young child in respect of whom the declaration was made, or

(b) a child of the partner of that parent;

"entitlement period" means a period determined in accordance with section 5 of the Childcare Payments Act 2014 (which relates to the receipt of money towards childcare costs).

When a parallel declaration ceases to have effect

26.—(1) This regulation applies if—   1.082

(a) a person has made a declaration in respect of a young child ("Declaration A"),

    (b) Declaration A has effect (see regulation 25),

    (c) another person makes a declaration in respect of the same child ("Declaration B"), and

    (d) the child is, in relation to Declaration B, determined to be a qualifying child of working parents.

(2) Declaration A ceases to have effect beginning with the day on which Declaration B has effect.

Eligibility for childcare

Period of eligibility for childcare

1.083   **27.**—(1) A child is eligible for childcare under section 1 of the Act for the period—

    (a) beginning with whichever of 1st January, 1st April or 1st September is the first date on or after the day on which a declaration in respect of the child has effect, and

    (b) ending before the day on which the child ceases to be a qualifying child of working parents.

(2) A year begins with the date calculated in accordance with paragraph (1) for the purposes of determining in relation to the child whether the duty in section 1(1) of the Act has been discharged.

Disclosure of information

Information relating to immigration and social security

1.084   **28.**—(1) The Secretary of State may disclose to the Commissioners any information held by the Secretary of State for the purposes of their functions relating to any of the following—

    (a) immigration control;

    (b) social security.

(2) The Commissioners may use the information only in connection with the making of a determination as to whether a child is a qualifying child of working parents.

Information relating to qualifying child of working parents

1.085   **29.** The Secretary of State, the Commissioners and an English local authority may disclose information to each other for the purpose of checking any of the following—

    (a) whether a declaration in respect of a child has been made;

    (b) if a declaration in respect of a child has been made, whether the child was determined to be a qualifying child of working parents (see regulations 22 and 24);

    (c) if a child was determined to be a qualifying child of working parents, whether the declaration in respect of the child has effect (see regulations 25 and 26).

Part 4

Offences and penalties

Offences

Offence relating to onward disclosure of personal information

30.—(1) A person commits an offence if—   1.086
(a) the person discloses information in contravention of regulation 28 or 29,
(b) the disclosure relates to any person whose identity—
    (i) is specified in the disclosure, or
    (ii) can be deduced from it, and
(c) the disclosure is made other than in accordance with—
    (i) an enactment,
    (ii) an order of a court, or
    (iii) the written consent of the person to whom the information relates.

(2) It is a defence for a person charged with an offence under this regulation to prove that the person reasonably believed—
(a) that the disclosure was lawful, or
(b) that the information had already and lawfully been made available to the public.

(3) A person guilty of an offence under this regulation is liable—
(a) on conviction on indictment, to imprisonment for a term not exceeding two years, to a fine or to both, or
(b) on summary conviction—
    (i) in England and Wales, to imprisonment for a term not exceeding 12 months, to a fine or to both;
    (ii) in Northern Ireland, to imprisonment for a term not exceeding 6 months, to a fine not exceeding the statutory maximum or to both;
    (iii) in Scotland, to imprisonment for a term not exceeding 12 months, to a fine not exceeding the statutory maximum or to both.

Penalties

Penalty for dishonest conduct

31.—(1) A person is liable to a penalty under this regulation if the   1.087
person engages in dishonest conduct in connection with the process of
making a determination of a child's eligibility for childcare under section
1 of the Act.

(2) The amount of the penalty must not exceed £3,000.

Penalty for false or misleading information

32.—(1) A person is liable to a penalty under this regulation if the   1.088
person, by reason of a failure to take reasonable care, provides false or

misleading information, or makes or provides a false or misleading statement, in connection with a determination of a child's eligibility for childcare under section 1 of the Act.

(2) Despite paragraph (1), the person is not liable to the penalty if the person—

    (a) becomes aware of the false or misleading information or statement, and

    (b) takes reasonable steps to inform the Commissioners or the responsible local authority (as the case may be).

(3) The amount of the penalty must not exceed £500.

Penalty for material inaccuracy in declaration

1.089   **33.**—(1) A person is liable to a penalty under this regulation if, by reason of a failure to take reasonable care, the person includes a material inaccuracy in a declaration.

(2) The amount of the penalty must not exceed £300.

Assessment of penalty

1.090   **34.**—(1) If a person becomes liable to a penalty under any of regulations 31, 32 or 33—

    (a) the Commissioners may, subject to paragraph (3), assess the penalty, and

    (b) if they do so, they must notify the person.

(2) The notification must include a statement to the effect that the person has—

    (a) a right to apply to the Commissioners for a review of the penalty or its amount (see regulation 36), and

    (b) a right to appeal to the First-tier Tribunal against the determination, but only after the Commissioners have considered an application for a review (see regulation 40).

(3) The Commissioners must not assess a penalty in relation to a person after the end of whichever of the following ends first—

    (a) the period of one year beginning with the day on which the Commissioners first believed, or had reasonable grounds for believing, the person was liable to the penalty;

    (b) in the case of a penalty under regulation 31, the period of 20 years beginning with the day on which the person became liable to the penalty;

    (c) in the case of a penalty under regulation 32, the period of four years beginning with the day on which the person became liable to the penalty.

Enforcement of penalty

1.091   **35.**—(1) This regulation applies if the Commissioners notify a person of a penalty (see regulation 34).

(2) The person must pay the penalty—

    (a) if the person does not apply for a review (see regulation 36)—

        (i) within 30 days of the day on which the notification is made, or

    (ii) if the person is granted an extension to their right to apply for a review, on or before the date notified under regulation 37(5)(a)(ii);

(b) if the person applies for a review, unless the penalty is set aside, within 30 days of the day on which the person is notified of the outcome of the review (see regulation 38(5));

(c) if the person gives notice of appeal (see regulation 39), unless the penalty is set aside, on or before the day after the day on which—

    (i) the First-tier Tribunal gives a decision (see regulation 42), or

    (ii) if the person gives notice of the withdrawal of their case, the First-tier Tribunal consents to that withdrawal.

(3) A penalty may be enforced as if it were income tax charged in an assessment and due and payable.

PART 5

REVIEWS AND APPEALS

Reviews

Right to apply for review

36.—(1) This regulation applies if the Commissioners notify a person   **1.092** of any of the following—

(a) a decision to decline to make a determination as to whether a child is a qualifying child of working parents (see regulation 23);

(b) a determination as to whether a child is a qualifying child of working parents (see regulation 22);

(c) the assessment of a penalty (see regulation 34).

(2) The person may apply to the Commissioners for a review of (as the case may be)—

(a) the decision,

(b) the determination, or

(c) the penalty or its amount.

(3) The application must—

(a) be made—

    (i) within 30 days of the day on which the notification is made, or

    (ii) if the person is granted an extension of their right to apply for a review, on or before the date notified under regulation 37(5)(a)(ii),

(b) be in the form and manner specified under paragraph (4) (if any), and

(c) include the person's reasons for the application.

(4) The Commissioners may specify—

(a) the form of an application, and

(b) the manner in which it is to be made (which may require electronic communications).

Extension of right to apply for review

1.093   **37.**—(1) This regulation applies if the Commissioners notify a person of a matter mentioned in regulation 36(1).

(2) The person may apply to the Commissioners for an extension of their right to apply for a review.

(3) The application must—

(a) be made within seven months of the day on which the notification is made,

(b) be in the form and manner specified under paragraph (6) (if any), and

(c) include the applicant's reasons why it is, or was, not practicable for the person to apply for the review within 30 days of the day on which the notification is made.

(4) The Commissioners may—

(a) grant the application if they are satisfied—

   (i) it is (or was) not practicable due to special circumstances for the person to apply for the review within 30 days of the day on which the notification is made, and

   (ii) the granting of the application is reasonable in all the circumstances of the case, or

(b) decline the application.

(5) If the Commissioners—

(a) grant the application, they must—

   (i) specify a date on or before which the applicant must apply for the review, and

   (ii) notify the applicant of that date;

(b) decline the application—

   (i) they must notify the applicant, and

   (ii) the applicant must not make any further application in respect of the matter.

(6) The Commissioners may specify—

(a) the form of the application, and

(b) the manner in which the application is made.

Review procedure

1.094   **38.**—(1) This regulation applies if a person ("the applicant") makes an application for a review.

(2) The Commissioners must—

(a) review (as the case may be)—

   (i) the decision to decline to make a determination as to whether a child is a qualifying child of working parents,

   (ii) the determination as to whether a child is a qualifying child of working parents, or

   (iii) the imposition of the penalty or its amount, and

(b) complete the review—

(i) if no request under paragraph (3) is made, within 30 days of the day on which the application is made,

(ii) if a request under paragraph (3) is made, within 44 days of the day on which the application is made, or

(iii) within any other period agreed between the Commissioners and the applicant.

(3) The Commissioners may ask the applicant to provide further information or evidence in support of their application.

(4) If the Commissioners ask for further information or evidence, the Commissioners—

(a) must consider any information or evidence the applicant provides to the Commissioners within 14 days of the day on which the request is made, and

(b) may disregard any information or evidence provided after that period.

(5) Following the review, the Commissioners must—

(a) confirm, revise or set aside (as the case may be)—

(i) the decision,

(ii) the determination, or

(iii) the penalty or its amount, and

(b) notify the applicant of the result of the review.

(6) If the Commissioners revise a determination to determine that a child is a qualifying child of working parents, the date of the determination is the date on which the determination is revised.

Appeals

Right to appeal following review

39.—(1) This regulation applies if a person makes an application to the Commissioners for a review of—

(a) a decision to decline to make a determination as to whether a child is a qualifying child of working parents,

(b) a determination as to whether a child is a qualifying child of working parents, or

(c) a penalty or its amount.

(2) Following the review, the person may appeal to the First-tier Tribunal(57) against (as the case may be)—

(a) the decision (see regulation 40),

(b) the determination (see regulation 41), or

(c) the penalty or its amount (see regulation 42).

Appeal against decision to decline to make a determination

40.—(1) This regulation applies if a person appeals to the First-tier Tribunal against a decision to decline to make a determination as to whether a child is a qualifying child of working parents.

(2) The Tribunal may—

(a) confirm the decision, or

(b) set aside the decision.

1.095

1.096

(3) If the Tribunal sets aside the decision, the Commissioners must comply with regulation 22(2) in respect of the declaration (which requires a determination as to whether a child is a qualifying child of working parents).

Appeal against determination as to qualifying child of working parents

1.097   **41.**—(1) This regulation applies if a person appeals to the First-tier Tribunal against a determination as to whether a child is a qualifying child of working parents.

(2) The Tribunal may—
(a) confirm the determination, or
(b) withdraw any part of the determination the Tribunal finds was—
    (i) based on an error in fact, or
    (ii) wrong in law.

(3) If the Tribunal withdraws a part of the determination—
(a) it must for that part substitute its own determination, and
(b) the substituted determination is to be treated as if it were a determination made by the Commissioners or the responsible local authority (as the case may be) on the date of the notice that states the Tribunal's decision.

Appeal against imposition of penalty or amount

1.098   **42.**—(1) This regulation applies if a person appeals to the First-tier Tribunal against the imposition of a penalty or its amount.

(2) The Tribunal may—
(a) uphold the imposition of the penalty,
(b) set aside the penalty, or
(c) substitute the amount of the penalty with an amount the Tribunal determines.

Power to settle appeals by agreement

1.099   **43.**—(1) This regulation applies if—
(a) a person has a right of appeal to the First-tier Tribunal (see regulation 39),
(b) the person starts proceedings in the Tribunal (by sending or delivering a notice of appeal to it), and
(c) the Tribunal has not finally disposed of all issues in the proceedings.

(2) The Commissioners may agree with the appellant, in writing or otherwise, that the Commissioners' decision, determination or penalty or its amount (as the case may be) is to be treated as—
(a) upheld without variation,
(b) as varied in a particular manner, or
(c) as discharged or cancelled.

(3) If the agreement is not in writing, the Commissioners must notify the appellant in writing of—
(a) the fact that an agreement was made,

(b) the terms agreed,

(c) the date of the agreement, and

(d) the appellant's right under paragraph (4) to repudiate or resile from the agreement.

(4) The appellant may, within 30 days of the day on which the agreement is made, give notice to the Commissioners that the appellant desires to repudiate or resile from the agreement.

(5) If the notice mentioned in paragraph (4) is not given—

(a) the Commissioners must send notice of the agreement to the First-tier Tribunal, and

(b) the Tribunal must treat the notice as if it were a request for a consent order.

(6) In this regulation—

"appellant" means the person mentioned in paragraph (1);

"consent order" means a consent order made by the First-tier Tribunal under rule 32 of the Tribunal Procedure (First-tier Tribunal) (Social Entitlement Chamber) Rules 2008;

PART 6

DUTIES OF ENGLISH LOCAL AUTHORITIES

Childcare for qualifying children of working parents

Duty to secure childcare available free of charge

44.—(1) An English local authority must secure that childcare is made available free of charge for every child in its area who is a qualifying child of working parents. **1.100**

(2) The childcare must be—

(a) provided by a childcare provider, and

(b) made available for 570 hours during no fewer than 38 weeks in each year.

Arrangements for provision of childcare

Duty to make arrangements with childcare provider chosen by parent

45.—(1) The parent of a child in the area of an English local authority may choose a childcare provider to provide the childcare the local authority must secure for the child (see regulation 44). **1.101**

(2) The local authority must make arrangements for the childcare if the provider is willing—

    (a) to provide the childcare to the child, and

    (b) to accept as part of the arrangements—

        (i) the local authority's terms as to payment for the childcare,

        (ii) the mandatory termination provision (see regulation 46), and

        (iii) any requirements the local authority seeks to impose (see regulation 47).

(3) Paragraph (2) does not apply if the provider is any of the following—

    (a) a childcare provider the local authority has grounds to believe would not be able to satisfy a requirement the authority would impose if arrangements were made;

    (b) a childminder registered with an early years childminder agency that—

        (i) fails in its most recent inspection report (if any) to achieve a grade of "effective" or better, or

        (ii) notifies the local authority that, in the agency's reasonable opinion, the childminder has ceased to provide childcare of satisfactory quality;

    (c) a childcare provider (other than a childminder registered with a childcare agency) that fails in its most recent inspection report (if any) to achieve Grade 3 ("requires improvement") or better for the overall effectiveness of its childcare.

(4) Paragraph (2)(b) does not apply if the provider is the governing body of a maintained school.

Arrangements to provide for termination

1.102   **46.** An English local authority must, as part of arrangements with a childcare provider under regulation 45(2), include provision authorising the local authority to terminate the arrangements if the provider—

    (a) ceases to be a childcare provider (see regulation 6), or

    (b) becomes a childcare provider mentioned in regulation 45(3)(b) or (c) (which relates to minimum standard of childcare).

Requirements permissible in arrangements

1.103   **47.**—(1) As part of any arrangements with a childcare provider under regulation 45(2), an English local authority may impose on the provider one or more of only the following requirements—

    (a) a requirement to enable the local authority to—

        (i) comply with its duty to make arrangements with a childcare provider chosen by the parent of a child (see regulation 45), and

        (ii) terminate the arrangements (see regulation 46);

    (b) a requirement for the purpose of satisfying one or more of the following objectives—

        (i) that the childcare is provided free of charge;

    (ii) that the childcare is provided in a pattern to suit the needs of the parents of the children for whom the childcare is provided;

    (iii) that any financial assistance provided by a local authority under the arrangements is used properly and in accordance with the arrangements;

(c) a requirement for the purpose of meeting the needs of a child—

    (i) to whom the local authority owes a duty under regulation 45, and

    (ii) who has a disability or special educational needs;

(d) a requirement that the provider actively promotes the fundamental British values of —

    (i) democracy,

    (ii) individual liberty,

    (iii) mutual respect and tolerance of those with different faiths and beliefs, and

    (iv) the rule of law;

(e) a requirement that views or theories contrary to established scientific or historical evidence and explanations are not promoted as evidence-based views or theories;

(f) a requirement that, if the childcare provider (being other than a childminder registered with a childcare agency) achieves in its most recent inspection report (if any) the minimum grade mentioned in regulation 45(3)(c) or worse, the provider takes the measures specified in the report—

    (i) to improve the overall effectiveness of its childcare, and

    (ii) which may include the participation in any training or other quality improvement programme specified in the report;

(g) a requirement necessary for the effective administration of the arrangements.

(2) In this regulation—

"disability" has the meaning given in section 6 of the Equality Act 2010;

"special educational needs" has the meaning given in section 20 of the Children and Families Act 2014.

Requirements prohibited in arrangements

48. An English local authority must not, as part of arrangements with a childcare provider under regulation 45(2), impose on the provider any of the following—   **1.104**

(a) a requirement that the provider attend a training or other quality improvement programme other than that specified in an inspection report;

(b) a requirement subjecting the provider to a quality assessment process conducted by the local authority relating to—

    (i) in the case of a childminder registered with an early years childminder agency, the quality of the agency's services, or

    (ii) in the case of any other childcare provider, the quality of the provider's childcare.

Duty of English local authority to have regard to guidance

1.105   **49.** An English local authority must, when discharging its duties under these Regulations, have regard to any guidance given from time to time by the Secretary of State.

SCHEDULE   **Regulation 3**

CONSEQUENTIAL AMENDMENTS AND REVOCATIONS

Consequential amendments

Amendment of the Childcare Act 2006 (Provision of Information to Parents) (England) Regulations 2007

1.106   **1.**—(1) The Childcare Act 2006 (Provision of Information to Parents) (England) Regulations 2007 are amended in accordance with paragraph (2).

(2) In regulation 1(2)—

(a) in the definition of "the extended entitlement", for "regulation 33 of the Childcare (Early Years Provision Free of Charge) (Extended Entitlement) Regulations 2016" substitute "regulation 44 of the Childcare (Free of Charge for Working Parents) (England) Regulations 2022";

(b) in the definition of "free early years provision", in paragraph (b), for "regulation 33 of the Childcare (Early Years Provision Free of Charge) (Extended Entitlement) Regulations 2016" substitute "regulation 44 of the Childcare (Free of Charge for Working Parents) (England) Regulations 2022".

Amendment of the First-tier Tribunal and Upper Tribunal (Chambers) Order 2010

1.107   **2.**—(1) The First-tier Tribunal and Upper Tribunal (Chambers) Order 2010 is amended in accordance with sub-paragraph (2).

(2) In Article 6(eb), for "the Childcare (Early Years Provision Free of Charge) (Extended Entitlement) Regulations 2016" substitute "the Childcare (Free of Charge for Working Parents) (England) Regulations 2022".

Amendment of the Childcare Payments Regulations 2015

1.108   **3.**—(1) The Childcare Payments Regulations 2015 are amended on accordance with sub-paragraph (2).

(2) In regulation 5(1)(d), for "regulation 15 of the Childcare (Early Years Provision Free of Charge) (Extended Entitlement) Regulations 2016" substitute "regulation 25 of the Childcare (Free of Charge for Working Parents) (England) Regulations 2022".

Amendment of the Childcare (Early Years Provision Free of Charge) (Extended Entitlement) Regulations 2016

1.109   **4.**—(1) The Childcare (Early Years Provision Free of Charge) (Extended Entitlement) Regulations 2016 are amended in accordance with sub-paragraphs (2) to (5)

(2) In the title to the instrument, for "Childcare (Early Years Provision Free of Charge) (Extended Entitlement)" substitute "Childcare Act 2016 (Consequential Amendments)".

(3) In regulation 1(1), for "Childcare (Early Years Provision Free of Charge) (Extended Entitlement)" substitute "Childcare Act 2016 (Consequential Amendments)".

(4) In regulation 1(2), for "1, 2, 3" substitute "1";

(5) Omit—

(a) regulation 1(3) (which relates to the commencement of Part 4);

(b) regulation 2 (interpretation);

(c) Part 2 (a qualifying child of working parents);

(d) Part 3 (information, reviews, appeals and penalties);

(e) Part 4 (local authorities' duty to secure early years provision).

Amendment of the Childcare (Disqualification) and Childcare (Early Years Provision Free of Charge) (Extended Entitlement) (Amendment) Regulations 2018

5.—(1) The Childcare (Disqualification) and Childcare (Early Years Provision Free of   **1.110** Charge) (Extended Entitlement) (Amendment) Regulations 2018 are amended in accordance with sub-paragraph (2).

(2) Omit Part 3 (amendment of the Childcare (Early Years Provision Free of Charge) (Extended Entitlement) Regulations 2016).

Amendment of the Parental Bereavement Leave and Pay (Consequential Amendments to Subordinate Legislation) Regulations 2020

6.—(1) The Parental Bereavement Leave and Pay (Consequential Amendments to   **1.111** Subordinate Legislation) Regulations 2020 are amended in accordance with sub-paragraph (2).

(2) Omit regulation 40 (Childcare (Early Years Provision Free of Charge) (Extended Entitlement) Regulations 2016).

Amendment of the Tax Credits, Childcare Payments and Childcare (Extended Entitlement) (Coronavirus and Miscellaneous Amendments) Regulations 2020

7.—(1) The Tax Credits, Childcare Payments and Childcare (Extended Entitlement)   **1.112** (Coronavirus and Miscellaneous Amendments) Regulations 2020 are amended in accordance with sub-paragraph (2).

(2) Omit regulation 5 (Amendment of the Childcare (Early Years Provision Free of Charge) (Extended Entitlement) Regulations 2016).

Amendment of the Criminal Justice Act 2003 (Commencement No. 33) and Sentencing Act 2020 (Commencement No. 2) Regulations 2022

8.—(1) The Criminal Justice Act 2003 (Commencement No. 33) and Sentencing Act   **1.113** 2020 (Commencement No. 2) Regulations 2022 are amended in accordance with sub-paragraph (2).

(2) In the Schedule, in Part 2, in the table, in Column 1, omit the words "Regulation 19(5) of the Childcare (Early Years Provision Free of Charge) (Extended Entitlement) Regulations 2016 (S.I. 2016/1257)".

Revocations

Revocations

9. The enactments cited in the table are revoked.   **1.114**

Enactment	Citation
The Childcare (Early Years Provision Free of Charge) (Extended Entitlement) (Amendment) Regulations 2017	S.I. 2017/1160
The Childcare (Early Years Provision Free of Charge) (Extended Entitlement) (Coronavirus) (Amendment) Regulations 2020	S.I. 2020/712
The Childcare (Early Years Provision Free of Charge) (Extended Entitlement) (Amendment) Regulations 2021	S.I. 2021/674
The Childcare (Early Years Provision Free of Charge) (Extended Entitlement) (Amendment) (No. 2) Regulations 2021	S.I. 2021/1168

The Tax Credits Act 2002 (Additional Payments Modification and Disapplication) Regulations 2022

(SI 2022/1208)

The Commissioners for His Majesty's Revenue and Customs, in exercise of the powers conferred by sections 6(5) and (6) and 10(1) of the Social Security (Additional Payments) Act 2022, make the following Regulations.

Citation, commencement and interpretation

1.115   **1.**—(1) These Regulations may be cited as the Tax Credits Act 2002 (Additional Payments Modification and Disapplication) Regulations 2022 and come into force on 22nd December 2022 but regulations 2 to 6 have effect from 28th June 2022.

(2) In these Regulations "additional payment" means payments made by His Majesty's Revenue Customs in accordance with section 1(2) or 4(1) or (2) of the Social Security (Additional Payments) Act 2022.

Modification and disapplication of the Tax Credits Act 2002

1.116   **2.** The Tax Credits Act 2002 is modified as follows.

3. In respect of an additional payment, made to a person who is, or persons who are, not entitled to the additional payment, sections 14 to 19 are disapplied.

4. Section 20 has effect as if after subsection (5), there were inserted—

"(5A) Where the Board have reasonable grounds for believing that an additional payment has been paid to a person, or two persons jointly, by reference to a child tax credit or working tax credit and that the person or persons had no entitlement to the payment, the Board may decide that the additional payment was paid incorrectly.

(5B) But no decision may be made under subsection (5A) after the period of five years beginning with the end of the tax year in which the additional payment is made."

5. Section 28 has effect as if—
(a) in subsection (1)—
   (i) after "sections 18 to 21C)," there were inserted "or where the Commissioners have decided that an additional payment was paid incorrectly,",
   (ii) after "any part of it," there were inserted "or the incorrectly paid additional payment, or any part of it,",
(b) in subsection (2), after "an excess" there were inserted "or incorrectly paid additional payment",
(c) in subsections (3) and (4), after "awarded" there were inserted "or to whom the additional payment was made".

6. Section 67 has effect as if, at the appropriate place, there were inserted—

""additional payment" means a payment made under section 1(2) or 4(1) or (2) of the Social Security (Additional Payments) Act 2022 or a payment purporting to be a payment under any of those provisions."

The Cessation of EU Law Relating to Prohibitions on Grounds of Nationality and Free Movement of Persons Regulations 2022

(SI 2022/1240)

Made 28th November 2022

The Secretary of State, in exercise of the powers conferred by section 8(1) of, and paragraph 21 of Schedule 7 to, the European Union (Withdrawal) Act 2018 makes the following Regulations.

In accordance with paragraph 1(3) of Schedule 7 to that Act, a draft of this instrument has been laid before Parliament and approved by a resolution of each House of Parliament.

Citation, commencement and interpretation

1.117   **1.**—(1) These Regulations may be cited as the Cessation of EU Law Relating to Prohibitions on Grounds of Nationality and Free Movement of Persons Regulations 2022.

(2) These Regulations come into force on the day after the day on which they are made.

(3) In these Regulations, "relevant matters" are the matters set out in the Schedule.

(4) Nothing in these Regulations is to be construed as implying in any respect the continued application, recognition or availability in domestic law of—

(a) the prohibitions referred to in regulation 2;

(b) the rights, powers, liabilities, obligations, restrictions, remedies and procedures referred to in regulation 3; or

(c) Article 7(2) of Regulation (EU) No 492/2011 of the European Parliament and of the Council of 5th April 2011 on freedom of movement for workers within the Union.

Cessation of prohibitions on grounds of nationality

1.118   **2.** The prohibitions on the grounds of nationality which—

(a) continue by virtue of section 4(1) of the European Union (Withdrawal) Act 2018; and

(b) are derived from—

(i) Article 18 of the Treaty on the Functioning of the European Union;

(ii) Article 4 of the EEA Agreement; and

(iii) Article 2 of the Agreement between the European Community and its Member States and the Swiss Confederation on the free movement of persons signed at Brussels on 21st June 1999,

so far as they relate to relevant matters, cease to be recognised and available in domestic law (and to be enforced, allowed and followed accordingly).

Cessation of free movement of persons

1.119   **3.** Any rights, powers, liabilities, obligations, restrictions, remedies and procedures which—

54

(a) continue by virtue of section 4(1) of the European Union (Withdrawal) Act 2018; and

(b) are derived (directly or indirectly) from—

    (i) Article 21 or 45 of the Treaty on the Functioning of the European Union;

    (ii) Article 28 or 29 of the EEA Agreement; or

    (iii) Articles 3(6), 9(2), (3) and (6), and 15 of Annex 1 to the Agreement between the European Community and its Member States and the Swiss Confederation on the free movement of persons signed at Brussels on 21st June 1999,

so far as they relate to relevant matters, cease to be recognised and available in domestic law (and to be enforced, allowed and followed accordingly).

Amendment of Regulation (EU) No 492/2011

4.—(1) Regulation (EU) No 492/2011 of the European Parliament and of the Council of 5th April 2011 on freedom of movement for workers within the Union is amended as follows.   **1.120**

(2) In Article 7—

(a) after paragraph 2, insert—

"**2A.**

Paragraphs 1 and 2 do not apply in relation to the matters set out in the Schedule to the Cessation of EU Law Relating to Prohibitions on Grounds of Nationality and Free Movement of Persons Regulations 2022 (relevant matters).";

(b) omit paragraph 3.

(3) Omit Articles 9 and 10.

SCHEDULE

Relevant Matters

Social security and statutory payments

1.— (1) Social security, including—   **1.121**

(a) any scheme providing financial assistance to or in respect of individuals, in particular providing such assistance to or in respect of individuals—

    (i) who qualify by reason of old age, survivorship, bereavement, disability, sickness, incapacity, injury, unemployment, maternity, paternity, the care they provide to other individuals or having responsibility for other individuals;

    (ii) who qualify by reason of low income; or

    (iii) in relation to their housing costs; and

(b) tax credits under Part 1 of the Tax Credits Act 2002.

(2) The following payments under the following Parts of the Social Security Contributions and Benefits Act 1992—

(a) statutory adoption pay under Part 12ZB;

(b) statutory maternity pay under Part 12;

(c) statutory parental bereavement pay under Part 12ZD;

(d) statutory paternity pay under Part 12ZA;

(e) statutory shared parental pay under Part 12ZC; and

(f) statutory sick pay under Part 11.

(3) Sub-paragraph (2) is without prejudice to sub-paragraph (1).

Social assistance

1.122   2.—(1) Social assistance, within the meaning of Directive 2004/38/EC of the European Parliament and of the Council of 29th April 2004 on the right of citizens of the Union and their family members to move and reside freely within the territory of the Member States ("the Directive").

(2) The reference in subparagraph (1) to the Directive includes a reference to the case law of the Court of Justice of the European Union which interprets the concept of social assistance.

Housing

1.123   3.—(1) Housing, including—

(a) any accommodation provided to homeless persons; and

(b) mobile homes.

(2) "Mobile home" means caravan, motor vehicle, boat or other movable structure designed or adapted for human habitation, but does not include—

(a) any railway rolling stock which is for the time being on rails forming part of a railway system; or

(b) any tent.

Education, training and apprenticeships

1.124   4. Education, training and apprenticeships, including—

(a) social and physical training (including the promotion of the development of young children);

(b) vocational training (including that which helps people prepare for, obtain and retain employment);

(c) the charging of fees in connection with education and training; and

(d) the provision of financial assistance or financial resources in connection with education, training or apprenticeships.

Childcare, employer-supported childcare and the childcare payment scheme, etc.

1.125   5.—(1) Childcare, including—

(a) the provision of childcare free of charge; and

(b) the provision of financial assistance or financial resources in connection with the provision of childcare, including—

(i) childcare vouchers, within the meaning given in section 84 of the Income Tax (Earnings and Pensions) Act 2003 ("the 2003 Act"), or a scheme to which section 270A of that Act applies;

(ii) a scheme to which section 318 of the 2003 Act applies (employer-provided childcare);

(iii) a scheme to which section 318A of the 2003 Act applies (employer-contracted childcare);

(iv) a scheme under section 1 of the Childcare Payments Act 2014 (childcare payment scheme).

(2) "Childcare", for the purposes of this paragraph, means any form of care for a child but does not include—

(a) any form of health care for a child;

(b) care provided for a child if the care—

(i) is provided in any of the following establishments as part of the establishment's activities—

(aa) a children's home;

(bb) a care home;

(cc) a hospital in which the child is a patient;

(dd) a residential family centre; and

(ii) is so provided by the person carrying on the establishment or a person employed by the establishment (including a person who is employed under a contract of services); or

(c) care provided for a child who is detained in—

(i) a young offender institution;

(ii) a secure training college; or

(iii) a secure college.

(3) In this paragraph—

"care home", "children's home" and "residential family centre" have the same meaning as in the Care Standards Act 2000;

"child" means a person under the age of 18, except for the purposes of sub-paragraph (1)(b)(i) to (iv);

"hospital" has the meaning given by section 275 of the National Health Service Act 2006.

NEW SCOTTISH STATUTORY INSTRUMENTS

The Disability Assistance for Working Age People (Transitional Provisions and Miscellaneous Amendment) (Scotland) Regulations 2022

(SSI 2022/517)

Made	*21st June 2022*
Coming into force	*29th August 2022*

The Scottish Ministers make the following Regulations in exercise of the powers conferred by sections 31(2), 36(2), 43(5), 52 and 95 of the Social Security (Scotland) Act 2018 and all other powers enabling them to do so.

In accordance with section 96(2) of that Act, a draft of these Regulations has been laid before and approved by resolution of the Scottish Parliament.

In accordance with section 97(2) of that Act, the Scottish Ministers have informed the Scottish Commission on Social Security of their proposals, notified the Scottish Parliament that they have done so and made their proposals publicly available by such means as they consider appropriate.

PART 1

INTRODUCTORY AND INTERPRETATION

Citation, commencement and extent

1.126   **1.**—(1) These Regulations may be cited as the Disability Assistance for Working Age People (Transitional Provisions and Miscellaneous Amendment) (Scotland) Regulations 2022 and come into force on 29 August 2022.

(2) These Regulations extend to Scotland only.

Interpretation

1.127   **2.** In Parts 1, 2 and 3 of these Regulations—

"the 2018 Act" means the Social Security (Scotland) Act 2018,

"the ADP Regulations" means the Disability Assistance for Working Age People (Scotland) Regulations 2022,

"Adult Disability Payment" means disability assistance for adults given in accordance with the ADP Regulations,

"date of transfer" means the date when a transferring individual's entitlement to Adult Disability Payment begins by virtue of a transfer determination,

"daily living component of Adult Disability Payment" has the same meaning as "daily living component" in regulation 2 of the ADP Regulations,

"Disability Living Allowance" means a disability living allowance under section 71 of the Social Security Contributions and Benefits Act 1992,

"mobility component of Adult Disability Payment" has the same meaning as "mobility component" in regulation 2 of the ADP Regulations,

"notice of intention to transfer" means the notice required by regulation 3,

"relevant individual" means an individual who—

    (a) has an award of Disability Living Allowance who appears to the Scottish Ministers to be likely to be eligible for Adult Disability Payment—

        (i) who has—

            (aa) notified a change of circumstances in terms of regulation 32 of the Social Security (Claims and Payments) Regulations 1987, or

            (bb) made a claim for personal independence payment in terms of regulation 4 of the Personal Independence Payment (Transitional Provisions) Regulations 2013,

        (ii) whose award is due to be renewed, or

        (iii) who has requested to be transferred to Adult Disability Payment after 29 August 2022,

    (b) was aged 16 years old or older but under 65 years old on 8 April 2013,

    (c) is—

        (i) ordinarily resident in Scotland, or

        (ii) someone to whom regulation 15(3) (residence and presence conditions), regulation 17(1) (serving members of Her Majesty's forces, civil servants and their family members) or regulation 20(2) of the ADP Regulations (persons residing outside the United Kingdom to whom a relevant EU Regulation applies) applies,

"review determination" means the determination required by regulation 12(1),

"transfer determination" means the determination required by regulation 4(1),

"transferred individual" means an individual whose entitlement to Adult Disability Payment is given under a transfer determination, and "transferring individual" means an individual on whom the Scottish Ministers have served a notice of intention to transfer in accordance with regulation 3.

PART 2

TRANSFER TO ADULT DISABILITY PAYMENT

Notice of intention to transfer to Adult Disability Payment

1.128   **3.**—(1) The Scottish Ministers are to notify each relevant individual of their intention to transfer that individual's entitlement to disability assistance from an entitlement to Disability Living Allowance to an entitlement to Adult Disability Payment.

(2) Notice under paragraph (1) must—

(a) be given in a way that leaves the relevant individual with a record of the information which they can show to, or otherwise share with, others, and

(b) inform the relevant individual that—

    (i) they have been identified as a relevant individual for the purposes of transfer to Adult Disability Payment,

    (ii) the Scottish Ministers will make a determination, without receiving an application, to transfer the individual's entitlement to Disability Living Allowance to an entitlement to Adult Disability Payment within a period to be specified within the notice (the individual will be notified when the transfer determination is made and informed about their award and start date of Adult Disability Payment),

    (iii) the individual's award of Disability Living Allowance will cease—

        (aa) immediately before the award of Adult Disability Payment begins, or

        (bb) where a transferring individual was paid Disability Living Allowance one week in advance and 3 weekly in arrears, the date one week after the date their entitlement to Adult Disability Payment begins,

    (iv) except where the individual is subject to the special rules for terminal illness in regulation 9, the Scottish Ministers will make a review determination of the individual's entitlement to Adult Disability Payment within 12 months of the date of the notice.

(3) Where a notice under paragraph (1) is given in error where the individual is neither—

(a) ordinarily resident in Scotland, nor

(b) an individual who is habitually resident in an EEA state, Gibraltar or Switzerland and has a genuine and sufficient link to Scotland,

the duty on the Scottish Ministers in regulation 4(1) does not apply.

(4) Where paragraph (3) applies in respect of an individual and a transfer determination has not been made, the Scottish Ministers are to notify the individual that the duty on the Scottish Ministers in regulation 4(1) does not apply.

(5) In paragraph (3), "sufficient" means a link to Scotland that is sufficiently close that regulation 15(3) or 20(2) of the ADP Regulations would be incompatible with the applicable agreement mentioned in either of those regulations, if the relevant individual were not entitled to Adult Disability Payment.

Transfer determination without application of entitlement to Adult Disability Payment

4.—(1) The Scottish Ministers are to make a determination in respect 1.129
of a transferring individual, without receiving an application, of that individual's entitlement to Adult Disability Payment.

(2) A transfer determination must be made on the assumption that the transferring individual—

(a) other than Disability Living Allowance, is not entitled to any of the benefits set out in regulation 4, and

(b) meets the residence and presence conditions set out in regulations 15 to 21, of the ADP Regulations.

(3) Entitlement to Adult Disability Payment under a transfer determination begins on the date specified in the notice of determination given to the transferring individual in accordance with section 40 of the 2018 Act.

(4) The transfer determination is to be made on the basis of—

(a) such information as the Scottish Ministers have received from the Secretary of State for Work and Pensions in respect of the transferring individual's entitlement to Disability Living Allowance, and

(b) any other information available to the Scottish Ministers that appears to them to be relevant.

(5) Subject to regulation 9, a transfer determination must be made in accordance with regulation 5.

(6) The transfer determination does not need to be made on the basis of the information mentioned in paragraph (4)(b) where—

(a) the individual—

(i) before receiving notice under regulation 3(1), reported a change of circumstances to the Secretary of State for Work and Pensions, which has not been taken into account for the individual's entitlement to Disability Living Allowance, or

(ii) has, since receiving a notice under regulation 3(1), notified a change of circumstances to the Scottish Ministers, and

(b) following the transfer determination, a review determination is to be made.

(7) A determination under paragraph (1)—

(a) may be made on the assumption that whatever can be discerned about the transferring individual's circumstances from the information mentioned in paragraph (4) remains accurate on the date on which the determination is made,

(b) must be made no later than the end of the period specified within the notice of intention to transfer unless the Scottish Ministers have—

(i) good reason to extend that period,

(ii) agreed the period for extension with the Secretary of State for Work and Pensions, and

(iii) notified the transferring individual of the extension and the reason for it.

Entitlement to Adult Disability Payment

1.130   **5.**—(1) For the purposes of a transfer determination, an individual may be awarded the daily living component of Adult Disability Payment at the transitional rate specified in regulation 6(1) instead of being awarded that component at the standard or the enhanced rate in accordance with regulation 5(2) or (3) of the ADP Regulations.

(2) A transfer determination is to be made on the basis that a transferring individual who had been entitled to the—

(a) lowest rate of the care component of Disability Living Allowance immediately prior to the date of transfer is entitled to the transitional rate of the daily living component of Adult Disability Payment,

(b) middle rate of the care component of Disability Living Allowance immediately prior to the date of transfer is entitled to the standard rate of the daily living component of Adult Disability Payment,

(c) highest rate of the care component of Disability Living Allowance immediately prior to the date of transfer is entitled to the enhanced rate of the daily living component of Adult Disability Payment,

(d) lower rate of the mobility component of Disability Living Allowance immediately prior to the date of transfer is entitled to the standard rate of the mobility component of Adult Disability Payment,

(e) higher rate of the mobility component of Disability Living Allowance immediately prior to the date of transfer is entitled to the enhanced rate of the mobility component of Adult Disability Payment.

(3) A transferring individual mentioned in paragraph (2)(e) is to be treated as though they have obtained the maximum points for each activity listed in column 1 of the table in Part 3 of schedule 1 of the ADP Regulations.

Amount and form and time of payment of Adult Disability Payment

1.131   **6.**—(1) The weekly rate of payment of the daily living component of Adult Disability Payment is, where the transferring individual is entitled to the transitional rate, £24.45.

(2) Where an award of Adult Disability Payment is made to a transferring individual, the Scottish Ministers are to make—

(a) the first payment of assistance on a date specified in the notice of determination, and

(b) any subsequent payment—
    (i) 4 weekly in arrears,
    (ii) weekly in advance, or
    (iii) where the Scottish Ministers consider that it would be unjust not to do so, at such intervals as may be specified in the notice of determination.

Effect of determination on entitlement to Disability Living Allowance

7.—(1) Where a transfer determination is made that the transferring individual is entitled to Adult Disability Payment, the transferring individual's entitlement to Disability Living Allowance will cease on— **1.132**

(a) the date their entitlement to Adult Disability Payment begins,

(b) where a transferring individual was paid Disability Living Allowance one week in advance and 3 weekly in arrears, the date one week after the date their entitlement to Adult Disability Payment begins, or

(c) where regulation 9 applies, the date their entitlement to Adult Disability Payment would have begun had regulation 9(2) not applied to set an earlier date of entitlement.

(2) Where paragraph (1)(b) applies—

(a) section 71(7) (disability living allowance) of the Social Security Contributions and Benefits Act 1992, and

(b) regulation 4(d) of the ADP Regulations (entitlement to other benefits),

do not apply in respect of the first week of entitlement to Adult Disability Payment.

Periods in respect of a re-determination request in relation to a transfer determination

8.—(1) The period for requesting a re-determination of entitlement to Adult Disability Payment under section 41 of the 2018 Act (right to request re-determination) in relation to a transfer determination is 42 days beginning with the day that the individual is informed, in accordance with section 40 of the 2018 Act (notice of determination) of the right to make the request. **1.133**

(2) In relation to determining entitlement to Adult Disability Payment, the period allowed for re-determination in respect of a transfer determination (within the meaning of section 43 of the 2018 Act (duty to re-determine)) is as soon as reasonably practicable and not more than 182 days beginning with—

(a) the day that the request for a re-determination is received by the Scottish Ministers,

(b) in a case where the request for a re-determination is received by the Scottish Ministers outwith the period prescribed in paragraph (1), the day on which it is decided by the Scottish Ministers or (as the case may be) the First-tier Tribunal for Scotland that the individual in question has a good reason for not requesting a re-determination sooner, or

(c) in a case where the Scottish Ministers have informed the individual of their decision that the request for re-determination was not made in such form as the Scottish Ministers require, the day on which it is subsequently decided by the First-tier Tribunal for Scotland that the individual in question has made the request in such form as the Scottish Ministers require.

Special rules for terminal illness—exception to regulation 4(5)

1.134   **9.**—(1) Where the Scottish Ministers have—

(a) received information from the Secretary of State for Work and Pensions that the transferring individual is terminally ill in terms of section 72(5) of the Social Security Contributions and Benefits Act 1992 immediately before the date of transfer, or

(b) not received information from the Secretary of State for Work and Pensions that the transferring individual is terminally ill in terms of section 72(5) of the Social Security Contributions and Benefits 1992, but become aware, before they have made a transfer determination, that a transferring individual has a terminal illness in terms of regulation 26(7) of the ADP Regulations,

the transfer determination must be made on the basis that the transferring individual satisfies the conditions for the enhanced rate of both the daily living component and the mobility component of Adult Disability Payment.

(2) Where paragraph (1) applies—

(a) paragraphs (4) to (6) of regulation 26 of the ADP Regulations do not apply, and

(b) the transferring individual's entitlement to Adult Disability Payment will commence on whichever is the later of—

    (i) the date that the ADP Regulations came into force,

    (ii) the day that the clinical judgement was made in accordance with regulation 26(7) of the ADP Regulations, or

    (iii) the day one year before the date of the transfer determination.

Modification of the ADP Regulations: transferring individuals

1.135   **10.** The ADP Regulations apply to a transferring individual on and after the date of transfer with the following modifications—

(a) regulation 3(3) (overview) is to be read as if—

    (i) for "2 weekly rates of the daily living component" there were substituted "3 weekly rates of the daily living component", and

    (ii) after "(amount and form of Adult Disability Payment)" there were inserted "and regulation 6(1) of the Disability Assistance for Working Age People (Transitional Provisions and Miscellaneous Amendment) (Scotland) Regulations 2022",

(b) regulation 5 (daily living component) is to be read as if—

(i) in paragraph (1) after "the enhanced rate" there were inserted "or, where the individual is a transferring individual as defined in regulation 2 of the Disability Assistance for Working Age People (Transitional Provisions and Miscellaneous Amendment) (Scotland) Regulations 2022, at the transitional rate,

(ii) after paragraph (3) there were inserted—

"(3A) An individual is entitled to the daily living component at the transitional rate where regulation 5(2)(a) of the Disability Assistance for Working Age People (Transitional Provisions and Miscellaneous Amendment) (Scotland) Regulations 2022 applies to the individual." and

(iii) after paragraph (4)(c) there were inserted—

"(d) "the transitional rate" in relation to the daily living component means the weekly rate of the daily living component set in regulation 6(1) of the Disability Assistance for Working Age People (Transitional Provisions and Miscellaneous Amendment) (Scotland) Regulations 2022",

(c) regulation 32 (entitlement beginning while in alternative accommodation) is to be read as if—

(i) in paragraph (1) after "begins" there are the words "in terms of these Regulations", and

(ii) in paragraph (2) for "that day" there were substituted "the day on which the individual has been entitled to Adult Disability Payment for 28 days",

(d) regulation 35 (when an application is to be treated as made and beginning of entitlement to assistance) is treated as omitted,

(e) regulation 36 (time of payment) is treated as omitted,

(f) regulation 45 (when an increase in level of entitlement takes effect) is treated as omitted,

(g) regulation 46 (when a decrease in level or cessation of entitlement takes effect) is treated as omitted,

(h) regulation 54 (periods in respect of a re-determination request) is treated as omitted in relation to a request for a re-determination in respect of a transfer determination,

(i) where regulation 9 of these Regulations applies, for the period between the date when entitlement to Adult Disability Payment begins and the date of the transfer determination, regulation 4 (entitlement to other benefits) is treated as omitted.

Appointees

11.—(1) A person appointed by the Secretary of State for Work and   1.136
Pensions under regulation 33 of the Social Security (Claims and Payments) Regulations 1987 (persons unable to act) to receive Disability Living Allowance on behalf of a transferring individual is to be treated on and after the date of transfer as though appointed by the Scottish Ministers to act on behalf of that transferring individual under section 85B of the 2018 Act.

(2) As soon as reasonably practicable after the date of transfer, the Scottish Ministers must—

(a) consider whether the conditions for making an appointment in respect of the transferring individual are met (having regard to section 85B(3) of the 2018 Act),

(b) consider whether to terminate the appointment that is treated as having been made by virtue of sub-paragraph (1) and terminate it if they consider it appropriate, and

(c) if they have terminated an appointment in pursuance of head (b), appoint under section 85B of the 2018 Act another person to act on the transferring individual's behalf if they consider it appropriate to do so.

PART 3

REVIEW OF ENTITLEMENT TO ADULT DISABILITY PAYMENT

Review determination without application of entitlement to Adult Disability Payment

1.137   **12.**—(1) The Scottish Ministers are to make a determination in respect of a transferred individual, without receiving an application, of that individual's entitlement to Adult Disability Payment within the period of 12 months beginning with the date of that individual's notice of intention to transfer.

(2) Paragraph (1) does not apply—

(a) to transferred individuals to whom regulation 9 applies, or

(b) where a transferred individual has requested a re-determination under section 41 of the 2018 Act, or made an appeal under section 46 of the 2018 Act, in relation to the transfer determination.

(3) Subject to regulations 15 (when an increase in level of entitlement takes effect) and 16 (when a decrease in level or cessation of entitlement takes effect), entitlement to Adult Disability Payment under a determination under paragraph (1) begins on the date specified in the notice of determination given to the transferred individual in accordance with section 40 of the 2018 Act.

(4) The determination under paragraph (1) is to be made on the basis of any information that—

(a) the Scottish Ministers have received from the Secretary of State for Work and Pensions in respect of the transferred individual's entitlement to Disability Living Allowance,

(b) the Scottish Ministers requested from the transferred individual, and

(c) is available to the Scottish Ministers that appears to them to be relevant.

Time of payment

13. Where an award of Adult Disability Payment is made under a 1.138
review determination, the Scottish Ministers are to make—
  (a) the first payment of assistance on a date specified in the notice of
      determination, and
  (b) any subsequent payment—
     (i) 4 weekly in arrears,
     (ii) weekly in advance, or
     (iii) where the Scottish Ministers consider that it would be unjust
           not to do so, at such intervals as may be specified in the
           notice of determination.

Change of circumstances

14. Where the Scottish Ministers are making a review determination 1.139
of an individual's entitlement to Adult Disability Payment, where the
individual—
  (a) before receiving a notice under regulation 3(1), reported a change
      of circumstances to the Secretary of State for Work and Pensions,
      which had not been taken into account for the individual's entitle-
      ment to Disability Living Allowance, or
  (b) has, since receiving a notice under regulation 3(1), notified a
      change of circumstances to the Scottish Ministers,
the change of circumstances—
  (c) is not to be regarded as relating to the individual's entitlement to
      Disability Living Allowance, and
  (d) is to be taken into consideration by the Scottish Ministers in
      making the review determination.

When an increase in level of entitlement takes effect

15.—(1) Where, as a result of a review determination, the amount of 1.140
Adult Disability Payment payable in respect of an individual is increased,
or their entitlement to a component is awarded, the change takes effect
on the date of transfer.

(2) Where an individual has previously received Adult Disability Payment for a period under a transfer determination and a review determination has subsequently been made that the same individual is entitled to
Adult Disability Payment at a higher rate for that period, that individual
is entitled to be paid the difference between the value of entitlement to
Adult Disability Payment under the review determination and the value
of Adult Disability Payment to which that individual was previously
entitled under the transfer determination.

When a decrease in level or cessation of entitlement takes effect

16. Where an individual's entitlement to Adult Disability Payment is 1.141
determined in the review determination to be at a lower rate than, or the
same rate as awarded by, the transfer determination, entitlement under
the review determination will take effect on the day that the Scottish
Ministers make the review determination.

PART 4

MISCELLANEOUS AMENDMENTS

Amendment of the Personal Independence Payment (Transitional Provisions) Regulations 2013

1.142 **17.** *See the supplementary annotations to the 2013 Regulations in Part 2 of this Supplement.*

Amendment of the Disability Assistance for Children and Young People (Scotland) Regulations 2021

1.143 **18.** *See the supplementary annotations to the 2021 Regulations in Part 5 of this Supplement.*

Amendment of the Disability Assistance for Working Age People (Scotland) Regulations 2022

1.144 **19.** *See the supplementary annotations to the 2022 Regulations in Part 5 of this Supplement.*

PART II

UPDATING MATERIAL
VOLUME I

NON MEANS TESTED BENEFITS

Commentary by

Ian Hooker

John Mesher

Edward Mitchell

Christopher Ward

Nick Wikeley

p.101, *amendment to the Social Security Contributions and Benefits Act 1992 s.64 (Attendance allowance)*

With effect from March 21, 2022, reg.2 of the Scotland Act 2016   2.001
(Social Security) (Adult Disability Payment and Child Disability Payment) (Amendment) Regulations 2022 (SI 2022/335) amended subs.(1A) by inserting after para.(a) the following:

"(aa) adult disability payment;".

p.114, *annotation to the Social Security (Contributions and Benefits) Act 1992 s.70(3) (Invalid Care Allowance—restriction on entitlement)*

In line 1 of this note for the words "not in full-time education"   2.002
substitute the words "not receiving full-time education".

p.117, *amendment to the Social Security Contributions and Benefits Act 1992 s.71 (Disability living allowance)*

With effect from July 26, 2021, reg.2 of the Scotland Act 2016 (Social   2.003
Security) (Consequential Provision) (Miscellaneous Amendment) Regulations 2021 (SI 2021/804) amended s.71 by adding after subs.(6) the following:

"(7) A person shall not be entitled to a disability living allowance while they are entitled to Child Disability Payment."

With effect from March 21, 2022, reg.2 of the Scotland Act 2016 (Social Security) (Adult Disability Payment and Child Disability Payment) (Amendment) Regulations 2022 (SI 2022/335) further amended s.71 by deleting the words "Child Disability Payment" and substituting the words "adult disability payment or child disability payment".

p.236, *amendment to the Social Security Contributions and Benefits Act 1992 s.122 (Interpretation of Parts I to VI and supplementary provisions)*

With effect from July 26, 2021, reg.2 of the Scotland Act 2016 (Social   2.004
Security) (Consequential Provision) (Miscellaneous Amendment) Regulations 2021 (SI 2021/804) amended s.122 by inserting, after the definition of "child", the following:

""Child Disability Payment" means assistance under regulation 3 of the Disability Assistance for Children and Young People (Scotland) Regulations 2021;"

Note that with effect from March 21, 2022, this definition was superseded by the definition in reg.2 of the Scotland Act 2016 (Social Security) (Adult Disability Payment and Child Disability Payment) (Amendment) Regulations 2022 (SI 2022/335) as it appears in the current edition of Volume I of this work.

p.325, *introductory annotation to the new style Jobseekers Act 1995*

2.005   Note that the discretion given to the Secretary of State under reg.4 of the Transitional Provisions Regulations 2014 to determine (for administrative reasons) that no claims for universal credit are to be accepted in an area or category of case has been removed with effect from July 25, 2022 by reg.2 of the Universal Credit (Transitional Provisions) Amendment Regulations 2022 (SI 2022/752). There is thus now no exception, however remote, to the proposition that any new claim for JSA can only be for new style JSA.

pp.332–335, *annotation to the new style Jobseekers Act 1995 s.2 (The contribution-based conditions)*

2.006   The Social Security Advisory Committee's paper on *The future of working age benefits for those not in paid work* (Occasional Paper No.26, dated July 2022, but not added to the website until October 28, 2022) details at p.48 some ways in which it considers the current operation of the contribution conditions to be inequitable, e.g. the arbitrariness in when recent contributions come into play depending on the accident of when in the year the jobseeking period begins and the exclusion of claimants who have paid in for maybe 30 years and then are excluded by an insufficiency of contributions in two recent years.

Note that claimants in receipt of JSA are automatically credited with contributions under reg.8A(2)(a) of the Social Security (Credits) Regulations 1975, but unemployed people not so in receipt must make a claim within a reasonable time (reg.8A(2)(b)–(d) and (3)). See *SM v SSWP (JSA)* [2021] UKUT 179 (AAC) and *KL v SSWP (JSA)* [2022] UKUT 270 (AAC).

p.337, *annotation to the new style Jobseekers Act 1995 s.4 (Amount payable by way of jobseeker's allowance)*

2.007   The Social Security Advisory Committee's paper on *The future of working age benefits for those not in paid work* (Occasional Paper No.26, dated July 2022, but not added to the website until October 28, 2022) at pp.58–59 takes the view that the means-testing of a contributory benefit against pension income sits oddly in a world where the majority of private sector pension schemes are defined-contribution and members are free to draw flexibly from the funds through retirement. Nor was it clear why only that form of non-earned income should be identified for means-testing. It recommends that the test should be reviewed and consideration given to removing it. It may also be relevant to that view that the pension freedoms kick in at age 55 and the taking of benefits may not be an indication of withdrawal (or complete withdrawal) from the labour market.

Although the notes in the main volume at one point refer to the deduction pound for pound of earnings over £50 a week, note that the calculation of the amount of earnings in accordance with Pt 7 of the JSA

Regulations 2013 brings in the disregards in the Schedule to the Regulations (see regs 59(2) and 61(2)) and in particular the disregard of at least £5 per week (para.5).

p.368, *annotation to the new style Jobseekers Act 1995 s.6J (Higher-level sanctions)*

The Social Security Advisory Committee's paper on *The future of working age benefits for those not in paid work* (Occasional Paper No.26, dated July 2022, but not added to the website until October 28, 2022) contains further information on the question of the application of sanctions in new style JSA before November 2021. There is a specific reference on p.37 to the non-application of sanctions in that period where claimants did not uphold their responsibilities under their claimant commitment, but on p.70 it is said that there was an operational impediment in that the JSAPS computer payment system would not allow the application of reductions of benefit for sanctions. That impediment would seem to have applied to all forms of sanction.

p.413, *correction to new style Jobseekers Act 1995 s.22 (Members of the forces)*

Replace the text of s.22 with the following: 2.008A

"**22.**—(1) Regulations may modify any provisions of this Act, in such manner as the Secretary of State thinks proper, in its application to persons who are or have been members of Her Majesty's forces.

(2) [¹ . . .]

(3) For the purposes of this section, Her Majesty's forces shall be taken to consist of such establishments and organisations in which persons serve under the control of the Defence Council as may be prescribed."

AMENDMENT

1. Welfare Reform Act 2021 Sch.14 Pt 4 (trigger date on or after April 29, 2013).

DEFINITIONS

"prescribed"—see s.35(1).
"regulations"—*ibid.*

p.459, *amendment to the Welfare Reform Act 2007 s.1C (Claimant commitment) (not yet in force)*

Insert after the annotation to s.1B and before s.2 the following text: 2.009

"**Claimant commitment**

    1C.—*(not yet in force)*"

Section 1C of the Welfare Reform Act 2007 was inserted by s.54(3) of the Welfare Reform Act 2012 but has yet to be brought into force. However, much of its work is done by s.11A of the 2007 Act (see below).

p.470, *annotation to the Welfare Reform Act 2007 s.11A (Claimant commitment)*

2.010 See also the note to s.1C above, a provision which has yet to be brought into force. Much of its work is done by s.11A.

p.521, *amendment to the Welfare Reform Act 2012 s.77 (Personal independence payment)*

2.011 With effect from July 26, 2021, reg.3 of the Scotland Act 2016 (Social Security) (Consequential Provision) (Miscellaneous Amendment) Regulations 2021 (SI 2021/804) amended s.77 by adding after subs.(3) the following:

"(4) A person is not entitled to personal independence payment while they are entitled to Child Disability Payment.".

With effect from March 21, 2022, reg.3 of the Scotland Act 2016 (Social Security) (Adult Disability Payment and Child Disability Payment) (Amendment) Regulations 2022 (SI 2022/335) further amended s.77 by deleting the words "Child Disability Payment" and substituting the words "adult disability payment or child disability payment".

p.534, *amendment to the Welfare Reform Act 2012 s.95 (Interpretation of Part 4)*

2.012 With effect from July 26, 2021, reg.3 of the Scotland Act 2016 (Social Security) (Consequential Provision) (Miscellaneous Amendment) Regulations 2021 (SI 2021/804) amended s.95 by inserting before the definition of "daily living activities" the following:

""Child Disability Payment" means assistance under regulation 3 of the Disability Assistance for Children and Young People (Scotland) Regulations 2021;".

With effect from March 21, 2022, reg.3(3)(a) of the Scotland Act 2016 (Social Security) (Adult Disability Payment and Child Disability Payment) (Amendment) Regulations 2022 (SI 2022/335) further amended s.95 by inserting before the definition of "Child Disability Payment" as provided above the following:

"adult disability payment" means disability assistance given in accordance with the Disability Assistance for Working Age People (Scotland) Regulations 2022;";

And reg.3(3)(b) deleted the definition of "Child Disability Payment" as provided above and substituted the following:

"child disability payment" means disability assistance given in accordance with the Disability Assistance for Children and Young People (Scotland) Regulations 2021 (SSI 2021/174);

p.562, *annotation to the Pensions Act 2014 s.30 (Bereavement support payment)*

The reference to *O'Donnell v Department for Communities* [2020] NICA 36 should be to the note following s.31 below (not above). See also *R. (Jwanczuk) v SSWP* [2022] EWHC 2298 (Admin), currently under appeal to the Court of Appeal.
   2.013

pp.573–574, *annotation to the Pensions Act 2014 s.31 (Bereavement support payment: contribution condition and amendments)*

Note that the decision in *O'Donnell v Department for Communities* was considered in *R. (Jwanczuk) v SSWP* [2022] EWHC 2298 (Admin). The judge (Kerr J) was not bound by the decision of the Court of Appeal in Northern Ireland and considered the matter afresh, ultimately reaching a similar result. An appeal to the Court of Appeal is pending at the time of writing.
   2.014

pp.610–611, *annotation to the Social Security (Credits) Regulations 1975 (SI 1975/556) reg.8A (Credits for unemployment)*

For confirmation that reg.8A can apply to unemployed people who are not claiming JSA, see *KL v SSWP (JSA)* [2022] UKUT 270 (AAC). The decision also confirms that whether the claim was made "within such further time as may be reasonable in the circumstances of the case" (within reg.8A(3)) is ultimately a question of fact (see *CIB/2445/2006*, decided under reg.8B).
   2.015

pp.613–614, *annotation to the Social Security (Credits) Regulations 1975 (SI 1975/556) reg.8B (Credits for incapacity for work or limited capability for work)*

For a case involving the operation of reg.8B, and the potential linkage to a claim for universal credit, see *JW v SSWP (UC)* [2022] UKUT 117 (AAC).
   2.016

pp.657–658, *amendment to the Social Security Benefit (Computation of Earnings) Regulations 1996 (SI 1996/2745) reg.2 (Interpretation)*

With effect from July 1, 2022, the Health and Care Act 2022 (Consequential and Related Amendments and Transitional Provisions) Regulations 2022 (SI 2022/634) reg.12 deletes the definition of "clinical commissioning group" and replaces it after the definition of "employment" by:
   2.017

""integrated care board" means an integrated care board established under Chapter A3 of Part 2 of the National Health Service Act 2006".

p.772, *amendment to the Social Security (Attendance Allowance) Regulations 1991 (SI 1991/2740) reg.2 (Conditions as to residence and presence in Great Britain)*

2.018   With effect from March 21, 2022, reg.5 of the Scotland Act 2016 (Social Security) (Adult Disability Payment and Child Disability Payment) (Amendment) Regulations 2022 (SI 2022/335) amended reg.2 by inserting after reg.2(1) the following:

"(1ZA) A person to whom regulation 53(1) of the Disability Assistance for Working Age People (Scotland) Regulations 2022 applies shall be treated for the period set out in that regulation as though he does not satisfy the condition in paragraph (1)(a)(i) of this regulation.".

p.775, *amendment to the Social Security (Attendance Allowance) Regulations 1991 (SI 1991/2740) reg.2C (Refugees and certain persons with leave to enter or remain in the United Kingdom)*

2.019   With effect from March 22, 2022, reg.4 of the Social Security (Habitual Residence and Past Presence) (Amendment) Regulations 2022 (SI 2022/344) amended para.(1)(d) by omitting the word "or" and inserted after para.(e) the following:

"or
    (f) leave to enter or remain in the United Kingdom granted under or outside the immigration rules or a right of abode in the United Kingdom within the meaning given in section 2 of the Immigration Act 1971 where the person—
        (i) was residing in Ukraine immediately before 1st January 2022; and
        (ii) left Ukraine in connection with the Russian invasion which took place on 24th February 2022.".

Note: this regulation applies only to England and Wales. Identical provision is made for Scotland, with effect from the same date, by the Social Security (Residence Requirements) (Ukraine) (Scotland) Regulations 2022 (SSI 2022/108).

With effect from October 18, 2022, this regulation is further amended by reg.3 of the Social Security (Habitual Residence and Past Presence) (Amendment) (No. 2) Regulations 2022 (SI 2022/990) as follows:
    (a) at the end of para.(1)(e), for "or" substitute "; or";
    (b) in para.(1)(f):
        (i) for "or a right" substitute ", a right";
        (ii) after "1971" insert "or does not require leave to enter or remain in the United Kingdom in accordance with section 3ZA of that Act,".

p.789, *amendment to the Social Security (Disability Living Allowance) Regulations 1991 (SI 1991/2890) reg.2 (Conditions as to residence and presence in Great Britain)*

With effect from July 26, 2021, reg.5 of the Scotland Act 2016 (Social Security) (Consequential Provision) (Miscellaneous Amendment) Regulations 2021 (SI 2021/804) amended reg.2 by the insertion before para.(2) of the following: 2.020

"(1ZA) A person to whom regulation 36(1) of the Disability Assistance for Children and Young People (Scotland) Regulations 2021 applies shall be treated for the period set out in that regulation as though he does not satisfy the condition in paragraph (1)(a)(i) of this regulation.".

With effect from March 21, 2022, reg.6 of the Scotland Act 2016 (Social Security) (Adult Disability Payment and Child Disability Payment) (Amendment) Regulations 2022 (SI 2022/335) further amended reg.2 by adding after reg.2(1ZA) the following:

"(1ZB) A person to whom regulation 53(1) of the Disability Assistance for Working Age People (Scotland) Regulations 2022 applies shall be treated for the period set out in that regulation as though he does not satisfy the condition in paragraph (1)(a)(i) of this regulation.".

p.794, *amendment to the Social Security (Disability Living Allowance) Regulations 1991 (SI 1991/2890) reg.2C (Refugees and certain persons with leave to enter or remain in the United Kingdom)*

With effect from March 22, 2022, reg.4 of the Social Security (Habitual Residence and Past Presence) (Amendment) Regulations 2022 (SI 2022/344) amended para.(1)(d) by omitting the word "or" and inserted after para.(e) the following: 2.021

"or
  (f) leave to enter or remain in the United Kingdom granted under or outside the immigration rules or a right of abode in the United Kingdom within the meaning given in section 2 of the Immigration Act 1971 where the person—
    (i) was residing in Ukraine immediately before 1st January 2022; and
    (ii) left Ukraine in connection with the Russian invasion which took place on 24th February 2022.".

Note: this regulation applies only to England and Wales. Identical provision is made for Scotland, with effect from the same date, by the Social Security (Residence Requirements) (Ukraine) (Scotland) Regulations 2022 (SSI 2022/108).

With effect from October 18, 2022, this regulation is further amended by reg.3 of the Social Security (Habitual Residence and Past Presence) (Amendment) (No. 2) Regulations 2022 (SI 2022/990) as follows:

(a) at the end of para.(1)(e), for "or" substitute "; or";
(b) in para.(1)(f):
    (i) for "or a right" substitute ", a right";
    (ii) after "1971" insert "or does not require leave to enter or remain in the United Kingdom in accordance with section 3ZA of that Act,".

p.865, *amendment to the Social Security (Invalid Care Allowance) Regulations 1976 (SI 1976/409) reg.9C (Refugees and certain persons with leave to enter or remain in the United Kingdom)*

2.022   With effect from March 22, 2022, reg.4 of the Social Security (Habitual Residence and Past Presence) (Amendment) Regulations 2022 (SI 2022/344) amended para.(1)(d) by omitting the word "or" and inserted after para.(e) the following:

"or
    (f) leave to enter or remain in the United Kingdom granted under or outside the immigration rules or a right of abode in the United Kingdom within the meaning given in section 2 of the Immigration Act 1971 where the person—
        (i) was residing in Ukraine immediately before 1st January 2022; and
        (ii) left Ukraine in connection with the Russian invasion which took place on 24th February 2022.".

Note: this regulation applies only to England and Wales. Identical provision is made for Scotland, with effect from the same date, by the Social Security (Residence Requirements) (Ukraine) (Scotland) Regulations 2022 (SSI 2022/108).

    With effect from October 18, 2022, this regulation is further amended by reg.3 of the Social Security (Habitual Residence and Past Presence) (Amendment) (No. 2) Regulations 2022 (SI 2022/990) as follows:
    (a) at the end of para.(1)(e), for "or" substitute "; or";
    (b) in para.(1)(f):
        (i) for "or a right" substitute ", a right";
        (ii) after "1971" insert "or does not require leave to enter or remain in the United Kingdom in accordance with section 3ZA of that Act,".

p.904, *amendment to the Social Security (Personal Independence Payment) Regulations 2013 (SI 2013/377) (Part 4 Residence and presence conditions)*

2.023   With effect from July 26, 2021, reg.6 of the Scotland Act 2016 (Social Security) (Consequential Provision) (Miscellaneous Amendment) Regulations 2021 (SI 2021/804) amended these regulations by the insertion before reg.23A of the following:

"Persons in receipt of an equivalent Scottish benefit who move from Scotland to England or Wales

23ZA. Where regulation 36(1) of the Disability Assistance for Children and Young People (Scotland) Regulations 2021 applies to C, regulation 16(c) of these Regulations is treated as not satisfied for the period set out in regulation 36(1) of those Regulations.".

With effect from March 21, 2022, reg.7 of the Scotland Act 2016 (Social Security) (Adult Disability Payment and Child Disability Payment) (Amendment) Regulations 2022 (SI 2022/335) amended reg.23ZA by renumbering it as reg.23ZA(1) and adding the following:

"(2) Where regulation 53(1) of the Disability Assistance for Working Age People (Scotland) Regulations 2022 applies to C, regulation 16(c) of these Regulations is treated as not satisfied for the period set out in regulation 53(1) of those Regulations."

p.905, *amendment to the Social Security (Personal Independence Payment) Regulations 2013 (SI 2013/377) reg.23A (Refugees and certain persons with leave to enter or remain in the United Kingdom)*

With effect from March 22, 2022, reg.4 of the Social Security (Habitual Residence and Past Presence) (Amendment) Regulations 2022 (SI 2022/344) amended para.(1)(d) by omitting the word "or" and inserted after para.(e) the following: **2.024**

"or
   (f) leave to enter or remain in the United Kingdom granted under or outside the immigration rules or a right of abode in the United Kingdom within the meaning given in section 2 of the Immigration Act 1971 where the person—
      (i) was residing in Ukraine immediately before 1st January 2022; and
      (ii) left Ukraine in connection with the Russian invasion which took place on 24th February 2022.".

Note: this regulation applies only to England and Wales. Identical provision is made for Scotland, with effect from the same date, by the Social Security (Residence Requirements) (Ukraine) (Scotland) Regulations 2022 (SSI 2022/108).

With effect from October 18, 2022, this regulation is further amended by reg.3 of the Social Security (Habitual Residence and Past Presence) (Amendment) (No. 2) Regulations 2022 (SI 2022/990) as follows:
   (a) at the end of para.(1)(e), for "or" substitute "; or";
   (b) in para.(1)(f):
      (i) for "or a right" substitute ", a right";
      (ii) after "1971" insert "or does not require leave to enter or remain in the United Kingdom in accordance with section 3ZA of that Act,".

p.908, *annotation to the Social Security (Personal Independence Payment) Regulations 2013 (SI 2013/377) reg.27 (Revision and supersession of an award after the person has reached the relevant age)*

2.025   The operation of this regulation has been examined in detail by Judge Wikeley in *SC v SSWP (PIP)* [2022] UKUT 97 (AAC). The claimant had been in receipt of both components of DLA. She was transferred to PIP shortly after her 65th birthday with an award of both mobility and daily living components at the standard rate. But following a review, the mobility component was withdrawn. The HCP who examined her then took the view that her mobility had improved following a knee replacement operation. Two years later in the course of another review it was accepted that the claimant's condition had worsened and that, but for her age, she would have qualified for the mobility component at the standard rate. No award could be made, however, because none of the exceptions provided for in regs 25, 26, or 27 applied and in particular, reg.27(4) could not apply because more than a year had elapsed since she had last been entitled to that component. Judge Wikeley clarifies the meaning to be given to the words "original award" as used in this regulation. He finds that, to make sense of para.(4), the words must refer to the current award on which the revision is based and not to a previous award in which the claimant was entitled to mobility component.

p.922, *annotation to the Social Security (Personal Independence Payment) Regulations 2013 (SI 2013/377) Sch.1 (Personal independence payment assessment)*

2.026   An attempt to have the rest of the amendments made to these regulations by reg.2(2) and (3) of the amending regulations (those affecting Activity 3—Managing therapy or monitoring a health condition) to be found to be invalid failed in *CK v SSWP (PIP); JM v SSWP (PIP)* [2022] UKUT 122 (AAC). Judge Ward was asked to find those amendments invalid on the grounds that they were either made without consultation, or that they were *ultra vires*, or that they were discriminatory. He rejected the argument on all three grounds.

p.933, *annotation to the Social Security (Personal Independence Payment) Regulations 2013 (SI 2013/377) Sch.1 (Activity 2—Taking nutrition)*

2.027   In *CW v SSWP (PIP)* [2022] UKUT 281 (AAC) Judge Hemingway has decided that each of the elements of the definition of "taking nutrition" should be taken separately and not cumulatively when considering a claimant's entitlement under Descriptor 2.b.(i). The claimant had suffered an injury to his hand that resulted in the amputation of one finger and in consequence of which he needed to use specially adapted cutlery to cut up food. The claimant had been awarded 2 points under Activity 2 but, on appeal, the FTT decided that the claimant could qualify for those points only if he were able to show that he required an aid to accomplish each of the elements specified in "taking nutrition". In other words, he would need to show that he needed an aid not only to cut up food, but also to move it to his mouth, and then an aid to chew it, and again an aid to swallow it. The FTT observed that the elements of the definition were separated only by commas and should therefore be read cumulatively. As well, they thought that to give a purposive interpretation to the Descriptor meant that they should read it so as to restrict entitlement in accordance with the Government's intention expressed when enacting the PIP legislation. Judge Hemingway disagreed. He thought that to give a purposive interpretation required that the elements be treated separately. In his view a claimant who would require an aid or appliance (or even a series of separate items) to accomplish each of these elements would be so rare as to be almost non-existent. If so, it would mean that Descriptor 2.b.(i) had been stripped of any meaningful function at all. (And note that the Secretary of State had conceded that this was the correct interpretation and that the *PIP Assessment Guidance* for HCP provides for the award of points in these circumstances).

This was much the same point on which Judge Hemingway had expressed a non-binding (*obiter*) opinion in *CB v SSWP (PIP)* [2022] UKUT 100 (AAC). There, the claimant suffered from an ulcerated throat so that she was able to swallow food only after it had been processed by a liquidiser or similar machine. It seemed to be accepted that this meant she needed to use an aid to swallow, though not to chew. The definition of "take nutrition" required that an aid was needed to "chew and swallow". In that case the judge expressed the opinion that each word should be taken separately and in doing so he observes that to read the definition as if it were cumulative would envisage "an aid or appliance of considerable and quite probably unrealistic versatility" such that the only sensible interpretation was to treat each element separately.

But the point of real contention in this case was whether artificial dentures could be regarded as an aid or appliance. The claimant had argued that her false teeth were an aid that she needed to chew her food. Judge Hemingway declined the invitation to comment on this point, but the separation of each element of the definition means that such an argument could be raised. It seems likely that an award of points will be refused on the basis that the use of false teeth is so widespread in the general population that it cannot be regarded as any indication of disablement—see *CW v SSWP (PIP)* [2016] UKUT 197 (AAC) discussed in notes following reg.2 above.

p.935, *annotation to the Social Security (Personal Independence Payment) Regulations 2013 (SI 2013/377) Sch.1 (Activity 3—Managing therapy or monitoring a health condition)*

An attempt to have the amendments made to this Activity and to the definitions provided in Pt 1 of this Schedule by reg.2(2) and (3) of the amending regulations found to be invalid failed in *CK v SSWP (PIP); JM v SSWP (PIP)* [2022] UKUT 122 (AAC). Judge Ward was asked to find those amendments invalid on the grounds that they were either made without consultation, or that they were *ultra vires*, or that they were discriminatory. He rejected the argument on all three grounds.

2.028

p.1128, *annotation to the Jobseeker's Allowance Regulations 2013 (SI 2013/378) reg.1 (Citation, commencement and application)*

2.029   Note that the discretion given to the Secretary of State under reg.4 of the Transitional Provisions Regulations 2014 to determine (for administrative reasons) that no claims for universal credit are to be accepted in an area or category of case has been removed with effect from July 25, 2022 by reg.2 of the Universal Credit (Transitional Provisions) Amendment Regulations 2022 (SI 2022/752). There is thus now no exception, however remote, to the proposition that any new claim for JSA can only be for new style JSA.

pp.1136–1138, *annotation to the Jobseeker's Allowance Regulations 2013 (SI 2013/378) reg.5 (Application of regulations where there is dual entitlement)*

2.030   The Social Security Advisory Committee's paper on *The future of working age benefits for those not in paid work* (Occasional Paper No.26, dated July 2022, but not added to the website until October 28, 2022) contains further information on the question of the application of sanctions in new style JSA before November 2021. There is a specific reference on p.37 to the non-application of sanctions in that period where claimants did not uphold their responsibilities under their claimant commitment, but on p.70 it is said that there was an operational impediment in that the JSAPS computer payment system would not allow the application of reductions of benefit for sanctions. That impediment would seem to have applied to all forms of sanction.

pp.1152–1155, *annotation to the Jobseeker's Allowance Regulations 2013 (SI 2013/378) reg.14(3) (Work search requirement and work availability requirement: limitations—previous work)*

2.031   On June 23, 2022 (published on the internet on July 6, 2022), the Chair of the SSAC wrote to the Secretary of State to say that after careful consideration the Committee had decided not to take the regulations shortening the "permitted period" on formal reference, but wished to record a number of concerns and make some advisory recommendations. It is worth setting out in full the statement of concerns relating to the role of the regulatory changes in enhancing the overall policy intent (footnotes have been omitted):

"Scale of the challenge

In order to assess whether the regulation change could deliver and was proportionate to the policy intent, we were keen to understand the relative size of the role of the regulatory change in combination with the other measures as part of the Way to Work scheme, and the scale of the increase in off-flow into work that would be expected to be required to achieve the 500k target. Officials were unable to provide an

estimate of the overall scale of the change from the combined programme or of the expected contribution of the regulatory change. We
appreciate that this is difficult to do, but whether this goal involves an
increase in off-flow rates of 10%, 50% or 100% compared to an
expected counterfactual has a material impact on the proportionality
of the policy response.

Given that the off-flow from benefits into employment for the
month of February (which would be unlikely to have yet been significantly affected by the programme's components) had been estimated at around 114K—so that on average only 96.5K per month
needed to be achieved over the remaining four months to meet the
target—it seems as if the required impact could be at the lower end of
the scale, and more aligned to avoiding a drop in off-flow rates rather
than appreciably boosting them.

We also sought to understand the number of jobseekers whose
search expectations would be changed by these regulations for the
duration of the scheme. Unfortunately, officials were not in a position
to provide an estimate of the scale of the change.

Evidence base

We were informed that the rationale for the reduction in the duration of the permitted period was that there was a unique moment in
the labour market as, post-COVID, there were significantly higher
than normal levels of sectoral shift and high levels of vacancies—which
meant there would be greater benefit from jobseekers expanding their
search into new sectors at an earlier point.

We have sought access to evidence that could underpin the basis of
the decision to shorten the permitted period. We understand that the
choice of four weeks as the new duration was a judgment informed by
feedback from work coaches. However, no data or explanation has
been made available to indicate what the impact would be of making
the change. In fact, the evidence offered indicated that there was no
noticeable increase in the historic off-flow rate after the 13-week point,
suggesting that the extant pattern of broadening of the work-search
expectations, at least at this point, did not have a discernible
impact.

Our concerns are compounded by the lack of a clear positive outcome expected as a result of the reduction in the permitted period. We
are told that no estimate is available of what a positive outcome would
be either in terms of the number claiming the benefits, or the fiscal
impact though presumably these have been incorporated in the latest
forecasts produced by the Office for Budget Responsibility and
adopted by the Government in the Spring Statement.

We asked your officials for an assessment of the baseline (historic)
patterns of off-flow, and how these might have been expected to evolve
in coming months absent these change in these regulations, alongside
any early indication of patterns in the early months of the programme
(see Appendix for details). Unfortunately, this information has not
been shared with the Committee.

Potential negative impact

At the time of our scrutiny, no assessment had been made of the risk of individuals entering roles that were inconsistent with their qualifications/experience, or simply wrong for them in terms of their career path and ambitions, nor of the risk that increased competition from more highly qualified people would make it more difficult for longer-term unemployed people to find work. Similarly, no consideration had been made of the impact on those with part-time, or other flexible, job-search expectations for whom the four-week cut-off could be disproportionate and one that will certainly vary by protected characteristics, most obviously sex and disability.

There was some acknowledgement that there may be negative consequences from these changes, for example increased cycling on and off benefits, and job mismatches leading to more churn for employers and to claimants potentially having career paths hindered. However, there was no analysis of how to mitigate against negative effects, particularly where those with protected characteristics might be disproportionately impacted.

Evaluating the effectiveness of the permitted period change

These regulations were brought in to deal with a unique moment in the economy as it reopened from COVID restrictions, resulting in a very high number of labour market vacancies. However, the regulations do not have a sunset clause and the Committee would be concerned that, without a proper review of the impact of these regulations, they may be left on the statute book, despite the labour market situation having substantially changed. Therefore, the Committee very much welcomes that in your letter to me of 3 February, you committed to undertake such an evaluation of the regulations at the end of June to assess their effectiveness and whether they should be retained.

The way in which the regulations would be reviewed in terms of (a) by what criteria they would be deemed a success, and (b) how such criteria would be evaluated is in need of detailed thought. It will also be important to differentiate the criteria on which the regulations are evaluated with respect to the current unique point in time and the assessment whether they should be retained for what should then be much more normal times ahead. However, when we asked officials how they plan to undertake this, it was clear that such thinking had not yet matured.

Urgency

The regulations had been laid under the urgency provision before being presented to this Committee for scrutiny. I have previously written to you seeking a better understanding of the nature of the urgency in this instance. As you know, this Committee is supportive of the use of "urgency" where legislation is being brought forward as a direct consequence of either an external factor or a fiscal event. Indeed we welcomed the use of urgency, and expedited our own statutory scrutiny process, to ensure that essential support could be introduced quickly in response to recent crises in Afghanistan and Ukraine. However, a compelling argument for urgency in this specific case remains unclear to us.

We were informed that the regulations had to bypass the scrutiny of the Committee before coming into force, as "every day" was essential in ensuring that the Government can meet its own target. However, there was no explanation of what impact there might be in waiting a few weeks for the Committee to complete its statutory scrutiny —either on the specific issue of the target or in terms of the broader proposals.

Similarly, it is not clear why the target could not simply have been put back a short period, or why the rest of the Way to Work programme could not proceed whilst the permitted period proposals were considered by the Committee."

Despite that politely devastating analysis, success of the Way to Work campaign was declared on June 30, 2022 by way of a tweet and a press release asserting that over half a million people had been helped into work by the campaign in five months (later quoted in the House of Commons by the then Prime Minister on July 6, 2022). That declaration was apparently based on an answer to a Parliamentary Question on June 30, 2022 revealing an estimate using management information that as of June 29, 2022 at least 505,400 unemployed universal credit and JSA claimants had moved into work during the campaign. That use of the figures was castigated by the Director General for Regulation in the Office for Statistics Regulation in his letter of July 29, 2022 to the Permanent Secretary of the DWP. He concluded that it was difficult to attribute and quantify the impact of the campaign in the absence of a clearly defined and published target and details of how it would be measured and reported, so that the way that the DWP had communicated information did not uphold the principles of being trustworthy, of high quality and offering public value. A more targeted point might have been to note the speciousness of using evidence of the numbers who moved into work *during* the campaign to support the assertion that all those claimants had been helped into work *by* the campaign. A further written answer to a Parliamentary Question on September 5, 2022 revealed that no estimate had been made of the number of unemployed universal credit and JSA claimants who would have moved into work between January and June 2022 in the absence of the Way to Work campaign.

Overall, it is hard to avoid the conclusion that this whole shabby episode was little more than a small-scale exercise in grandiose posturing with every appearance of having been foisted on the DWP with no time for thought or preparation. However, the episode is not over. There has been no public sign of the promised evaluation of the effectiveness of the amending regulations and of whether they should be retained (the September 2022 written answer suggests that there has been no attempt at any real evaluation or at meeting the concerns of the SSAC or of the

Office for Statistics Regulations). But the amendments are unlikely to be reversed while a high level of job vacancies continues, even though that state of affairs is likely to produce a high level of off-flow from benefit independently of the amendments' effect.

p.1159, *amendment to the Jobseeker's Allowance Regulations 2013 (SI 2013/378) reg.16(5)(b)(ii) (Circumstances in which requirements must not be imposed)*

2.032 With effect from July 1, 2022, reg.4(4)(a) of the Social Security (Medical Evidence) and Statutory Sick Pay (Medical Evidence) (Amendment) (No. 2) Regulations 2022 (SI 2022/630) omitted the words "by a doctor" after "statement given".

pp.1205–1207, *annotation to the Jobseeker's Allowance Regulations 2013 (SI 2013/378) reg.42(2) (Remunerative work—determination of hours engaged)*

2.033 In *KN v DfC (JSA)* [2022] NICom 21, a claim was made after the claimant lost his full-time work but continued to work for the employer on a casual basis, the weekly hours apparently being completely ad hoc. He was paid fortnightly. Since the claimant had said on his claim form that he had been sacked, the effect of that work on entitlement was not examined until some months had passed. The DfC considered that the pattern of fortnightly payment meant that there was a recognisable cycle of work under the equivalent of reg.42(2)(b)(ii), so that the claimant was not entitled to JSA for fortnights in which the hours worked averaged at least 16 per week and was not excluded by the remunerative work rule for fortnights in which the average fell below that level. The appeal tribunal endorsed that approach. On further appeal, Northern Ireland Commissioner Stockman accepted the DfC's submission that the conflation of the issue of a recognisable cycle of *work* with the period of payment of remuneration was an error of law and that the equivalent of reg.42(2)(b)(i) should have been applied. The case was remitted to a new tribunal for reconsideration after the DfC had made a fresh submission on the application of that provision to the evidence. The Commissioner expressed no opinion on the claimant's contention that the hours worked should be averaged over the whole period concerned (20 weeks). Thus, the question of whether that approach or a rolling five-week average should be adopted was left open.

p.1221, *amendment to the Jobseeker's Allowance Regulations 2013 (SI 2013/378) reg.46A(2)(a) (Extended period of sickness)*

2.034 With effect from July 1, 2022, reg.4(4)(b) of the Social Security (Medical Evidence) and Statutory Sick Pay (Medical Evidence) (Amendment) (No. 2) Regulations 2022 (SI 2022/630) omitted the words "a doctor's" between "form of" and "statement".

p.1240, *amendment to the Jobseeker's Allowance Regulations 2013 (SI 2013/378) reg.60(2)(c)(v) (Earnings of self-employed earners—payments not included)*

With effect from July 1, 2022, reg.65 of the Health and Care Act 2022   2.035
(Consequential and Related Amendments and Transitional Provisions)
Regulations 2022 (SI 2022/634) amended reg.60(2)(c) by substituting
the following for head.(v):

> "(v)   an integrated care board established under Chapter A3 of Part 2
> of the National Health Service Act 2006;"

p.1256, *annotation to the Jobseeker's Allowance Regulations 2013 (SI 2013/378) Sch. (Sums to be disregarded in the calculation of earnings)*

The reference to reg.62 should be to reg.61.   2.036

p.1290, *amendment to the Employment and Support Allowance Regulations 2013 (SI 2013/379) reg.17 (Information required for determining capability for work)*

With effect from July 1, 2022, reg.4(5) of the Social Security (Medical   2.037
Evidence) and Statutory Sick Pay (Medical Evidence) (Amendment)
(No. 2) Regulations 2022 (SI 2022/630) omitted the word "doctor's"
after "the form of" in reg.17(1)(a).

p.1303, *amendment to the Employment and Support Allowance Regulations 2013 (SI 2013/379) reg.37(7)(b)(iv) (A claimant who works to be treated as not entitled to an employment and support allowance)*

With effect from July 1, 2022, reg.66 of the Health and Care Act 2022   2.038
(Consequential and Related Amendments and Transitional Provisions)
Regulations 2022 (SI 2022/634) substituted for para.(7)(b)(v) the fol-
lowing:

> "(v)   an integrated care board established under Chapter A3 of Part 2
> of the National Health Service Act 2006;".

p.1378, *amendment to the Employment and Support Allowance Regulations 2008 (SI 2008/794) reg.21 (Information required for determining capability for work)*

With effect from July 1, 2022, reg.4(2) of the Social Security (Medical   2.039
Evidence) and Statutory Sick Pay (Medical Evidence) (Amendment)
(No. 2) Regulations 2022 (SI 2022/630) omitted the word "doctor's"
after "the form of" in reg.21(1)(a).

p.1570, *annotation to the Social Security (Industrial Injuries) (Prescribed Diseases) Regulations 1985 (SI 1985/967) reg.36 (Time for claiming benefit in respect of occupational asthma)*

See now *NP v SSWP (II)* [2022] UKUT 279 (AAC), discussed   2.040
further in relation to Sch.1, PD D7, in which Judge Wikeley dismissed

an appeal from a tribunal which had found that the claimant's workplace exposure to various agents had exacerbated his pre-existing constitutional asthma rather than triggered occupational asthma. The judge further ruled that even if coal dust was "any other sensitising agent" within the terms of D7(x) the claim would in any event have failed as it was time barred under reg.36: "The Appellant was employed by the National Coal Board between 1964 and 1977. His claim for industrial disablement benefit was not made until January 2017. It follows that, even if coal dust was indeed 'any other sensitising agent', and so working underground at a colliery was a prescribed occupation for the purposes of PD D7, the claim on that basis was necessarily way out of time and in effect statute-barred" (para.43).

pp.1622–1623, *annotation to Social Security (Industrial Injuries) (Prescribed Diseases) Regulations 1985 (SI 1985/967) Sch.1 (D7 (occupational asthma))*

2.041   See now *NP v SSWP (II)* [2022] UKUT 279 (AAC), in which Judge Wikeley dismissed an appeal from a tribunal which had found that the claimant's workplace exposure to various agents had exacerbated his pre-existing constitutional asthma rather than triggered occupational asthma. Judge Wikeley explained as follows:

"Work-related asthma in general means asthma where there is some association between increased symptoms and workplace exposure. There are generally accepted to be two types of work-related asthma. The first is work-aggravated asthma, meaning (as the label implies) asthma that is aggravated, but not caused, by exposure to an inhaled agent at work. This type of asthma is not compensated under the industrial injuries scheme. The second is occupational asthma, being asthma that is caused by exposure to an inhaled agent at work. Occupational asthma may be one of two types. The first is occupational asthma with sensitisation, typically where a worker has developed an allergy or sensitisation to an inhaled agent at work. Depending on the circumstances, this may be covered by the prescribed disease provisions for PD D7 in the industrial injuries scheme. The second is acute irritant induced asthma, where asthma develops after a single very high dose exposure (or perhaps multiple symptomatic high doses) to inhaled irritants. This type of asthma may be covered by the accident provisions in the industrial injuries scheme (rather than under the prescribed disease rules)" (para.15).

Judge Wikeley held that the tribunal had provided an adequately reasoned conclusion for its finding that the claimant experienced work-*aggravated* asthma rather than work-*caused* occupational asthma.

In addition, the judge ruled that " . . . in stating that coal dust is not a sensitising agent [within D7(x)] the FTT was simply reflecting and stating the prevailing view in medical science. It certainly had no persuasive evidence before it that coal dust was recognised as a sensitising agent for the purposes of PD D7" (para.40). Indeed, the Secretary of State's representative had relied on the fact that the UK Occupational Asthma

Sensitising Information Service (OASIS) specifically lists coal dust as a *non*-sensitising agent for the purposes of PD D7. Given that OASIS is the in-house system operated by the Centre for Health and Disability Assessment, which conducts medical assessments on behalf of the DWP, and its listings are not available online, Judge Wikeley observed that "if DWP decision-makers are routinely relying on OASIS listings when deciding prescribed disease claims it would seem only fair that such material is made publicly available" (para.41).

PART III

UPDATING MATERIAL
VOLUME II

UNIVERSAL CREDIT, STATE PENSION CREDIT AND THE SOCIAL FUND

Commentary by

John Mesher

Tom Royston

Nick Wikeley

p.49, *Universal Credit—General note: Challenges of transition*

In November 2022, the Government announced that the managed   3.001
migration of "legacy" benefit claimants to UC, initially intended to be
complete by 2017, and expected earlier in 2022 to be complete by 2024,
would be delayed to 2028: Autumn Statement 2022 (CP 751, November
2022), para.5.15. This is expected to save several hundred million
pounds per year (*ibid*, p.61 para.53). That is for two reasons: some
legacy claimants who will be better off on UC will move slower than they
would have done; some legacy claimants who will be worse off on UC
will move due to "natural" migration instead of managed migration, and
therefore will not receive transitional protection.

pp.56–57, *Universal Credit—General note: Calculation of income*

The General Note discusses *R. (Pantellerisco) v SSWP* [2021] EWCA   3.002
Civ 1454; [2021] PTSR 1922. The Supreme Court has now refused
permission to appeal, so the Court of Appeal's decision is final.

p.58, *Universal Credit—General note: The benefit cap*

Until recently the benefit cap rates had not been changed, or even   3.003
reviewed, since its rates were inserted into s.96 of the Act in 2016.
However, the Government has announced that those rates will be raised
in line with inflation, along with other benefit levels, in April 2023:
Autumn Statement 2022 (CP 751, November 2022), para.2.47.

p.59, *Universal Credit—General note: Claimant responsibilities and the*
claimant commitment

Until 2022, a person in work but with very low earnings would   3.004
generally be subjected to "light touch" conditionality rather than intensive requirements, by virtue of reg.99(6) of the 2013 Regulations. With
effect from September 26, 2022 the Universal Credit (Administrative
Earnings Threshold) (Amendment) Regulations 2022 (SI 2022/886)
expanded the "intensive requirements" group by an additional 120,000
people, to anyone with earnings of less than the equivalent of 12 hours
per week (h.p.w.) at minimum wage (19 h.p.w. for couples). The government stated in September 2022 that it planned to increase this threshold
further, to 15 h.p.w. (24 h.p.w. for couples) from January 2023: *Growth*
Plan 2022 (CP 743, September 2022), para.4.30.

p.61, *Universal Credit—General note: Sanctions*

The government stated in September 2022 that it "will be strengthen-   3.005
ing the sanctions regime to set clear work expectations—including applying for jobs, attending interviews or increasing the hours—in return for
receiving UC": *Growth Plan 2022* (CP 743, September 2022), para.4.31.
It is not clear what precisely this will entail.

p.78, *annotation to the Welfare Reform Act 2012 s.14 (Claimant commitment)*

3.006   Paragraph 4.31 of the September 2022 *Growth Plan 2022* (CP 743) said that the government would be strengthening the universal credit sanctions regime to set clear expectations, including applying for jobs, attending interviews or increasing hours, but it was left unclear exactly what that was to entail or whether any legislative change was envisaged. It is not known whether the plan, such as it was, has survived the change of administration.

p.112, *annotation to the Welfare Reform Act 2012 s.26 (Higher-level sanctions)*

3.007   Paragraph 4.31 of the September 2022 *Growth Plan 2022* (CP 743) said that the government would be strengthening the universal credit sanctions regime to set clear expectations, including applying for jobs, attending interviews or increasing hours, but it was left unclear exactly what that was to entail or whether any legislative change was envisaged. It is not known whether the plan, such as it was, has survived the change of administration.

For a summary of past government reactions to official reports and studies on the effectiveness or fairness of sanctions regimes see pp.210–211 of the 2021/22 edition of Vol.V of this series. More recently, a letter dated June 15, 2022 from the Chair of the House of Commons Work and Pensions Committee, Sir Stephen Timms, to the then Secretary of State, noted that the Committee's 2019 report on *Benefit Sanctions* had recommended that the Department "urgently evaluate the effectiveness of reforms to welfare conditionality" and that the government had accepted the recommendation, saying that it would focus its evaluation on "whether the sanctions regime within Universal Credit is effective at supporting claimants to search for work". At that stage publication in late spring 2019 was envisaged and in June 2020 an official (Neil Couling) told the House of Lords Economic Affairs Committee that the DWP still had "every intention of fulfilling" the commitment to provide the research to the Committee. In 2022 a Freedom of Information request for the report was rejected by the DWP and a spokesperson told the press that it "could not publish the report because it did not present a comprehensive picture of sanctions". Sir Stephen asked in the letter of June 15, 2022 if the DWP would provide the Committee with a copy of the evaluation report, as it had committed to doing. The then Secretary of State's reply, in her letter of July 15, 2022, was as follows:

> "We no longer plan to publish the report. This was commissioned by a previous administration. The notion of a sanction acts not only through its imposition on a claimant but importantly also through its effect as a deterrent. Due to the way the report was commissioned, we were unable to assess the deterrent effect and therefore this research does not present a comprehensive picture of sanctions."

The Public Law Project published a distinctly critical report, *Benefit Sanctions: a Presumption of Guilt*, on July 20, 2022.

p.159, *annotation to the Welfare Reform Act 2012 s.96A (Benefit cap: review)*

A difficulty with s.96A(1)–(2) is that those provisions are not accom-   **3.008** panied by any obligation to publish the outcome of a review unless it results in a change to the cap levels. That omission obstructs the ability of an external observer to know whether the requirement to conduct five-yearly reviews is being complied with. In July 2022 a minister informed Parliament that there had not ever been a review of benefit cap levels under s.96A(1): PQ UIN 27503, July 4, 2022. Then, in November 2022 the Government announced that it had decided to raise the cap levels (implying that it had at some point after July 2022 finally conducted a review): *Autumn Statement 2022* (CP 751, November 2022), para.2.47. It follows that the s.96A(1) duty will next *require* a review at some point between July and November 2027—unless the Secretary of State meanwhile chooses to conduct a review, which would restart the clock.

p.164, *amendment to the Welfare Reform Act 2012 Sch.3 para.14 (Abolition of benefits: consequential amendments—Capital Allowances Act 2001)*

With effect from April 1, 2020, s.33(2)(c)(viii)(a) of the Finance Act   **3.009** 2019 revoked para.14.

p.167, *annotation to the Welfare Reform Act 2012 Sch.4 (Housing credit element of State Pension Credit)*

This Schedule is still not in force. In November 2022, the Govern-   **3.010** ment announced that the movement of pensioners from housing benefit to housing credit (and therefore the commencement of this Schedule) would be delayed to 2028–29: *Autumn Statement 2022* (CP 751, November 2022), para.5.14.

p.172, *erratum—Welfare Reform Act 2012 Sch.6 (Migration to Universal Credit)*

There is an error in the first sentence of the General Note to Sch.6.   **3.011** This Schedule is fully in force (and has been since July 18, 2019: Welfare Reform Act 2012 (Commencement No. 33) Order (SI 2019/1135) art.2).

p.192, *amendment to the Universal Credit Regulations 2013 (SI 2013/376) reg.2 (Interpretation)*

With effect from May 4, 2022, reg.2 of the Universal Credit (Local   **3.012** Welfare Provision Disregard) (Amendment) Regulations 2022 (SI

2022/448) amends reg.2 of the 2013 Regulations. The amendment inserts, after the definition of "local authority":

> ""local welfare provision" means occasional financial or other assistance given by a local authority, the Scottish Ministers or the Welsh Ministers, or a person authorised to exercise any function of, or provide a service to, them, to or in respect of individuals for the purpose of—
>
> (a) meeting, or helping to meet, an immediate short term need—
>   (i) arising out of an exceptional event, or exceptional circumstances; and
>   (ii) that requires to be met in order to avoid a risk to the well-being of an individual; or
> (b) enabling individuals to establish or maintain a settled home, where those individuals have been or, without the assistance, might otherwise be—
>   (i) in prison, hospital, a residential care establishment or other institution; or
>   (ii) homeless or otherwise living an unsettled way of life;".

p.204, *amendment to the Universal Credit Regulations 2013 (SI 2013/376) reg.8 (Cases where the minimum age is 16)*

3.013   With effect from July 1, 2022, reg.4(3)(a) of the Social Security (Medical Evidence) and Statutory Sick Pay (Medical Evidence) (Amendment) (No. 2) Regulations 2022 (SI 2022/630) amended reg.8(1)(b) by omitting the phrase "by a registered medical practitioner".

p.208, *amendments to the Universal Credit Regulations 2013 (SI 2013/376) reg.9 (Persons treated as not being in Great Britain)*

3.014   With effect from October 18, 2022, reg.2 of the Social Security (Habitual Residence and Past Presence) (Amendment) (No. 2) Regulations 2022 (SI 2022/990) amended reg.9(4)(zc) of the 2013 Regulations as follows:

(a) at the end of para.(i) omit "or";
(b) at the end of para.(ii) insert "or";
(c) after para.(ii) insert:
   "(iii) does not require leave to enter or remain in the United Kingdom in accordance with section 3ZA of that Act;"

p.220, *annotation to the Universal Credit Regulations 2013 (SI 2013/376) reg.12(2)(a) (Meaning of "receiving education")*

3.015   Upper Tribunal Judge Rowley ruled as follows in *BK v SSWP (UC)* [2022] UKUT 73 (AAC), an appeal in which the issue was the meaning of "undertaking a full-time course of advanced education" under reg.12(2)(a):

"19. The following propositions may be gleaned from the jurisprudence:

a. Whether or not a person is undertaking a full-time course is a question of fact for the tribunal having regard to the circumstances in each particular case (*R/SB 40/83* at [13]; *R(SB) 41/83* at [12]). Parameters have been set, as appear below:

b. The words "full-time" relate to the course and not to the student. Specifically, they do not permit the matter to be determined by reference to the amount of time which the student happens to dedicate to their studies (*R/SB 40/83* at [14], [15]; *R(SB) 2/91* at [7]; *R(SB) 41/83* at [11]).

c. Evidence from the educational establishment as to whether or not the course is full-time is not necessarily conclusive, but it ought to be accepted as such unless it is inconclusive on its face, or is challenged by relevant evidence which at least raises the possibility that it ought to be rejected (*R/SB 40/83* at [18]), and any evidence adduced in rebuttal should be weighty in content (*R/SB 41/83* at [12]). See also *Flemming v Secretary of State for Work and Pensions* [2002] EWCA Civ 641, [2002] 1 WLR 2322 at [21]–[22] and [38]; and *Deane v Secretary of State for Work and Pensions* [2010] EWCA Civ 699, [2011] 1 WLR 743 where the Court of Appeal repeated an earlier statement in *Flemming* that:

"38 . . . A tribunal of fact should, I think be very slow to accept that a person expects or intends to devote—or does, in fact, devote—significantly less time to the course than those who have conduct of the course expect of him, and very slow to hold that a person who is attending a course considered by the educational establishment to be a part-time course is to be treated as receiving full-time education because he devote significantly more time than that which is expected of him . . . "

d. If the course is offered as full-time course, the presumption is that the recipient is in full-time education. There may be exceptions to the rule, such where a student is granted exemptions from part of the course: *Deane* [51]."

p.223, *annotation to the Universal Credit Regulations 2013 (SI 2013/376) reg.14 (Exceptions to the requirement not to be receiving education)*

The Court of Appeal has dismissed an appeal by the claimant against the decision of Swift J in *R. (Kays) v SSWP* [2022] EWHC 167 (Admin). The unsuccessful grounds of appeal were that (1) the decision to make the 2020 Regulations without consultation was irrational; (2) the 2020 Regulations achieved their purpose in an irrational and arbitrary way; (3) the purpose of those regulations was irrational and discriminatory; and (4) the Respondent had not had due regard to the public sector equality duty: see *R. (Kays) v SSWP* [2022] EWCA Civ 1593. According to Lewis LJ (at [37]):

3.016

"The respondent is entitled to make different provision for different classes, both as a matter of general principle and under the regulation-making powers conferred by section 42(2) of the 2012 Act. In the present case, the respondent has made different provision for two different groups where there is a rational distinction between those two groups. The respondent is entitled to make such distinctions. The choice may seem to some to be a hard choice. It may, in due course, emerge that there are different and better choices, as Underhill LJ recognised at paragraph 59 of his judgment in *Pantellerisco*. That, however, does not mean that the distinction that the respondent has made at present is irrational. It reflects a rational difference between two groups: one of whom will be taking decisions about whether to pursue full-time education on the basis of the student finance available and one who will be taking decisions when they are already in receipt of certain benefits."

p.276, *annotation to the Universal Credit Regulations 2013 (SI 2013/376) reg.46 (What is included in capital?)*

3.017 At some point, the valuation of digital assets, such as non-fungible tokens, cryptocurrency etc., may have to be addressed, including how they fit into the notions of capital and of personal possessions. There is extensive discussion of the existing legal framework in the Law Commission's *Digital Assets: Consultation Paper* (Law Com. No.256, July 28, 2022).

p.288, *annotation to the Universal Credit Regulations 2013 (SI 2013/376) reg.46 (What is included in capital?—Claimant holding as trustee)*

3.018 Note the decision of the Supreme Court, by a majority of three to two, in *Guest v Guest* [2022] UKSC 27; [2022] 3 W.L.R. 911 on proprietary estoppel and the nature of the remedies available in equity. Lord Briggs, giving the majority judgment, conducted an exhaustive survey of the English and Australian case law, as well as academic debate, and rejected the theory that the aim of the remedy was to compensate the person given a promise or assurance about the acquisition of property for the detriment suffered in reliance on the promise or assurance, rather than primarily to hold the person who had given the promise or assurance to the promise or assurance, which would usually prevent the unconscionability inherent in the repudiation of the promise or assurance that had been detrimentally relied on (paras 71 and 61). However, the remedy was a flexible one dependent on the circumstances. Lord Briggs summarised the principles as follows:

"74. I consider that, in principle, the court's normal approach should be as follows. The first stage (which is not in issue in this case) is to determine whether the promisor's repudiation of his promise is, in the light of the promisee's detrimental reliance upon it, unconscionable at all. It usually will be, but there may be circumstances (such as the promisor falling on hard times and needing to sell the property to pay his creditors, or to pay for expensive medical treatment or social care for himself or his wife) when it may not be. Or the promisor may have announced or carried out only a partial repudiation of the promise, which may or may not have been unconscionable, depending on the circumstances.

75. The second (remedy) stage will normally start with the assumption (not presumption) that the simplest way to remedy the unconscionability constituted by the repudiation is to hold the promisor to the promise. The promisee cannot (and probably would not) complain, for example, that his detrimental reliance had cost him more than the value of the promise, were it to be fully performed. But the court may have to listen to many other reasons from the promisor (or his executors) why something less than full performance will negate the unconscionability and therefore satisfy the equity. They may be based on one or more of the real-life problems already outlined. The court may be invited by the promisor to consider one or more proxies for performance of the promise, such as the transfer of less property than promised or the provision of a monetary equivalent in place of it, or a combination of the two.

76. If the promisor asserts and proves, the burden being on him for this purpose, that specific enforcement of the full promise, or monetary equivalent, would be out of all proportion to the cost of the detriment to the promisee, then the court may be constrained to limit the extent of the remedy. This does not mean that the court will be seeking precisely to compensate for the detriment as its primary task, but simply to put right a disproportionality which is so large as to stand in the way of a full specific enforcement doing justice between the parties. It will be a very rare case where the detriment is equivalent in value to the expectation, and there is nothing in principle unjust in a full enforcement of the promise being worth more than the cost of the detriment, any more than there is in giving specific performance of a contract for the sale of land merely because it is worth more than the price paid for it. An example of a remedy out of all proportion to the detriment would be the full enforcement of a promise by an elderly lady to leave her carer a particular piece of jewellery if she stayed on at very low wages, which turned out on valuation by her executors to be a Faberge worth millions. Another would be a promise to leave a generous inheritance if the promisee cared for the promisor for the rest of her life, but where she unexpectedly died two months later."

Thus, in circumstances where proprietary estoppel might be in play (as would probably now be the case on similar facts to *R(SB) 23/85* and *R(SB) 7/87*), great care would be needed in establishing the primary facts and, outside the clearest cases, in a deeper investigation of the principles of law governing the nature of any remedy available. And would a repudiation of a promise when the promisor would otherwise be forced to rely on a means-tested benefit be unconscionable? However, even if it were to be concluded that the claimant did not hold the property in question on trust for someone else, the possibility of a claim in equity, e.g. for some monetary compensation, might well affect the valuation of the property.

pp.342–348, *annotation to the Universal Credit Regulations 2013 (SI 2013/376) reg.55 (Employed earnings)*

3.019   Note the decision of the Court of Appeal in *Commissioners for HMRC v Murphy* [2022] EWCA Civ 1112; [2023] 1 W.L.R. 51 on the meaning of "profit" in s.62(2)(b) of ITEPA. In a complex settlement of police officers' group claims for compensation for underpayment of overtime and certain allowances, the principal sum agreed to be paid by the Metropolitan Police Service ("the Met") covered only some of the claimants' costs. It did not include the amount of their solicitors' and counsel's "success fee" under a "damages-based agreement" or the amount of the premium paid on a policy insuring them against the risk of having to pay the Met's costs. But those amounts were deducted from the principal sum and only the balance of the principal sum paid to the individual claimants. Mr Murphy had succeeded before the Upper Tribunal (Tax and Chancery Chamber) ("UTTCC") in an argument that his proportionate share of those amounts should be deducted from his share of the whole principal sum in calculating the "profit" within s.62(2)(b), as they were necessarily incurred in order to obtain the sum derived from his employment. The Court of Appeal held that to have been an error of law. In the context of the statutory scheme, all earnings from employment are taxable, subject only to the deductions allowed under the legislation. In s.62(2)(b) "profit" is used in the sense of "a material benefit derived from a property, position etc; income, revenue", one of the definitions in the Oxford English Dictionary. The expenditure not being allowable deductions nor having been incurred in the performance of Mr Murphy's duties, the sole question was whether the profit was "from" employment as a reward for services, as it clearly was, the principal settlement sum relating to amounts alleged to be due under the claimants' contracts of employment. It did not matter that they were left to meet some of their own costs.

E.ON UK Plc v Commissioners of HMRC [2022] UKUT 196 (TCC) also concerned the "from" test in s.9(2) of ITEPA, for universal credit purposes applied by reg.52(a). E.ON made a one-off payment, called a facilitation payment, to employees who were members of its final salary pension scheme, in which prospective changes adverse to members were being made. The UTTCC overturned the FtT's decision upholding HMRC's view that the payment was taxable. After a very full analysis of the complex package of which the facilitation payment was a part, the UTTCC concluded that the particular payment was not an inducement to provide future services on different terms, but in return for employees' consent to the adverse changes in the pension scheme and thus was not taxable. It was not even a case within the principle of *Kuehne and Nagel Drinks Logistics Ltd v Commissioners for HMRC* [2012] EWCA Civ 34; [2012] S.T.C. 840 where there are two or more reasons for a payment and it is enough that one related to employment was sufficiently sub-stantial. There was extensive discussion of tax cases relating to pensions that might possibly have to be consulted if similar circumstances arise.

pp.374–375, *annotation to the Universal Credit Regulations 2013 (SI 2013/376) reg.61(3) and (4) (Information for calculating earned income—real time information etc.—Paragraphs (3) and (4))*

In relation to the argument mentioned on these pages that para.(2)(b)   **3.020** of the pre-November 16, 2020 form of reg.61 (information received from HMRC incorrect in a material respect) could have been engaged if the employer had reported a payment as made on the actual date of payment rather than on the date specified in HMRC guidance/instruc-tions, *DfC v OS (UC)* [2022] NICom 29 can be added to the lack of judicial support also mentioned on these pages. However, it is submitted that the decision adds little weight against the argument, which in any event should now be almost entirely of historical interest only.

The claimant's last day of work was November 9, 2018. He claimed universal credit on November 19, 2018. In the assessment period ending on December 18, 2018 he received payments relating to his work down to November 9. Although the DfC appeared not to have identified the amounts accurately in its initial decision, it was agreed before Northern Ireland Commissioner Stockman that the relevant payments were a payment of £404.34 in final wages on November 23 and a payment of £225.52 in accrued holiday pay on November 30. Those amounts were apparently reported by the employer through RTI on those dates. The appeal tribunal erroneously applied the post-November 16, 2020 form of the equivalent of reg.61 (which of course was not in force at the relevant time) in holding that no payments fell to be attributed to the assessment period ending on December 18, because the payments were not *for* that assessment period. It was agreed on the DfC's appeal that the tribunal's decision should be set aside for applying the wrong legislation and that the Commissioner should substitute a decision on the under-lying appeal. The argument made for the claimant was that he had been entitled to be made the two payments on November 16 (presumably as the next normal or contractual pay-day) and that in accordance with the PAYE legislation and HMRC guidance pay should be recorded on the date on which the employee is entitled to be paid. Therefore, the infor-mation provided by HMRC (presumably) on November 23 and/or 30 was incorrect in a material respect because the payment date should have been November 16.

Commissioner Stockman rejected that argument, though finding some force in it. He considered that the key word in issue was "incor-rect" and continued in para.35:

"The term "incorrect", when applied to information, it appears to me, has the meaning of being inaccurate or being wrong. I can find no authority for construing the expression "the information received from HMRC is incorrect . . . in some material respect" to encompass the situation where otherwise accurate information is not recorded on the correct date. There may well be a legitimate expectation that information should be provided on a particular date under legislation and guidance. A failure to do so may well be an incorrect application of the relevant PAYE rules. However, in the absence of persuasive authority, I cannot hold that this procedural failing renders the information "incorrect" when it amounts to accurate information being provided at the wrong date."

It is submitted that "incorrect" was not the sole key word, but that the word "information" was of equal significance and that the payment date included in the RTI information received from HMRC could be regarded as inaccurate or wrong if the identification of the date did not follow HMRC instructions. Nor is it clear how the absence of existing persuasive authority was relevant to construing the meaning of the relevant provision. In other cases, even under the current form of reg.61, there may be difficult issues following the ending of employment about when particular payments are due to be made and how that fits in with PAYE and RTI reporting obligations.

pp.464–467, *annotation to the Universal Credit Regulations 2013 (SI 2013/376) reg.97(4) and (5) (Work search requirement and work availability requirement—limitations—previous work)*

3.021   On June 23, 2022 (published on the internet on July 6, 2022), the Chair of the SSAC wrote to the Secretary of State to say that after careful consideration the Committee had decided not to take the regulations shortening the "permitted period" on formal reference, but wished to record a number of concerns and make some advisory recommendations. It is worth quoting the statement of concerns relating to the role of the regulatory changes in enhancing the overall policy intent verbatim (footnotes have been omitted):

"Scale of the challenge

In order to assess whether the regulation change could deliver and was proportionate to the policy intent, we were keen to understand the relative size of the role of the regulatory change in combination with the other measures as part of the Way to Work scheme, and the scale of the increase in off-flow into work that would be expected to be required to achieve the 500k target. Officials were unable to provide an estimate of the overall scale of the change from the combined programme or of the expected contribution of the regulatory change. We appreciate that this is difficult to do, but whether this goal involves an increase in off-flow rates of 10%, 50% or 100% compared to an expected counterfactual has a material impact on the proportionality of the policy response.

Given that the off-flow from benefits into employment for the month of February (which would be unlikely to have yet been significantly affected by the programme's components) had been estimated at around 114K—so that on average only 96.5K per month needed to be achieved over the remaining four months to meet the target—it seems as if the required impact could be at the lower end of the scale, and more aligned to avoiding a drop in off-flow rates rather than appreciably boosting them.

We also sought to understand the number of jobseekers whose search expectations would be changed by these regulations for the duration of the scheme. Unfortunately, officials were not in a position to provide an estimate of the scale of the change.

Evidence base

We were informed that the rationale for the reduction in the duration of the permitted period was that there was a unique moment in the labour market as, post-COVID, there were significantly higher than normal levels of sectoral shift and high levels of vacancies—which meant there would be greater benefit from jobseekers expanding their search into new sectors at an earlier point.

We have sought access to evidence that could underpin the basis of the decision to shorten the permitted period. We understand that the choice of four weeks as the new duration was a judgment informed by feedback from work coaches. However, no data or explanation has been made available to indicate what the impact would be of making the change. In fact, the evidence offered indicated that there was no noticeable increase in the historic off-flow rate after the 13-week point, suggesting that the extant pattern of broadening of the work-search expectations, at least at this point, did not have a discernible impact.

Our concerns are compounded by the lack of a clear positive outcome expected as a result of the reduction in the permitted period. We are told that no estimate is available of what a positive outcome would be either in terms of the number claiming the benefits, or the fiscal impact though presumably these have been incorporated in the latest forecasts produced by the Office for Budget Responsibility and adopted by the Government in the Spring Statement.

We asked your officials for an assessment of the baseline (historic) patterns of off-flow, and how these might have been expected to evolve in coming months absent these change in these regulations, alongside any early indication of patterns in the early months of the programme (see Appendix for details). Unfortunately, this information has not been shared with the Committee.

Potential negative impact

At the time of our scrutiny, no assessment had been made of the risk of individuals entering roles that were inconsistent with their qualifications/ experience, or simply wrong for them in terms of their career path and ambitions, nor of the risk that increased competition from more highly qualified people would make it more difficult for longer-term unemployed people to find work. Similarly, no consideration had been made of the impact on those with part-time, or other flexible, job-search expectations for whom the four-week cut-off could be disproportionate and one that will certainly vary by protected characteristics, most obviously sex and disability.

There was some acknowledgement that there may be negative consequences from these changes, for example increased cycling on and off benefits, and job mismatches leading to more churn for employers and to claimants potentially having career paths hindered. However, there was no analysis of how to mitigate against negative effects, particularly where those with protected characteristics might be disproportionately impacted.

Evaluating the effectiveness of the permitted period change

These regulations were brought in to deal with a unique moment in the economy as it reopened from COVID restrictions, resulting in a very high number of labour market vacancies. However, the regulations do not have a sunset clause and the Committee would be concerned that, without a proper review of the impact of these regulations, they may be left on the statute book, despite the labour market situation having substantially changed. Therefore, the Committee very much welcomes that in your letter to me of 3 February, you committed to undertake such an evaluation of the regulations at the end of June to assess their effectiveness and whether they should be retained.

The way in which the regulations would be reviewed in terms of (a) by what criteria they would be deemed a success, and (b) how such criteria would be evaluated is in need of detailed thought. It will also be important to differentiate the criteria on which the regulations are evaluated with respect to the current unique point in time and the assessment whether they should be retained for what should then be much more normal times ahead. However, when we asked officials how they plan to undertake this, it was clear that such thinking had not yet matured.

Urgency

The regulations had been laid under the urgency provision before being presented to this Committee for scrutiny. I have previously written to you seeking a better understanding of the nature of the urgency in this instance. As you know, this Committee is supportive of the use of "urgency" where legislation is being brought forward as a direct consequence of either an external factor or a fiscal event. Indeed we welcomed the use of urgency, and expedited our own statutory scrutiny process, to ensure that essential support could be introduced quickly in response to recent crises in Afghanistan and Ukraine. However, a compelling argument for urgency in this specific case remains unclear to us.

We were informed that the regulations had to bypass the scrutiny of the Committee before coming into force, as "every day" was essential in ensuring that the Government can meet its own target. However, there was no explanation of what impact there might be in waiting a few weeks for the Committee to complete its statutory scrutiny —either on the specific issue of the target or in terms of the broader proposals.

Similarly, it is not clear why the target could not simply have been put back a short period, or why the rest of the Way to Work programme could not proceed whilst the permitted period proposals were considered by the Committee."

Despite that politely devastating analysis, success of the Way to Work campaign was declared on June 30, 2022 by way of a tweet and a press release asserting that over half a million people had been helped into work by the campaign in five months (later quoted in the House of Commons by the then Prime Minister on July 6, 2022). That declaration was apparently based on an answer to a Parliamentary Question on June 30, 2022 revealing an estimate using management information that as of June 29, 2022 at least 505,400 unemployed universal credit and JSA claimants had moved into work during the campaign. That use of the figures was castigated by the Director General for Regulation in the Office for Statistics Regulation in his letter of July 29, 2022 to the Permanent Secretary of the DWP. He concluded that it was difficult to attribute and quantify the impact of the campaign in the absence of a clearly defined and published target and details of how it would be measured and reported, so that the way that the DWP had communicated information did not uphold the principles of being trustworthy, of high quality and offering public value. A more targeted point might have been to note the speciousness of using evidence of the numbers who moved into work *during* the campaign to support the assertion that all those claimants had been helped into work *by* the campaign. A further written answer to a Parliamentary Question on September 5, 2022 revealed that no estimate had been made of the number of unemployed universal credit and JSA claimants who would have moved into work between January and June 2022 in the absence of the Way to Work campaign.

Overall, it is hard to avoid the conclusion that this whole shabby episode was little more than a small-scale exercise in grandiose posturing with every appearance of having been foisted on the DWP with no time for thought or preparation. However, the episode is not over. There has been no public sign of the promised evaluation of the effectiveness of the amending regulations and of whether they should be retained (the September 2022 written answer suggests that there has been no attempt at any real evaluation or at meeting the concerns of the SSAC or the Office for Statistics Regulations). But the amendments are unlikely to be reversed while a high level of job vacancies continues, even though that state of affairs is likely to produce a high level of off-flow from benefit independently of the amendments' effect.

p.471, *amendment to the Universal Credit Regulations 2013 (SI 2013/376) reg.99(4)(b)(ii) (Circumstances in which requirements must not be imposed)*

3.022   With effect from July 1, 2022, reg.4(3)(b) of the Social Security (Medical Evidence) and Statutory Sick Pay (Medical Evidence) (Amendment) (No. 2) Regulations 2022 (SI 2022/630) omitted the words "by a doctor" after "statement given".

p.473, *amendment to the Universal Credit Regulations 2013 (SI 2013/376) reg.99(6) (Circumstances in which requirements must not be imposed)*

3.023   With effect from September 26, 2022, reg.2 of the Universal Credit (Administrative Earnings Threshold) (Amendment) Regulations 2022 (SI 2022/886) substituted the following for para.(6) of reg.99:

"(6) This paragraph applies where—
  (a) the claimant has monthly earnings (excluding any that are not employed earnings) that are equal to, or more than, the amount that a person would be paid at the hourly rate set out in regulation 4 of the National Minimum Wage Regulations for 12 hours per week, converted to a monthly amount by multiplying by 52 and dividing by 12; or
  (b) the claimant is a member of a couple whose combined monthly earnings (excluding any that are not employed earnings) are equal to, or more than, the amount that a person would be paid at the hourly rate set out in regulation 4 of the National Minimum Wage Regulations for 19 hours per week, converted to a monthly amount by multiplying by 52 and dividing by 12."

Regulation 4 of the National Minimum Wage Regulations 2015 (see the definition in reg.2), as amended, sets the hourly rate (£9.50 as from April 2022) for employees aged at least 23, what the government calls the national living wage. Thus, as confirmed in the Explanatory Memorandum to SI 2022/886, the monthly rates prescribed under the new para.(6) are £494 (sub-para.(a) for individual claimants) and £782 (sub-para.(b) for couples). The figures under the previous form of para.(6) were £355 and £567 respectively. If employed earnings (not self-employed earnings or income from other paid work under reg.52(a)(iii)) equal or exceed the relevant figure, the so-called administrative earnings threshold (AET), work search and work availability requirements may not be imposed, unless the claimant falls within one of the pilot schemes and is to be treated as if para.(6) does not exist.

The rationale for the increase in the threshold, exposing more claimants to the more rigorous parts of the conditionality and sanctions regime, is set out as follows in the revised Explanatory Memorandum (the original version was found to be inadequate by the House of Lords Secondary Legislation Scrutiny Committee: *13th Report of Session 2022–23*, HL Paper 68, October 13, 2022):

"7.1 The current AET is equivalent to an individual claimant working 8.62 hours per week earning the National Living Wage (NLW). The current AET for couples is equivalent to them working 13.77 hrs per week between them earning the National Living Wage (NLW).

7.2 When Universal Credit (UC) claimants earn more than their Conditionality Earnings Threshold (CET) they move into the Working Enough conditionality group, where no conditionality requirements are applied, and the claimants do not regularly interact with a work coach. The CET is a flexible threshold which is calculated based on the number of hours an individual claimant can reasonably be expected to undertake work or work-related activities based on their circumstances. In most cases, it is set at the rate equivalent to working 35 hours at the NLW, but this can be adjusted to take account of health conditions or caring responsibilities.

7.3 Where a UC claimant is subject to all work-related requirements, the Administrative Earnings Threshold (AET) is used to determine which conditionality regime the claimant is allocated to. UC claimants are placed in the Intensive Work Search (IWS) regime if they are earning less than their AET, or placed in the Light Touch regime if they are earning at or above their AET but below their CET. Those in the IWS regime are required to accept a Claimant Commitment agreeing work search requirements and work availability requirements as well as work preparation and work-focused interview requirements. Whereas those in Light Touch are not required to comply with work search requirements or work availability requirements.

7.4 This instrument will support UC claimants to progress in work by extending work coach support to more UC claimants on low incomes. Work coaches provide regular on-going tailored support, and claimants will be able to access a comprehensive range of training and skills provision based on their needs.

7.5 Departmental analysts have estimated that this change to the AET will bring in an estimated additional 114,000 claimants into the IWS regime from the Light Touch regime (16.5% of Light Touch claimants). This change will require impacted claimants to review and agree a new Claimant Commitment with a work coach, agreeing appropriate work search requirements which will be revised and updated regularly.

7.6 The policy intent is to support those who find themselves in low income to help them access opportunities to increase their earnings. This might be by increasing their hours, progressing in their current role/sector, or switching careers."

Paragraph 7.4 might be thought somewhat disingenuous in that there seems nothing to have prevented more extensive work coach support being provided to claimants in the light touch regime through the operation of the work-focused interview and work preparation requirements. Nor does the Memorandum explain what was wrong with the previous method of calculating the AET. That was done more explicitly in the

DWP's presentation to the Social Security Advisory Committee. Paragraph 3.3 of the revised minutes of the SSAC meeting of January 26, 2022 (publication of the minutes of this item having been delayed until SI 2022/886 was laid) contains the explanation that the effect was to return the AET to the real level set in 2015, which had been eroded since because wages had risen faster than benefit levels, which had featured in the previous method of calculation.

Paragraph 4.30 of the September 2022 *Growth Plan 2022* (CP 743) said that the government was going to increase the AET further from January 2023, to 15 hours at the national living wage for individual claimants and 24 hours for couples. That would seem to produce very significant increases to £617 and £988 per month respectively. It was estimated that about 120,000 additional claimants would be moved into the intensive work search regime, in which it was said that they would have to attend weekly or fortnightly appointments. Paragraph 3.7 of the *Autumn Statement* (CP 751, November 17, 2022) confirmed that that proposal was to go ahead, as was implemented with effect from January 30, 2023 by reg.2 of the Universal Credit (Administrative Earnings Threshold) (Amendment) Regulations 2023 (SI 2023/7). The statements in the Explanatory Memorandum that the AET for an individual will be £618 per month seem to have ignored the rule on rounding in reg.6(1A)(b) of the Universal Credit Regulations and the amount was corrected to £617 in the Minister of State's statement to Parliament on January 30, 2023 and a press release.

In addition, para.5.11 of the *Autumn Statement* promised a nationwide rollout, to be phased from September 2023, of the In-Work Progression Offer, announced in the Spending Review 2021. That appears to be a reference to the promise of funding of £99 million over three years to expand work coach support to help people progress once they are in work (para.4.99 of *Autumn Budget and Spending Review 2021* (HC 822, October 27, 2021)). It is estimated that over 600,000 claimants will eventually be affected, unless exempted by having earnings reaching the conditionality earnings threshold under reg.90. Further details were given in the DWP's December 2022 publication *Helping people secure, stay and succeed in higher quality, higher paying jobs*, the UK Government's response to the In-Work Progression Commission's report—supporting progression out of low pay: a call to action.

pp.479–481, *annotation to the Universal Credit Regulations 2013 (SI 2013/376) reg.99(6) (Circumstances in which requirements must not be imposed)*

3.024   See the amendment noted in the entry for p.473 and the plans for 2023 noted there. The revised minutes of the SSAC meeting of January 26, 2022, mentioned in that entry, also contain some further information on developments in knowledge and official thinking on in-work progression and the aftermath of the randomised control trial.

pp.526–539, *amendments to the Universal Credit Regulations 2013 (SI 2013/376) Schedule 4 (Housing costs element for renters)*

With effect from October 1, 2022, reg.3 of the Housing Benefit and Universal Credit (Victims of Domestic Abuse and Victims of Modern Slavery) (Amendment) Regulations 2022 (SI 2022/942) amended Sch.4 of the 2013 Regulations as follows: 3.025

In para.2 (interpretation):
(a) before "exempt accommodation" insert:
""domestic violence" has the meaning given by regulation 98(4);";
(b) after "registered social landlord", insert:
""relative" has the meaning given by section 63(1) of the Family Law Act 1996;".

In para.29 (renters excepted from shared accommodation):
(a) in sub-para.(1) for "(9A)" substitute "(9C)";
(b) after sub-para.(9A) insert:
  "(9B) E is under 35 years old and—
    (a) after attaining the age of 16 had domestic violence inflicted upon or threatened against them ("the victim") by their partner or former partner, or by a relative; and
    (b) provides evidence from a person acting in an official capacity which demonstrates that—
    (i) the victim's circumstances are consistent with their having had domestic violence inflicted upon or threatened against them; and
    (ii) the victim has contacted a person acting in an official capacity in relation to such an incident.
  (9C) E is under 35 years old and has been the subject of a positive conclusive grounds determination relating to modern slavery.";
(c) in sub-para.(10):
    (i) after the definition of ""care home", "registered charity" and "voluntary organisation"" insert:
      ""competent authority" means a person who is a competent authority within the meaning of the Trafficking Convention;
      "compulsory labour", "forced labour", "servitude" and "slavery" have the same meaning as in Article 4 of the Convention for the Protection of Human Rights and Fundamental Freedoms, agreed by the Council of Europe at Rome on 4th November 1950 as it has effect for the time being in relation to the United Kingdom;";
    (ii) after the definition of "hostel for homeless people" insert:
      ""person acting in an official capacity" means a health care professional (within the meaning given by regulation 98(4)), a police officer, a registered social worker (within the meaning given by regulation 98(4)), the victim's employer, or any public, voluntary, or charitable body

109

which has had direct contact with the victim in connection with domestic violence;

"positive conclusive grounds determination relating to modern slavery" means a determination made by a competent authority that an individual is a victim of trafficking in human beings, slavery, servitude or forced or compulsory labour;

"the Trafficking Convention" means the Council of Europe Convention on Action against Trafficking in Human Beings (done at Warsaw on 16th May 2005);

"trafficking in human beings" has the same meaning as in the Trafficking Convention.".

In para.36 (under-occupancy deduction), sub-para.(6)(b):

(a) for ""domestic violence" and "person acting in an official capacity" have the meaning given to them in regulation 98(4) of these Regulations;" substitute ""person acting in an official capacity" has the meaning given to it in regulation 98(4) of these Regulations;";

(b) omit the definition of "relative".

p.561, *amendment to the Universal Credit Regulations 2013 (SI 2013/376) Sch.10 (Capital to be disregarded)*

3.026
With effect from May 4, 2022, reg.2(3) of the Universal Credit (Local Welfare Provision Disregard) (Amendment) Regulations 2022 (SI 2022/448) amended Sch.10 by inserting the following after para.18:

"**18A.** A payment received within the past 12 months by way of local welfare provision including arrears and payments in lieu of local welfare provision.".

A new definition of "local welfare provision" has been inserted into reg.2 (see the entry for p.192). The amendment brings the Universal Credit Regulations into line with those for the "legacy" benefits. The scope and meaning of the amendment was summarised on p.563 of the main volume.

p.600, *annotation to the Loans for Mortgage Interest Regulations 2017 (SI 2017/725)*

3.027
In November 2022, the Government announced an intention to legislate such that by Spring 2023 it "will allow those on UC to apply for a loan to help with interest repayments after three months, instead of nine" and "will also abolish the zero earnings rule to allow claimants to continue receiving support while in work and on UC": *Autumn Statement 2022* (CP 751, November 2022), para.5.16. At the time of writing no draft legislation had been published, but its plans will require amendment to the definition of "qualifying period" in reg.2(1), and to the earned income exclusion in reg.3(4).

p.679, *amendment to the Universal Credit (Transitional Provisions) Regulations 2014 (SI 2014/1230) reg.2(4) (Interpretation)*

With effect from July 25, 2022, reg.11 of, and Sch. para.1(2) to, the Universal Credit (Transitional Provisions) Amendment Regulations 2022 (SI 2022/752) omitted the reference to "and regulation 47 (notified persons who claim as a different benefit unit)" in reg.2(4).   **3.028**

p.681, *revocation of the Universal Credit (Transitional Provisions) Regulations 2014 (SI 2014/1230) reg.4 (Secretary of State discretion to determine that claims for universal credit may not be made)*

With effect from July 25, 2022, reg.2 of the Universal Credit (Transitional Provisions) Amendment Regulations 2022 (SI 2022/752) revoked reg.4.   **3.029**

p.686, *amendment to the Universal Credit (Transitional Provisions) Regulations 2014 (SI 2014/1230) reg.5 (Exclusion of entitlement to certain benefits)*

With effect from July 25, 2022, reg.11 of, and Sch. para.1(3) to, the Universal Credit (Transitional Provisions) Amendment Regulations 2022 (SI 2022/752) substituted "or 46(1)" for ", 46(1) or 47(2)" in para.(2)(ab).   **3.030**

pp.687–690, *revocation of the Universal Credit (Transitional Provisions) Regulations 2014 (SI 2014/1230) reg.6 (Exclusion of claims for certain existing benefits)*

With effect from July 25, 2022, reg.3 of the Universal Credit (Transitional Provisions) Amendment Regulations 2022 (SI 2022/752) revoked reg.6.   **3.031**

p.692, *insertion of the Universal Credit (Transitional Provisions) Regulations 2014 (SI 2014/1230) reg.6A (Restriction on claims for housing benefit, income support or a tax credit)*

With effect from July 25, 2022, reg.4 of the Universal Credit (Transitional Provisions) Amendment Regulations 2022 (SI 2022/752) inserted a new reg.6A immediately before reg.7 (Termination of awards of certain existing benefits: new claimant partners):   **3.032**

"Restriction on claims for housing benefit, income support or a tax credit

6A.—(1) Except as provided by paragraphs (2) to (7) a person may not make a claim for housing benefit, income support, or a tax credit.

(2) Paragraph (1) does not apply to a claim for housing benefit in respect of specified accommodation or temporary accommodation.

(3) Paragraph (1) does not apply to a claim for housing benefit that is made during the last assessment period of an award of universal credit, where the claimant reaches the qualifying age for state pension credit and paragraph 26 of Schedule 1 to the Decisions and Appeals Regulations applies, in respect of entitlement arising from the date the claimant reaches that age.

(4) Paragraph (1) does not apply to a claim for housing benefit by a single person who has reached the qualifying age for state pension credit, or a member of a State Pension Credit Act couple where both members have reached that age or a member of a polygamous marriage where all members have reached that age.

(5) Paragraph (1) does not apply to a claim for housing benefit where—

    (a) the claim is made by a member of a State Pension Credit Act couple who has reached the qualifying age for state pension credit and the other member has not reached that age; and

    (b) one of the savings in the sub-paragraphs of article 4(1) of the Welfare Reform Act 2012 (Commencement No. 31 and Savings and Transitional Provisions and Commencement No. 21 and 23 and Transitional and Transitory Provisions (Amendment)) Order 2019 applies and the saving has not ceased to have effect under article 4(2) of that Order.

(6) Paragraph (1) does not apply to a claim for a tax credit where a person makes or persons make a claim for child tax credit or working tax credit and on the date on which he or she (or they) makes or make the claim he or she (or they) has or have an award of working tax credit or child tax credit respectively.

(7) Paragraph (1) does not apply to a claim for a tax credit where a person has or had, or persons have or had, an award of child tax credit or working tax credit in respect of a tax year and that person or those persons makes or make (or is or are treated as making) a claim for that tax credit for the next tax year.

(8) For the purposes of this regulation—

    (a) "polygamous marriage" has the same meaning as in regulation 3(5) of the Universal Credit Regulations;

    (b) "State Pension Credit Act couple" means a couple as defined in section 17(1) of the State Pension Credit Act 2002,

and a reference to the date on which a claim for a tax credit is made is a reference to the date on which such claim is made or treated as made as provided for in the Tax Credits (Claims and Notifications) Regulations 2002."

p.692, *amendments to the Universal Credit (Transitional Provisions) Regulations 2014 (SI 2014/1230) reg.7 (Termination of awards of certain existing benefits: new claimant partners)*

3.033   With effect from July 25, 2022, reg.5(2) of the Universal Credit (Transitional Provisions) Amendment Regulations 2022 (SI 2022/752) amended reg.7(1) by inserting "and" at the end of sub-para.(b) and omitting sub-para.(d) together with the "and" preceding it.

p.694, *amendments to the Universal Credit (Transitional Provisions) Regulations 2014 (SI 2014/1230) reg.8 (Termination of awards of certain existing benefits: other claimants)*

With effect from July 25, 2022, reg.5(3) of the Universal Credit **3.034** (Transitional Provisions) Amendment Regulations 2022 (SI 2022/752) amended reg.8 by (1) inserting ", whether or not subsequently withdrawn" after "is made" in para.(1)(a); (2) omitting sub-para.(b) and the "and" preceding it; and (3) inserting after para.(2A):

"(2B) This regulation does not apply in the case of a single claimant who has reached the qualifying age for state pension credit or in the case of joint claimants who have both reached the qualifying age for state pension credit."

p.696, *amendment to the Universal Credit (Transitional Provisions) Regulations 2014 (SI 2014/1230) reg.8A (Transitional housing payment)*

With effect from July 25, 2022, reg.11 of, and Sch. para.1(4) to, the **3.035** Universal Credit (Transitional Provisions) Amendment Regulations 2022 (SI 2022/752) substituted "or 46" for ", 46 or 47" in the preliminary text and substituted "or 46(1)" for ", 46(1) or 47(2)" in paras.(a) and (b).

p.697, *amendment to the Universal Credit (Transitional Provisions) Regulations 2014 (SI 2014/1230) reg.8B (Effect on universal credit award of two week run-on etc.)*

With effect from July 25, 2022, reg.11 of, and Sch. para.1(5) to, the **3.036** Universal Credit (Transitional Provisions) Amendment Regulations 2022 (SI 2022/752) substituted "or 46(1)" for ", 46(1) or 47(2)".

pp.703–704, *amendments to the Universal Credit (Transitional Provisions) Regulations 2014 (SI 2014/1230) reg.12 (Modification of tax credits legislation: overpayments and penalties)*

With effect from July 25, 2022, reg.5(4) of the Universal Credit **3.037** (Transitional Provisions) Amendment Regulations 2022 (SI 2022/752) amended reg.12(1) by inserting "and" at the end of sub-para.(a) and omitting sub-para.(c) together with the "and" preceding it.

pp.704–705, *amendments to the Universal Credit (Transitional Provisions) Regulations 2014 (SI 2014/1230) reg.12A (Modification of tax credits legislation: finalisation of tax credits)*

With effect from July 25, 2022, reg.5(5) of the Universal Credit **3.038** (Transitional Provisions) Amendment Regulations 2022 (SI 2022/752) amended reg.12A(1) by inserting "and" at the end of sub-para.(a) and omitting sub-para.(c) together with the "and" preceding it.

p.706, *amendment to the Universal Credit (Transitional Provisions) Regulations 2014 (SI 2014/1230) reg.13 (Appeals etc relating to certain existing benefits)*

3.039   With effect from July 25, 2022, reg.11 of, and Sch. para.1(6) to, the Universal Credit (Transitional Provisions) Amendment Regulations 2022 (SI 2022/752) substituted "or 46" for ", 46 or 47" in para.(3).

p.717, *annotation to the Universal Credit (Transitional Provisions) Regulations 2014 (SI 2014/1230) reg.21 (Other claimants with limited capability for work: credits only cases)*

3.040   In *JW v SSWP (UC)* [2022] UKUT 117 (AAC) the claimant had been entitled to income-related ESA at the support group rate but her claim ended when her partner took up full-time work. Six months later, the claimant applied for universal credit. The decision-maker and tribunal concluded, applying the general rule in reg.28 of the UC Regulations 2013, that she had to wait for a further three months from the start of her universal credit claim before the limited capability for work-related activity (LCWRA) element became payable. However, Judge Wikeley observed that none of the exceptions to the general rule in reg.28 dealt with the situation in which a claimant had previously been entitled to a legacy benefit. Such cases required consideration of the UC (Transitional) Regulations 2014 and especially reg.21. Having concluded that the claimant fell within the terms of reg.8B(2)(a)(iv) of the Social Security (Credits) Regulations 1975 (see reg.21(1))—namely that a person can receive NI credits equivalent to the lower earnings limit for the relevant period if the only reason they are not entitled to ESA is that they did not satisfy the contribution conditions—Judge Wikeley held, allowing the claimant's appeal and re-making the decision under appeal, that reg.21(4) and (5) provided the mechanism for the payment of the LCWRA element from the start of the claimant's universal credit claim rather than after a further waiting period of three months.

p.742, *amendment to the Universal Credit (Transitional Provisions) Regulations 2014 (SI 2014/1230) reg.44 (Migration notices)*

3.041   With effect from July 25, 2022, reg.11 of, and Sch. para.1(7) to, the Universal Credit (Transitional Provisions) Amendment Regulations 2022 (SI 2022/752) inserted "or" at the end of para.(5)(a) and omitted para.(5)(b).

p.742, *annotation to the Universal Credit (Transitional Provisions) Regulations 2014 (SI 2014/1230) reg.44 (Migration notice)*

3.042   Regulation 2 of the Universal Credit (Managed Migration Pilot and Miscellaneous Amendments) Regulations 2019 (SI 2019/1152), limiting the number of cases migrated to a maximum of 10,000 awards was revoked with effect from July 25, 2022, by reg.10 of the Universal Credit

(Transitional Provisions) Amendment Regulations 2022 (SI 2022/752).

p.745, *amendment to the Universal Credit (Transitional Provisions) Regulations 2014 (SI 2014/1230) reg.46 (Termination of existing benefits if no claim before the deadline)*

With effect from July 25, 2022, reg.11 of, and Sch. para.1(8) to, the   **3.043** Universal Credit (Transitional Provisions) Amendment Regulations 2022 (SI 2022/752) omitted para.(5).

pp.746–747, *revocation of the Universal Credit (Transitional Provisions) Regulations 2014 (SI 2014/1230) reg.47 (Notified persons who claim as a different benefit unit)*

With effect from July 25, 2022, reg.6(1) of the Universal Credit   **3.044** (Transitional Provisions) Amendment Regulations 2022 (SI 2022/752) revoked reg.47.

p.748, *amendment to the Universal Credit (Transitional Provisions) Regulations 2014 (SI 2014/1230) reg.50 (Secretary of State to determine whether transitional protection applies)*

With effect from July 25, 2022, reg.6(2) of the Universal Credit   **3.045** (Transitional Provisions) Amendment Regulations 2022 (SI 2022/752) amended reg.50(2) by deleting "where regulation 47 (notified persons who claim as a different benefit unit) applies" and substituting:

"where—
(a) notified persons who were a couple for the purposes of an award of an existing benefit when the migration notice was issued are single persons or members of a different couple for the purposes of a claim for universal credit; or
(b) notified persons who were single for the purposes of an award of an existing benefit when the migration notice was issued are a couple for the purposes of a claim for universal credit; or
(c) notified persons who were members of a polygamous marriage for the purposes of an award of an existing benefit when the migration notice was issued are a couple or single persons for the purposes of a claim for universal credit."

pp.755–756, *amendment to the Universal Credit (Transitional Provisions) Regulations 2014 (SI 2014/1230) reg.55 (The transitional element—initial amount and adjustment where other elements increase)*

With effect from July 25, 2022, reg.7 of the Universal Credit (Transi-   **3.046** tional Provisions) Amendment Regulations 2022 (SI 2022/752) amended reg.55 by inserting ", subject to paragraph (5)," after ""relevant increase" is" in para.(4) and after the end of para.(4) inserting the following new paragraphs:

"(5) In cases where the LCW element is replaced by the LCWRA element, the "relevant increase" is to be treated as the difference between the amounts of those elements.

(6) In this regulation, "LCW element" and "LCWRA element" have the same meaning as in regulation 2 of the Universal Credit Regulations."

p.758, *amendment to the Universal Credit (Transitional Provisions) Regulations 2014 (SI 2014/1230) reg.58 (Qualifying claim—Secretary of State may set later commencement day)*

3.047   With effect from July 25, 2022, reg.11 of, and Sch. para.1(9) to, the Universal Credit (Transitional Provisions) Amendment Regulations 2022 (SI 2022/752) omitted "or 47(4)".

p.759, *amendment to the Universal Credit (Transitional Provisions) Regulations 2014 (SI 2014/1230) reg.60 (Protection for full-time students until course completed)*

3.048   With effect from July 25, 2022, reg.8 of the Universal Credit (Transitional Provisions) Amendment Regulations 2022 (SI 2022/752) amended reg.60 such that the existing text becomes para.(1) and after para.(1) is inserted:

"(2) Paragraph (1) does not apply to any assessment period in respect of which a transitional element or transitional capital disregard would (if the claimant had been entitled to that element or that disregard) have ceased to apply by virtue of regulation 56 (circumstances in which transitional protection ceases) or regulation 57 (application of transitional protection to a subsequent award)."

p.762, *revocation of the Universal Credit (Transitional Provisions) Regulations 2014 (SI 2014/1230) reg.64 (Discretionary hardship payments)*

3.049   With effect from July 25, 2022, reg.9 of the Universal Credit (Transitional Provisions) Amendment Regulations 2022 (SI 2022/752) revoked reg.64.

p.787, *amendment to the State Pension Credit Regulations 2002 (SI 2002/1792) reg.2 (Persons not in Great Britain)*

3.050   With effect from October 18, 2022, reg.2(1) and (2)(c) of the Social Security (Habitual Residence and Past Presence) (Amendment) (No. 2) Regulations 2022 (SI 2022/990) amended reg.2(4)(zzc) by (1) omitting "or" at the end of para.(i); (2) inserting "or" at the end of para.(ii); and (3) after para.(ii) inserting the following:

"(iii) does not require leave to enter or remain in the United Kingdom in accordance with section 3ZA of that Act;".

p.827, *amendment to the State Pension Credit Regulations 2002 (SI 2002/1792) reg.17B (Earnings of self-employed earners)*

With effect from July 1, 2022, reg.99 of and the Sch. to the Health and Care Act 2022 (Consequential and Related Amendments and Transitional Provisions) Regulations 2022 (SI 2022/634) substituted "an integrated care board established under Chapter A3 of Part 2 of the National Health Service Act 2006" for "a clinical commissioning group established under section 14D of the National Health Service Act 2006" in para.(2)(d)(iva) as substituted by reg.17B(4). **3.051**

p.886, *amendment to the Social Fund Cold Weather Payments (General) Regulations 1988 (SI 1988/1724) reg.1 (Citation, commencement and interpretation)*

With effect from November 1, 2022, reg.1(2) of the 1988 Regulations is amended by art.2 of the Social Security (Scotland) Act 2018 (Winter Heating Assistance) (Consequential Modifications) Order 2022 (SI 2022/1018). In the definition of "home", after the word "separately" omit the words "in particular, in Scotland, any croft land on which the dwelling is situated". **3.052**

p.890, *amendment to the Social Fund Cold Weather Payments (General) Regulations 1988 (SI 1988/1724) reg.1A (Prescribed description of persons)*

With effect from November 1, 2022, reg.1A of the 1988 Regulations is amended by art.2 of the Social Security (Scotland) Act 2018 (Winter Heating Assistance) (Consequential Modifications) Order 2022 (SI 2022/1018). After para.(7) insert: **3.053**

"(8) The fifth condition is that the person's home is in England or Wales.".

p.902, *modifications to the Social Fund Winter Fuel Payment Regulations 2000 (SI 2000/729) reg.2 (Social fund winter fuel payments)*

With effect from September 19, 2022, concerning social fund winter fuel payments in respect of the winter that follows the qualifying week beginning on 19 September 2022, reg.2 of the Social Fund Winter Fuel Payment (Temporary Increase) Regulations 2022 (SI 2022/813) modified the 2000 Regulations as follows: **3.054**

reg.2 is applied as if:
    (a) the references to £100 (in both places) were to £250;
    (b) in paras (1)(i), (2)(a) and (3), the reference to £200 were to £500;
    (c) in para.(2)(b), the reference to £200 were to £350;
    (d) in para.(2)(b), the reference to £150 were to £300; and
    (e) the references to £300 (in both places) were to £600.

pp.905–906, *erratum—Social Fund Winter Fuel Payment Regulations 2000 (SI 2000/729) reg.3 (Persons not entitled to a winter fuel payment)*

3.055   There is an error in the General Note to reg.3 of the 2000 Regulations. Sub-paragraph (a) should read:

"partners of people who were entitled to state pension credit, income-based jobseekers allowance or income-related employment and support allowance throughout the qualifying week (reg.3(1)(a)(i)). This is to prevent double payment;"

pp.969–970, *amendments to the Social Security (Immigration and Asylum) Consequential Amendments Regulations 2000 (SI 2000/636) reg.2 (Persons not excluded from specified benefits under section 115 of the Immigration and Asylum Act 1999)*

3.056   With effect from May 3, 2022, reg.2 of the Social Security and Council Tax Reduction Schemes (Amendment) Regulations 2022 (SI 2022/449) amends reg.2 of the 2000 Regulations. The amendments are as follows:
  (a) in para.(1):
      (i) after "a social fund payment," insert "or"; and
      (ii) omit "housing benefit under the Contributions and Benefits Act"; and
      (iii) omit ", or state pension credit under the State Pension Credit Act 2002";
  (b) in para.(1A):
      (i) after "entitlement to" insert "housing benefit under the Contributions and Benefits Act, state pension credit under the State Pension Credit Act 2002, or"; and
      (ii) after "universal credit" insert ", as the case may be,".

PART IV

UPDATING MATERIAL
VOLUME III

ADMINISTRATION, ADJUDICATION AND
THE EUROPEAN DIMENSION

Commentary by

Mark Rowland

Christopher Ward

p.11, *Social Security Administration Act 1992 (Arrangement of Sections)*

Note that a number of sections not included in Vol.III may be found   4.001
in Vol.IV: ss.13A, 14, 15, 113A, 113B, 122AA, 129–132.

p.20, *annotation to the Social Security Administration Act 1992 s.1(1)*
(Entitlement to benefit dependent on claim)

The issue in *AM v SSWP (UC)* [2022] UKUT 242 (AAC) was   4.002
whether a claimant needed expressly to have applied for his award of
universal credit to commence within the one month period before the
date of his claim, in the circumstances for which reg.26 of the Universal
Credit, Personal Independence Payment, Jobseeker's Allowance and
Employment and Support Allowance (Claims and Payments) Regulations 2013 (SI 2013/380) provides. A three-judge panel held that s.1 was
concerned with the manner and time of a claim and not with its content.

p.20, *annotation to the Social Security Administration Act 1992*
s.1(1A)–(1C) (Entitlement to benefit dependent on claim)

The operation of s.1(1B)(b) was examined by a three-judge panel in   4.003
R. (Bui) v SSWP and R. (Onekoya) v SSWP [2022] UKUT 189 (AAC).
The panel considered that the basis for the view taken in *CH/4085/2007*
was not explained and considered the interpretation afresh. Noting that
the amendment introducing these subsections had been introduced by
the Social Security Administration (Fraud) Act 1997, their origin in an
anti-fraud measure led the panel to conclude that s.1(1B)(b) was only
fulfilled once SSWP had completed verification of the material submitted by a claimant rather than, as submitted on behalf of the claimants, once documents had been submitted which could in principle lead
to a NINO being issued. The Court of Appeal has granted permission to
appeal and a hearing is awaited at the time of writing.

p.42, *annotation to the Social Security Administration Act 1992 s.5*
(Regulations about claims for and payments of benefit)

The issue in *AM v SSWP (UC)* [2022] UKUT 242 (AAC) was   4.004
whether a claimant needed expressly to have applied for his award of
universal credit to commence within the one month period before the
date of his claim, in the circumstances for which reg.26 of the Universal
Credit, Personal Independence Payment, Jobseeker's Allowance and
Employment and Support Allowance (Claims and Payments) Regulations 2013 (SI 2013/380) provides. A three-judge panel held that the
regulation-making power in s.5 was concerned with the manner and time
of a claim rather than with its content.

p.64, *annotation to the Social Security Administration Act 1992 s.71*
(Overpayments—general—Misrepresentation)

The second sub-paragraph in 1.102 should read "However, it is   4.005
essential in every case to identify with some accuracy exactly what the

misrepresentation is on which the Secretary of State relies in making the recoverability decision: see, for example, *NS v SSWP (CA)* [2014] UKUT 7 (AAC).

pp.101–102, *amendments to the Social Security Administration Act 1992 s.108 (Reduction of expenditure on income support: certain maintenance orders to be enforceable by the Secretary of State)*

4.006   A number of amendments are required to the text of subs.(4), both in consequence of Brexit and otherwise. The text is correctly shown below. The Amendments shown below are the corrected list that should appear on p.102 and are compiled by reference to the whole of s.108.

"(4) The powers conferred on the Secretary of State by subsection (2)(a) above include power—
    (a) to apply for the registration of the maintenance order under—
        (i) section 17 of the Maintenance Orders Act 1950; [² or]
        (ii) section 2 of the Maintenance Orders Act 1958;
        [⁷ . . .] [⁸ . . .]
        [⁷ . . .] [⁹ . . .]
        [¹⁰ . . .]
[¹¹ (ab) to apply for recognition and enforcement of the maintenance order under the Convention on the International Recovery of Child Support and other forms of Family Maintenance done at The Hague on 23rd November 2007, to the extent permitted by Article 36 of that Convention; and]
(b) to make an application under section 2 of the Maintenance Orders (Reciprocal Enforcement) Act 1972 (application for enforcement in reciprocating country)."

Section 108(9) should be replaced by
[¹⁰ . . .]

AMENDMENTS

1. Access to Justice Act 1999 Sch.4 para.48 (April 1, 2000).
2. Civil Jurisdiction and Judgments (Amendment) (EU Exit) Regulations 2019 (SI 2019/479) Pt 2 reg.66(a) (December 31, 2020).
3. Child Maintenance and Other Payments Act 2008 Sch.7 para.2(2) (October 27, 2008).
4. The Welfare Reform Act 2012 (Commencement No. 9 and Transitional and Transitory Provisions and Commencement No. 8 and Savings and Transitional Provisions (Amendment)) Order 2013 (SI 2013/983) art.3(1)(b) (April 29, 2013).
5. Legal Aid, Sentencing and Punishment of Offenders Act 2012 Sch.5(1) para.41 (April 1, 2013).
6. Civil Jurisdiction and Judgments Order 2011 (SI 2011/1484) Sch.7 para.14 (June 18, 2011).
7. Civil Jurisdiction and Judgments (Amendment) (EU Exit) Regulations 2019 (SI 2019/479) Pt 2 reg.66(b) (December 31, 2020).
8. Civil Jurisdiction and Judgments Order 2001 (SI 2001/3929) Sch.3 para.24(a) (March 1, 2002).
9. Civil Jurisdiction and Judgments (Maintenance) Regulations 2011 (SI 2011/1484) Sch.7 para.14(a)(ii) (June 18, 2011).

10. Jurisdiction and Judgments (Family) (Amendment etc.) (EU Exit) Regulations 2019 (SI 2019/519) Sch. para.21 (December 31, 2020).
11. International Recovery of Maintenance (Hague Convention 2007 etc.) Regulations 2012 (SI 2012/2814) Sch.4 para.6(b) (August 1, 2014).

pp.123–124, *amendments to the Social Security Administration Act 1992 s.124 (Provisions relating to age, death and marriage)*

With effect from July 12, 2016, Immigration Act 2016 Sch.15 para.36 made the following amendments: 4.007

In subs.(3), for the words from "a fee" to "Wales and" substitute "the appropriate fee in England and Wales and a fee of".

In subs.(3A), for para.(b) substitute:

"(b) on payment of the appropriate fee;".

In subs.(5), in para.(a) after the opening words insert:

""the appropriate fee" means the fee payable to the registrar or superintendent registrar for a certified copy of an entry in the register concerned by virtue of section 38A of the Births and Deaths Registration Act 1953, section 71A of the Marriage Act 1949 or section 9 of the Marriage (Same Sex Couples) Act 2013."

Errata: The definition of "register of conversions" should appear before the definition of "Registrar General" in subs.(5)(a) and not in subs.(5)(b).

Footnote 10 should refer to para.12 of the Schedule to SI 2014/3168 (and not to art.12).

pp.222–226, *annotation to the Social Security Act 1998 s.8 (Decisions by Secretary of State)*

Section 6 of the Social Security (Additional Payments) Act 2022 provides that, for the purposes relating to the administration of an additional payment, any provision applying in relation a benefit or tax credit by reference to which that additional payment is made is to apply in relation to that payment as if it were a payment or award of the benefit or tax credit in question, subject to any necessary modifications. This would appear to have the effect that, among other provisions, ss.8, 9, 10 and 12 of the 1998 Act apply to at least some extent where the additional payment is paid by reference to a benefit to which they apply. However, s.6(2)(a) provides that the legislation that may be applied includes "provision relating to overpayments and recovery, and appeals relating to overpayments and recovery (but not provision relating to appeals or reviews about entitlement to the social security benefit, tax credit or disability benefit in question)". This raises two questions. The first is whether revision and supersession fall within the scope of "review". It is certainly arguable that the legislation is to be read literally and that review is excluded in tax credit cases, but revision and supersession are not excluded in ordinary social security cases. The second question is whether the words in parenthesis are intended to prevent a person from   4.008

challenging an overpayment or recovery decision on the ground that he or she was entitled to the additional payment or whether they are merely intended to emphasise that there is no right of appeal save in the context of an overpayment or recovery. These points may be fairly academic because, given the nature of the payments, it seems unlikely that there will in fact be many disputes, save where it is alleged that the related benefit was wrongly paid.

pp.227–232, *annotation to the Social Security Act 1998 s.9 (Revision of decisions)*

4.009   See the supplementary annotation to s.8, above.

pp.233–235, *annotation to the Social Security Act 1998 s.10 (Decisions superseding earlier decisions)*

4.010   See the supplementary annotation to s.8, above.

pp.239–264, *annotation to the Social Security Act 1998 s.12 (Appeal to First-tier Tribunal)*

4.011   See the supplementary annotation to s.8, above.

pp.270–274, *annotation to the Social Security Act 1998 s.17 (Finality of decisions)*

4.012   Where an interim assessment of disablement is made on a claim for disablement benefit, it is made in respect of a specific period and the decision is final only for that period. Thus, the decision that must be made in respect of a following period does not involve any revision or supersession of the interim decision in respect of the earlier period (*DW v SSWP (II)* [2022] UKUT 183 (AAC)); it is simply a further decision on the claim.
See also the supplementary annotation to s.8, above.

p.504, *annotation to the Social Security (Claims and Payments) Regulations (SI 1987/1968) reg.35 (Deductions which may be made from benefit and paid to third parties)*

4.013   In *R. (Timson) v SSWP* [2022] EWHC 2392 (Admin) Cavanagh J conducted a lengthy examination of law, policy and practice relating to third party deductions in the context of a challenge to SSWP's guidance to decision-makers on common law and human rights grounds. The claim for judicial review succeeded only on the aspect that SSWP's written guidance to decision-makers in relation to third party deductions was unlawful because, by implication and omission, it had the effect that, read as a whole, it presented a misleading picture of the true legal position to decision-makers, in that it did not make clear that claimants should be offered the opportunity to make representations and/or provide relevant information to the decision-maker before the decision whether to make a third party deduction was taken. The claims in relation to the ECHR were dismissed. The Court of Appeal has granted permission to appeal and a hearing is awaited at the time of writing.

p.568, *annotation to the Universal Credit, Personal Independence Payment, Jobseeker's Allowance and Employment and Support Allowance (Claims and Payments) Regulations 2013 (SI 2013/380) reg.26 (Time within which a claim for universal credit is to be made)*

The issue in *AM v SSWP (UC)* [2022] UKUT 242 (AAC) was whether a claimant needed expressly to have applied for his award of universal credit to commence within the one month period before the date of his claim, in the circumstances for which reg.26(2) provides. A three-judge panel having found that SSAA 1992 ss.1 and 5 were concerned with the manner and time of a claim and not with its content, turned to reg.26. Although all judges agreed in the result, there was a divergence of reasoning. Judges Wikeley and Wright considered that while reg.26(1) plainly assumes that the Secretary of State's decision-maker must at some point establish "the period in respect of which the claim is made", that does not create a requirement that the claim must itself have intended or identified any period. The enabling legislation would not permit it to do so. A contrary construction of reg.26 would be problematic. The decision of a Tribunal of Commissioners in *R(SB) 8/94* in relation to supplementary benefit could be distinguished on a number of grounds. Judge Jacobs preferred to base his conclusion on the view that: **4.014**

> "It is the decision-maker's decision that has this effect [i.e. that entitlement can begin on the date requested], not the claimant's request, application, claim or any other word you choose to use. The result of the decision-maker deciding that entitlement begins earlier than the date of claim is that the claim was not made on the first day of the relevant period. And by virtue of regulation 26(2) that triggers the duty to extend the period for claiming. And the effect of that is that section 1(1)(a) of the Administration Act is satisfied."

pp.645–649, *annotation to the Social Security and Child Support (Decisions and Appeals) Regulations 1999 (SI 1999/991) reg.3ZA (Consideration of revision before appeal)*

HMRC has applied to the Court of Appeal for permission to appeal against the decision in *AB v HMRC (TC)* [2021] UKUT 328 (AAC), mentioned on p.647 of the main work. It is expected that the application will be determined in early 2023. **4.014A**

pp.650–651, *annotation to the Social Security and Child Support (Decisions and Appeals) Regulations 1999 (SI 1999/991) reg.4 (Late application for a revision)*

HMRC has applied to the Court of Appeal for permission to appeal against the decision in *AB v HMRC (TC)* [2021] UKUT 328 (AAC), **4.014B** mentioned on p.651 of the main work. It is expected that the application will be determined in early 2023.

pp.763–764, *annotation to the Universal Credit, Personal Independence Payment, Jobseeker's Allowance and Employment and Support Allowance (Decisions and Appeals) Regulations 2013 (SI 2013/381) reg.26 (Medical evidence and limited capability for work etc.)*

4.015   Following the decision in *MH v SSWP (PIP)* [2020] UKUT 185 (AAC), mentioned on p.764 of the main work, reg.27(2) of the Social Security (Personal Independence Payment) Regulations 2013 was amended with effect from November 30, 2020 so as to refer expressly to both reg.23 and reg.26 of the Decisions and Appeals Regulations, rather than implicitly just to reg.23 (see Vol.I of the main work). Thus, the difficulty identified in *MH* has been removed.

pp.869–870, *amendment to the Social Security (Medical Evidence) Regulations 1976 (SI 1976/615) reg.1 (Citation, commencement and interpretation)*

4.016   With effect from July 1, 2022, reg.2 of the Social Security (Medical Evidence) and Statutory Sick Pay (Medical Evidence) (Amendment) (No. 2) Regulations 2022 (SI 2022/630) added the following definition after the definition of "doctor" in subs.(2):

"healthcare professional" means a person, not being the patient, who is—
   (a) a registered medical practitioner;
   (b) a registered nurse;
   (c) a registered occupational therapist or registered physiotherapist;
   (d) a registered pharmacist within the meaning of article 3 of the Pharmacy Order 2010;

With effect from April 17, 2002, the Nursing and Midwifery Order 2001 (Consequential Amendments) Order (SI 2002/881) Sch.1 para.1 amended the definition of "registered midwife" so that it means "a midwife who is registered as a midwife with the Nursing and Midwifery Council under the Nursing and Midwifery Order 2001". Entry 1 in the list of amendments on p.870 is to be amended accordingly.

p.870, *amendment to the Social Security (Medical Evidence) Regulations 1976 (SI 1976/615) reg.2 (Evidence of incapacity for work, limited capability for work and confinement)*

4.017   With effect from July 1, 2022, reg.2 of the Social Security (Medical Evidence) and Statutory Sick Pay (Medical Evidence) (Amendment) (No. 2) Regulations 2022 (SI 2022/630) substituted "healthcare professional" for "doctor" in reg.2(1).

p.872, *amendment to the Social Security (Medical Evidence) Regulations 1976 (SI 1976/615) reg.5 (Self-certification for first 7 days of a spell of incapacity for work or limited capability for work)*

With effect from July 1, 2022, reg.2 of the Social Security (Medical Evidence) and Statutory Sick Pay (Medical Evidence) (Amendment) (No. 2) Regulations 2022 (SI 2022/630) substituted "healthcare professional" for "doctor" in reg.5(1). **4.018**

pp.872–876, *amendments to the Social Security (Medical Evidence) Regulations 1976 (SI 1976/615) Sch.*

With effect from July 1, 2022, reg.2 of the Social Security (Medical Evidence) and Statutory Sick Pay (Medical Evidence) (Amendment) (No. 2) Regulations 2022 (SI 2022/630) made substantial amendments to the Schedule. The Schedule is reproduced below, as it stands following those amendments: **4.019**

SCHEDULE 1   Regulation 2(1)

PART 1

RULES

1. In these rules, unless the context otherwise requires— **2.856**
   "assessment" means either a consultation between a patient and a healthcare professional which takes place in person or by telephone or a consideration by a healthcare professional of a written report by another healthcare professional or other health professional;
   "condition" means a specific disease or bodily or mental disability;
   "other health professional" means a person (other than a healthcare professional and not being the patient) who is a registered midwife or a member of any profession regulated by a body mentioned in section 25(3) of the National Health Service Reform and Health Care Professions Act 2002;
   "patient" means the person in respect of whom a statement is given in accordance with these rules.

2. Where a healthcare professional issues a statement to a patient in accordance with an obligation arising under a contract, agreement or arrangement under Part 4 of the National Health Service Act 2006 or Part 4 of the National Health Service (Wales) Act 2006 or Part 1 of the National Health Service (Scotland) Act 1978 the healthcare professional's statement shall be in a form set out at Part 2 or Part 2A of this Schedule.

3. Where a healthcare professional issues a statement in any case other than in accordance with rule 2, the healthcare professional's statement shall be in the form set out in Part 2 or Part 2A of this Schedule or in a form to like effect.

4. A healthcare professional's statement must be based on an assessment made by that healthcare professional.

5. A healthcare professional's statement shall contain the following particulars—
   (a) the patient's name;
   (b) the date of the assessment (whether by consultation or consideration of a report as the case may be) on which the healthcare professional's statement is based;
   (c) the condition in respect of which the healthcare professional advises the patient they are not fit for work;

127

    (d) a statement, where the healthcare professional considers it appropriate, that the patient may be fit for work;

    (e) a statement that the healthcare professional will or, as the case may be will not, need to assess the patient's fitness for work again;

    (f) the date on which the healthcare professional's statement is given;

    (g) the address of the healthcare professional; and

    (h) the name of the healthcare professional (whether in the form of a signature or otherwise); and

    (i) the profession of the healthcare professional.

5A. Where the healthcare professional's statement is in the form set out in Part 2 of this Schedule—

    (a) the healthcare professional's name shall, irrespective of their profession, be recorded next to the words "doctor's signature";

    (b) the healthcare professional's address shall, irrespective of their profession, be recorded next to the words "doctor's address"; and

    (c) the healthcare professional shall record their profession within the statement in such place as appears to them to be appropriate.

6. Subject to rule 8, the condition in respect of which the healthcare professional is advising the patient is not fit for work or, as the case may be, which has caused the patient's absence from work shall be specified as precisely as the healthcare professional's knowledge of the patient's condition at the time of the assessment permits.

7. Where a healthcare professional considers that a patient may be fit for work the healthcare professional shall state the reasons for that advice and where this is considered appropriate, the arrangements which the patient might make, with their employer's agreement, to return to work.

8. The condition may be specified less precisely where, in the healthcare professional's opinion, disclosure of the precise condition would be prejudicial to the patient's well-being, or to the patient's position with their employer.

9. A healthcare professional's statement may be given on a date after the date of the assessment on which it is based, however no further statement shall be furnished in respect of that assessment other than a healthcare professional's statement by way of replacement of an original which has been lost, in which case it shall be clearly marked "duplicate".

10. Where, in the healthcare professional's opinion, the patient will become fit for work on a day not later than 14 days after the date of the assessment on which the healthcare professional's statement is based, the healthcare professional's statement shall specify that day.

11. Subject to rules 12 and 13, the healthcare professional's statement shall specify the minimum period for which, in the healthcare professional's opinion, the patient will not be fit for work or, as the case may be, for which they may be fit for work.

12. The period specified shall begin on the date of the assessment on which the healthcare professional's statement is based and shall not exceed 3 months unless the patient has, on the advice of a healthcare professional, refrained from work for at least 6 months immediately preceding that date.

13. Where—

    (a) the patient has been advised by a healthcare professional that they are not fit for work and, in consequence, has refrained from work for at least 6 months immediately preceding the date of the assessment on which the healthcare professional's statement is based; and

    (b) in the healthcare professional's opinion, the patient will not be fit for work for the foreseeable future,

instead of specifying a period, the healthcare professional may, having regard to the circumstances of the particular case, enter, after the words "case for", the words "an indefinite period".

STATEMENT OF FITNESS FOR WORK
FOR SOCIAL SECURITY OR STATUTORY SICK PAY

2.857

Patient's name

Mr, Mrs, Miss, Ms

I assessed your case on:

/	/

and, because of the following
condition(s):

I advise you that:

☐ you are not fit for work.
☐ you may be fit for work taking account
of the following advice:

If available, and with your employer's agreement, you may benefit from:

☐ a phased return to work   ☐ amended duties
☐ altered hours   ☐ workplace adaptations

Comments, including functional effects of your condition(s):

This will be the case for

or from | / | / | to | / | / |

I will/will not need to assess your fitness for work again at the end of this period.
(*Please delete as applicable*)

Doctor's signature

Date of statement | / | / |

Doctor's address

129

2.858   **Statement of Fitness for Work
For social security or Statutory Sick Pay**

Patient's name	Mr, Mrs, Miss, Ms
I assessed your case on:	/ /
and, because of the following condition(s):	

I advise you that: ☐ you are not fit for work.

☐ you may be fit for work taking account of the following advice:

If available, and with your employer's agreement, you may benefit from:

☐ a phased return to work   ☐ amended duties

☐ altered hours   ☐ workplace adaptations

Comments, including functional effects of your condition(s):

This will be the case for	
or from	/ / to / /

I will/will not need to assess your fitness for work again at the end of this period.
(Please delete as applicable)

Issuer's name

Issuer's profession

Date of statement	/ /
Issuer's address	

p.937, *annotation to the Social Security (Payments on Account of Benefit) Regulations 2013 (SI 2013/383) reg.5 (Payment on account of benefit where there is no award of benefit)*

In *R. (Bui) v SSWP and R. (Onekoya) v SSWP* [2022] UKUT 189 (AAC), a three-judge panel considered the requirement in reg.5(1)(b) that it appear "likely", holding that in the cases before them, which concerned claimed entitlement before a NINO had been issued, it could not be met until the process of verification leading to the issue of a NINO had been completed. An application to the Court of Appeal for permission to appeal is pending at the time of writing.

4.020

p.938, *Social Security (Payments on Account of Benefit) Regulations 2013 (SI 2013/383) reg.7 (Definition of financial need)*

The omission of reg.7(2) is no longer justified. It reads:

4.021

"(2) Where the payment on account of benefit is to be on account of universal credit, the following are members of A's family for the purpose of paragraph (1)—
  (a) any child or qualifying young person for whom A is responsible; and
  (b) where A is a member of a couple, their partner."

p.939, *Social Security (Payments on Account of Benefit) Regulations 2013 (SI 2013/383) reg.13 (Earnings condition)*

The text in the main volume at para.2.968 should be replaced with the following:

4.022

Earnings condition

[¹ **13.**—(1) The earnings condition is satisfied—
  (a) in a case where regulation 12(2) (expenses necessarily related to obtaining or retaining employment) does not apply, where paragraph (2) is satisfied;
  (b) in a case where regulation 12(2) does apply, where paragraph (4) is satisfied.
(2) This paragraph is satisfied where—
  (a) if B is not a member of a couple, B does not have earned income exceeding £2,600, or
  (b) if B is a member of a couple, B and their partner jointly do not have earned income exceeding £3,600,
  over the relevant period.
(3) In paragraph (2), "the relevant period" means the period covered by the six complete assessment periods preceding the date of the application for the budgeting advance.
(4) This paragraph is satisfied where—
  (a) if B is not a member of a couple, B does not have earned income, or

(b) if B is a member of a couple, B and their partner jointly do not have earned income,

exceeding the permitted amount over the applicable period.

(5) In paragraph (4), "the permitted amount over the applicable period" is to be determined by the formula—

$$N \times \left(\frac{P}{6}\right)$$

where—

N is the number of complete assessment periods in the applicable period, and

P is—

(i) where sub-paragraph (4)(a) applies, £2,600;

(ii) where sub-paragraph (4)(b) applies, £3,600.

(6) For the purposes of paragraphs (4) and (5), "the applicable period" means—

(a) if there are six or more complete assessment periods immediately preceding the date of the application for the budgeting advance, the period covered by the six complete assessment periods immediately preceding the date of the application for the budgeting advance;

(b) if there are fewer than six complete assessment periods immediately preceding the date of the application for the budgeting advance, the number of complete assessment periods immediately preceding the date of the application for the budgeting advance.

(7) Earned income for each complete assessment period is to be calculated for the purposes of this regulation in accordance with Chapter 2 of Part 6 of the Universal Credit Regulations save that in relation to the earned income of a person who is in gainful self-employment for the purpose of regulation 64 of be disregarded.

(8) In this regulation, "assessment period" has the meaning given in regulation 21 of the Universal Credit Regulations.]

Amendment

1. Universal Credit and Miscellaneous Amendments Regulations 2015 (SI 2015/1754) Pt 1 reg.7 (November 4, 2015).

p.941, *Social Security (Payments on Account of Benefit) Regulations 2013 (SI 2013/383) reg.18 (Payment by direct credit transfer)*

4.023   The text in the main volume at 2.973 should be replaced with the following:

Payment by direct credit transfer

[[1] **18.** A budgeting advance may be paid by way of direct credit transfer into a bank account or other account nominated by B or a person acting on B's behalf.]

AMENDMENT

    1. Universal Credit and Miscellaneous Amendments (No.2) Regulations 2014 (SI 2014/2888) reg.5(1)(c) (November 26, 2014).

pp.1007–1008, *annotation to the Child Benefit and Guardian's Allowance (Administration) Regulations 2003 (SI 2003/492) reg.6 (Time within which claims to be made)*

In *HMRC v BZ (CHB)* [2022] UKUT 264 (AAC), the claimant had received a notification dated May 18, 2019 that she had been accepted as having refugee status but which indicated that she could not claim benefits until she had received her Biometric Residence Permit, which only occurred later. Judge Gullick KC held that, while the notification had indeed notified the claimant that she had been recorded as a refugee, the notification of May 18, 2019:   4.024

> "was not valid notification of the recording of refugee status for the purpose of Regulation 6(2)(d) of the 2003 Regulations. That is because the notification incorrectly stated that a claim for Child Benefit could not be made until receipt of the BRP. In my judgment, a notification of this sort which contains a statement denying the existence of the very right to claim an entitlement which it would otherwise confer cannot, in this context, be a valid notification. To construe the language of Regulation 6(2)(d) otherwise would, in my judgment, be to ignore its purpose and would be to adopt precisely the sort of 'purely linguistic' approach rejected by Singh LJ in [*R. (on the application of Kaitey) v Secretary of State for the Home Department* [2021] EWCA Civ 1875.]"

p.1015, *amendment to the Child Benefit and Guardian's Allowance (Administration) Regulations 2003 (SI 2003/492) reg.23 (Information to be given and changes to be notified)*

With effect from June 9, 2022, the following paragraph was added by Tax Credits and Child Benefit (Miscellaneous Amendments) Regulations 2022 (SI 2022/555) reg.3:   4.025

> "(3A) Where a person is in receipt of a benefit or allowance by means other than a direct credit transfer, in accordance with regulation 17, that person must, if required, within such time as the Board may determine, provide details of a bank or other account to which payment can be made."

p.1047, *amendment to the Child Benefit and Guardian's Allowance (Decisions and Appeals) Regulations 2003 reg.18 (Suspension in prescribed cases)*

With effect from June 9, 2022, reg.2(1) and (2) of the Tax Credits and Child Benefit (Miscellaneous Amendments) Regulations 2022 (SI 2022/555) amended reg.18(2) by substituting a semicolon for the full stop at the end of sub-para.(e) and adding as sub-para.(f):   4.026

> "(f) no details of a bank account or other account have been provided
> by a person who is in receipt of the benefit or allowance by means
> other than a direct credit transfer and that person has been
> requested by the Board under regulation 23 of the Child Benefit
> and Guardian's Allowance (Administration) Regulations 2003 to
> provide details of an account into which the benefit or allowance
> can be paid."

p.1048, *amendment to the Child Benefit and Guardian's Allowance
(Decisions and Appeals) Regulations 2003 reg.19 (Provision of information
or evidence)*

4.027   With effect from June 9, 2022, reg.2(1) and (3) of the Tax Credits and
Child Benefit (Miscellaneous Amendments) Regulations 2022 (SI
2022/555) amended reg.19(1) by substituting "; or" for the full stop at
the end of sub-para.(b) and adding as sub-para.(c):

> "(c) suspended under regulation 18."

pp.1067–1096, *annotation to the Tribunals, Courts and Enforcement Act
2007 s.3 (The First-tier Tribunal and the Upper Tribunal)*

4.028   The reference on p.1067 to Sch.5 to the Coronavirus Act 2020 should
be to Sch.25, but para.2 of that Schedule has anyway effectively been
replaced by Pt 7ZA of the Courts Act 2003 (Transmission and recording
of court and tribunal proceedings), inserted by ss.198 and 199 of the
Police, Crime, Sentencing and Courts Act 2022 with effect from April
28, 2022, and the Remote Observation and Recording (Courts and
Tribunals) Regulations 2022 (see Part 1 of this Supplement).

In *Soriano v Forensic News LLC* [2021] EWCA Civ 1952; [2022] 2
W.L.R. 1952, it was pointed out at [62] by Warby LJ, with whom the
other members of the Court agreed, that, while on conventional principles, an English court cannot take judicial notice of foreign law so that,
if it is disputed, a question of foreign law must be proved by expert
evidence or else it may be presumed that foreign law is no different from
English law, "modern cases show much greater practicality and flexibility
in their approach to these principles". Thus, even in the courts, expert
evidence is not always necessary when a finding of foreign law is
required.

pp.1097–1098, *annotation to the Tribunals, Courts and Enforcement Act
2007 s.7 (Chambers: jurisdiction and Presidents)*

4.029   With effect from December 1, 2022, reg.3 of, and para.2 of Sch.3 to,
the Childcare (Free of Charge for Working Parents) (England) Regulations 2022 (SI 2022/1134) amended art.6(eb) of the First-tier Tribunal
and Upper Tribunal (Chambers) Order 2010 (set out within the annotation) by substituting for "the Childcare (Early Years Provision Free of
Charge) (Extended Entitlement) Regulations 2016" the words "the

Childcare (Free of Charge for Working Parents) (England) Regulations 2022".

pp.1107–1127, *annotation to the Tribunals, Courts and Enforcement Act 2007 s.11 (Right to appeal to Upper Tribunal)*

Where a party alleges that there was a breach of the rules of natural justice because questioning by a member of the First-tier Tribunal was oppressive, the Upper Tribunal may listen to a recording. It did so in *GJ v SSWP (PIP)* [2022] UKUT 349 (AAC) and concluded that the questioning had been "in an entirely appropriate inquisitorial style which cannot fairly be described as 'cross-examination' or 'oppressive questioning'".   **4.030**

DD v Sussex Partnership NHS Foundation Trust [2022] UKUT 166 (AAC) contains a useful survey of the case law on the question whether appeals that have become academic should still be decided. The fact that the appellant patient had legal representation, which is not always the case in the Upper Tribunal, was one reason for deciding the academic point in that case, together with the likelihood of the issue arising again in other cases.

Note that the new s.11A of the 2007 Act, see below, very severely restricts the power of the Administrative Court to consider challenges to a refusal by the Upper Tribunal to give permission to appeal to the Upper Tribunal from the First-tier Tribunal on an application under s.11(4)(b), although it does not affect refusals under other legislation to give permission to appeal from other bodies.

p.1127, *insertion of the Tribunals, Courts and Enforcement Act 2007 s.11A (Finality of decisions by Upper Tribunal about permission to appeal)*

With effect from July 14, 2022, s.2(1) of the Judicial Review and Courts Act 2022 inserted a new s.11A into the 2007 Act: **4.031**

"Finality of decisions by Upper Tribunal about permission to appeal

11A.—(1) Subsections (2) and (3) apply in relation to a decision by the Upper Tribunal to refuse permission (or leave) to appeal further to an application under section 11(4)(b).

(2) The decision is final, and not liable to be questioned or set aside in any other court.

(3) In particular—
(a) the Upper Tribunal is not to be regarded as having exceeded its powers by reason of any error made in reaching the decision;
(b) the supervisory jurisdiction does not extend to, and no application or petition for judicial review may be made or brought in relation to, the decision.

(4) Subsections (2) and (3) do not apply so far as the decision involves or gives rise to any question as to whether—
(a) the Upper Tribunal has or had a valid application before it under section 11(4)(b),

(b) the Upper Tribunal is or was properly constituted for the purpose of dealing with the application, or

(c) the Upper Tribunal is acting or has acted—
  (i) in bad faith, or
  (ii) in such a procedurally defective way as amounts to a fundamental breach of the principles of natural justice.

(5) Subsections (2) and (3) do not apply so far as provision giving the First-tier Tribunal jurisdiction to make the first-instance decision could (if the Tribunal did not already have that jurisdiction) be made by—

(a) an Act of the Scottish Parliament, or

(b) an Act of the Northern Ireland Assembly the Bill for which would not require the consent of the Secretary of State.

(6) The court of supervisory jurisdiction is not to entertain any application or petition for judicial review in respect of a decision of the First-tier Tribunal that it would not entertain (whether as a matter of law or discretion) in the absence of this section.

(7) In this section—

"decision" includes any purported decision;

"first-instance decision" means the decision in relation to which permission (or leave) to appeal is being sought under section 11(4)(b);

"the supervisory jurisdiction" means the supervisory jurisdiction of—

(a) the High Court, in England and Wales or Northern Ireland, or

(b) the Court of Session, in Scotland,

and "the court of supervisory jurisdiction" is to be read accordingly."

By virtue of s.2(2) of the 2022 Act, this section does not apply in relation to a decision (including any purported decision) of the Upper Tribunal made before July 14, 2022.

pp.1127–1133, *annotation to the Tribunals, Courts and Enforcement Act 2007 s.12 (Proceedings on appeal to Upper Tribunal)*

4.031A   In *AEB v Secretary of State for the Home Department* [2022] EWCA Civ 1512, the Court of Appeal held the Immigration Appeals Chamber of the Upper Tribunal to have erred in law in not remitting a case for rehearing after it had set aside the First-tier Tribunal's decision for errors of law that had resulted in the appellant being denied a fair hearing before that tribunal. It accepted that the Upper Tribunal had a discretion as to whether to remit a case or re-make the decision itself, but considered that reasons were required if the Upper Tribunal decided not to remit and that insufficient reasons had been given. The Court's decision was based partly on a Practice Statement applicable in the Immigration Appeals Chamber of the Upper Tribunal, but the Court also expressed itself in wider terms, pointing out that not remitting a case meant that the losing party would be denied the opportunity of appealing to the Upper Tribunal against a re-made decision, rather than to the Court.

pp.1136–1146, *annotation to the Tribunals, Courts and Enforcement Act 2007 s.13 (Right to appeal to Court of Appeal etc.)*

Where the Secretary of State or HMRC seeks permission to appeal in what will be a test case affecting many others, and the proposed respondent is not represented, the appellate court (and the party applying for permission) may wish to take steps with a view to ensuring that the case is properly argued, either by encouraging the respondent to obtain representation or by arranging for the Attorney General to be asked to appoint an advocate to the court. Thus, in *Carrington v Revenue and Customs Commissioners* [2021] EWCA Civ 1724; [2022] 1 W.L.R. 2546 at [17]–[23], it is recorded that HMRC undertook not to apply for costs if it were successful and that the Court suggested that Mrs Carrington seek assistance from Advocate (the Bar Council's pro bono unit). At HMRC's suggestion, the Court also arranged for an advocate to the court to be appointed although, after the advocate had made written submissions, Mrs Carrington obtained pro bono representation and so the Court was able to dispense with further assistance from the advocate. 4.032

Note that the new s.11A of the 2007 Act, see above, very severely restricts the power of the Administrative Court to consider challenges to a refusal by the Upper Tribunal to give permission to appeal to the Upper Tribunal from the First-tier Tribunal, although it does not affect refusals to give permission to appeal from other bodies and does not apply where permission to appeal from the First-tier Tribunal was refused before July 14, 2022.

When the Administrative Court is considering an application for judicial review of a refusal of the Upper Tribunal to give permission to appeal to the Upper Tribunal against a decision of a body other than the First-tier Tribunal, a *"Cart* approach", as required by CPR r.54.7A(7)(b), is not appropriate (*R. (Reid) v Upper Tribunal (Administrative Appeals Chamber)* [2022] EWHC 2180 (Admin)) at [8]–[17]. It was also held at [34]–[41] that, where an appeal lies to the Upper Tribunal on questions of fact, as well as law, but only with permission, the Upper Tribunal is entitled to refuse permission if an appeal appears to have no reasonable prospect of success.

In *DJ v Secretary of State for the Home Department* [2022] EWCA Civ 1057, the Court of Appeal held that a decision of the Immigration and Asylum Chamber of the Upper Tribunal under r.43 of the Tribunal Procedure (Upper Tribunal) Rules 2008 could not be the subject of an appeal to the Court of Appeal. However, that was because a r.43 decision made in the context of the type of asylum claim in issue in that case was an "excluded decision" within the scope of art.3(m) of the Appeals (Excluded Decisions) Order 2009 (SI 2009/275), made under para.(8)(f) of this section.

p.1156, *amendment to the Tribunals, Courts and Enforcement Act 2007 s.17 (Quashing orders under section 15(1): supplementary provision)*

4.033   With effect from July 14, 2022, s.1(3) of the Judicial Review and Courts Act 2022 amended s.17 of the 2007 Act by inserting before subs.(1) a new subs.(A1):

"(A1) In cases arising under the law of England and Wales, section 29A of the Senior Courts Act 1981 applies in relation to a quashing order under section 15(1)(c) of this Act as it applies in relation to a quashing order under section 29 of that Act."

It also amends subs.(2)(b) by substituting for "decision is quashed" the words "quashing order is made".

Section 29A of the 1981 Act, inserted by s.1(1) of the 2022 Act, provides that quashing orders may be suspended, that any retrospective effect of a quashing order may be removed or limited and that a quashing order may be made subject to conditions.

By virtue of s.1(4) of the 2022 Act, these amendments do not affect proceedings commenced before July 14, 2022.

p.1165, *annotation to the Tribunals, Courts and Enforcement Act 2007 s.23 (Practice directions)*

4.033A   The distinction between Practice Directions and Practice Statements was considered in *AEB v Secretary of State for the Home Department* [2022] EWCA Civ 1512, where the Court was content to adopt the view expressed in *DT v SSWP (II)* [2015] UKUT 509 (AAC) that the Senior President of Tribunals' authority for making Practice Statements is derived from s.3(4) of this Act under which he presides over both the First-tier Tribunal and the Upper Tribunal. The purpose of Practice Statements "is to provide guidance, both to Tribunal Judges and to Tribunal users, so as to encourage consistency of approach and under-standing" (*AEB* at [15]), whereas Practice Directions made under s.23 impose obligations on those to whom they are directed.

p.1171, *annotation to the Tribunals, Courts and Enforcement Act 2007 s.29(1) (Costs or expenses)*

4.033B   With effect from June 28, 2022, s.48(2) of the Judicial Review and Courts Act 2022 inserted a new s.194A into the Legal Services Act 2007 so as to give the First-tier Tribunal and the Upper Tribunal the same power as courts in England and Wales have under s.194 of the 2007 Act (mentioned in the annotation in the main work) to order a person to make a payment to a prescribed charity where, but for the fact that that a party's representation was provided free of charge, the tribunal would have had the power to order that person to make a payment to that party in respect of the representation. The new power extends across the United Kingdom, save where proceedings are within devolved compe-tence (see s.194A(11) and (12)). It has little relevance in social security cases, because tribunals generally lack any power to award costs in such cases. However, it may be exercised in other contexts. The charity prescribed under the Legal Services Act 2007 (Prescribed Charity) Order 2008 (SI 2008/2680) (which has effect in relation to s.194A by virtue of s.194C(4)) is the Access to Justice Foundation.

pp.1188–1191, *repeal of the Coronavirus Act 2020 s.55 and Sch.25 (Public participation in proceedings conducted by video or audio)*

With effect from June 28, 2022, s.201(2) of the Police, Crime, Sentencing and Courts Act 2022 repealed s.55 of, and Sch.25 to, the Coronavirus Act 2020, subject to a saving that had the effect that temporary amendments to Tribunal Procedure Rules that were to expire when the Act ceased to be in force remained in force until September 25, 2022 (see the Police, Crime, Sentencing and Courts Act 2022 (Commencement No. 2) Regulations 2022 (SI 2022/704)).   **4.034**

Section 55 and Sch.25 have been superseded by Pt 7ZA of the Courts Act 2003 (Transmission and recording of court and tribunal proceedings), inserted by ss.198 and 199 of the 2022 Act with effect from April 28, 2022, and regulations made under those new provisions (see Part I of this Supplement). The explanatory memorandum to the commencement order mentioned above suggests that it was anticipated that the temporary amendments to the Tribunal Procedure Rules would be replaced by permanent amendments in the light of the new provisions in the 2003 Act, but it appears that such permanent amendments have not been considered necessary.

pp.1212–1213, *annotation to the Tribunal Procedure (First-tier Tribunal) (Social Entitlement Chamber) Rules 2008 (SI 2008/2685) r.4 (Delegation to staff)*

Tribunal Case Workers have become Legal Officers. The Senior President of Tribunals has issued the following Practice Statement, with effect from July 26, 2022:   **4.035**

"Practice Statement authorising Legal Officers to carry out functions of a judicial nature in the First-tier Tribunal (Social Entitlement Chamber)

1. The Senior President of Tribunals hereby authorises any appropriately trained member of staff appointed under section 40(1) of the Tribunals, Courts and Enforcement Act 2007 or section 2(1) of the Courts Act 2003 and designated as a 'Legal Officer' by the Chamber President to carry out the functions of the Tribunal Procedure (First-tier Tribunal) (Social Entitlement Chamber) Rules 2008 set out in paragraph 3 below.
2. A Legal Officer must have been authorised by the Chamber President to exercise those functions. All functions must be exercised under the supervision of a judge and in accordance with guidance issued by the Chamber President.

3. A Legal Officer may make all decisions that a judge assigned to the Social Security and Child Support or Criminal Injuries Compensation jurisdiction may make under the Tribunal Procedure (First-tier Tribunal) (Social Entitlement Chamber) Rules 2008 save those which are substantive final decisions.

4. In accordance with rule 4(3) of the Tribunal Procedure (First-tier Tribunal) (Social Entitlement Chamber) Rules 2008, within 14 days after the date that the Tribunal sends notice of a decision made by a Legal Officer pursuant to an authorisation under paragraph 1 above that party may apply in writing to the Tribunal for the decision to be considered afresh by a judge."

pp.1214–1224, *annotation to the Tribunal Procedure (First-tier Tribunal) (Social Entitlement Chamber) Rules 2008 (SI 2008/2685) r.5 (Case management powers)*

4.036 In *LJT v SSWP (PIP)* [2019] UKUT 21 (AAC), mentioned on p.1221 of the main work, the Upper Tribunal was critical (at [16]) of the First-tier Tribunal for having adjourned on an earlier occasion in order to obtain a copy of the claimant's GP records without, it appeared, having considered first taking evidence from the claimant that might have made the adjournment unnecessary.

p.1224, *expiry of the Tribunal Procedure (First-tier Tribunal) (Social Entitlement Chamber) Rules 2008 (SI 2008/2685) r.5A (Coronavirus temporary rule (decisions without a hearing))*

4.037 This rule expired on September 25, 2022 and has not been replaced (see the supplementary annotation to the Coronavirus Act 2020, above).

pp.1259–1260, *annotation to the Tribunal Procedure (First-tier Tribunal) (Social Entitlement Chamber) Rules 2008 (SI 2008/2685) r.22(8) (Cases in which the notice of appeal is to be sent to the Tribunal—Paragraph (8))*

4.037A A very detailed analysis of the cases mentioned in para.3.325 and other cases on extending the absolute time-limit for appealing, so as to avoid a breach of the European Convention on Human Rights, is to be found in *GJ v SSWP (PIP)* [2022] UKUT 340 (AAC), in which it is unsurprisingly concluded that the scope for such an extension "is very narrowly drawn indeed".

pp.1275–1289, *annotation to the Tribunal Procedure (First-tier Tribunal) (Social Entitlement Chamber) Rules 2008 (SI 2008/2685) r.27 (Decision with or without a hearing)*

4.038 In *CF v SSWP (CSM)* [2022] UKUT 271 (AAC), a hearing took place, following which the judge issued directions requiring further evidence to be provided. Another judge then, without the parties having consented to the case being decided without a hearing and without them having been provided with the judge's note of what was said at the first hearing, decided it on the papers, having regard to the fact the parties had had the opportunity to attend a hearing "and taking account of the factors in the overriding objective, including the delay from the date of decision, the need for finality in appeals, proportionality and the issues in the case". The decision was unsurprisingly set aside by the Upper Tribunal on the ground that, although the condition in r.27(1)(b) might have been satisfied, the condition in r.27(1)(a) clearly was not. This is not to say that, following a hearing, the First-tier Tribunal may never issue directions requiring further evidence and then decide the case without a further hearing, but the hearing must have been complete except as regards the further evidence, the decision must be made by the judge or panel who had heard the case and the parties must generally have agreed to make any further representations in writing rather than orally (*CF* at [24]). There may perhaps be cases where the additional evidence merely confirms what had already been said and there is clearly nothing further that the losing party could have said about it at a hearing, but a decision is liable to be set aside if a party subsequently shows that a hearing might conceivably have made a difference.

Video evidence from abroad

In *Raza v Secretary of State for the Home Department* [2023] EWCA Civ 29, it was argued that a decision of the First-tier Tribunal was wrong in law in the light of *Re Agbabiaka (evidence from abroad, Nare guidance) Nigeria* [2021] UKUT 286 (IAC) (mentioned in the main work on p.1283) because evidence had been received from Pakistan without the Pakistani authorities' consent. The Court of Appeal rejected that submission, Elizabeth Laing LJ, with whom the other members of the Court agreed, said at [76]:

> "The primary question for this Court is whether there is any provision or rule of domestic law which shows that the FtT hearing was unlawful and a nullity. There is none. The [Nationality, Immigration and Asylum Act 2002] expressly requires some appeals to be made from, and some to be continued from, abroad. The 2002 Act does not provide that the lawfulness of such appeals depends on any condition, such as the obtaining of permission from a foreign state. The Rules assume that a hearing can be conducted partly by video link. The Rules do not provide for any further conditions in relation to the taking of evidence from abroad. Neither *Nare* nor *Agbabiaka* suggests that the taking of video evidence from abroad without the permission of the state concerned is unlawful, or that it makes the hearing a nullity. *Agbabiaka* suggests that such a hearing might be contrary to the public interest because of its potential to damage international relations, and, thus contrary to the interests of justice, but that is a different point. I accept Mr Kovats's submission that the sanctions for such conduct are diplomatic, not legal."

Oral evidence

The fact that a witness has lied on one occasion does not necessarily mean that the whole of his or her evidence is unreliable (*SSWP v AM (IS)* [2010] UKUT 428 (AAC) at [26]; *MW v Leeds CC (HB)* [2018] UKUT 319 (AAC) at [8]). Nor does dishonesty within the proceedings before the Tribunal. In *VS v SSWP (ESA)* [2017] UKUT 274 (AAC), the First-tier Tribunal was criticised for giving the impression that it was more interested in investigating and condemning the claimant's behaviour in concealing an adverse psychological report than with whether she actually had limited capability for work. However, repeated references to a claimant's dishonesty in a statement of reasons may be justified, as in *MH v SSWP (PIP)* [2022] UKUT 248 (AAC) where the Upper Tribunal said at [25]:

" . . . this was not a case like *VS* where it appears the F-tT had become rather fixated upon one particular aspect of the appeal and the damage to credibility that it thought that had caused. The F-tT, in the case now before me, did properly apply its adverse credibility conclusions. Its frequent references to the lack of credibility, when explaining and justifying its conclusion with respect to each activity in issue, was perhaps unnecessarily repetitive as I have touched upon but on my reading what it was doing was simply stressing its disbelief with respect to each compartmentalised consideration of each activity for the sake of thoroughness."

p.1291, *expiry of the Tribunal Procedure (First-tier Tribunal) (Social Entitlement Chamber) Rules 2008 (SI 2008/2685) r.30(3A) (Public and private hearings)*

4.039 Paragraph (3A) expired on September 25, 2022 (see the supplementary annotation to the Coronavirus Act 2020, above).

pp.1292–1295, *annotation to the Tribunal Procedure (First-tier Tribunal) (Social Entitlement Chamber) Rules 2008 (SI 2008/2685) r.30 (Public and private hearings)*

4.040 Part 7ZA of the Courts Act 2003 (Transmission and recording of court and tribunal proceedings), inserted by ss.198 and 199 of the 2022 Act with effect from April 28, 2022, together with the Remote Observation and Recording (Courts and Tribunals) Regulations 2022 (see Part 1 of this Supplement), make provision for the transmission of remote hearings that are public or that, although in private, may be attended by "specific categories of person, or specific individuals, who are not taking part in the proceedings". They also make provision for the recording of remote hearings.

Paragraph (3A) and r.30A expired on September 25, 2022 (see the supplementary annotation to the Coronavirus Act 2020, above) and have not been replaced, it presumably being considered that the new legislation is an adequate substitute. In effect, practicality does not now govern whether the hearing is formally in public; instead, it governs whether the general public can in practice exercise their right to watch, or at least listen to, public proceedings. Even if live streaming cannot take place, it may be possible to transmit a recording later.

pp.1295–1296, *expiry of the Tribunal Procedure (First-tier Tribunal) (Social Entitlement Chamber) Rules 2008 (SI 2008/2685) r.30A (Coronavirus temporary rule (recording of remote hearings))*

This rule expired on September 25, 2022 and has not been replaced (see the supplementary annotations to the Coronavirus Act 2020 and to r.30, above).   4.041

pp.1303–1317, *annotation to the Tribunal Procedure (First-tier Tribunal) (Social Entitlement Chamber) Rules 2008 (SI 2008/2685) r.34 (Reasons for decisions)*

In *DW v SSWP (II)* [2022] UKUT 183 (AAC), the Upper Tribunal considered the extent to which the First-tier Tribunal, when it includes a registered medical practitioner among its members, is required to give reasons for any medical opinion that it expresses.   4.042

"17. In courts, medical expertise is provided by witnesses who are entitled to give opinion evidence. If there is a dispute as to the evidence, the witnesses may be required to give reasons for their opinions and the court is then required to consider that reasoning. As was said in *Flannery v Halifax Estate Agencies Ltd* [1999] EWCA Civ 811; [2000] 1 W.L.R. 377 at 382B—'. . . where the dispute involves something in the nature of an intellectual exchange, with reasons and analysis advanced on either side, the judge must enter into the issues canvassed before him and explain why he prefers one case over the other.' Otherwise, the court may simply rely on the opinion offered. Where a tribunal includes a registered medical practitioner as a member and so has its own expertise, it is required to give reasons for its conclusion but is generally entitled to rely on its own expertise. I do not accept that the First-tier Tribunal is obliged to give reasons for its reasons in the absence of reasoned evidence that contradicts its opinion. It may be that, on an appeal to the Upper Tribunal, a party is entitled to adduce evidence for the purpose of showing that there is a contradictory body of medical opinion and that, in the circumstances of a particular case, the First-tier Tribunal's reliance on its unexplained opinion is inadequate, but that has not been done here as regards Mr Rogers' paragraph 88 point. On the contrary, he readily accepts that '[w]hat the Tribunal states may be correct'."

p.1349, *expiry of the Tribunal Procedure (Upper Tribunal) Rules 2008 (SI 2008/2698) r.5A (Coronavirus temporary rule (decisions without a hearing))*

This rule expired on September 25, 2022 and has not been replaced (see the supplementary annotation to the Coronavirus Act 2020, above).   4.043

pp.1358–1360, *annotation to Tribunal Procedure (Upper Tribunal) Rules 2008 (SI 2008/2698) r.10 (Orders for costs)*

4.043A   With effect from June 28, 2022, s.48(2) of the Judicial Review and Courts Act 2022 inserted a new s.194A into the Legal Services Act 2007 so as to give the First-tier Tribunal and the Upper Tribunal the same power as courts in England and Wales have under s.194 of the 2007 Act to order a person to make a payment to a prescribed charity where, but for the fact that that a party's representation was provided free of charge, the tribunal would have had the power to order that person to make a payment to that party in respect of the representation. The new power extends across the United Kingdom, save where proceedings are within devolved competence (see s.194A(11) and (12)). It has little relevance in social security cases, where tribunals generally lack any power to award costs. However, it may be exercised in other contexts. The charity prescribed under the Legal Services Act 2007 (Prescribed Charity) Order 2008 (SI 2008/2680) (which has effect in relation to s.194A by virtue of s.194C(4)) is the Access to Justice Foundation.

p.1373, *insertion of the Tribunal Procedure (Upper Tribunal) Rules 2008 (SI 2008/2698) r.20B (Application for an authorised costs order)*

4.044   With effect from November 1, 2022, r.5(1) and (2) of the Tribunal Procedure (Amendment No. 2) Rules 2022 (SI 2022/1030) inserted r.20B into the 2008 Rules. However, as this rule is concerned only with applications by charities under s.324A of the Charities Act 2011 and is not relevant to social security cases, it is not set out here.

p.1387, *amendment of the Tribunal Procedure (Upper Tribunal) Rules 2008 (SI 2008/2698) r.26A (Cases transferred or referred to the Upper Tribunal, applications made directly to the Upper Tribunal, cases where an offence has been certified and proceedings without notice to a respondent)*

4.045   With effect from November 1, 2022, r.5(1) and (3) of the Tribunal Procedure (Amendment No. 2) Rules 2022 (SI 2022/1030) amended r.26A(2)(aa) by substituting for "Schedule 1D of the Charities Act 1993" the words "section 325 or 326 of the Charities Act 2011".

pp.1390–1391, *annotation to the Tribunal Procedure (Upper Tribunal) Rules 2008 (SI 2008/2698) r.28 (Application for permission to bring judicial review proceedings)*

4.046   The view expressed in *R. (Spahiu) v Secretary of State for the Home Department* [2018] EWCA Civ 2604; [2019] 1 W.L.R. 1297 that the Civil Procedure Rules apply by analogy to judicial review proceedings in the Upper Tribunal may suggest that, in the light of *R. (Good Law Project Ltd) v Secretary of State for Health and Social Care* [2022] EWCA Civ 355; [2022] 1 W.L.R. 2339, a particularly strict approach must be taken to whether an application under r.28 has been made in time and that time should not be extended unless the applicant took all reasonable steps to comply with r.28 but was unable to do so.

p.1400, *expiry of the Tribunal Procedure (Upper Tribunal) Rules 2008 (SI 2008/2698) r.37(2ZA) (Public and private hearings)*

Paragraph (2ZA) expired on September 25, 2022 (see the supplemen-   4.047
tary annotation to the Coronavirus Act 2020, above).

pp.1401–1402, *annotation to the Tribunal Procedure (Upper Tribunal) Rules 2008 (SI 2008/2698) r.37 (Public and private hearings)*

Part 7ZA of the Courts Act 2003 (Transmission and recording of   4.048
court and tribunal proceedings), inserted by ss.198 and 199 of the 2022
Act with effect from April 28, 2022, together with the Remote Observation and Recording (Courts and Tribunals) Regulations 2022 (see Part
1 of this Supplement), make provision for the transmission of remote
hearings that are public or that, although in private, may be attended by
"specific categories of person, or specific individuals, who are not taking
part in the proceedings". They also make provision for the recording of
remote hearings.
Paragraph (2ZA) of this rule and r.37A both expired on September
25, 2022 (see the supplementary annotation to the Coronavirus Act
2020, above) and have not been replaced, it presumably being considered that the new legislation is an adequate substitute. In effect,
practicality does not now govern whether the hearing is formally in
public; instead, it governs whether the general public can in practice
exercise their right to watch, or at least listen to, public proceedings.
Even if live streaming cannot take place, it may be possible to transmit a
recording later.

p.1402, *expiry of the Tribunal Procedure (Upper Tribunal) Rules 2008 (SI 2008/2698) r.37A (Coronavirus temporary rule (recording of remote hearings))*

This rule expired on September 25, 2022 and has not been replaced   4.049
(see the supplementary annotations to the Coronavirus Act 2020 and to
r.37, above).

p.1407, *annotation to the Tribunal Procedure (Upper Tribunal) Rules 2008 (SI 2008/2698) r.43 (Setting aside a decision which disposes of proceedings)*

In *DJ v Secretary of State for the Home Department* [2022] EWCA Civ   4.050
1057, the Court of Appeal held that a decision of the Immigration and
Asylum Chamber of the Upper Tribunal under r.43 could not be the
subject of an appeal to the Court of Appeal. However, although there
was considerable discussion in Macur LJ's judgment as to why it should
be necessary to appeal against a r.43 decision rather than the substantive

decision that had not been set aside or that had been substituted for a decision that had been set aside, the basis of the Court's decision was actually that a r.43 decision was an "excluded decision" within the scope of art.3(m) of the Appeals (Excluded Decisions) Order 2009 (SI 2009/275), made under s.13(8)(f) of the Tribunals, Courts and Enforcement Act 2007, which applies only to certain types of decision in chambers of the Upper Tribunal other than the Administrative Appeals Chamber. Accordingly, the decision has no relevance to social security cases in the Administrative Appeals Chamber, save that some of the reasoning may suggest that, if an application for permission to appeal against a r.43 decision were to be made in such a case, consideration should be given to whether it might be better directed at a relevant substantive decision.

pp.1444–1447, *annotation to the Human Rights Act 1998 s.7 (Proceedings—Standing to raise the complaint: the victim requirement)*

4.051 In *Taylor v Department for Communities* [2022] NICA 21, the Court of Appeal in Northern Ireland dismissed an appeal by the claimant who had brought judicial review proceedings based on art.14 in relation to his housing benefit, primarily on the ground that he was not a "victim". The Court observed:

> "[19] In *Senator Lines GMBH v Austria and Others* [2006] 21 BHRC 640 the Grand Chamber of the ECtHR, in determining whether the particular application was admissible, reflected on the concept of "*potential victim.*" Referring to concrete examples in its jurisprudence, the court recalled one case where an alien's removal had been ordered but not enforced and another where a law prohibiting homosexual acts was capable of being, but had not been, applied to a certain category of the population which included the applicant. The judgment continues, at page 11:

>> "However, for an applicant to be able to claim to be a *victim* in such a situation *he must produce reasonable and convincing evidence of the likelihood that a violation affecting him personally will occur; mere suspicion or conjecture is insufficient . . .* " [emphasis added]

> [21] Rejecting his argument, the Grand Chamber reasoned and concluded as follows. In order to be able to lodge a petition in pursuance of article 34, a person, non-governmental organisation or group of individuals had to be able to claim to be *the victim* of a violation of the convention rights. In order to claim to be a victim of a violation, a person had to be directly affected by the impugned measure. The ECHR did not, therefore, envisage the bringing of an *actio popularis* for the interpretation of the rights set out therein or permit individuals to complain about a provision of national law simply because they considered, without having been directly affected by it, that it might contravene the convention. It was, however, open to a person to contend that a law violated his rights, in the absence of an

individual measure of implementation, if he was required either to modify his conduct or risk being prosecuted or if he was a member of a class of people *at "real risk"* of being directly affected by the legislation. Given their age, the wills they had made and the value of the property each owned, the applicants had established that there was a real risk that, in the not too distant future, one of them would be required to pay substantial inheritance tax on the property inherited from her sister. Accordingly, both were directly affected by the impugned legislation and thus had victim status.

[22] Plainly a vague or fanciful possibility of a future Convention violation will not suffice. In short, *"risk"* in this context denotes *real risk*. This requires, per *Senator Lines*, a reasonable and convincing evidential foundation."

pp.1475–1477, *annotation to Human Rights Act 1998 Sch.1 Pt I (Article 8—Right to respect for private and family life—Benefit, family life and private life)*

In *Jivan v Romania* (App.62250/19) the Court found a breach of art.8   4.052 in the State's failure (including on the part of the appeal court) adequately to assess the degree of disability of an older man. The Court's reasoning is somewhat brief, but suggests that the State may have focussed on the main presenting medical issue (a partial amputation) to the exclusion of a wider range of medical and social factors. It observed:

"The Court reiterates that a wide margin is usually allowed to the State under the Convention in issues of general policy, including social, economic, and healthcare policies (see, for instance, *McDonald*, cited above, § 54, with further references). However, if a restriction on fundamental rights applies to a particularly vulnerable group in society that has suffered considerable discrimination in the past, such as persons with disabilities, or elderly dependent people, then the State's margin of appreciation is substantially narrower and it must have very weighty reasons for the restrictions in question (see *Guberina v. Croatia*, no. 23682/13, § 73, 22 March 2016, in the context of discrimination of a physically disabled child; *Alajos Kiss v. Hungary*, no. 38832/06, § 42, 20 May 2010, in the context of the restriction of a mentally disabled person's right to vote; and *Cînţa v. Romania*, no. 3891/19, § 41, 18 February 2020, in the context of the restriction of a mentally ill parent's right to contact with his child)."

In *Beeler v Switzerland* (App.78630/12) (Grand Chamber) the Strasbourg Court has reviewed existing authorities on when benefits issues may fall within the ambit of art.8. The issue arose acutely in the case, as Switzerland has not ratified Protocol 1, so a claim based on art.14 could only succeed if taken together with art.8. The Court observed:

"66. An analysis of the case-law summarised above indicates that the Court has not always been entirely consistent in defining the factors

147

leading it to find that complaints concerning social welfare benefits fell within the ambit of Article 8 of the Convention.

67. The Court notes at the outset that all financial benefits generally have a certain effect on the way in which the family life of the person concerned is managed, although that fact alone is not sufficient to bring them within the ambit of Article 8. Otherwise, all welfare benefits would fall within the ambit of that Article, an approach which would be excessive.

68. It is therefore necessary for the Court to clarify the relevant criteria in order to specify, or indeed to circumscribe, what falls within the ambit of Article 8 in the sphere of welfare benefits.

69. It can also be seen from the case-law summarised above that in the field of social welfare benefits, the sphere of protection of Article 1 of Protocol No. 1 and that of Article 8 of the Convention intersect and overlap, although the interests secured under those Articles are different. In determining which complaints fall within the ambit of Article 8, the Court must redress the inconsistencies noted under Article 8, particularly when read in conjunction with Article 14 of the Convention (see paragraphs 64–65 above).

It follows that the Court can no longer simply accept either a legal presumption to the effect that in providing the benefit in question, the State is displaying its support and respect for family life (see the case-law cited in paragraph 65 above), or a hypothetical causal link whereby it ascertains whether the grant of a particular benefit is "liable to affect the way in which family life is organised" (see the case-law cited in paragraph 64 above).

70. In the Court's view, the Grand Chamber judgment in *Konstantin Markin* (cited above) should be taken as the main reference point here:

"*(i) On whether Article 14 taken in conjunction with Article 8 is applicable*

129. The Court must determine at the outset whether the facts of the case fall within the scope of Article 8 and hence of Article 14 of the Convention. It has repeatedly held that Article 14 of the Convention is pertinent if 'the subject matter of the disadvantage . . . constitutes one of the modalities of the exercise of a right guaranteed . . . ', or if the contested measures are 'linked to the exercise of a right guaranteed

. . . For Article 14 to be applicable, it is enough for the facts of the case to fall within the ambit of one or more of the provisions of the Convention (see *Thlimmenos v. Greece* [GC], no. 34369/97, § 40, ECHR 2000-IV; *E.B. v. France*, cited above, §§47–48; and *Fretté v. France*, no.36515/97, §31, ECHR 2002-I, with further references).

130. It is true that Article 8 does not include a right to parental leave or impose any positive obligation on States to provide parental-leave allowances. At the same time, by enabling one of the parents to stay at home to look after the children, parental *leave* and related *allowances* promote family life and *necessarily affect the way in*

which it is organised [emphasis added *in original*]. Parental leave and parental allowances therefore come within the scope of Article 8 of the Convention. It follows that Article 14, taken together with Article 8, is applicable. Accordingly, if a State does decide to create a parental-leave scheme, it must do so in a manner which is compatible with Article 14 of the Convention (see *Petrovic*, cited above, §§ 26–29)."

71. In the context of *Konstantin Markin*, the applicability of Article 14 of the Convention in conjunction with Article 8 stemmed from the fact that the parental leave and the corresponding allowance had *"necessarily affect[ed] the way in which [family life was] organised"* (compare and contrast the approach followed in the cases referred to in paragraphs 64 and 65 above), both measures having been aimed at enabling one of the parents to remain at home to look after the children (in this case, infants). Thus, a close link between the allowance associated with parental leave and the enjoyment of family life was considered necessary.

72. Accordingly, for Article 14 of the Convention to be applicable in this specific context, the subject matter of the alleged disadvantage must constitute one of the modalities of exercising the right to respect for family life as guaranteed by Article 8 of the Convention, in the sense that the measures seek to promote family life and necessarily affect the way in which it is organised. The Court considers that a range of factors are relevant for determining the nature of the benefit in question and that they should be examined as a whole. These will include, in particular: the aim of the benefit, as determined by the Court in the light of the legislation concerned; the criteria for awarding, calculating and terminating the benefit as set forth in the relevant statutory provisions; the effects on the way in which family life is organised, as envisaged by the legislation; and the practical repercussions of the benefit, given the applicant's individual circumstances and family life throughout the period during which the benefit is paid."

pp.1480–1482, *annotation to Human Rights Act 1998 Sch. 1 Pt I (Article 14—Prohibition of discrimination—The Strasbourg approach to art. 14 in the social security context)*

For a recent decision in which the Strasbourg Court held in a case of discrimination on the ground of nationality that the necessary "weighty reasons" existed, see *Savickis v Latvia* (App.49270/11) (Grand Chamber). **4.053**

pp.1493–1494, *annotation to Human Rights Act 1998 Sch. 1 Pt I (National authorities on art. 14 read with art. 1 of Protocol 1 in relation to specific benefits—(c) Bereavement)*

The decision in *O'Donnell v Department for Communities* was considered in *R. (Jwanczuk) v SSWP* [2022] EWHC 2298 (Admin). The **4.054** judge was not bound by the decision of the Court of Appeal in Northern Ireland and considered the matter afresh, ultimately reaching a similar result. An appeal to the Court of Appeal is pending at the time of writing.

A challenge to the exclusion of cohabiting couples from (old-style) bereavement benefits has recently failed in *HM and MK v SSWP (BB)* [2023] UKUT 15 (AAC).

p.1501, *annotation to Human Rights Act 1998 Sch.1 Pt I (National authorities on art.14 read with art.1 of Protocol 1 in relation to specific benefits—(i) Universal credit)*

4.055 The Court of Appeal have refused SSWP permission to appeal.

pp.1504–1505, *annotation to Human Rights Act 1998 Sch.1 Pt I (Article 14 in conjunction with art.8)*

4.056 For the observations in *Beeler v Switzerland* (App.78630/12) (Grand Chamber) concerning the ambit of art.8 in social security cases, see under Article 8 above.

pp.1506–1509, *annotation to Human Rights Act 1998 Sch.1 Pt II (Article 1—Protection of property—General Note)*

4.057 In *Beeler v Switzerland* (App.78630/12) (Grand Chamber) the Strasbourg Court took the opportunity to review existing authority, observing:

> "[T]he Court observes that its case-law has now taken on sufficient maturity and stability for it to give a clear definition of the threshold required for the applicability of Article 1 of Protocol No. 1, including in the sphere of social welfare benefits. It should be reiterated in this connection that that Article does not create a right to acquire property or to receive a pension of a particular amount. Its protection applies only to existing possessions and, under certain circumstances, to the "legitimate expectation" of obtaining an asset; for the recognition of a possession consisting in a legitimate expectation, the applicant must have an assertable right which may not fall short of a sufficiently established, substantive proprietary interest under the national law (see *Bélané Nagy*, cited above, §§ 74–79).
>
> 58. Thus, where the applicant does not satisfy, or ceases to satisfy, the legal conditions laid down in domestic law for entitlement to any particular form of benefits or pension, there is no interference with the rights under Article 1 of Protocol No 1 if the conditions had changed before the applicant became eligible for the benefit in question. Where the suspension or diminution of a pension was not due to any changes in the applicant's own circumstances, but to changes in the law or its implementation, this may result in an interference with the rights

under Article 1 of Protocol No. 1. Accordingly, where the domestic legal conditions for entitlement to any particular form of benefits or pension have changed and where, as a result, the person concerned no longer fully satisfies them, a careful consideration of the individual circumstances of the case—in particular, the nature of the change in the conditions—may be warranted in order to verify the existence of a sufficiently established, substantive proprietary interest under the national law (ibid., §§ 86–89).

p.1512, *annotation to the Human Rights Act 1998 Sch.2 (Remedial orders)*

A draft of the Bereavement Benefits (Remedial Order) 2022 was laid before Parliament on October 11, 2022. Following consultation, it contains a number of changes from the version proposed in 2021. **4.058**

pp.1523–1526, *annotation to the European Union (Withdrawal) Act 2018 s.4 (Saving for rights etc. under section 2(1) of the ECA)*

With effect from November 29, 2022, The Cessation of EU Law Relating to Prohibitions on Grounds of Nationality and Free Movement of Persons Regulations 2022 (SI 2022/1240) make provision seeking to guard against EU provisions relating to the matters referred to in the title of the Regulations (in particular arts 18, 21 and 45 TFEU) having any continuing effect in the UK via s.4(1) of the Act. They also amend Regulation (EU) No.492/2011. The text is set out in the "New Legislation" section of this Supplement. **4.059**

p.1526, *European Union (Withdrawal) Act 2018 s.5 (Exceptions to savings and incorporation)*

In *SSWP v AT (UC)* [2022] UKUT 330 (AAC), AT had moved to the UK exercising her rights under art.21 TFEU before the end of the Brexit transition period and claimed universal credit after it. The case was an appeal against the decision of the First-tier Tribunal, which had relied on s.5(5) to apply the principles of the Charter as "fundamental rights or principles which exist irrespective of the Charter". However, on appeal, neither party sought to uphold this reasoning. A three-judge panel nonetheless held that the Charter did apply, relying principally on s.7A of this Act and arts 4 and 13 of the Withdrawal Agreement. SSWP has been given permission to appeal to the Court of Appeal. **4.060**

p.1534, *European Union (Withdrawal) Act 2018 s.7A (General implementation of remainder of withdrawal agreement)*

The section creates, in respect of the matters derived from the Withdrawal Agreement listed in s.7A(1), a "conduit pipe", similar to the **4.061** effect previously given by s.2 of the European Communities Act 1972: *SSWP v AT (UC)* [2022] UKUT 330 (AAC) at [67]–[69].

pp.1537–1539, *annotation to the European Union (Withdrawal) Act 2018 s.8 (Dealing with deficiencies arising from withdrawal)*

4.062   Regulations made under this section include, in relation to social security, the Cessation of EU Law Relating to Prohibitions on Grounds of Nationality and Free Movement of Persons Regulations 2022 (SI 2022/1240) (in force from November 29, 2022). The text is set out in the "New Legislation" section of this Supplement. In summary, the Regulations seek to guard against EU provisions relating to the matters referred to in the title of the Regulations (in particular arts 18, 21 and 45 TFEU) having any continuing effect in the UK via this s.4(1) of the Act. They also amend Regulation (EU) No.492/2011.

p.1575, *annotation to Extracts from the Agreement on the Withdrawal of the United Kingdom art.4 (Methods and principles relating to the effect, the implementation and the application of this Agreement)*

4.063   As the definition of "Union law" in art.2 includes the Charter, it was among the "methods and general principles of Union law" for the purposes of art.4(3). Accordingly, the "methods" in accordance with which the provisions of the Withdrawal Agreement were to be interpreted and applied include those of the Charter (*SSWP v AT (UC)* [2022] UKUT 330 (AAC) at [105]); *CG* had established that the UK was implementing or acting in the scope of EU law (art.21 TFEU) when it had granted CG a domestic law right of residence (Pre-settled status) and the same applied to AT: *SSWP v AT (UC)* at [106].

p.1581, *annotation to Extracts from the Agreement on the Withdrawal of the United Kingdom art.13 (Residence rights)*

4.064   In *SSWP v AT (UC)* [2022] UKUT 330 (AAC), SSWP submitted that art.13(1) created a unique type of right *("sui generis")*, subject to the limitations and conditions referred to in the article, but not the right under art.21 TFEU on which AT had relied to move to the UK (as had the claimant in *CG v Department for Communities* (C-709/20)). The argument was rejected at [96]–[102], the panel concluding:

> "What AT retained, after the end of the transition period, was that part of her bundle of Article 21 TFEU rights which entitled her to continue to reside in the UK. CG shows that that right continues to generate legal effects even when the residence does not comply with the conditions in the [Citizens' Rights Directive], at least for those who have a right of residence granted under national law" [at 102].

SSWP has been given permission to appeal to the Court of Appeal.

p.1606, *annotation to Treaty on the Functioning of the European Union (updating commentary)*

4.065

Para(s) in 2020–21 edition	Updating commentary
3.92–3.93	*Art.18 TFEU* Following *CG v Department for Communities* (C-709/20), see under art.21 below for the discussion of *SSWP v AT (UC)* [2022] UKUT 330 (AAC).
3.108–3.117	*Art.21 TFEU* In *CG v Department for Communities* (C-709/20), the CJEU held that when CG was granted pre-settled status, the UK was implementing or acting in the scope of art.21. The same principle was followed by a three-judge panel in the post-transition period case of *SSWP v AT (UC)*. Permission has been given to appeal to the Court of Appeal.

p.1607, *annotation to Charter of Fundamental Rights of the European Union (updating commentary)*

Updating commentary to be read together with 2020–21 edition, paras 3.150–3.212

4.066

Para(s) in 2020–21 edition	Updating commentary
3.152	*Art.1 Human dignity* In *CG v Department for Communities* (C-709/20) (which related to a decision before the end of the Brexit transition period) the CJEU had relied on arts 1, 7 and 24 of the Charter to hold that the claimant who had moved in the exercise of her right under art.21 TFEU and had then been granted Pre-settled status could not be refused universal credit without the State ensuring that she could nevertheless live with her children in dignified conditions. In *SSWP v AT (UC)* [2022] UKUT 330 (AAC) a three-judge panel of the Upper Tribunal applied *CG* to a decision which post-dated the end of the transition period. It held that where *CG* was applicable, as in

Para(s) in 2020–21 edition	Updating commentary
	the case before it, an individualised assessment was required: [111]–[118]. It explained what art.1 required by reference to the decisions of the CJEU in *Jawo v Germany* (C-163/17) and *Haqbin v Federaal Agentschap voor de opvang van asielzoekers* (C-233/18), concluding at [125] that:
	" . . . [The] range of matters with which Article 1 is concerned, albeit strictly limited, extends to the provision of support for a person's "most basic needs". These will no doubt vary from person to person, though typically they will include housing (which we take as including a basic level of heating adequate for a person's health), food, clothing and hygiene. *Haqbin* also shows that the state may breach its obligations under Article 1 if a person lacks these things even for a very limited time, though it is right to note that the applicant in that case, as an unaccompanied minor asylum-seeker, was particularly vulnerable. In cases where a person is deprived of the means to meet his most basic needs for a very short time, the question whether Article 1 is breached will be sensitive to contextual matters of this kind."
	SSWP has been given permission to appeal to the Court of Appeal.
3.159	*Art.7 Respect for private and family life (General Note)*
	The article was referred to, with art.24, in both *CG v Department for Communities* (C-709/20) and *SSWP v AT (UC)* [2022] UKUT 330 (AAC), but both were very much ancillary to art.1 in the respective decisions. See under art.1 for more detail.
3.177	*Art.24 The Rights of the Child (General Note)*
	The article was referred to, with art.7, in both *CG v Department for Communities* (C-709/20) and *SSWP v AT (UC)* [2022] UKUT 330 (AAC), but both were very much ancillary to art.1 in the respective decisions. See under art.1 for more detail.

pp.1607–1608, *annotation to Regulation (EU) No.492/2011 (updating commentary)*

4.067

Para(s) in 2020–21 edition	Updating commentary
3.215–3.222	*Art.7* With effect from November 29, 2022, the Cessation of EU Law Relating to Prohibitions on Grounds of Nationality and Free Movement of Persons Regulations 2022 (SI 2022/1240) reg.4: inserts the following as a new para.2A: "Paragraphs 1 and 2 do not apply in relation to the matters set out in the Schedule to The Cessation of EU Law Relating to Prohibitions on Grounds of Nationality and Free Movement of Persons Regulations 2022 (relevant matters)." and omits para.3 from art.7. The text of the Regulations is set out in the "New Legislation" section of this book. The "relevant matters" in the Schedule appear to be designed to catch anything to do with social security or social assistance.
3.223–3.225	*Art.9* With effect from November 29, 2022, the Cessation of EU Law Relating to Prohibitions on Grounds of Nationality and Free Movement of Persons Regulations 2022 (SI 2022/1240) reg.4 omits art.9.
3.226–3.230	*Art.10* With effect from November 29, 2022, the Cessation of EU Law Relating to Prohibitions on Grounds of Nationality and Free Movement of Persons Regulations 2022 (SI 2022/1240) reg.4 omits art.10.

pp.1608–1611, *annotation to Directive 2004/38/EC (updating commentary)*

4.068

Para(s) in 2020–21 edition	Updating commentary
3.238	*Art.2(2)(d)—family members* In *ZK and MS v Minister for Justice and Equality* (C-248/22), the High Court of Ireland has asked

Para(s) in 2020–21 edition	Updating commentary
	whether Council Directive 2004/38/EC prohibits the simultaneous conferral of derived rights of residence on the estranged spouse and the de facto, durable partner of a European Union citizen lawfully exercising his right of free movement as a worker under the Directive.
3.244–3.249	*Art.3(2)(a)—beneficiaries* In *SRS and AA v Minister for Justice and Equality* (C-22/21) (September 15, 2022; text rectified October 28, 2022) the Court held: Point (a) of the first subparagraph of Article 3(2) of Directive 2004/38/EC ... must be interpreted as meaning that the concept of 'any other family members who are members of the household of the Union citizen having the primary right of residence', mentioned in that provision, refers to persons who have a relationship of dependence with that citizen, based on close and stable personal ties, forged within the same household, in the context of a shared domestic life going beyond a mere temporary cohabitation entered into for reasons of pure convenience.
3.277–3.278	In the light of *VI*, SSWP accepted that a history of apparent affiliation to the NHS was sufficient in *WH v Powys CC and SSWP (HB)* [2022] UKUT 203 (AAC).
3.296	By order dated April 29, 2022, *KR v Staatssecretaris van Justitie en Veiligheid* (C-637/21) has been removed from the Court's register.

pp.1612–1615, *annotation to Regulation 883/2004 (updating commentary)*

4.069

Para(s) in 2020–21 edition	Updating commentary
3.349 and 3.351	*Art.1—definitions* *AH v SSWP* is no longer "stood out" and (as *Harrington v SSWP*) is awaiting hearing in February 2023.

Para(s) in 2020–21 edition	Updating commentary
3.523	*Art.81—claims declarations or appeals* In *FS v Chief Appeals Officer* (C-3/21) September 29, 2022 the Court held: 1. Article 81 of Regulation (EC) No 883/2004 of the European Parliament and of the Council of 29 April 2004 on the coordination of social security systems must be interpreted as meaning that the concept of 'claim' in that article refers only to an application made by a person who has exercised his or her right to freedom of movement to the authorities of a Member State which is not competent under the conflict rules laid down by that regulation. Therefore, that concept does not include either the initial application made under the legislation of a Member State by a person who has not yet exercised his or her right to freedom of movement or the periodic payment, by the authorities of that Member State, of a benefit normally payable, at the time of that payment, by another Member State. 2. EU law, and in particular the principle of effectiveness, does not preclude the application of national legislation which makes the retroactive effect of an application for child benefit subject to a limitation period of 12 months, since that period does not render practically impossible or excessively difficult the exercise by the migrant workers concerned of the rights conferred by Regulation No.883/2004.

pp.1617–1618, *annotation to Extracts from the Trade and Cooperation Agreement*

A process of revision of the Trade and Cooperation Agreement affecting its numbering was completed. The definitive text can be found at: **4.070**
https://eur-lex.europa.eu/legal-content/EN/TXT/?uri=uriserv%3AOJ.L_.2021.149.01.0010.01.ENG.
The following changes to numbering from the text used in the 2022–23 edition should be noted:

Page	Old Number	New Number
1617	INST.2	8
1617	Ch.SSC.1	488

Page	Old Number	New Number
1617	Ch.SSC.2	489
1618	Ch.SSC.3	490

The numbering of the Protocol on Social Security Coordination is unaffected.

PART V

UPDATING MATERIAL
VOLUME IV

HMRC-ADMINISTERED SOCIAL SECURITY BENEFITS AND SCOTLAND

Commentary by

Ian Hooker

Edward Mitchell

Mark Rowland

Nick Wikeley

p.xvi, *Contents—heading to Part IIA (Tax credits)*

For the purposes of clarification, delete the heading to Part A "TAX   5.001
CREDITS COMMENCEMENT ORDERS AND TRANSITIONAL
PROVISIONS" and replace with the heading "PROVISIONS FOR
THE ROLL-OUT OF UNIVERSAL CREDIT TO REPLACE TAX
CREDITS".

p.xx, *Contents—Part XIII*

Errata: Five sets of regulations are missing from this part of the list of   5.001A
contents in the main work and one has been wrongly included.
After the seventh entry (SSI 2020/352), insert:

For the last entry (SSI 2020/482), substitute:

p.186, *annotation to the Tax Credits Act 2002 s.14 (Initial decisions)*

*Additional payments under the Social Security (Additional Payments) Act
2022*

Sections 14 to 19 are disapplied in relation to a person who is, or   5.002
persons who are, not entitled to an additional payment under ss.1(2) or
4(1) or (2) of the Social Security (Additional Payments) Act 2022. This
prevents a person from making a request for mandatory reconsideration
of, or appealing against, a decision that the person is not entitled to a
HMRC-administered additional payment. Since the additional payments decision is not a decision taken under the Tax Credits Act 2002,
the usual mechanisms for challenging decisions taken under the Act do
not apply.

The House of Lords' Secondary Legislation Scrutiny Committee
raised concerns that HMRC might seek to recover additional payments
made due to official error (21st Report of Session 2022–23, HL Paper
111, December 8, 2022). HMRC's response was described as follows at
p.3, para.8 of the Committee's report (emphasis in the original):

"HMRC assured us that it will exercise discretion in seeking to recover monies, including if a recipient is experiencing financial hardship. HMRC also said that it has well-established processes to enable repayments to be tailored to a customer's circumstances, for example allowing repayment by instalments over a time period they can manage. HMRC will not reduce the person's underlying tax credit award. *We encourage HMRC to consider carefully whether and how they recover payments made as a result of official error.*"

p.200, *modification of the Tax Credits Act 2002 s.20 (Decisions on discovery)*

5.003   With effect from June 28, 2022, reg.4 of the Tax Credits Act 2002 (Additional Payments Modification and Disapplication) Regulations 2022 (SI 2022/1208) modified s.20 as if after subs.(5) there were inserted:

"(5A) Where the Board have reasonable grounds for believing that an additional payment has been paid to a person, or two persons jointly, by reference to a child tax credit or working tax credit and that the person or persons had no entitlement to the payment, the Board may decide that the additional payment was paid incorrectly.

(5B) But no decision may be made under subsection (5A) after the period of five years beginning with the end of the tax year in which the additional payment is made."

p.202, *annotation to the Tax Credits Act 2002 s.20 (Decisions on discovery)*

5.004   Subsection (5A) permits HMRC to decide that an additional payment made by HMRC under the Social Security (Additional Payments) Act 2022 was paid incorrectly where a person had no entitlement to such a payment. Linked modifications to s.28 of the Act define the incorrect payment as an overpayment so that it may be recovered in the same way as an overpayment of a tax credit.

p.210, *modification of the Tax Credits Act 2002 s.28 (Overpayments)*

5.005   With effect from June 28, 2022, reg.5 of the Tax Credits Act 2002 (Additional Payments Modification and Disapplication) Regulations 2022 (SI 2022/1208) modified s.28 as follows:
(a) in subsection (1)—
    (i) after "sections 18 to 21C)," there were inserted "or where the Commissioners have decided that an additional payment was paid incorrectly,",
    (ii) after "any part of it," there were inserted "or the incorrectly paid additional payment, or any part of it,",
(b) in subsection (2), after "an excess" there were inserted "or incorrectly paid additional payment",

(c) in subsections (3) and (4), after "awarded" there were inserted "or to whom the additional payment was made".

p.212, *annotation to the Tax Credits Act 2002 s.28 (Overpayments)*

Section 20(5) permits HMRC to decide that an additional payment **5.006** under the Social Security (Additional Payments) Act 2022 was paid incorrectly. Modifications made to s.28 treat the incorrect payment as an overpayment, which means that the payment, or part of it, may be recovered from the person to whom it was paid in the same way as an overpayment of tax credit.

p.251, *modification of the Tax Credits Act 2002 s.67 (Interpretation)*

With effect from June 28, 2022, reg.6 of the Tax Credits Act 2002 **5.007** (Additional Payments Modification and Disapplication) Regulations 2022 (SI 2022/1208) modified s.67 as if, at the appropriate place, there were inserted:

""additional payment" means a payment made under section 1(2) or 4(1) or (2) of the Social Security (Additional Payments) Act 2022 or a payment purporting to be a payment under any of those provisions."

p.278, *amendment to the Income Tax (Earnings and Pensions) Act (ITEPA) 2003 s.7(5) (Meaning of "employment income", "general earnings" and "specific employment income")*

With effect from April 6, 2018, s.5(2) of the Finance (No. 2) Act 2017 **5.008** inserted in s.7(5) a new sub-para.(ca) as follows:

"(ca) section 402B (termination payments, and other benefits, that cannot benefit from section 403 threshold),".

p.322, *amendment to the Income Tax (Earnings and Pensions) Act 2003 s.677 (UK social security benefits wholly exempt from tax: Table B)*

With effect from June 1, 2022, for tax year 2021–22 and subsequent **5.009** years subs.(1), Table B—Part 1 (Benefits payable under primary legislation and Northern Ireland Welfare Supplementary Payments), is amended by reg.2 of the Income Tax (Exemption of Social Security Benefits) Regulations 2022 (SI 2022/529), by the addition of the following entry at the appropriate place in Table B—Part 1:

"

Adult Disability Payment	SS(S)A 2018	Sections 24 and 31.

"

p.323, *modification of the Income Tax (Earnings and Pensions) Act 2003 s.677 (UK social security benefits wholly exempt from tax: Table B)*

5.010   With effect from June 1, 2022, for tax year 2021-22 and subsequent years, subs. (1), Table B—Part 1 (Benefits payable under primary legislation and Northern Ireland Welfare Supplementary Payments), is modified by reg.5(a)(i) of the Income Tax (Exemption of Social Security Benefits) Regulations 2022 (SI 2022/529), so that it has effect as of the following entries were inserted at the appropriate places in Table B—Part 1:

"

Payments made under the scheme known as the Council Tax Rebate Discretionary Fund	LGA 2003 Section 31
Payments made pursuant to any scheme or grant in Scotland, Wales or Northern Ireland corresponding to the Council Tax Rebate Discretionary Fund	

"

p.323, *modification of the Income Tax (Earnings and Pensions) Act 2003 s.677 (UK social security benefits wholly exempt from tax: Table B)*

5.011   With effect from June 1, 2022, for tax year 2020–21 and subsequent years, subs.(1), Table B—Part 1 (Benefits payable under primary legislation and Northern Ireland Welfare Supplementary Payments), is modified by reg.5(a)(ii) of the Income Tax (Exemption of Social Security Benefits) Regulations 2022 (SI 2022/529), so that it has effect as if the following entries were inserted at the appropriate places in Table B—Part 1:

"

Payments under the scheme known as the Household Support Fund Grant	LGA 2003 Section 31
Payments made pursuant to any scheme or grant in Scotland, Wales or Northern Ireland corresponding to the Household Support Fund Grant	

"

p.325, *modification of the Income Tax (Earnings and Pensions) Act 2003 s.677 (UK social security benefits wholly exempt from tax: Table B)*

5.012   With effect from June 1, 2022, s.677 is modified by reg.5(b) of the Income Tax (Exemption of Social Security Benefits) Regulations 2022 (SI 2022/529), so that it has effect as if the following were inserted after subs.(3):

"(4) In this section—

(a) "the Council Tax Rebate Discretionary Fund" means the grant that was the subject of guidance published by the Department for Levelling up, Housing and Communities on 23 February 2022 (and as updated from time to time).

(b) "the Household Support Fund Grant" means any grant paid under the Household Support Fund Grant Determination No 31/5787 and subsequent determinations made under section 31 of LGA 2003 to provide support of a similar nature.

(5) References in this section to payments made pursuant to any scheme or grant in Scotland, Wales or Northern Ireland corresponding to any scheme or grant defined in subparagraphs (a) and (b) of section 4 are references only to payments made pursuant to such a scheme or grant for the tax year 2021–22 and subsequent tax years."

p.460, *annotation to the Welfare Reform Act 2012 Sch.6 (Migration to Universal Credit)*

Separate, but inter-linked legislation, prevents certain individuals from making a claim for a tax credit. The most important are the Welfare Reform Act 2012 Commencement Orders Nos 9 (SI 2013/983), 23 (SI 2015/634) and 29 (SI 2017/664), and the Universal Credit (Transitional Provisions) Regulations 2014 (SI 2014/1230). For an explanation of the combined operation of this legislation, see the note to art.14 of the Welfare Reform Act 2012 (Commencement No. 29 and Commencement No. 17, 19, 22, 23 and 24 and Transitional and Transitory Provisions (Modification)) Order 2017 (SI 2017/664), below in this volume.   5.013

p.535, *annotation to the Coronavirus Act 2020 s.1 (Meaning of "coronavirus" and related terminology)*

GENERAL NOTE

The purpose of the Coronavirus Act was to enable the Government to respond to an emergency situation and manage the effects of the Covid-19 pandemic. The Act for the most part contained temporary measures designed either to amend existing legislative provisions or to introduce new statutory powers intended to mitigate these impacts.   5.014

p.536, *annotation to the Coronavirus Act 2020 s.40 (Statutory sick pay: power to disapply waiting period limitation)*

GENERAL NOTE

This section expired with effect from March 25, 2022 (see Coronavirus Act 2020 ss.89 and 90). It enabled regulations to be made disapplying the waiting period for new SSP claims—see further the General Note to the Statutory Sick Pay (Coronavirus) (Suspension of Waiting Days) (Saving Provision) Regulations 2022 (SI 2022/381) in Part I of this Supplement.   5.015

p.536, *annotation to the Coronavirus Act 2020 s.76 (HMRC functions)*

GENERAL NOTE

5.016   This section remains in force at the time of writing. The power to make a direction as conferred by this section may be exercised by means of a notice published in *The Gazette*.

p.539, *heading to Part IIA (Tax credits)*

5.017   For the purposes of clarification, delete the heading to Part A "TAX CREDITS COMMENCEMENT ORDERS AND TRANSITIONAL PROVISIONS" and replace with the heading "PROVISIONS FOR THE ROLL-OUT OF UNIVERSAL CREDIT TO REPLACE TAX CREDITS".

p.548, *amendment to the Welfare Reform Act 2012 (Commencement No.23 and Transitional and Transitory Provisions) Order 2015 (SI 2015/634) art.7 (Transitional provision: claims for housing benefit, income support or a tax credit)*

5.018   With effect from March 30, 2022, art.5 and Sch. para.3 of the Welfare Reform Act 2012 (Commencement No. 34 and Commencement No. 9, 21, 23, 31 and 32 and Transitional and Transitory Provisions (Amendment)) Order 2022 (SI 2022/302) amended art.7(2) by omitting "or by virtue of article 4(11) of the Welfare Reform Act 2012 (Commencement No. 32 and Savings and Transitional Provisions) Order 2019".

pp.548–549, *revocation of the Welfare Reform Act 2012 (Commencement No.23 and Transitional and Transitory Provisions) Order 2015 (SI 2015/634) art.7 (Transitional provision: claims for housing benefit, income support or a tax credit)*

5.019   With effect from July 25, 2022, reg.11 of, and Sch. para.6 to, the Universal Credit (Transitional Provisions) Amendment Regulations 2022 (SI 2022/752) revoked art.7.

p.552, *annotation to the Welfare Reform Act 2012 (Commencement No.29 and Commencement No.17, 19, 22, 23 and 24 and Transitional and Transitory Provisions (Modification)) Order 2017 (SI 2017/664) art.14 (Modification of the No 23 Order: claims for housing benefit, income support or a tax credit)*

5.020   The modifications to earlier commencement orders made by prior articles of this Order removed the requirement for the "gateway conditions" to be met in order for a person living in a designated postcode area to be able to make a claim for universal credit. The result was a significant expansion of the numbers of tax credit recipients to whom the universal credit provisions applied. The next stop in the paper chase is reg.6A of the Universal Credit (Transitional Provisions) Regulations 2014 (SI 2014/1230) (which makes provision previously contained in art.7 of the No. 23 Order (SI 2015/634)). This prevents a person to whom the universal credit provisions apply from making a claim for a tax credit. It is by this route that art.14 of this Order rendered large numbers of tax credits recipients, subject to exceptions, unable to make a new claim for a tax credit.

The transitional picture is further complicated by savings provisions in the Welfare Reform Act 2012 (Commencement No. 32 and Savings and Transitional Provisions) Order 2019 (SI 2019/167) (below in this volume). This Order commences s.33(1)(f) of the Welfare Reform Act 2012, which abolishes tax credits, with effect from February 1, 2019. However, it also includes a number of savings provisions, especially for those with existing awards of tax credits. For those falling within the savings provisions, tax credits are not abolished so that existing awards may be maintained and, provided that a person is not prevented from claiming a tax credit by reg.6A of the Universal Credit (Transitional Provisions) Regulations 2014, new claims may be also made (since tax credits are awarded annually, a new claim is required each year).

p.554, *amendment to the Welfare Reform Act 2012 (Commencement No. 32 and Savings and Transitional Provisions) Order 2019 (SI 2019/167) art.1 (Citation and interpretation)*

With effect from March 30, 2022, art.4(3) of the Welfare Reform Act   5.021
2012 (Commencement No. 34 and Commencement No. 9, 21, 23, 31 and 32 and Transitional and Transitory Provisions (Amendment)) Order 2022 (SI 2022/302) amended art.1 by omitting para.(3).

p.557, *amendment to the Welfare Reform Act 2012 (Commencement No. 32 and Savings and Transitional Provisions) Order 2019 (SI 2019/167) art.4 (Appointed day—coming into force of universal credit provisions and abolition of income-related employment and support allowance and income-based jobseeker's allowance: persons resident outside Great Britain)*

With effect from March 30, 2022, art.4(4) of the Welfare Reform Act   5.022
2012 (Commencement No. 34 and Commencement No. 9, 21, 23, 31 and 32 and Transitional and Transitory Provisions (Amendment)) Order 2022 (SI 2022/302) amended art.4 by omitting para.(11).

p.560, *annotation to the Welfare Reform Act 2012 (Commencement No. 32 and Savings and Transitional Provisions) Order 2019 (SI 2019/167) art.5 (Amendment of the No. 9, No. 21 and No. 23 Orders)*

Cases 2 and 3—persons who may claim Universal Credit

Cases 2 and 3 refer to a person who may claim UC. The Universal   5.023
Credit (Transitional Provisions) Regulations 2014 (SI 2014/1230) set out the categories of person who are capable of claiming UC. The general rule is that a person who is able to make a claim for UC is unable to claim a tax credit (reg.6A of the 2014 Regulations).

p.566, *revocation of the Universal Credit (Transitional Provisions) Regulations 2014 (SI 2014/1230) reg.4 (Secretary of State discretion to determine that claims for universal credit may not be made)*

5.024   With effect from July 25, 2022, reg.2 of the Universal Credit (Transitional Provisions) Amendment Regulations 2022 (SI 2022/752) revoked reg.4.

pp.567–568, *revocation of the Universal Credit (Transitional Provisions) Regulations 2014 (SI 2014/1230) reg.6 (Exclusion of claims for certain existing benefits)*

5.025   With effect from July 25, 2022, reg.3 of the Universal Credit (Transitional Provisions) Amendment Regulations 2022 (SI 2022/752) revoked reg.6.

p.569, *insertion of the Universal Credit (Transitional Provisions) Regulations 2014 (SI 2014/1230) reg.6A (Restriction on claims for housing benefit, income support or a tax credit)*

5.026   With effect from July 25, 2022, reg.4 of the Universal Credit (Transitional Provisions) Amendment Regulations 2022 (SI 2022/752) inserted a new reg.6A immediately before reg.7 (Termination of awards of certain existing benefits: new claimant partners):

"Restriction on claims for housing benefit, income support or a tax credit

6A.—(1) Except as provided by paragraphs (2) to (7) a person may not make a claim for housing benefit, income support, or a tax credit.

(2) Paragraph (1) does not apply to a claim for housing benefit in respect of specified accommodation or temporary accommodation.

(3) Paragraph (1) does not apply to a claim for housing benefit that is made during the last assessment period of an award of universal credit, where the claimant reaches the qualifying age for state pension credit and paragraph 26 of Schedule 1 to the Decisions and Appeals Regulations applies, in respect of entitlement arising from the date the claimant reaches that age.

(4) Paragraph (1) does not apply to a claim for housing benefit by a single person who has reached the qualifying age for state pension credit, or a member of a State Pension Credit Act couple where both members have reached that age or a member of a polygamous marriage where all members have reached that age.

(5) Paragraph (1) does not apply to a claim for housing benefit where—

(a) the claim is made by a member of a State Pension Credit Act couple who has reached the qualifying age for state pension credit and the other member has not reached that age; and

168

(b) one of the savings in the sub-paragraphs of article 4(1) of the Welfare Reform Act 2012 (Commencement No. 31 and Savings and Transitional Provisions and Commencement No. 21 and 23 and Transitional and Transitory Provisions (Amendment)) Order 2019 applies and the saving has not ceased to have effect under article 4(2) of that Order.

(6) Paragraph (1) does not apply to a claim for a tax credit where a person makes or persons make a claim for child tax credit or working tax credit and on the date on which he or she (or they) makes or make the claim he or she (or they) has or have an award of working tax credit or child tax credit respectively.

(7) Paragraph (1) does not apply to a claim for a tax credit where a person has or had, or persons have or had, an award of child tax credit or working tax credit in respect of a tax year and that person or those persons makes or make (or is or are treated as making) a claim for that tax credit for the next tax year.

(8) For the purposes of this regulation—

(a) "polygamous marriage" has the same meaning as in regulation 3(5) of the Universal Credit Regulations;

(b) "State Pension Credit Act couple" means a couple as defined in section 17(1) of the State Pension Credit Act 2002,

and a reference to the date on which a claim for a tax credit is made is a reference to the date on which such claim is made or treated as made as provided for in the Tax Credits (Claims and Notifications) Regulations 2002."

p.569, *annotation to the Universal Credit (Transitional Provisions) Regulations (SI 2022/752), reg.6A (Restriction on claims for housing benefit, income support or a tax credit)*

Paragraph (1) enacts the general rule that no one may make a claim for a tax credit. The general rule is subject to two exceptions. Firstly, where, at the date of claim, the person (or couple) has an award of a tax credit (reg.6A(6)). According to HMRC, this allows tax credit awards to continue to be renewed annually pending a claimant's transfer to Universal Credit. Secondly, where a person (or couple) has or had an award of a tax credit for a particular tax year and makes (or is treated as making) a claim for the same type of tax credit for the next tax year (reg.6A(7)). 5.027

Regulation 6A is a re-enactment of much of art.7 of the Welfare Reform Act 2012 (Commencement No. 23 and Transitional and Transitory Provisions) Order 2015 (SI 2015/634). The provisions were relocated to the main transitional regulations in order to "simplify and improve the legislative position so it can be read in conjunction with the other provisions relating to the transition to UC" (Explanatory Memorandum to the amending instrument, SI 2022/752).

Regulation 6A(7) re-enacts without alteration art.7(6) of the 2015 Order. Accordingly, Upper Tribunal Judge Mitchell's construction of the provision in *W v HMRC* (TC) [2020] UKUT 239 (AAC) remains applicable. Judge Mitchell held that the exception in art.7(6) (now reg.6A(7)) was not satisfied where a person whose original award was as a member of a couple subsequently claimed a tax credit as a single person:

"11 . . . After the introductory injunction ('paragraph (1) does not apply to a claim for a tax credit'), Article 7(6) contains two components whose purpose is to identify the class of individuals that benefit from that injunction:

    (a) the first component identifies a wide class comprised of two groups: (i) a person who has or had an award of a tax credit; and (ii) persons who have or had an award of tax credit;

    (b) the second component narrows down that wide class. In doing so, it maintains, and operates on, the distinction drawn by the first component between sole and joint claimants, as is shown by it use of the referential pronouns 'that' and 'those'.

For a person within group (i) under what I have described as the first component, 'that person' must make a claim for tax credit for the next tax year to avoid being filtered out of article 7(6) [now regulation 6A(7)]. For persons within group (ii), 'those persons' must make a claim.

12. A person in Mr W's position, that is a person residing in a UC 'Full Service Area' who jointly claimed a tax credit in the previous tax year, will only benefit from article 7(6) [now regulation 6A(7)] if he re-claims together with the previous year's partner."

The issue in *HMRC v RS (No.2)* [2022] UKUT 246 (AAC) was the meaning of "for the next tax year", a component of the exception provided for by reg.6A(7) (the issue arose under art.7 of the No. 23 commencement order but, as mentioned above, that provision was relocated to reg.6A(7)). In particular, whether a claim made part-way through a tax year was made "for the next tax year". The claimant had a tax credit award for 2018/19, which terminated with effect from June 26, 2019, and he made a new claim on August 1, 2019; the question was whether that claim was made for 2019/20, which was the "next tax year". Upper Tribunal Judge Wikeley held that it was not so that the claimant did not satisfy the exception. A tax year runs from April 6 in one calendar year to April 5 in the next year (Tax Credits Act 2002 s.48). The legislative intention, therefore, must have been that the phrase "for the next tax year" meant the whole of the next tax year. Since the claimant had not made a claim for the (whole of) the next tax year, he fell outside the exception and was therefore caught by the general legislative prohibition on new claims being made for tax credits.

p.569, *amendments to the Universal Credit (Transitional Provisions) Regulations 2014 (SI 2014/1230) reg.7 (Termination of awards of certain existing benefits: new claimant partners)*

5.028   With effect from July 25, 2022, reg.5(2) of the Universal Credit (Transitional Provisions) Amendment Regulations 2022 (SI 2022/752) amended reg.7(1) by inserting "and" at the end of sub-para.(b) and omitting sub-para.(d) together with the "and" preceding it.

pp.569–570, *amendments to the Universal Credit (Transitional Provisions) Regulations 2014 (SI 2014/1230) reg.8 (Termination of awards of certain existing benefits: other claimants)*

With effect from July 25, 2022, reg.5(3) of the Universal Credit   5.029
(Transitional Provisions) Amendment Regulations 2022 (SI 2022/752) amended reg.8 by (1) inserting ", whether or not subsequently withdrawn" after "is made" in para.(1)(a); (2) omitting sub-para.(b) and the "and" preceding it; and (3) inserting after para.(2A):

> "(2B) This regulation does not apply in the case of a single claimant who has reached the qualifying age for state pension credit or in the case of joint claimants who have both reached the qualifying age for state pension credit."

p.570, *annotation to the Universal Credit (Transitional Provisions) Regulations 2014 (SI 2014/1230), reg.8 (Termination of awards of certain existing benefits: other claimants)*

As originally enacted, reg.8 made its termination of entitlement to a   5.030
tax credit, consequent on the making of a Universal Credit (UC) claim, conditional on a Secretary of State determination that an individual satisfied the UC basic conditions specified in reg.8(1)(b). Since July 25, 2022, at which date reg.8(1)(b) was revoked, no such determination has been required.

In *HMRC v SSWP and SA (TC)* [2022] UKUT 350 (AAC), a three-judge panel of the Upper Tribunal considered the pre-July 25, 2022 requirement for the Secretary of State to be satisfied that a claimant met the UC basic conditions specified in reg.8(1)(b). The basic condition in question required a person to be "in Great Britain" (Welfare Reform Act 2012 s.4(1)(c)). Whether a person is "in Great Britain" is determined in accordance with reg.9 of the Universal Credit Regulations 2013 which requires a person to have a qualifying right to reside in the UK (or certain islands). The issue was whether the First-tier Tribunal, on an appeal consequent on a reg.8 termination of benefit, would consider whether the Secretary of State had been entitled to determine that a claimant met the UC basic conditions or if it was restricted to considering whether, in fact, the Secretary of State had been satisfied that the conditions were met. Given the complexities of right to reside law, it would often not be obvious whether the Secretary of State had been entitled to determine that a claimant was "in Great Britain". The Upper Tribunal held that the First-tier Tribunal could not decide if the Secretary of State had been entitled to make a particular UC basic conditions determination. That would involve reading words into reg.8(1)(b) for which there was no justification. The only issue for the tribunal is one of fact—did the Secretary of State make a UC basic conditions determination. Typically, this will be evidenced by the "stop notice" used by the DWP to inform HMRC of a reg.8(1) determination.

The three-judge panel in *SA* disapproved Upper Tribunal Judge Poynter's observation in *MR v HMRC* (TC) (CTC/923/2018) that if, following termination of benefit under reg.8, the Secretary of State decided that a claimant was not, after all, entitled to UC, that would tend to show that the Secretary of State had not been satisfied, for reg.8(1)(b) purposes, that the basic conditions were satisfied. Under the three-judge panel's decision, the only issue is one of pure fact namely whether the Secretary of State determined that the UC basic conditions were met, and no qualitative considerations arise.

As originally enacted, reg.8(1)(a) said nothing about withdrawal of a UC claim. As subsequently amended, reg.8(1)(a) expressly provides that withdrawal of a UC claim makes no difference to its application. Therefore, the Upper Tribunal decisions considered below, about the legal consequences for reg.8 of withdrawal, or purported withdrawal, of UC claims, are only relevant to the operation of reg.8 before July 25, 2022.

In *HMRC v AB* [2021] UKUT 209 (AAC), HMRC accepted that a claimant withdrew her UC claim before the Secretary of State had determined whether the UC basic conditions were met. HMRC argued that withdrawal of the claim made no difference to the operation of reg.8 so that, despite withdrawal, the subsequent determination that the UC basic conditions were met triggered reg.8(2) and terminated entitlement to tax credits. Upper Tribunal Judge Mitchell rejected HMRC's argument and held that, if a UC claim were withdrawn before the Secretary of State had made a UC basic conditions determination under reg.8(1)(b), reg.8(2) did not operate to terminate entitlement to a tax credit.

In *JL v Calderdale MBC and SSWP* [2022] UKUT 9 (AAC) the claimant attempted to withdraw his UC claim about three hours after it was made online. By that time, the DWP's computer systems had already accepted that the claimant met the UC basic conditions and notified the local authority responsible for the claimant's housing benefit award. The local authority decided that, under reg.8(2), the claimant's housing benefit award had been terminated. Upper Tribunal Judge Jacobs held that a DWP computer made a valid computerised determination that the UC basic conditions were met (s.2 of the Social Security Act 1998 provides authority, in certain circumstances, for decisions and determinations to be made by a computer). In other words, the claimant was too late. When he attempted to withdraw his UC claim, a determination had already been made that the UC basic conditions were met, and the UC claim could not be withdrawn because a determination had been made on it (reg.31(1) of the Universal Credit [etc.] (Claims and Payments) Regulations 2013). Judge Jacobs' related decision in *SK v HMRC and SSWP* [2022] UKUT 10 (AAC) describes the DWP's evidence about their computerised decision/determination-making processes. If that evidence is accepted, as it was in *SK*, it follows that "the making of the claim and the determination under regulation 8(1)(b) take effect simultaneously through the universal credit system". On this approach, a claimant has no opportunity to withdraw a UC claim before a UC basic conditions determination is made and there was no need for reg.8(1) to have been amended to provide that withdrawal of a UC claim has no effect on the operation of reg.8.

In *HMRC v SSWP v GS* [2023] UKUT 9 (AAC), Upper Tribunal Judge West approached the decisions in *AB* and *SK* on the basis that they were in conflict, and it was necessary to choose which one to follow. However, that was not strictly accurate. The difference between the decisions was evidential or factual rather than principled. *AB* proceeded on the agreed factual basis that a UC claim was in fact withdrawn *before* a UC basic conditions determination had been made. By contrast, *SK* involved an attempt to withdraw a UC claim *after* a basic conditions determination had been made. *SK* did not address the legal consequences of withdrawal of a UC claim in advance of a UC basic conditions determination because the judge accepted evidence that this was impossible under the DWP's computerised decision-making arrangements. Be that as it may, Judge West said that *SK* and *AB* were inconsistent decisions and that he would follow *SK* because it was more recent decision and a cogent reason for not following *SK* was absent. The judge said that this approach was mandated by the Court of Appeal in *Re Lune Metal Products Ltd* [2006] EWCA Civ 1720, although that decision dealt with the case "where a first instance judge is faced with a point on which there are two previous inconsistent decisions from judges of co-ordinate jurisdiction". In fact, there are conflicting decisions as to whether this approach to choosing between inconsistent decisions applies in the jurisdiction now exercised by the Upper Tribunal (in *CIS/3101/2007* Social Security Commissioner Jacobs thought not; in *R(IS) 13/01* Social Security Commissioner Rowland thought it did apply).

Regulation 8 does not apply to single claimants who have reached the qualifying age for state pension credit or joint claimants both of whom have reached that age (reg.8(2B)).

p.574, *amendments to the Universal Credit (Transitional Provisions) Regulations 2014 (SI 2014/1230) reg.12 (Modification of tax credits legislation: overpayments and penalties)*

With effect from July 25, 2022, reg.5(4) of the Universal Credit   5.031
(Transitional Provisions) Amendment Regulations 2022 (SI 2022/752) amended reg.12(1) by inserting "and" at the end of sub-para.(a) and omitting sub-para.(c) together with the "and" preceding it.

p.575, *amendments to the Universal Credit (Transitional Provisions) Regulations 2014 (SI 2014/1230) reg.12A (Modification of tax credits legislation: finalisation of tax credits)*

With effect from July 25, 2022, reg.5(5) of the Universal Credit   5.032
(Transitional Provisions) Amendment Regulations 2022 (SI 2022/752) amended reg.12A(1) by inserting "and" at the end of sub-para.(a) and omitting sub-para.(c) together with the "and" preceding it.

p.582, *amendment to the Universal Credit (Transitional Provisions) Regulations 2014 (SI 2014/1230) reg.44 (Migration notice)*

5.033 With effect from July 25, 2022, reg.11 of, and Sch. para.1(7) to, the Universal Credit (Transitional Provisions) Amendment Regulations 2022 (SI 2022/752) inserted "or" at the end of para.(5)(a) and omitted para.(5)(b).

p.583, *annotation to the Universal Credit (Transitional Provisions) Regulations 2014 (SI 2014/1230) reg.44 (Migration notice)*

5.034 Regulation 2 of the Universal Credit (Managed Migration Pilot and Miscellaneous Amendments) Regulations 2019 (SI 2019/1152), limiting the number of cases migrated to a maximum of 10,000 awards was revoked with effect from July 25, 2022, by reg.10 of the Universal Credit (Transitional Provisions) Amendment Regulations 2022 (SI 2022/752).

p.584, *amendment to the Universal Credit (Transitional Provisions) Regulations 2014 (SI 2014/1230) reg.46 (Termination of existing benefits if no claim before the deadline)*

5.035 With effect from July 25, 2022, reg.11 of, and Sch. para.1(8) to, the Universal Credit (Transitional Provisions) Amendment Regulations 2022 (SI 2022/752) omitted para.(5).

pp.584–585, *revocation of the Universal Credit (Transitional Provisions) Regulations 2014 (SI 2014/1230) reg.47 (Notified persons who claim as a different benefit unit)*

5.036 With effect from July 25, 2022, reg.6(1) of the Universal Credit (Transitional Provisions) Amendment Regulations 2022 (SI 2022/752) revoked reg.47.

p.585, *annotation to the Universal Credit (Transitional Provisions) Regulations 2014 (SI 2014/230) reg.47 (Notified persons who claim as a different benefit unit)*

5.037 Regulation 47 dealt with claimants who were part of a couple upon receipt of a managed migration notice, but who had become single claimants, or members of a different couple, by the time that Universal Credit (UC) was claimed. For instance, where the couple had separated by the time of the UC claim or where claimants had been treated as a couple for tax credits purposes but single for UC purposes. In such cases, existing entitlements of both members of the original couple ceased upon either one of them claiming UC.

With effect from 25 July 2022, reg.47 was revoked. The reason for its revocation was described as follows by the Explanatory Memorandum that accompanied the amendment regulations:

174

"The [original provision] does not align with the current treatment of cases of natural migration following couple separation. In these situations, where one of the separated couple makes a single claim for UC, their ex-partner (provided they were the lead claimant for their legacy benefit) will remain entitled to their existing benefits which will be reassessed for them as single awards. The removal of regulation 47 . . . means that there will be consistency between when couples separate and naturally claim UC due to the change of circumstance and the position for couples who separate after being issued with a migration notice. In both cases, the claimant who is receiving the benefit payments can remain on that benefit until they make a new Universal Credit (UC) claim."

p.586, *amendment to the Universal Credit (Transitional Provisions) Regulations 2014 (SI 2014/1230) reg.50 (Secretary of State to determine whether transitional protection applies)*

With effect from July 25, 2022, reg.6(2) of the Universal Credit (Transitional Provisions) Amendment Regulations 2022 (SI 2022/752) amended reg.50(2) by deleting "where regulation 47 (notified persons who claim as a different benefit unit) applies" and substituting: **5.038**

"where—
   (a) notified persons who were a couple for the purposes of an award of an existing benefit when the migration notice was issued are single persons or members of a different couple for the purposes of a claim for universal credit; or
   (b) notified persons who were single for the purposes of an award of an existing benefit when the migration notice was issued are a couple for the purposes of a claim for universal credit; or
   (c) notified persons who were members of a polygamous marriage for the purposes of an award of an existing benefit when the migration notice was issued are a couple or single persons for the purposes of a claim for universal credit."

p.590, *amendment to the Universal Credit (Transitional Provisions) Regulations 2014 (SI 2014/1230) reg.55 (The transitional element—initial amount and adjustment where other elements increase)*

With effect from July 25, 2022, reg.7 of the Universal Credit (Transitional Provisions) Amendment Regulations 2022 (SI 2022/752) amended reg.55 by inserting ", subject to paragraph (5)," after ""relevant increase" is" in para.(4) and after the end of para.(4) inserting the following new paragraphs: **5.039**

"(5) In cases where the LCW element is replaced by the LCWRA element, the "relevant increase" is to be treated as the difference between the amounts of those elements.
   (6) In this regulation, "LCW element" and "LCWRA element" have the same meaning as in regulation 2 of the Universal Credit Regulations."

p.594, amendment to the Universal Credit (Transitional Provisions) Regulations 2014 (SI 2014/1230) reg.58 (Qualifying claim—Secretary of State may set later commencement day)

5.040   With effect from July 25, 2022, reg.11 of, and Sch. para.1(9) to, the Universal Credit (Transitional Provisions) Amendment Regulations 2022 (SI 2022/752) omitted "or 47(4)".

p.595, amendment to the Universal Credit (Transitional Provisions) Regulations 2014 (SI 2014/1230) reg.60 (Protection for full-time students until course completed)

5.041   With effect from July 25, 2022, reg.8 of the Universal Credit (Transitional Provisions) Amendment Regulations 2022 (SI 2022/752) amended reg.60 such that the existing text becomes para.(1) and after para.(1) is inserted:

> "(2) Paragraph (1) does not apply to any assessment period in respect of which a transitional element or transitional capital disregard would (if the claimant had been entitled to that element or that disregard) have ceased to apply by virtue of regulation 56 (circumstances in which transitional protection ceases) or regulation 57 (application of transitional protection to a subsequent award)."

p.595, annotation to the Universal Credit (Transitional Provisions) Regulations 2014 (SI 2014/1230) reg.60 (Protection for full-time students until course completed)

5.042   Regulation 60(2), effective from July 25, 2022, prevents the student exemption under reg.60(1) from being reapplied if a student's Universal Credit award ends, unless the claimant would continue to qualify for transitional protection. It also has the effect of removing the student exemption in circumstances which would, in other migration cases, bring to an end the Transitional Element and Transitional Capital Disregard provided for by these Regulations.

p.596, revocation of the Universal Credit (Transitional Provisions) Regulations 2014 (SI 2014/1230) reg.64 (Discretionary hardship payments)

5.043   With effect from July 25, 2022, reg.9 of the Universal Credit (Transitional Provisions) Amendment Regulations 2022 (SI 2022/752) revoked reg.64.

p.612, amendment to the Working Tax Credit (Entitlement and Maximum Rate) Regulations 2002 (SI 2002/2005) reg.4(1A) (Entitlement to basic element of working tax credit: qualifying remunerative work)

5.044   With effect from June 9, 2022, reg.5(2) of the Tax Credits and Child Benefit (Miscellaneous Amendments) Regulations 2022 (SI 2022/555) amended reg.4(1A) by omitting sub-paras (c) and (da).

p.625, *amendment to the Working Tax Credit (Entitlement and Maximum Rate) Regulations 2002 (SI 2002/2005) reg.7D (Ceasing to undertake work or working for less than 16, 24 or 30 hours per week)*

With effect from June 9, 2022, reg.5(3) of the Tax Credits and Child Benefit (Miscellaneous Amendments) Regulations 2022 (SI 2022/555) amended reg.7D by omitting reg.7D(3). **5.045**

pp.626–630, *repeal of the Working Tax Credit (Entitlement and Maximum Rate) Regulations 2002 (SI 2002/2005) reg.7E (Alteration in hours worked due to coronavirus)*

With effect from June 9, 2022, reg.5(4) of the Tax Credits and Child Benefit (Miscellaneous Amendments) Regulations 2022 (SI 2022/555) repealed reg.7E. **5.046**

pp.637–638, *amendments to the Working Tax Credit (Entitlement and Maximum Rate) Regulations 2002 (SI 2002/2005) reg.10 (30 hour element)*

With effect from June 9, 2022, reg.5(5) of the Tax Credits and Child Benefit (Miscellaneous Amendments) Regulations 2022 (SI 2022/555) omitted the words ", except where paragraph (4) applies" in para.(1) and omitted paras (4) and (5). **5.047**

pp.643–646, *amendments to the Working Tax Credit (Entitlement and Maximum Rate) Regulations 2002 (SI 2002/2005) reg.14 (Entitlement to child care element of working tax credit)*

With effect from June 9, 2022, reg.5(6) of the Tax Credits and Child Benefit (Miscellaneous Amendments) Regulations 2022 (SI 2022/555) made the following amendments to reg.14: **5.048**
- (a) in para.(1A)(d), for "Article 5(3)(d) of the Tax Credits (Approval of Child Care Providers)(Wales) Scheme 2007" substituted "Article 5(2)(d) of The Approval of Home Childcare Providers (Wales) Scheme 2021";
- (b) in para.(1B)(c), in the definition of "foster parent":
  - (i) in the definition for England in sub-para.(i), for "the Fostering Services Regulations 2002" substituted "the Care Planning, Placement and Case Review (England) Regulations 2010";
  - (ii) in the definition for Wales in sub-para.(ii) for "the Fostering Service (Wales) Regulations 2003", substituted "the Care Planning, Placement and Case Review (Wales) Regulations 2015";
- (c) in para.(2)(f)(vii), omitted the words "the Tax Credits (Approval of Child Care Providers) (Wales) Scheme 2007 or", and
- (d) in para.(2D)(b), omitted the words "the Tax Credits (Approval of Child Care Providers)(Wales) Scheme 2007 or".

p.649, *annotation to the Working Tax Credit (Entitlement and Maximum Rate) Regulations 2002 (SI 2002/2005) reg.14 (Entitlement to child care element of working tax credit)*

5.049 The paragraph beginning "With regard to reg.14(2)(f) . . . " is to be omitted.

p.719, *amendment to the Tax Credits (Definition and Calculation of Income) Regulations 2002 (SI 2002/2006) reg.19 (General disregards in the calculation of income)*

5.050 With effect from July 1, 2022, reg.99 of and the Sch. to the Health and Care Act 2022 (Consequential and Related Amendments and Transitional Provisions) Regulations 2022 (SI 2022/634) substituted "an integrated care board established under Chapter A3 of Part 2 of the National Health Service Act 2006" for "a clinical commissioning group established under section 14D of the National Health Service Act 2006" in Table 8 item 3(da).

p.780, *amendments to the Tax Credits (Claims and Notifications) Regulations 2002 (SI 2002/2014) reg.2 (Interpretation)*

5.051 With effect from June 9, 2022, reg.6(2) of the Tax Credits and Child Benefit (Miscellaneous Amendments) Regulations 2022 (SI 2022/555) amended reg.1 by omitting the definitions of "Coronavirus Job Retention Scheme" and "critical worker".

p.785, *annotation to the Tax Credits (Claims and Notifications) Regulations 2002 (SI 2002/2014) reg.5 (Manner in which claims to be made)*

5.052 In *HMRC v RS (No.2)* [2022] UKUT 246 (AAC), the Upper Tribunal was informed that, in consequence of the migration of tax credit claimants to Universal Credit, HMRC have not produced an approved tax credits claim form since the 2018/19 tax year. In relation to that (dwindling) category of individuals who remain entitled to claim a tax credit, HMRC has exercised its discretion under reg.5(2)(b) to permit claims to be made by telephone. Upper Tribunal Judge Wikeley observed that, given the altered claims landscape under which written claims no longer appear to be a feasible option, the issue determined in in *MK* might need to be revisited in the light of current circumstances.

pp.791–792, *amendments to the Tax Credits (Claims and Notifications) Regulations 2002 (SI 2002/2014) reg.11 (Circumstances in which claims to be treated as—notices containing provision under section 17(2)(a), 4(a) or 6(a) of the Act)*

5.053 With effect from June 9, 2022, reg.6(3) of the Tax Credits and Child Benefit (Miscellaneous Amendments) Regulations 2022 (SI 2022/555) amended reg.11(3) by (i) inserting "or" at the end of sub-para.(b); (ii) substituting "." for "; or" at the end of sub-para.(c); and (iii) omitting sub-para.(d).

p.793, *annotation to the Tax Credits (Claims and Notifications) Regulations 2002 (SI 2002/2014) reg.11 (Circumstances in which claims to be treated as made—notices containing provision under section 17(2)(a), (4)(a) or (6)(a) of the Act)*

As originally enacted, para.(3)(d) contained a sweep-up provision 5.054 which provided for a late declaration to a s.17 notice to be treated as a new claim. With effect from June 9, 2022, this provision was revoked since, generally, no new claims to tax credits have been permitted since March 30, 2022.

p.800, *amendments to the Tax Credits (Claims and Notifications) Regulations 2002 (SI 2002/2014) reg.21 (Requirement to notify changes of circumstances which may decrease the rate at which a person or persons is or are entitled to tax credit or mean that entitlement ceases)*

With effect from June 9, 2022, reg.6(4) of the Tax Credits and Child 5.055 Benefit (Miscellaneous Amendments) Regulations 2022 (SI 2022/555) amended reg.21 by omitting para.(4).

pp.802–803, *repeal of the Tax Credits (Claims and Notifications) Regulations 2002 (SI 2002/2014) reg.21A (Coronavirus—date of notification—cases where change of circumstances which may decrease the rate at which a person is, or persons are, entitled to tax credit or mean entitlement to that tax credit ceases)*

With effect from June 9, 2022, reg.6(5) of the Tax Credits and Child 5.056 Benefit (Miscellaneous Amendments) Regulations 2022 (SI 2022/555) repealed reg.21A.

p.805, *amendment to the Tax Credits (Claims and Notifications) Regulations 2002 (SI 2002/2014) reg.25 (Date of notification—cases where change of circumstances which may increase the maximum rate)*

With effect from June 9, 2022, reg.6(6) of the Tax Credits and Child 5.057 Benefit (Miscellaneous Amendments) Regulations 2022 (SI 2022/555) amended reg.25 by omitting para.(4).

p.805, *annotation to the Tax Credits (Claims and Notifications) Regulations 2002 (SI 2002/2014) reg.25 (Date of notification—cases where change of circumstances which may increase the maximum rate)*

The words "(unless the claimant is a critical worker who satisfies the 5.058 requirements of regulation 25A)" are to be omitted.

pp.805–806, *repeal of the Tax Credits (Claims and Notifications) Regulations 2002 (SI 2002/2014) reg.25A (Coronavirus—date of notification—cases where change of circumstances may increase the maximum rate)*

5.059   With effect from June 9, 2022, reg.6(7) of the Tax Credits and Child Benefit (Miscellaneous Amendments) Regulations 2022 (SI 2022/555) repealed reg.25A.

p.806, *amendment to the Tax Credits (Claims and Notifications) Regulations 2002 (SI 2002/2014) reg.26 (Date of notification—disability element and severe disability element of working tax credit)*

5.060   With effect from June 9, 2022, reg.6(8) of the Tax Credits and Child Benefit (Miscellaneous Amendments) Regulations 2022 (SI 2022/555) amended reg.26 by omitting para.(4).

p.807, *amendment to the Tax Credits (Claims and Notifications) Regulations 2002 (SI 2002/2014) reg.26A (Date of notification—disability element where child is disabled or severely disabled)*

5.061   With effect from June 9, 2022, reg.6(9) of the Tax Credits and Child Benefit (Miscellaneous Amendments) Regulations 2022 (SI 2022/555) amended reg.26A by omitting para.(5).

pp.808–809, *repeal of the Tax Credits (Claims and Notifications) Regulations 2002 (SI 2002/2014) reg.26B (Coronavirus—date of notification of disability)*

5.062   With effect from June 9, 2022, reg.6(10) of the Tax Credits and Child Benefit (Miscellaneous Amendments) Regulations 2022 (SI 2022/555) repealed reg.26B.

p.817, *amendment to the Tax Credits (Payments by the Commissioners) Regulations 2002 (SI 2002/2173) reg.3 (Child tax credit and child care element—member of a couple prescribed for the purposes of section 24(2) of the Act)*

5.063   With effect from June 9, 2022, reg.7 of the Tax Credits and Child Benefit (Miscellaneous Amendments) Regulations 2022 (SI 2022/555) amended reg.3 by substitute "twenty" for "nineteen" in para.(5)(a).

p.944, *amendment to the Statutory Sick Pay (General) Regulations 1982 (SI 1982/894) reg.2 (Persons deemed incapable of work)*

5.064   With effect from March 25, 2022, reg.2(2) of the Statutory Sick Pay (General) (Coronavirus Amendment) Regulations 2022 (SI 2022/380) inserted "or" in sub-para.(1)(a)(iii), after the words "contract of service," and omitted sub-paras (c) and (d).

p.945, *amendment to the Statutory Sick Pay (General) Regulations 1982 (SI 1982/894) reg.2 (Persons deemed incapable of work)*

With effect from March 25, 2022, reg.2(3) of the Statutory Sick Pay (General) (Coronavirus Amendment) Regulations 2022 (SI 2022/380) omitted para.(4).   **5.065**

pp.966–971, *amendments to the Statutory Sick Pay (General) Regulations 1982 (SI 1982/894) Schs 1 and 2 (Isolation due to coronavirus and Shielding due to coronavirus)*

With effect from March 25, 2022, reg.2(4) of the Statutory Sick Pay (General) (Coronavirus Amendment) Regulations 2022 (SI 2022/380) omitted Schs 1 and 2.   **5.066**

p.979, *amendments to the Statutory Sick Pay (Medical Evidence) Regulations 1985 (SI 1985/1604) reg.1 (Citation, commencement and interpretation)*

With effect from July 1, 2022, reg.3(2) of the Social Security (Medical Evidence) and Statutory Sick Pay (Medical Evidence) (Amendment) (No. 2) Regulations 2022 (SI 2022/630) amended reg.1(2) by inserting after the definition of the "1992 Act" the following new definition: **5.067**

""healthcare professional" means a person, not being the patient, who is—
  (a) a registered medical practitioner;
  (b) a registered nurse;
  (c) a registered occupational therapist or registered physiotherapist;
  (d) a registered pharmacist within the meaning of article 3 of the Pharmacy Order 2010;".

With effect from April 6, 2022, reg.3(2) of the Social Security (Medical Evidence) and Statutory Sick Pay (Medical Evidence) (Amendment) Regulations 2022 (SI 2022/298) amended reg.1(2) by omitting "; and "signed" shall be construed accordingly" in the definition of "signature".

p.979, *amendment to the Statutory Sick Pay (Medical Evidence) Regulations 1985 (SI 1985/1604) reg.2 (Medical information)*

With effect from July 1, 2022, reg.3(3) of the Social Security (Medical Evidence) and Statutory Sick Pay (Medical Evidence) (Amendment) (No. 2) Regulations 2022 (SI 2022/630) amended reg.2(1)(a) by substituting "healthcare professional" for "doctor".   **5.068**

pp.980–981, *amendment to the Statutory Sick Pay (Medical Evidence) Regulations 1985 (SI 1985/1604) Sch.1 Pt 1*

With effect from April 6, 2022, reg.3(3)–(5) of the Social Security (Medical Evidence) and Statutory Sick Pay (Medical Evidence)   **5.069**

181

(Amendment) Regulations 2022 (SI 2022/298) and with effect from July 1, 2022, reg.3(4)–(17) of the Social Security (Medical Evidence) and Statutory Sick Pay (Medical Evidence) (Amendment) (No. 2) Regulations 2022 (SI 2022/630) both amended Sch.1 so that it now reads as follows:

"SCHEDULE 1

Part 1

Rules

1. In these rules, unless the context otherwise requires—

"assessment" means either a consultation between a patient and a healthcare professional which takes place in person or by telephone or a consideration by a healthcare professional of a written report by another healthcare professional or other health professional;
"condition" means a specific disease or bodily or mental disability;
"other health professional" means a person (other than a healthcare professional and not being the patient) who is a registered midwife, or a member of any profession regulated by a body mentioned in section 25(3) of the National Health Service Reform and Health Care Professions Act 2002;
"patient" means the person in respect of whom a statement is given in accordance with these rules.

2. Where a healthcare professional issues a statement to a patient in accordance with an obligation arising under a contract, agreement or arrangement under Part 4 of the National Health Service Act 2006 or Part 4 of the National Health Service (Wales) Act 2006 or Part 1 of the National Health Service (Scotland) Act 19783 the healthcare professional's statement shall be in a form set out at Part 2 or Part 2A of this Schedule.

3. Where a healthcare professional issues a statement in any case other than in accordance with rule 2, the healthcare professional's statement shall be in the form set out in Part 2 or Part 2A of this Schedule or in a form to like effect.

4. A healthcare professional's statement must be based on an assessment made by that healthcare professional.

5. A healthcare professional's statement shall contain the following particulars—
(a) the patient's name;
(b) the date of the assessment (whether by consultation or consideration of a report as the case may be) on which the healthcare professional's statement is based;
(c) the condition in respect of which the healthcare professional advises the patient they are not fit for work;
(d) a statement, where the healthcare professional considers it appropriate, that the patient may be fit for work;
(e) a statement that the healthcare professional will or, as the case may be will not, need to assess the patient's fitness for work again;
(f) the date on which the healthcare professional's statement is given;
(g) the address of the healthcare professional;
(h) the name of the healthcare professional (whether in the form of a signature or otherwise); and
(i) the profession of the healthcare professional.

5A. Where the healthcare professional's statement is in the form set out in Part 2 of this Schedule—
(a) the healthcare professional's name shall, irrespective of their profession, be recorded next to the words "doctor's signature";
(b) the healthcare professional's address shall, irrespective of their profession, be recorded next to the words "doctor's address"; and

(c) the healthcare professional shall record their profession within the statement in such place as appears to them to be appropriate.

6. Subject to rule 8, the condition in respect of which the healthcare professional is advising the patient is not fit for work or, as the case may be, which has caused the patient's absence from work shall be specified as precisely as the healthcare professional's knowledge of the patient's condition at the time of the assessment permits.

7. Where a healthcare professional considers that a patient may be fit for work the healthcare professional shall state the reasons for that advice and where this is considered appropriate, the arrangements which the patient might make, with their employer's agreement, to return to work.

8. The condition may be specified less precisely where, in the healthcare professional's opinion, disclosure of the precise condition would be prejudicial to the patient's well-being, or to the patient's position with their employer.

9. A healthcare professional's statement may be given on a date after the date of the assessment on which it is based, however no further statement shall be furnished in respect of that assessment other than a healthcare professional's statement by way of replacement of an original which has been lost, in which case it shall be clearly marked "duplicate".

10. Where, in the healthcare professional's opinion, the patient will become fit for work on a day not later than 14 days after the date of the assessment on which the healthcare professional's statement is based, the healthcare professional's statement shall specify that day.

11. Subject to rules 12 and 13 , the healthcare professional's statement shall specify the minimum period for which, in the healthcare professional's opinion, the patient will not be fit for work or, as the case may be, for which they may be fit for work.

12. The period specified shall begin on the date of the assessment on which the healthcare professional's statement is based and shall not exceed 3 months unless the patient has, on the advice of a healthcare professional, refrained from work for at least 6 months immediately preceding that date.

13. Where—
(a) the patient has been advised by a healthcare professional that they are not fit for work and, in consequence, has refrained from work for at least 6 months immediately preceding the date of the assessment on which the healthcare professional's is based; and
(b) in the healthcare professional's opinion, the patient will not be fit for work for the foreseeable future, instead of specifying a period, the healthcare professional may, having regard to the circumstances of the particular case, enter, after the words "case for", the words "an indefinite period".

14. [. . .]"

p.981, *amendment to the Statutory Sick Pay (Medical Evidence) Regulations 1985 (SI 1985/1604) Sch.1 Pt 2*

With effect from July 1, 2022, reg.3(18)(a) of the Social Security (Medical Evidence) and Statutory Sick Pay (Medical Evidence) (Amendment) (No. 2) Regulations 2022 (SI 2022/630) amended the heading to Pt 2 of Sch.1 so that it now reads "FORM OF HEALTHCARE PROFESSIONAL'S STATEMENT".   5.070

p.981, *amendment to the Statutory Sick Pay (Medical Evidence) Regulations 1985 (SI 1985/1604) Sch. 1 Pt 2*

5.071   With effect from April 6, 2022, reg.3(6) of the Social Security (Medical Evidence) and Statutory Sick Pay (Medical Evidence) (Amendment) Regulations 2022 (SI 2022/298) inserted a new PART 2A as follows under the heading "ALTERNATIVE FORM OF DOCTOR'S STATEMENT", although the heading was later amended to read "ALTERNATIVE FORM OF HEALTHCARE PROFESSIONAL'S STATEMENT" with effect from July 1, 2022 by reg.3(18)(b) of the Social Security (Medical Evidence) and Statutory Sick Pay (Medical Evidence) (Amendment) (No. 2) Regulations 2022 (SI 2022/630).

STATEMENT OF FITNESS FOR WORK
FOR SOCIAL SECURITY OR STATUTORY SICK PAY

Patient's name

Mr, Mrs, Miss, Ms

I assessed your case on:

/   /

and, because of the following
condition(s):

I advise you that:

☐ you are not fit for work.
☐ you may be fit for work taking account
of the following advice:

If available, and with your employer's agreement, you may benefit from:

☐ a phased return to work   ☐ amended duties
☐ altered hours   ☐ workplace adaptations

Comments, including functional effects of your condition(s):

This will be the case for

or from [/   /   ] to [/   /   ]

I will/will not need to assess your fitness for work again at the end of this period.
(*Please delete as applicable*)

Doctor's signature

Date of statement

/   /

Doctor's address

p.987, *annotation to the Statutory Sick Pay (Coronavirus) (Suspension of Waiting Days and General Amendment) Regulations 2020 (SI 2020/374)*

5.072   Delete the existing General Note and replace with the following:

GENERAL NOTE

These Regulations ceased to have effect on March 24, 2022. See further the General Note to the Statutory Sick Pay (Coronavirus) (Suspension of Waiting Days) (Saving Provision) Regulations 2022 (SI 2022/381) in Part I of this Supplement.

p.999, *annotation to the Statutory Sick Pay (Coronavirus) (Funding of Employers' Liabilities) Regulations 2022 (SI 2022/5)*

5.073   The end-date of "March 17, 2021" in line 4 of the General Note to these Regulations should read "March 17, 2022".

p.1006, *enactment of the Statutory Sick Pay (General) (Coronavirus Amendment) Regulations 2022 (SI 2022/380)*

5.074   See Part I of this Supplement for the text of SI 2022/380.

p.1006, *enactment of the Statutory Sick Pay (Coronavirus) (Suspension of Waiting Days) (Saving Provision) Regulations 2022 (SI 2022/381)*

5.075   See Part I of this Supplement for the text of SI 2022/381.

pp.1313–1314, *amendments to the Child Trust Funds Regulations 2004 (SI 2004/1450) reg.18A (Permitted withdrawals from an account where the child is terminally ill)*

5.076   With effect from March 21, 2022, reg.3(2) of the Social Security (Scotland) Act 2018 (Disability Assistance and Information-Sharing) (Consequential Provision and Modifications) Order 2022 (SI 2022/332) amended reg.18A by inserting ", or regulations for disability assistance for working age people," after "people" in para.(2)(b), under Case 1, para.(iii), and also by inserting "for disability assistance for children and young people, or regulations for disability assistance for working age people," after "regulations" in para.(6)(c).

p.1350, *amendment to the Childcare Payments (Eligibility) Regulations 2015 (SI 2015/448) reg.2 (Interpretation)*

5.077   With effect from December 1, 2022, reg.2(2)(a) of the Childcare Payments (Miscellaneous Amendments) Regulations 2022 (SI 2022/1148) amended reg.2 by substituting for para.(b) in the definition of "disability living allowance" the following:

"(b) disability assistance given in accordance with regulations made under section 31 of the Social Security (Scotland) Act 2018;"

p.1350, *amendment to the Childcare Payments (Eligibility) Regulations 2015 (SI 2015/448) reg.2 (Interpretation)*

With effect from December 1, 2022, reg.2(2)(b) of the Childcare Payments (Miscellaneous Amendments) Regulations 2022 (SI 2022/1148) amended reg.2 by substituting for "means engaged" in the definition of "employed" the phrase "means—(a) engaged" and inserting at the end the following new sub-paragraph:

5.078

"or
(b) an engagement in relation to which any of Chapters 7 to 10 of Part 2 of ITEPA 2003 applies (which relate to agency workers, workers under arrangements made by intermediaries and workers providing services through managed service companies);".

p.1357, *amendment to the Childcare Payments (Eligibility) Regulations 2015 (SI 2015/448) reg.9 (The requirement to be in qualifying paid work)*

With effect from December 1, 2022, reg.2(3) of the Childcare Payments (Miscellaneous Amendments) Regulations 2022 (SI 2022/1148) amended para.(1)(c) by substituting "and" for the "or" which appears after "as an employed person".

5.079

pp.1358–1359, *amendment to the Childcare Payments (Eligibility) Regulations 2015 (SI 2015/448) reg.10 (Calculation of expected income)*

With effect from December 1, 2022, reg.2(4) of the Childcare Payments (Miscellaneous Amendments) Regulations 2022 (SI 2022/1148) amended reg.10 by substituting ";" for "." at the end of para.(1)(b) and then inserting the following:

5.080

"(c) an engagement in relation to which any of Chapters 7 to 10 of Part 2 of ITEPA 2003 applies (which relate to agency workers, workers under arrangements made by intermediaries and workers providing services through managed service companies)."

p.1359, *amendment to the Childcare Payments (Eligibility) Regulations 2015 (SI 2015/448) reg.11 (Self-employed persons: start-up periods)*

With effect from December 1, 2022, reg.2(5) of the Childcare Payments (Miscellaneous Amendments) Regulations 2022 (SI 2022/1148) amended reg.11 by substituting for para.(1) the following:

5.081

"(1) A self-employed person does not have to meet the condition in regulation 9(1)(b) or (c) in respect of—
  (a) their first declaration of eligibility, if it is made within a start-up period; and
  (b) declarations of eligibility in each of the three entitlement periods immediately following that start-up period."

p.1362, *amendment to the Childcare Payments (Eligibility) Regulations 2015 (SI 2015/448) reg.13 (Qualifying paid work: caring, incapacity for work or limited capability for work)*

5.082 With effect from December 1, 2022, reg.2(6) of the Childcare Payments (Miscellaneous Amendments) Regulations 2022 (SI 2022/1148) amended reg.13 by omitting "or" at the end of para.(1)(b)(v), by substituting "; or" for "." at the end of para.(1)(b)(vi) and then inserting the following:

"(vii) carer's assistance given in accordance with regulations made under section 28 of the Social Security (Scotland) Act 2018, except young carer grants given under the Carer's Assistance (Young Carer Grants) (Scotland) Regulations 2019."

pp.1363–1364, *amendments to the Childcare Payments (Eligibility) Regulations 2015 (SI 2015/448) reg.15 (Income not to exceed a certain level)*

5.083 With effect from December 1, 2022, reg.2(7) of the Childcare Payments (Miscellaneous Amendments) Regulations 2022 (SI 2022/1148) amended reg.15 by omitting paras (1A) and (1B) and in para.(4) omitting the definition of "critical worker".

p.1371, *amendments to the Childcare Payments Regulations 2015 (SI 2015/522) reg.5 (Variation of entitlement periods)*

5.084 With effect from December 1, 2022, reg.3 and Sch. para.3 of the Childcare (Free of Charge for Working Parents) (England) Regulations 2022 (SI 2022/1134) amended reg.5(1)(d) by substituting "regulation 25 of the Childcare (Free of Charge for Working Parents) (England) Regulations 2022" for "regulation 15 of the Childcare (Early Years Provision Free of Charge) (Extended Entitlement) Regulations 2016".

p.1372, *amendments to the Childcare Payments Regulations 2015 (SI 2015/522) reg.6 (Declarations of eligibility)*

5.085 With effect from December 1, 2022, reg.3(2)(a) and (b) of the Childcare Payments (Miscellaneous Amendments) Regulations 2022 (SI 2022/1148) amended reg.6 by omitting "and" in para.(1)(b), substituting ";" for "." at the end of para.(1)(c) and then inserting "(d) be accompanied by a confirmation, if required by HMRC." From the same date reg.3(2)(c) of the same amending regulations substituted a new para.(7) as follows:

"(7) In this regulation—
"a confirmation" means a confirmation made to HMRC, orally or in writing, by a declarant or their partner that they have complied with the requirement in section 8(1)(a) of the Taxes Management Act 1970 within the period specified in section 8(1D), except where either section 8(1F) or 8(1G) applies where the time limit specified in that section applies;

"declarant" means a person who makes a declaration of eligibility for the purposes of either opening a childcare account or reconfirming eligibility."

p.1389, *amendment to the title to the Childcare (Early Years Provision Free of Charge) (Extended Entitlement) Regulations 2016 (SI 2016/1257)*

With effect from December 1, 2022, reg.3 and Sch. para.4(2) of the   5.086
Childcare (Free of Charge for Working Parents) (England) Regulations 2022 (SI 2022/1134) amended the title of the instrument by substituting "Childcare Act 2016 (Consequential Amendments)" for "Childcare (Early Years Provision Free of Charge) (Extended Entitlement)".

p.1391, *amendments to the Childcare (Early Years Provision Free of Charge) (Extended Entitlement) Regulations 2016 (SI 2016/1257) reg.1 (Citation and commencement)*

With effect from December 1, 2022, reg.3 and Sch. para.4(3) of the   5.087
Childcare (Free of Charge for Working Parents) (England) Regulations 2022 (SI 2022/1134) amended reg.1(1) by substituting "Childcare Act 2016 (Consequential Amendments)" for "Childcare (Early Years Provision Free of Charge) (Extended Entitlement)". With effect from the same date, reg.3 and Sch. para.4(4) of the same amending regulations substituted "1" for "1, 2, 3" in reg.1(2) while reg.3 and Sch. para. 4(5)(a) omitted reg.1(3).

pp.1392–1393, *omission of the Childcare (Early Years Provision Free of Charge) (Extended Entitlement) Regulations 2016 (SI 2016/1257) reg.2 (Interpretation)*

With effect from December 1, 2022, reg.3 and Sch. para.4(5)(b) of   5.088
the Childcare (Free of Charge for Working Parents) (England) Regulations 2022 (SI 2022/1134) omitted reg.2.

pp.1394–1421, *omission of the Childcare (Early Years Provision Free of Charge) (Extended Entitlement) Regulations 2016 (SI 2016/1257) Pt 2 (A qualifying child of working parents), Pt 3 (Information, reviews, appeals and penalties) and Pt 4 (Local authorities' duty to secure early years provision)*

With effect from December 1, 2022, reg.3 and Sch. para.4(5)(c)–(e)   5.089
of the Childcare (Free of Charge for Working Parents) (England) Regulations 2022 (SI 2022/1134) omitted Pts 2, 3 and 4.

p.1411, *amendment to the Childcare (Early Years Provision Free of Charge) (Extended Entitlement) Regulations 2016 (SI 2016/1257) reg.19(5) (Unauthorised disclosure of information received under regulation 18)*

With effect from December 1, 2020, s.410 of and para.446(1) of   5.090
Sch.24(6) to the Sentencing Act 2020 substituted "the commencement

of paragraph 24(2) of Schedule 22 to the Sentencing Act 2020" for "the commencement of section 154(1) of the Criminal Justice Act 2003". However, with effect from April 28, 2022, reg.5(2) and Sch.1 Pt 1 of the Criminal Justice Act 2003 (Commencement No. 33) and Sentencing Act 2020 (Commencement No. 2) Regulations 2022 (SI 2022/500) substituted "2nd May 2022" for "the commencement of paragraph 24(2) of Schedule 22 to the Sentencing Act 2020". Note that with effect from December 1, 2022, reg.3 and Sch. para.4(8) of the Childcare (Free of Charge for Working Parents) (England) Regulations 2022 (SI 2022/1134) omitted the words "Regulation 19(5) of the Childcare (Early Years Provision Free of Charge) (Extended Entitlement) Regulations 2016" in the Sch., in Pt 2, in the table, in Column 1 of the Criminal Justice Act 2003 (Commencement No. 33) and Sentencing Act 2020 (Commencement No. 2) Regulations 2022 (SI 2022/500).

p.1469, *annotation to the Social Security (Scotland) Act 2018 s.52A (Re-determination and appeal deadlines)*

5.091   The definition of "coronavirus" in s.1 of the Coronavirus (Scotland) Act 2020 continues in force for the purposes of ss.52A and 52B of the 2018 Act, by virtue of reg.2 of the Coronavirus (Scotland) Acts (Saving Provision) Regulations 2022 (SSI 2022/261), notwithstanding that it has expired for most other purposes.

p.1469, *annotation to the Social Security (Scotland) Act 2018 s.52B (Applications for assistance)*

5.092   See the supplementary annotation to s.52A, above.

pp.1509–1510, *amendment of the Early Years Assistance (Best Start Grants) (Scotland) Regulations 2018 (SSI 2018/370) reg.9 (Meaning of being responsible for a child)*

5.093   With effect from November 14, 2022, reg.2(1) and (2) of the Social Security (Miscellaneous Amendment and Transitional Provision) (Scotland) Regulations 2022 (SSI 2022/336) amended reg.9 of the 2018 Regulations by, in para.(1)(c), inserting "or section 54A" after "section 54"and, for para.(3), substituting:

"(3) For the purpose of paragraph (1)(g), an individual is a kinship carer for a child on a day if—
   (a) the individual is—
      (i) a person who is related to the child,
      (ii) a person who is known to the child and with whom the child has a pre-existing relationship, or
      (iii) a friend or acquaintance of a person related to the child, and
   (b) on that day, the child lives with the individual (exclusively or predominantly) under the terms of—
      (i) a kinship care order as defined in section 72(1) of the Children and Young People (Scotland) Act 2014,

   (ii) any other order under section 11(1) of the Children (Scotland) Act 1995 ("the 1995 Act"), or

  (iii) an agreement between the individual, the individual's partner or both of them and—

     (aa) a local authority by which the child is looked after within the meaning of section 17(6) of the 1995 Act,

     (bb) a local authority in England or Wales by which the child is looked after within the meaning of section 105(4) of the Children Act 1989 ("the 1989 Act"), or

     (cc) an authority in Northern Ireland by which the child is looked after within the meaning of article 25 of the Children (Northern Ireland) Order 1995 ("the 1995 Order").

(4) A person described in paragraph (3)(a) must not be—

(a) the parent of the child within the meaning of section 15(1) of the 1995 Act,

(b) a foster carer within the meaning of regulation 2 of the Looked After Children (Scotland) Regulations 2009,

(c) a local authority foster parent in England and Wales within the meaning of section 105(1) of the 1989 Act, or

(d) an authority foster parent in Northern Ireland within the meaning of article 27(3) of the 1995 Order.

(5) In paragraph (3)(a) "related" means related either by blood, marriage or civil partnership.".

p.1513, *amendment of the Early Years Assistance (Best Start Grants) (Scotland) Regulations 2018 (SSI 2018/370) Sch.1 (Procedural matters)*

With effect from November 28, 2022, reg.2(1) and (3) of the Social   5.094
Security (Miscellaneous Amendment and Transitional Provision) (Scotland) Regulations 2022 (SSI 2022/336) amended Pt 2 (Determination without application) of Sch.1 of the 2018 Regulations by, after para.5, inserting:

"Determination following award of Scottish child payment

5A.—(1) The Scottish Ministers are to make a determination of an individual's entitlement to an early learning grant or a school-age grant in connection with a child (without receiving an application) where the circumstances described in sub-paragraph (2) are met.

(2) The circumstances referred to in sub-paragraph (1) are that—

(a) a determination has been made that the individual is entitled to a Scottish child payment in respect of the child and the individual has an ongoing entitlement to that payment by virtue of regulation 19 of the Scottish Child Payment Regulations,

(b) the individual's Scottish child payment in respect of the child is not currently suspended within the meaning of regulation 19G(a) of the Scottish Child Payment Regulations, and

(c) it appears to the Scottish Ministers from the available information that the individual is likely to be entitled to an early learning grant or a school-age grant in respect of the child.

(3) Where a determination is to be, or has been, made without an application by virtue of this paragraph, references in these Regulations to the day the application is made are to be read as references to the day the determination is made.

(4) Where an individual who is entitled to a Scottish child payment requests that the Scottish Ministers do not make a determination (without receiving an application) of the individual's entitlement to an early leaning grant or school-age grant—

(a) the Scottish Ministers are not to make a determination (without receiving an application) under sub-paragraph (1), and

(b) accordingly, their duty to do so under sub-paragraph (1) ceases to apply.

(5) In this paragraph—

(a) "Scottish child payment" means Scottish child payment assistance given in accordance with the Scottish Child Payment Regulations,

(b) "Scottish Child Payment Regulations" means the Scottish Child Payment Regulations 2020, and

(c) "the available information" means—

(i) the information provided in the individual's application for the Scottish child payment,

(ii) any other information obtained by the Scottish Ministers in connection with that application, and

(iii) any other information available to them that is relevant to their consideration of whether the individual is entitled to an early learning grant or a school-age grant.".

pp.1514–1518, *amendment of the Early Years Assistance (Best Start Grants) (Scotland) Regulations 2018 (SSI 2018/370) Sch.2 (Pregnancy and baby grant)*

5.095   With effect from November 14, 2022, reg.2(1) and (4) of the Social Security (Miscellaneous Amendment and Transitional Provision) (Scotland) Regulations 2022 (SSI 2022/336) amended paras 1, 4 and 6 of, and inserts a new para.11 into, Sch.2 of the 2018 Regulations.

In para.1 (eligibility), sub-para.(f) is omitted, with a consequential moving of the word "and" that preceded it.

In para.4 (residence requirement), "has" is inserted before "leave" in sub-para.(2)(ab)(i), the word "or" is moved from the end of sub-para.(2)(ac)(i) to the end of sub-para.(2)(ac)(ii) and a new sub-para.(2)(ac)(iii) is inserted:

"(iii) does not require leave to enter or remain in the United Kingdom in accordance with section 3ZA of that Act,".

In para.6 (the basic amount), sub-para.(2)(b)(v) is substituted and a new sub-para.(2)(b)(vi) is inserted, so that those provisions read:

"(v) a child for whom neither the individual nor their partner is responsible,

(vi) a child in any one of the circumstances described in sub-paragraph (4), (5) or (6).".

Also in para.6, after sub-para.(3), sub-paras (4) to (7) are inserted:

"(4) The circumstance referred to in sub-paragraph (2)(b)(vi) is that—

(a) the child mentioned in sub-paragraph (2)(b)(vi) was, at the time of that child's birth, not a child of the—

(i) individual to whom the grant is to be given, or

(ii) individual's partner (where the individual has a partner on the day the application is made), and

(b) the individual first became responsible for the child mentioned in sub-paragraph (2)(b)(vi) when that child was aged 12 months or older.

(5) The circumstance referred to in sub-paragraph (2)(b)(vi) is that the individual to whom the grant is to be given has left their home with the child mentioned in sub-paragraph (2)(b)(vi) due to domestic abuse.

(6) The circumstance referred to in sub-paragraph (2)(b)(vi) is that—

(a) the child mentioned in sub-paragraph (2)(b)(vi) was born before the individual to whom the grant is to be given arrived in the United Kingdom, and

(b) the individual to whom the grant is to be given is one of the following—

(i) a person who has leave to enter or remain in the United Kingdom granted under the immigration rules made under section 3(2) of the Immigration Act 1971 ("the 1971 Act") by virtue of—

(aa) the Afghan Relocations and Assistance Policy, or

(bb) the previous scheme for locally-employed staff in Afghanistan (sometimes referred to as the ex-gratia scheme),

(ii) a person who has been granted discretionary leave outside the immigration rules as a dependant of a person referred to in sub-head (i),

(iii) a person who has leave granted under the Afghan Citizens Resettlement Scheme,

(iv) a person with leave to enter or remain in the United Kingdom granted under or outside the immigration rules made under section 3(2) of the 1971 Act, or with a right of abode in the United Kingdom within the meaning of section 2 of that Act or who does not require leave to enter or remain in the United Kingdom in accordance with section 3ZA of the Act, where the person—

(aa) was residing in Ukraine immediately before 1 January 2022, and

> (bb) left Ukraine in connection with the Russian invasion which took place on 24 February 2022,
>
> (v) a refugee within the definition in Article 1 of the Convention relating to the status of refugees done at Geneva on 28 July 1951, as extended by article 1(2) of the Protocol relating to the status of refugees done at New York on 31 January 1967, or
>
> (vi) a person who has humanitarian protection granted under the rules made under section 3(2) of the 1971 Act.

(7) In paragraph (6) "the Afghan Citizens Resettlement Scheme" has the same meaning as in paragraph 4.",

Paragraph 11 is inserted after para.10:

"Meaning of "domestic abuse"

11.—(1) Subject to sub-paragraph (3), in this schedule, "domestic abuse" means abusive behaviour within the meaning of sections 2 and 3 of the Domestic Abuse (Protection) (Scotland) Act 2021 ("the 2021 Act").

(2) For the purposes of this schedule, sections 2 and 3 of the 2021 Act apply as if—

> (a) references to "person A" were references to the partner or the ex-partner of the individual to whom the grant is to be given, and
>
> (b) references to "person B" were references to the individual to whom the grant is to be given.

(3) Sub-paragraphs (4) to (13) have effect until the day on which sections 2 and 3 of the 2021 Act come into force.

(4) "Abusive behaviour" means behaviour by the partner or ex-partner of the individual to whom the grant is to be given ("person A") which is abusive of the individual to whom the grant is to be given ("person B").

(5) Behaviour by person A is abusive of person B if a reasonable person would consider the behaviour to be likely to cause person B to suffer physical or psychological harm.

(6) Behaviour is behaviour of any kind, including (for example)—

> (a) saying or otherwise communicating as well as doing something,
>
> (b) intentionally failing—
>
> > (i) to do something,
> >
> > (ii) to say or otherwise communicate something.

(7) Behaviour directed at a person is such behaviour however carried out, including (in particular)—

> (a) by way of conduct towards property,
>
> (b) through making use of a third party,

as well as behaviour in a personal or direct manner.

(8) In sub-paragraph (5), the reference to psychological harm includes fear, alarm and distress.

(9) Behaviour may consist of a single incident or a course of conduct.

(10) Behaviour which is abusive of person B includes (in particular)—
  (a) behaviour directed at person B that is violent, threatening or intimidating,
  (b) behaviour directed at person B, at a child of person B or at another person that either—
    (i) has its purpose (or among its purposes) one or more of the relevant effects set out in sub-paragraph (11), or
    (ii) would be considered by a reasonable person to be likely to have one or more of the relevant effects set out in sub-paragraph (11).
(11) The relevant effects are of—
  (a) making person B dependent on, or subordinate to, person A,
  (b) isolating person B from friends, relatives or other sources of support,
  (c) controlling, regulating or monitoring person B's day-to-day activities,
  (d) depriving person B of, or restricting person B's, freedom of action,
  (e) frightening, humiliating, degrading or punishing person B.
(12) In sub-paragraph (10)(a), the reference to violent behaviour includes sexual violence as well as physical violence.
(13) Person A and person B are partners (and "ex-partners" is to be construed accordingly) if they are—
  (a) spouses or civil partners of each other, or
  (b) in an intimate personal relationship with each other.".

Note that, on p.1516 of the main work, para.4(2)(ab)(i)(ia) and (ib) should be further inset.

pp.1518–1519, *amendment of the Early Years Assistance (Best Start Grants) (Scotland) Regulations 2018 (SSI 2018/370) Sch.3 (Early learning grant)*

With effect from November 14, 2022, reg.2(1) and (5) of the Social 5.096 Security (Miscellaneous Amendment and Transitional Provision) (Scotland) Regulations 2022 (SSI 2022/336) amended paras 1 and 3 of Sch.3 of the 2018 Regulations.

In para.1 (eligibility), sub-para.(g) is omitted, with a consequential moving of the word "and" that preceded it.

In para.3 (residence requirement), the word "or" is moved from the end of sub-para.(2)(ac)(i) to the end of sub-para.(2)(ac)(ii) and a new sub-para.(2)(ac)(iii) is inserted:

"(iii) does not require leave to enter or remain in the United Kingdom in accordance with section 3ZA of that Act,".

Note that, on p.1519 of the main work, para.3(2)(ab)(i)(ia) and (ib) should be further inset.

pp.1521–1522, *amendment of the Early Years Assistance (Best Start Grants) (Scotland) Regulations 2018 (SSI 2018/370) Sch.4 (School-age grant)*

5.097　With effect from November 14, 2022, reg.2(1) and (6) of the Social Security (Miscellaneous Amendment and Transitional Provision) (Scotland) Regulations 2022 (SSI 2022/336) amended paras 1 and 4 of Sch.4 of the 2018 Regulations.

In para.1 (eligibility), sub-para.(g) is omitted, with a consequential moving of the word "and" that preceded it.

In para.4 (residence requirement), the word "or" is moved from the end of sub-para.(2)(ac)(i) to the end of sub-para.(2)(ac)(ii) and a new sub-para.(2)(ac)(iii) is inserted:

"(iii) does not require leave to enter or remain in the United Kingdom in accordance with section 3ZA of that Act,".

pp.1537–1538, *amendment of the Carer's Assistance (Young Carer Grants) (Scotland) Regulations 2019 (SSI 2019/324) reg.8 (Conditions relating to residence)*

5.098　With effect from November 14, 2022, reg.7 of the Social Security (Miscellaneous Amendment and Transitional Provision) (Scotland) Regulations 2022 (SSI 2022/336) amended reg.8(2) of the 2019 Regulations by moving "or" from the end of sub-para.(ab)(i) to the end of sub-para.(ab)(ii) and inserting a new sub-para.(ab)(iii):

"(iii) does not require leave to enter or remain in the United Kingdom in accordance with section 3ZA of that Act,".

p.1546, *substitution of the Scottish Child Payment Regulations 2020 (SSI 2020/351) reg.4 (References to the 2018 Act)*

5.099　With effect from November 14, 2022, reg.4(1) and (2) of the Social Security (Miscellaneous Amendment and Transitional Provision) (Scotland) Regulations 2022 (SSI 2022/336) amended the 2020 Regulations by substituting for reg.4 (and its heading):

"Interpretation

4. In these Regulations—
"the 2018 Act" means the Social Security (Scotland) Act 2018,
"child" means a person under the age of 16, and
"coronavirus" means severe acute respiratory syndrome coronavirus 2 (SARS CoV-2).".

pp.1547–1548, *substitution of the Scottish Child Payment Regulations 2020 (SSI 2020/351) reg.11 (Meaning of "kinship carer")*

5.100　With effect from November 14, 2022, reg.4(1) and (3) of the Social Security (Miscellaneous Amendment and Transitional Provision) (Scotland) Regulations 2022 (SSI 2022/336) amended the 2020 Regulations by substituting for reg.11:

"**11.**—(1) An individual is a kinship carer for a child on a day if—

  (a) the individual is—

    (i) a person who is related to the child,

    (ii) a person who is known to the child and with whom the child has a pre-existing relationship, or

    (iii) a friend or acquaintance of a person related to the child, and

  (b) on that day, the child lives with the individual (exclusively or predominantly) under the terms of—

    (i) a kinship care order as defined in section 72(1) of the Children and Young People (Scotland) Act 2014,

    (ii) any other order under section 11(1) of the Children (Scotland) Act 1995 ("the 1995 Act"), or

    (iii) an agreement between the individual, the individual's partner or both of them and—

      (aa) a local authority by which the child is looked after within the meaning of section 17(6) of the 1995 Act,

      (bb) a local authority in England or Wales by which the child is looked after within the meaning of section 105(4) of the Children Act 1989 ("the 1989 Act"), or

      (cc) an authority in Northern Ireland by which the child is looked after within the meaning of article 25 of the Children (Northern Ireland) Order 1995 ("the 1995 Order").

(2) A person described in paragraph (1)(a) must not be—

  (a) the parent of the child within the meaning of section 15(1) of the 1995 Act,

  (b) a foster carer within the meaning of regulation 2 of the Looked After Children (Scotland) Regulations 2009,

  (c) a local authority foster parent in England and Wales within the meaning of section 105(1) of the 1989 Act, or

  (d) an authority foster parent in Northern Ireland within the meaning of article 27(3) of the 1995 Order.

(3) In paragraph (1)(a) "related" means related either by blood, marriage or civil partnership.".

p.1550, *amendment of the Scottish Child Payment Regulations 2020 (SSI 2020/351) reg.18 (Eligibility for a Scottish child payment)*

With effect from November 14, 2022, reg.4(1) and (4) of the Social Security (Miscellaneous Amendment and Transitional Provision) (Scotland) Regulations 2022 (SSI 2022/336) amended reg.18(b) of the 2020 Regulations by substituting "16" for "6". This, and the amendment to reg.19 (see below) have the effect of extending the scope of child payments to those with children under 16, rather than only children under 6. Regulation 5 of the 2022 Regulations makes transitional provision: 5.101

"Transitional and consequential provision in connection with regulation 4

5.—(1) Any application for a Scottish child payment under the Scottish Child Payment Regulations in respect of a child who is aged 6 years old or older which is made before 14 November 2022 is to be treated for the purposes of those Regulations as having been made on 14 November 2022.

(2) Where the Scottish Ministers make a determination without receiving an application by virtue of Part 2 of the schedule of the Scottish Child Payment Regulations that an individual is entitled to a Scottish child payment in respect of—

(a) a period that includes one or more days falling before 14 November 2022, and

(b) a child who reached the age of 6 before that date, the individual's entitlement begins on 14 November 2022.

(3) In the case of any application to which paragraph (1) applies, regulation 18A of the Scottish Child Payment Regulations is to be read as though, for the words from "begins" to the end there were substituted "begins is 14 November 2022".

(4) In the case of any determination to which paragraph (2) applies, regulation 18A of the Scottish Child Payment Regulations does not apply.

(5) For the purposes of paragraph (1), an application is "made" on the date it is received by the Scottish Ministers."

See the supplementary annotation to reg.19, below, for further transitional provision in respect of those with ongoing entitlement in respect of children under 6.

p.1550, *insertion of the Scottish Child Payment Regulations 2020 (SSI 2020/351) reg.18A (Beginning of entitlement to assistance)*

5.102 With effect from November 14, 2022, reg.4(1) and (5) of the Social Security (Miscellaneous Amendment and Transitional Provision) (Scotland) Regulations 2022 (SSI 2022/336) amended the 2020 Regulations by inserting:

"Beginning of entitlement to assistance

18A. Where a determination is made that an individual is entitled to a Scottish child payment, the date on which entitlement begins is the date on which the application is made or treated as made in accordance with regulation 5.".

Note that this provision is disapplied where transitional provision is made in the light of the extension of eligibility to cover children up to 16, rather than up to 6 (see the supplementary annotations to regs 18 and 19, above and below respectively).

p.1550, *amendment of the Scottish Child Payment Regulations 2020 (SSI 2020/351) reg.19 (Ongoing entitlement)*

With effect from November 14, 2022, reg.2 of the Scottish Child **5.103** Payment (Ancillary Provision) Regulations 2022 (SSI 2022/326) amended reg.19(2)(b) of the 2020 Regulations by substituting "16" for "6". This amendment is consequential upon the similar amendment made by the Social Security (Miscellaneous Amendment and Transitional Provision) (Scotland) Regulations 2022 to reg.18(b) (see above), making provision for child payments in respect of children up to the age of 16, rather than only to those aged up to 6. Regulation 4 of the Scottish Child Payment (Ancillary Provision) Regulations 2022 makes transitional provision:

"Transitional provision: determination to extend existing award of Scottish child payment

4.—(1) The Scottish Ministers are to make a determination of an individual's entitlement to a Scottish child payment where paragraph (2) applies.

(2) On 14 November 2022, the individual has an ongoing entitlement to a Scottish child payment in accordance with regulation 19(1) of the 2020 Regulations (ongoing entitlement) by virtue of a determination that was made by the Scottish Ministers before that date.

(3) Subject to paragraph (4), a determination under paragraph (1) must be made—

   (a) on the assumption that the individual continues to meet the eligibility criteria set out in regulation 18 of the 2020 Regulations (eligibility for a Scottish child payment) on the date on which the determination is made, and

   (b) on the basis that the individual has an ongoing entitlement to a Scottish child payment on the basis described in regulation 19(2) of the 2020 Regulations.

(4) Where a determination is to be, or has been, made under this regulation—

   (a) the individual's entitlement begins on 14 November 2022,

   (b) regulation 18A of the 2020 Regulations (beginning of entitlement to assistance) does not apply, and

   (c) the determination is to be treated for the purposes of the 2020 Regulations as a determination made by the Scottish Ministers under paragraph 3 of the schedule of those Regulations (duty to make a determination of entitlement)."

p.1553, *amendment of the Scottish Child Payment Regulations 2020 (SSI 2020/351) reg.20 (Value and form of a Scottish child payment)*

With effect from November 14, 2022, reg.4(1) and (6) of the Social **5.104** Security (Miscellaneous Amendment and Transitional Provision) (Scotland) Regulations 2022 (SSI 2022/336) amended reg.20 of the 2020

Regulations by, in para.(1), substituting "£25" for "£20" and, after para.(4), inserting:

"(5) For each week in the period of 12 weeks ending with the death of the child, the amount of Scottish child payment that is to be given to the individual is the weekly rate, multiplied by two.".

These amendments are both subject to savings by virtue of Scottish Child Payment (Saving Provisions) Regulations 2022 (SSI 2022/302), reg.2 of which makes it plain that the increase in the value of child payments applies only from November 14, 2022 (and not to the period from April 1, 2022 to November 13, 2022) and reg.3 of which makes it plain that the new para.(5) "is of no effect in relation to the death of a child which occurred before 14 November 2022".

p.1554, *amendment of the Scottish Child Payment Regulations 2020 (SSI 2020/351) reg.21 (Time of payment)*

5.105   With effect from November 14, 2022, reg.4(1) and (7) of the Social Security (Miscellaneous Amendment and Transitional Provision) (Scotland) Regulations 2022 (SSI 2022/336) amended reg.21 of the 2020 Regulations by substituting for para.(2):

"(2) Except where paragraph (3) applies, where a determination is made that an individual is entitled to a Scottish child payment, the Scottish Ministers are to make—
    (a) the first payment of a Scottish child payment on a date specified in the determination, and
    (b) subsequent payments in the last week of each successive period of 4 weeks in which the individual continues to be entitled to a Scottish child payment for at least one week by virtue of regulation 19.".

pp.1560–1567, *amendment of the Scottish Child Payment Regulations 2020 (SSI 2020/351) Sch. (Procedural matters)*

5.106   With effect from November 14, 2022, reg.4(1) and (8) of the Social Security (Miscellaneous Amendment and Transitional Provision) (Scotland) Regulations 2022 (SSI 2022/336) amended paras 11(3), 12(5), 34 and 35 of the Sch. of the 2020 Regulations.

Paragraph 11(3) (determination following award of a Scottish child payment in respect of another child) is amended by inserting "where the child is under 6 years old" at the beginning of head (b), inserting "or" at the end of that head and, after that head, inserting:

"(c) where the child is 6 years old or older, such earlier day which is—
    (i) not more than 4 weeks before that day on which the child was recognised to be a child for whom the individual has responsibility in terms of an award of assistance mentioned in regulation 12(2)(a), and

(ii) on or after 14 November 2022.",

Paragraph 12(5) (determination following cessation of award of a Scottish child payment) is amended by substituting "the day on which the change of circumstances" for "the determination" and inserting "occurred" after "(3)". This amendment does not apply in respect of a determination described in para.12(3) that was made by the Scottish Ministers before November 14, 2022 (see reg.3 of the Scottish Child Payment (Ancillary Provision) Regulations 2022 (SSI 2022/326)).

In para.34 (re-determination and appeal deadlines), sub-para.(4) is omitted.

In para.35 (timing of applications for Scottish child payment), sub-para.(4) is omitted.

p.1594, *amendment of the Disability Assistance for Children and Young People (Scotland) Regulations 2021 (SSI 2021/174) reg.5 (Residence and presence conditions)*

With effect from November 14, 2022, reg.8 of the Social Security (Miscellaneous Amendment and Transitional Provision) (Scotland) Regulations 2022 (SSI 2022/336) amended reg.5(10A)(f) of the 2021 Regulations by substituting "has a right" for "or a right" and, after "1971", inserting "or does not require leave to enter or remain in the United Kingdom in accordance with section 3ZA of that Act".   5.107

p.1595, *amendment of the Disability Assistance for Children and Young People (Scotland) Regulations 2021 (SSI 2021/174) reg.6 (Interpretation—residence and presence conditions)*

With effect from August 29, 2022, reg.18(1) and (2) of the Disability Assistance for Working Age People (Transitional Provisions and Miscellaneous Amendment) (Scotland) Regulations 2022 (SSI 2022/217) amended reg.6 of the 2021 Regulations by omitting the definitions of "civil partnership" and "person who is living with another person as if they were in a civil partnership".   5.108

p.1615, *amendment of the Disability Assistance for Children and Young People (Scotland) Regulations 2021 (SSI 2021/174) reg.28 (When an increase in level of entitlement takes effect)*

With effect from August 29, 2022, reg.18(1) and (3) of the Disability Assistance for Working Age People (Transitional Provisions and Miscellaneous Amendment) (Scotland) Regulations 2022 (SSI 2022/217) amended reg.28 of the 2021 Regulations by inserting after para.(1)(c):   5.109

"(ca) in the case of a determination made in accordance with regulation 31(a), where the period that an individual has been—
   (i) for the purpose of regulation 17, resident in a care home,
   (ii) for the purposes of regulation 18, in legal detention, or

(iii) for the purposes of regulation 20, resident in a care home or in legal detention,

has come to an end, on the day on which the individual leaves that place, or".

p.1625, *amendment of the Disability Assistance for Children and Young People (Scotland) Regulations 2021 (SSI 2021/174) Sch. Pt 1 (Short-term assistance)*

5.110   With effect from August 29, 2022, reg.18(1) and (4) of the Disability Assistance for Working Age People (Transitional Provisions and Miscellaneous Amendment) (Scotland) Regulations 2022 (SSI 2022/217) amended Pt 1 of the Sch. of the 2021 Regulations by substituting for para.4:

"Reduction of payment of Child Disability Payment where short-term assistance is paid

4. Where an individual has received short-term assistance for a period and a determination is subsequently made that the individual is entitled to Child Disability Payment for the same period, any payment of Child Disability Payment to be made as a result of the subsequent determination for that period—

(a) where the individual is to be paid Child Disability Payment at the same rate as or a lower rate than any short-term assistance and any Child Disability Payment already paid to that individual for that period, is to be reduced to £0,

(b) in any other case, is to be reduced by any short-term assistance and any Child Disability Payment already paid to that individual for that period."

pp.1628–1629, *amendment of the Disability Assistance for Children and Young People (Scotland) Regulations 2021 (SSI 2021/174) Sch. Pt 3 (Transfer to child disability payment)*

5.111   With effect from August 29, 2022, reg.18(1) and (5) of the Disability Assistance for Working Age People (Transitional Provisions and Miscellaneous Amendment) (Scotland) Regulations 2022 (SSI 2022/217) amended para.13 (Modification of these Regulations: transferring individuals) in Pt 3 of the Sch. of the 2021 Regulations by, in sub-para.(za) substituting "11(2), 11(3)" for "11(3)", in sub-para.(b), omitting "and" and, after sub-para.(b), inserting:

", and

(c) regulation 25 (time of payment) is to be read as if for paragraph (b) there were substituted—

"(b) any subsequent payment—

(i) 4 weekly in arrears,

(ii) weekly in advance, or

(iii) where the Scottish Ministers consider that it would be unjust not to do so, at such intervals as may be specified in the notice of determination.""".

pp.1637–1638, *amendment of the Disability Assistance for Working Age People (Scotland) Regulations 2022 (SSI 2022/54) reg.2 (Interpretation)*

With effect from August 29, 2022, reg.19(1) and (2) of the Disability Assistance for Working Age People (Transitional Provisions and Miscellaneous Amendment) (Scotland) Regulations 2022 (SSI 2022/217) amended reg.2 of the 2022 Regulations by omitting the definitions of "EU withdrawal agreement" and "medical treatment" and, after the definition of "previous award", inserting: 5.112

""qualifying services" means accommodation, board and personal care,".

p.1640, *amendment of the Disability Assistance for Working Age People (Scotland) Regulations 2022 (SSI 2022/54) reg.7 (Determination of ability to carry out activities)*

With effect from August 29, 2022, reg.19(1) and (3) of the Disability Assistance for Working Age People (Transitional Provisions and Miscellaneous Amendment) (Scotland) Regulations 2022 (SSI 2022/217) amended reg.7(2)(a) of the 2022 Regulations by, after "schedule 1", inserting "or, as the case may be, column 2 of the table in Part 3 of schedule 1". 5.113

p.1645, *amendment of the Disability Assistance for Working Age People (Scotland) Regulations 2022 (SSI 2022/54) reg.15 (Residence and presence conditions)*

With effect from November 14, 2022, reg.9 of the Social Security (Miscellaneous Amendment and Transitional Provision) (Scotland) Regulations 2022 (SSI 2022/336) amended reg.15(7)(d) of these Regulations by substituting "has a right" for "of a right" and, after "1971", inserting "or does not require leave to enter or remain in the United Kingdom in accordance with section 3ZA of that Act". 5.114

p.1647, *amendment of the Disability Assistance for Working Age People (Scotland) Regulations 2022 (SSI 2022/54) reg.17 (Serving members of Her Majesty's forces, civil servants and their family members)*

With effect from August 29, 2022, reg.19(1) and (4) of the Disability Assistance for Working Age People (Transitional Provisions and Miscellaneous Amendment) (Scotland) Regulations 2022 (SSI 2022/217) amended reg.17(4) of the 2022 Regulations by omitting the definitions of "civil partnership" and "person who is living with another person as if they were in a civil partnership". 5.115

p.1651, *amendment of the Disability Assistance for Working Age People (Scotland) Regulations 2022 (SSI 2022/54) reg.24 (Persons who have reached the relevant age: other exceptions)*

5.116   With effect from August 29, 2022, reg.19(1) and (5) of the Disability Assistance for Working Age People (Transitional Provisions and Miscellaneous Amendment) (Scotland) Regulations 2022 (SSI 2022/217) amended reg.24 of the 2022 Regulations by, at the end of para.(b), omitting "or" and, after para.(c), inserting:

", or
   (d)   are a transferring individual in terms of the Disability Assistance for Working Age People (Transitional Provisions and Miscellaneous Amendment) (Scotland) Regulations 2022.".

p.1652, *amendment of the Disability Assistance for Working Age People (Scotland) Regulations 2022 (SSI 2022/54) reg.25 (Determination of an award after the person has reached the relevant age)*

5.117   With effect from August 29, 2022, reg.19(1) and (6) of the Disability Assistance for Working Age People (Transitional Provisions and Miscellaneous Amendment) (Scotland) Regulations 2022 (SSI 2022/217) amended reg.25 of the 2022 Regulations by, in para.(1)(a)(ii), omitting "of the mobility component", in para.(2), omitting sub-para.(a), and, in para.(3), after sub-para.(b), inserting:

"(c)   where the original award did not include an award of the mobility component, the Scottish Ministers may not award that component at either the standard or enhanced rate.".

p.1653, *amendment of the Disability Assistance for Working Age People (Scotland) Regulations 2022 (SSI 2022/54) reg.26 (Entitlement under special rules for terminal illness)*

5.118   With effect from August 29, 2022, reg.19(1) and (7) of the Disability Assistance for Working Age People (Transitional Provisions and Miscellaneous Amendment) (Scotland) Regulations 2022 (SSI 2022/217) amended reg.26 of the 2022 Regulations by substituting for para.(3):

"(3) An individual to whom this regulation applies is to be treated as though—
   (a)   they have obtained the maximum points for each activity listed in column 1 of the tables in Part 2 and Part 3 of schedule 1, and
   (b)   they have satisfied regulations 5(3) and 6(3).".

pp.1664–1665, *amendment of the Disability Assistance for Working Age People (Scotland) Regulations 2022 (SSI 2022/54) reg.45 (When an increase in level of entitlement takes effect)*

5.119   With effect from August 29, 2022, reg.19(1) and (8) of the Disability Assistance for Working Age People (Transitional Provisions and Miscellaneous Amendment) (Scotland) Regulations 2022 (SSI 2022/217) amended reg.45(1) of the 2022 Regulations so that it reads (with amendments in square brackets):

"(1) Where, as a result of a determination without an application, the amount of Adult Disability Payment payable in respect of an individual is increased or their entitlement to a component is awarded, the change takes effect—

(a) in the case of an increase pursuant to a determination made under regulation [48(c), 48(d) or 48(e)] (determination following change of circumstances etc.) on the day after the day on which Personal Independence Payment [or Disability Living Allowance] ceased to be paid in respect of the individual,

(b) in the case of an award of entitlement to a component or an increase pursuant to a determination made in accordance with regulation 48(a) that affects their eligibility under regulation 5 (daily living component) or regulation 6 (mobility component), on the date when—

   (i) if as a result of the individual reporting the change—

      (aa) if the individual reports the change within one month of the change occurring, the individual first satisfies the requirements for a higher rate of the daily living or mobility component,

      (bb) if the individual reports the change within more than one month but not more than 13 months of the change occurring, the individual first satisfies the requirements for a higher rate of the [daily living] or mobility component, but only if the Scottish Ministers consider that the individual had good reason for not notifying the change within one month, or

      (cc) in any other case, the individual reports the change.

   (ii) if as a result of the Scottish Ministers becoming aware that a determination of an individual's entitlement was made in ignorance of a material fact, on the date when the Scottish Ministers make the determination.

(c) in the case of an earlier determination which was based on official error [. . .] within the meaning of regulation 49 (determination following official error—underpayments) or on error within the meaning of regulation 50 (determination following error—overpayments), [. . .] on the date when the earlier determination took effect, [. . .]

[(ca) in the case of a determination made in accordance with regulation 48(a), where the period that an individual has been—

   (i) resident in a care home for the purpose of regulation 27,

   (ii) an in-patient in hospital or similar institution for the purpose of regulation 28,

   (iii) in legal detention for the purpose of regulation 30, or

> (iv) resident in a care home, an in-patient in a hospital or similar institution, or in legal detention for the purposes of regulation 32,
>
> has come to an end, on the day on which the individual leaves the place, or]
>
> (d) in any other case, on the date when the Scottish Ministers make the determination."

p.1665, *amendment of the Disability Assistance for Working Age People (Scotland) Regulations 2022 (SSI 2022/54) reg.46 (When a decrease in level or cessation of entitlement takes effect)*

5.120   With effect from August 29, 2022, reg.19(1) and (9) of the Disability Assistance for Working Age People (Transitional Provisions and Miscellaneous Amendment) (Scotland) Regulations 2022 (SSI 2022/217) amended reg.46(1) of the 2022 Regulations by, in sub-para.(a), substituting"48(c), 48(d) or 48(e)" for "48(c) or 48(d)" and inserting "or Disability Living Allowance" after "Personal Independence Payment" and, in sub-para.(c), omitting "or error".

p.1667, *amendment of the Disability Assistance for Working Age People (Scotland) Regulations 2022 (SSI 2022/54) reg.48 (Determination following change of circumstances etc.)*

5.121   With effect from August 29, 2022, reg.19(1) and (10) of the Disability Assistance for Working Age People (Transitional Provisions and Miscellaneous Amendment) (Scotland) Regulations 2022 (SSI 2022/217) amended reg.48 of the 2022 Regulations by inserting after para.(d):

> "(e) of an alteration of the component or rate of award of Disability Living Allowance which the individual was entitled to immediately before the date of transfer to Adult Disability Payment in accordance with regulation 4 (determination without application of entitlement to Adult Disability Payment) of the Disability Assistance for Working Age People (Transitional Provisions and Miscellaneous Amendment) (Scotland) Regulations 2022, as a result of a decision made pursuant to—
>
> > (i) revision under regulation 3 of the Social Security and Child Support (Decisions and Appeals) Regulations 1999 ("the 1999 Regulations"),
> >
> > (ii) a supersession under regulation 6 of the 1999 Regulations,
> >
> > (iii) an appeal under section 12 of the Social Security Act 1998 ("the 1998 Act"),
> >
> > (iv) a re-consideration under section 13 of the 1998 Act ,
> >
> > (v) an appeal to the Upper Tribunal under section 14 of the 1998 Act,
> >
> > (vi) a revision under article 10 of the Social Security (Northern Ireland) Order 1998 ("the 1998 Order"),
> >
> > (vii) a supersession under article 11 of the 1998 Order,

(viii) an appeal under article 13 of the 1998 Order, or

(ix) an appeal to the Commissioner under article 15 of the 1998 Order.".

p.1672, *amendment of the Disability Assistance for Working Age People (Scotland) Regulations 2022 (SSI 2022/54) reg.58 (Applications by individuals entitled to Child Disability Payment)*

With effect from August 29, 2022, reg.19(1) and (11) of the Disability Assistance for Working Age People (Transitional Provisions and Miscellaneous Amendment) (Scotland) Regulations 2022 (SSI 2022/217) amended reg.58 of the 2022 Regulations by, for para.(3), substituting: 5.122

"(3) Where an individual receives a determination that they are entitled to a rate of Adult Disability Payment which is higher than the rate of Child Disability Payment they were entitled to immediately before their entitlement to Adult Disability Payment begins, paragraph (4) applies.

(4) The individual is to receive a payment equal to the value of Adult Disability Payment they would have received for the period specified in paragraph (5), reduced by the amount of Child Disability Payment that they were entitled to for the same period.

(5) The period specified for the purposes of paragraph (4) is the period between the date—

(a) their entitlement to Adult Disability Payment would have begun if this regulation did not apply to the individual, in terms of regulation 35(4) to (6), and

(b) their entitlement to Adult Disability Payment begins in terms of paragraph (2).".

pp.1680–1682, *amendment of the Disability Assistance for Working Age People (Scotland) Regulations 2022 (SSI 2022/54) Sch.2 Pt 1 (Short-term assistance)*

With effect from August 29, 2022, reg.19(1) and (12) of the Disability Assistance for Working Age People (Transitional Provisions and Miscellaneous Amendment) (Scotland) Regulations 2022 (SSI 2022/217) amended Pt 1 of Sch.2 of the 2022 Regulations by, for para.4, substituting: 5.123

"Reduction of Adult Disability Payment where short-term assistance is paid

4. Where an individual has received short-term assistance for a period and a determination is subsequently made that the individual is entitled to Adult Disability Payment for the same period, any payment of Adult Disability Payment to be made as a result of the subsequent determination for that period—

(a) where the individual is to be paid Adult Disability Payment at the same rate as or a lower rate than any short-term assistance and any Adult Disability Payment already paid to that individual for that period, is to be reduced to £0, and

(b) in any other case, is to be reduced by any short-term assistance and any Adult Disability Payment already paid to that individual for that period.".

pp.1683–1686, *amendment of the Disability Assistance for Working Age People (Scotland) Regulations 2022 (SSI 2022/54) Pt 3 of Sch.2 (Transfer from personal independence payment to adult disability payment)*

5.124   With effect from August 29, 2022, reg.19(1) and (13) of the Disability Assistance for Working Age People (Transitional Provisions and Miscellaneous Amendment) (Scotland) Regulations 2022 (SSI 2022/217) amended Pt 3 of Sch.2 of the 2022 Regulations.

In para.7 (interpretation), in the definition of "transferring individual", "an individual" is substituted for "a relevant individual".

Paragraph 10 is substituted by:

"Effect of determination on entitlement to Personal Independence Payment

10.—(1) Where a determination is made under paragraph 9(1) that the transferring individual is entitled to Adult Disability Payment, the transferring individual's entitlement to Personal Independence Payment will cease on—

(a) the date their entitlement to Adult Disability Payment begins,

(b) where a transferring individual was paid Personal Independence Payment one week in advance and 3 weekly in arrears, the date one week after the date their entitlement to Adult Disability Payment begins, or

(c) where paragraph 11 applies, the date their entitlement to Adult Disability Payment would have begun had paragraph 11(2) not applied to set an earlier date of entitlement.

(2) Where paragraph (1)(b) applies—

(a) section 77(4) (personal independence payment) of the Welfare Reform Act 2012, and

(b) regulation 4(e) of these Regulations (entitlement to other benefits),

do not apply in respect of the first week of entitlement to Adult Disability Payment.",

Paragraph 11 (exceptions to para.9(5)) is amended by inserting after para.(1):

"(1A) Where the transferring individual reached the relevant age as defined in regulation 22(2) when they became terminally ill under section 82 of the Welfare Reform Act 2012 or in terms of regulation 26(7), the restrictions in sub-paragraph (1B) apply in relation to the determination under paragraph 9(1).

(1B) The restrictions referred to in sub-paragraph (1A) are—

(a) where the transferring individual was entitled to the mobility component of Personal Independence Payment at the standard rate immediately before the date of transfer, then regardless of whether the award would otherwise have been for the enhanced rate, the Scottish Ministers—

    (i) may only make an award for the standard rate of that component, and

    (ii) may only make such an award where the entitlement results from substantially the same condition or conditions in respect of which the mobility component of Personal Independence payment was given,

(b) where the transferring individual was entitled to the mobility component of Personal Independence Payment at the enhanced rate immediately before the date of transfer, the Scottish Ministers may only award that rate of that component where entitlement results from substantially the same condition or conditions in respect of which the mobility component of Personal Independence Payment was given,

(c) where the transferring individual was not entitled to the mobility component of Personal Independence Payment immediately before the date of transfer, the Scottish Ministers may not award that component at either the standard or enhanced rate."

In consequence, in sub-para.(1), "except where sub-paragraph (1A) applies," is inserted before "the determination made under paragraph 9(1)" and, in sub-para. (2), "or (1A)" is inserted after "sub-paragraph (1)".

In para.12 (change of circumstances), "care" is substituted for "daily living" in both sub-para. (4)(a)(i) and sub-para. 4(a)(ii) and, after sub-para.(6) there is inserted:

"(7) Where the change of circumstance notified under sub-paragraph (1) occurred after the person had reached the relevant age as defined in regulation 22(2), the restrictions in sub-paragraph (8) will apply in relation to the determination under sub-paragraph (1).

(8) The restrictions referred to in sub-paragraph (7) are—

(a) where the transfer determination awarded the mobility component at the standard rate then, regardless of whether the award would have otherwise been for the enhanced rate, the Scottish Ministers—

    (i) may only make an award for the standard rate of that component, and

    (ii) may only make such an award where entitlement results from substantially the same condition or conditions in respect of which the mobility component in the transfer determination was given,

(b) where the transfer determination awarded the mobility component at the enhanced rate, the Scottish Ministers may only award that rate of that component where entitlement results from substantially the same condition or conditions in respect of which the mobility component in the transfer determination was given,

(c) where the transfer determination did not include an award of the mobility component, the Scottish Ministers may not award that component at either the standard or enhanced rate."

In para.14 (modification of these regulations: transferring individuals), after sub-para.(b), there is inserted:

"(ba) in regulation 36, for sub-paragraph (b), substitute—
"(b) any subsequent payment—
(i) 4 weekly in arrears,
(ii) weekly in advance, or
(iii) where the Scottish Ministers consider that it would be unjust not to do so, at such intervals as may be specified in the notice of determination.",".

pp.1696–1698, *annotation to the Tribunals (Scotland) Act 2014 s.46 (Appeal from the Tribunal)*

5.125   In *South Lanarkshire Council v Boyd* [2022] CSIH 41, when dismissing an appeal from the Upper Tribunal, the Court of Session observed at [21] that, when it permitted a new argument, not advanced before the First-tier Tribunal, to be argued before it, the Upper Tribunal appeared not to have considered whether the evidence and the findings in facts might have been different if the argument had been in play before the First-tier Tribunal.

p.1700, *annotation to the Tribunals (Scotland) Act 2014 s.50 (Procedure on second appeal)*

5.126   Following the proceedings noted in the main work, the Court of Session appears to have given permission to appeal, but it ultimately dismissed the appeal (*South Lanarkshire Council v Boyd* [2022] CSIH 41).

p.1710, *amendment of the Tribunals (Scotland) Act 2014 Sch.10 (Index of expressions)*

5.127   With effect from May 13, 2022, s.16(8) of the Social Security Administration and Tribunal Membership (Scotland) Act 2020 modified Sch.10 by inserting after the entry for "extra judge (Upper)":

"extra judge (First-tier)   Section 19(4)".

This modification is consequential to modifications made by s.15 of the 2020 Act, which enable judges from UK, overseas or international courts or tribunals, and former judges of UK courts or tribunals, to sit temporarily in the First-tier Tribunal. Such judges could already be authorised to sit in the Upper Tribunal. Sections 15 and 16 were brought into force by the Social Security Administration and Tribunal Membership (Scotland) Act 2020 (Commencement No. 6) Regulations 2022 (SSI 2022/146).

p.1716, *annotation to the First-tier Tribunal for Scotland Social Security Chamber (Procedure) Regulations 2018 (SSI 2018/273) Sch. r.2 (Overriding objective and parties' obligation to co-operate with the First-tier Tribunal)*

The Upper Tribunal considered in *Kindreich v Slater, Hogg & Howison* [2022] UT 16 the extent to which the First-tier Tribunal is obliged, or is entitled, to assist an unrepresented party. Ultimately, the appellant failed because of the way he had argued the case before the First-tier Tribunal, but it is important to note that the overriding objective in the Housing and Property Chamber of the First-tier Tribunal is different from that in these Rules. The equivalent of r.2(2)(c) requires the First-tier Tribunal to ensure "so far as practicable that parties are on an equal footing procedurally and are able to participate fully in the proceedings, including assisting any party in the presentation of the party's case without advocating the course they should take". In these rules, the reference to equality is omitted, leaving the emphasis on the enabling role of the Tribunal, provided there is no unfairness to the opposing party. 5.128

Similarly, in *Woro v Brown* (decided on October 13, 2022 but not numbered), the Upper Tribunal held that in undefended housing proceedings, the First-tier Tribunal was required to raise any point as to competency but it was not entitled to raise a point as to relevancy—in other words, it was bound to consider whether it had jurisdiction to determine the proceedings, but was not entitled to go into the merits of points not raised by a party. However, that conclusion was reached after considering the function of a sheriff in such proceedings before jurisdiction was transferred to the First-tier Tribunal. In contrast, it has long been held at the highest level that social security proceedings are not adversarial (see *Kerr v Department for Social Development* [2004] UKHL 23; [2004] 1 W.L.R 1372 (also reported as an appendix to *R1/04(SF)*), noted at pp.1069 to 1071 in Vol.III of the main work).

In relation to proceeding in the absence of a party, see the supplementary annotation to r.27, below.

p.1721, *amendment of the First-tier Tribunal for Scotland Social Security Chamber (Procedure) Regulations 2018 (SSI 2018/273) Sch. r.14 (Disclosure of documents and information)*

With effect from June 21, r.2 of the First-tier Tribunal for Scotland Social Security Chamber and Upper Tribunal for Scotland (Rules of Procedure) (Miscellaneous Amendment) Regulations 2022 (SSI 2022/162) amended r.14 of the 2018 Rules by numbering the former text as para.(1) and adding: 5.129

"(2) The First-tier Tribunal may at any stage of the proceedings, on its own initiative or on the request of one or more of the parties, give a direction prohibiting disclosure of a document or information to a person ("the recipient") if—
(a) the document or information relates to the physical or mental health of a person,

(b) a registered medical practitioner or a registered nurse has informed either the First-tier Tribunal, or one or more of the parties, that disclosure of the document or information would be likely to cause serious harm to the physical or mental health of the recipient or some other person,

(c) the First-tier Tribunal is satisfied that such disclosure would be likely to cause serious harm to the physical or mental health of the recipient or some other person, and

(d) the First-tier Tribunal is satisfied, having regard to the interests of justice, that it is proportionate to give such a direction.

(3) If a party considers that the First-tier Tribunal should give a direction under paragraph (2) prohibiting the disclosure of a document or information to a person ("the recipient"), the party must provide to the First-tier Tribunal the document or information, and the reason the party is requesting that it be withheld, so that the First-tier Tribunal may decide whether the document or information should be disclosed to the recipient or should be subject of a direction under paragraph (2).

(4) The First-tier Tribunal must conduct proceedings as appropriate in order to give effect to a direction given under paragraph (2).

(5) If the First-tier Tribunal gives a direction under paragraph (2) which prevents disclosure to a party who has a representative, or any other person acting on their behalf, the First-tier Tribunal may give a direction that the document or information be disclosed to that representative or person if the First-tier Tribunal is satisfied that—

(a) disclosure to the representative or person would be in the interests of the party, and

(b) the representative or person will act in accordance with paragraph (6).

(6) Documents or information disclosed to a representative or person in accordance with a direction under paragraph (5) must not be disclosed either directly or indirectly to any other person without the First-tier Tribunal's consent.".

The new paragraphs are in terms very similar to those of r.14(2)–(6) of the Tribunal Procedure (First-tier Tribunal) (Social Entitlement Chamber) Rules 2008 (see Vol.III of the main work), save that it is expressly provided that the relevant documents and the feared harm must both relate to a person's health.

p.1734, *annotation to the First-tier Tribunal for Scotland Social Security Chamber (Procedure) Regulations 2018 (SSI 2018/273) Sch. r.27 (Hearings in a party's absence)*

5.130   In *Devine v Bailo* [2022] UT 14, the Upper Tribunal set aside a decision of the First-tier Tribunal given in the absence of a party at a hearing by telephone conference, when the absent party had submitted an email setting out in detail why he considered a telephone hearing to be inadequate. In its reasons for decision, the First-tier Tribunal had explained why a telephone conference was permitted and referred to the overriding objective which, as in the present Rules, provides that dealing with cases justly includes "avoiding delay, so far as compatible with the proper consideration of the issues". However, while it had referred to the need to avoid delay, it had not addressed the absent party's arguments and had therefore failed to show that it had considered whether its decision was compatible with the proper consideration of the issues. The Upper Tribunal said:

> "[13] In deciding whether to proceed in the face of an application to postpone it is likely that the FtT will have regard to the reason put forward by a party together with the nature of the dispute and whether that may be adjudicated upon fairly absent one of the parties. When delay is recognised as inevitable (in the event of acceding to the application to postpone) the FtT may have to assess what effect that will have upon the determination and what prejudice will be suffered by parties. If either or both parties are legally represented that may have a bearing on the assessment. Parties' ability to deal with the proposed means of convening the hearing (here at the telephone) will have to be weighed in the overall evaluation of whether to proceed or not. That will inevitably involve an assessment of what is said by parties about how they would react to telephone or video hearings. The scope of the hearing and how it is envisaged that the matter will be resolved—for example, with reference to oral testimony alone —may well be a relevant consideration. Documentary material including witness statements may well go some way to resolving, or assisting in the resolution of, disputed issues. The availability of alternative means of convening the hearing and informed estimates about when those may be accessed by the FtT may affect whether the application to postpone may be given effect to. These sorts of considerations may well have been relevant to the FtT's decision to postpone. The FtT decision is silent on what it made of these other factors, aside from delay, in the exercise of its discretion."

pp.1735–1737, *annotation to the First-tier Tribunal for Scotland Social Security Chamber (Procedure) Regulations 2018 (SSI 2018/273) Sch. r.29 (Reasons for decisions)*

The Council's appeal against the decision in *South Lanarkshire Council v Boyd* [2021] UT 24, mentioned in the main work, was dismissed by the Court of Session, who observed at [21] that, when it permitted new argument, not advanced before the First-tier Tribunal, to be argued before it, the Upper Tribunal appeared not to have considered whether the evidence and the findings in facts might have been different if the argument had been in play before the First-tier Tribunal, and also that the evidence led by the Council before the First-tier Tribunal appeared to have been "somewhat scant and lacking in clarity" (*South Lanarkshire Council v Boyd* [2022] CSIH 41). 5.131

p.1752, *amendment of the Upper Tribunal for Scotland (Social Security Rules of Procedure) Regulations 2018 (SSI 2018/274) Sch. r.17 (Disclosure of documents and information)*

5.132   With effect from June 21, r.3 of the First-tier Tribunal for Scotland Social Security Chamber and Upper Tribunal for Scotland (Rules of Procedure) (Miscellaneous Amendment) Regulations 2022 (SSI 2022/162) amended r.17 of the 2018 Rules by numbering the former text as para.(1) and adding:

"(2) The Upper Tribunal may at any stage of proceedings, on its own initiative or on the request of one or more of the parties, give a direction prohibiting disclosure of a document or information to a person ("the recipient") if—

(a) the document or information relates to the physical or mental health of a person,

(b) a registered medical practitioner or registered nurse has informed either the Upper Tribunal, or one or more of the parties, that disclosure of the information would be likely to cause serious harm to the physical or mental health of the recipient or some other person,

(c) the Upper Tribunal is satisfied that such disclosure would be likely to cause serious harm to the physical or mental health of the recipient or some other person, and

(d) the Upper Tribunal is satisfied, having regard to the interests of justice, that it is proportionate to give such a direction.

(3) If a party considers that the Upper Tribunal should give a direction under paragraph (2) prohibiting the disclosure of a document or information to a person ("the recipient"), the party must provide to the Upper Tribunal the document or information, and the reason the party is requesting that it be withheld, so that the Upper Tribunal may decide whether the document or information should be disclosed to the recipient or should be subject of a direction under paragraph (2).

(4) The Upper Tribunal must conduct proceedings as appropriate in order to give effect to a direction given under paragraph (2).

(5) If the Upper Tribunal gives a direction under paragraph (2) which prevents disclosure to a party who has a representative, or any other person acting on their behalf, the Upper Tribunal may give a direction that the document or information be disclosed to that representative or person if the Upper Tribunal is satisfied that—

(a) disclosure to the representative or person would be in the interests of the party, and

(b) the representative or person will act in accordance with paragraph (6).

(6) Documents or information disclosed to a representative or person in accordance with a direction under paragraph (5) must not be disclosed either directly or indirectly to any other person without the Upper Tribunal's consent.".

The new paragraphs are in terms very similar to those of r.14(2) to (6) of the Tribunal Procedure (Upper Tribunal) Rules 2008 (see Vol.III of the main work), save that it is expressly provided that the relevant documents and the feared harm must both relate to a person's health.

PART VI

CUMULATIVE UPDATING MATERIAL
VOLUME V

INCOME SUPPORT AND THE LEGACY
BENEFITS

Commentary by

John Mesher

Tom Royston

Nick Wikeley

Replace Vol.II pp.993–1110 with the following:

PART I

SOCIAL SECURITY STATUTES

p.15, *amendment to the Social Security Contributions and Benefits Act 1992 s.126(7) (Trade disputes)*

With effect from April 11, 2022, art.23 of the Social Security Benefits **6.001** Uprating Order 2022 (SI 2022/292) substituted "£42.50" for "£41" in subs.(7).

p.18, *annotation to the Social Security Contributions and Benefits Act 1992 s.126(5)(b) (Trade disputes—relevant sum)*

Note that the amount of the "relevant sum" for the purposes of **6.002** s.126(5)(b) is specified in subs.(7), not (6). With effect from April 11, 2022 the sum was increased to £42.50 (see the entry for p.15).

pp.19–20, *annotation to the Social Security Contributions and Benefits Act 1992 s.134(1) (Exclusions from benefit)*

In the Institute for Government and the Social Security Advisory **6.003** Committee's 2021 joint report *Jobs and benefits: The Covid-19 challenge* it was noted that if the capital limit had risen in line with prices since 2006 it would be close to £23,500 (or £25,000: different figures are given) and recommended that the limit should be increased to £25,000 and subsequently automatically indexed to maintain its real value (pp.22 and 31). That recommendation was summarily rejected in the Government's response of March 22, 2022.

p.72, *annotation to the Jobseekers Act 1995 s.13(1) (Income and capital: income-based jobseeker's allowance)*

In the Institute for Government and the Social Security Advisory **6.004** Committee's 2021 joint report *Jobs and benefits: The Covid-19 challenge* it was noted that if the capital limit had risen in line with prices since 2006 it would be close to £23,500 (or £25,000: different figures are given) and recommended that the limit should be increased to £25,000 and subsequently automatically indexed to maintain its real value (pp.22 and 31). That recommendation was summarily rejected in the Government's response of March 22, 2022.

p.81, *annotation to the old style Jobseekers Act 1995 s.15(2) (Effect on other claimants—trade disputes)*

With effect from April 11, 2022 the "prescribed sum" for the purposes **6.005** of s.15(2)(d) was increased to £42.50 (see the entry for p.1086).

p.133, *annotation to the old style Jobseekers Act 1995 s.35 (Interpretation—definition of "employment officer")*

6.006   Note in relation to the schemes whose providers have been designated as employment officers that the Work Programme has ceased to operate and that reg.8(3) of the SAPOE Regulations has been revoked with effect from March 22, 2022 (see the entry for p.1187).

PART II

INCOME SUPPORT REGULATIONS

p.229, *amendments to the Income Support (General) Regulations 1987 (SI 1987/1967) reg.2 (Interpretation)*

6.007   With effect from July 26, 2021, Sch.1 para.2 of the Social Security (Scotland) Act 2018 (Disability Assistance for Children and Young People) (Consequential Modifications) Order 2021 (SI 2021/786) inserts the following definitions:

"child disability payment" has the meaning given in regulation 2 of the DACYP Regulations;
"DACYP Regulations" means the Disability Assistance for Children and Young People (Scotland) Regulations 2021;

With effect from January 1, 2022, reg.2(2) of the Social Security (Income and Capital Disregards) (Amendment) Regulations 2021 (SI 2021/1405) inserts the following definitions:

"child abuse payment" means a payment from a scheme established or approved by the Secretary of State for the purpose of providing compensation in respect of historic institutional child abuse in the United Kingdom;"
"Windrush payment" means a payment made under the Windrush Compensation Scheme (Expenditure) Act 2020;"

With effect from January 1, 2022, reg.2(2) of the Social Security (Income and Capital Disregards) (Amendment) Regulations 2021 (SI 2021/1405) inserts ", a child abuse payment or a Windrush payment" into the definition of "qualifying person", after "Grenfell Tower payment".

With effect from March 21, 2022, art.2(2) of the Social Security (Disability Assistance for Working Age People) (Consequential Amendments) Order 2022 (SI 2022/177) inserts the following definition:

"adult disability payment" has the meaning given in regulation 2 of the Disability Assistance for Working Age People (Scotland) Regulations 2022;

p.275, *amendments to the Income Support (General) Regulations 1987 (SI 1987/1967) reg.4 (Temporary absence from Great Britain)*

With effect from July 26, 2021, Sch.1 para.3 of the Social Security **6.008** (Scotland) Act 2018 (Disability Assistance for Children and Young People) (Consequential Modifications) Order 2021 (SI 2021/786) makes the following amendment:

In reg.4(2)(c)(v)(aa) after "allowance", insert ", the care component of child disability payment at the highest rate in accordance with the DACYP Regulations (see regulation 11(5) of those Regulations)".

With effect from March 21, 2022, art.2(3) of the Social Security (Disability Assistance for Working Age People) (Consequential Amendments) Order 2022 (SI 2022/177) makes the following amendment:
In reg.4(2)(c)(v)(aa) (temporary absence from Great Britain):
(a) for "or" after "armed forces independence payment" substitute ", ";
(b) after "personal independence payment" insert "or the enhanced rate of the daily living component of adult disability payment".

pp.329–331, *amendment to the Income Support (General) Regulations 1987 (SI 1987/1967) reg.21AA (Special cases: supplemental—persons from abroad)*

The text in the main volume at para.2.167 should be replaced with the **6.009** following:

"[1] Special cases: supplemental—persons from abroad

21AA.—(1) "Person from abroad" means, subject to the following provisions of this regulation, a claimant who is not habitually resident in the United Kingdom, the Channel Islands, the Isle of Man or the Republic of Ireland.

(2) No claimant shall be treated as habitually resident in the United Kingdom, the Channel Islands, the Isle of Man or the Republic of Ireland unless he has a right to reside in (as the case may be) the United Kingdom, the Channel Islands, the Isle of Man or the Republic of Ireland other than a right to reside which falls within paragraph (3) [12 or (3A)].

(3) A right to reside falls within this paragraph if it is one which exists by virtue of, or in accordance with, one or more of the following—
(a) regulation 13 of the [12 Immigration (European Economic Area) Regulations 2016];
(b) regulation 14 of those Regulations, but only in a case where the right exists under that regulation because the claimant is—
  (i) a jobseeker for the purpose of the definition of "qualified person" in regulation 6(1) of those Regulations, or
  (ii) a family member (within the meaning of regulation 7 of those Regulations) of such a jobseeker; [14 or]

[⁷ [¹² (bb) regulation 16 of those Regulations, but only in a case where the right exists under that regulation because the claimant satisfies the criteria in paragraph (5) of that regulation;]]

[¹⁴ (c)–(e) . . .]

[¹² (3A) A right to reside falls within this paragraph if it exists by virtue of a claimant having been granted limited leave to enter, or remain in, the United Kingdom under the Immigration Act 1971 by virtue of—

(a) Appendix EU to the immigration rules made under section 3(2) of that Act; [¹⁵ . . .]

(b) being a person with a Zambrano right to reside as defined in Annex 1 of Appendix EU to the immigration rules made under section 3(2) of that Act.]

[¹⁵; or (c) having arrived in the United Kingdom with an entry clearance that was granted under Appendix EU (Family Permit) to the immigration rules made under section 3(2) of that Act.]

[¹³ (3B) Paragraph (3A)(a) does not apply to a person who—

(a) has a right to reside granted by virtue of being a family member of a relevant person of Northern Ireland; and

(b) would have a right to reside under the [¹² Immigration (European Economic Area) Regulations 2016] if the relevant person of Northern Ireland were an EEA national, provided that the right to reside does not fall within paragraph (3).]

(4) A claimant is not a person from abroad if he is—

[¹⁷ (zza) a person granted leave in accordance with the immigration rules made under section 3(2) of the Immigration Act 1971, where such leave is granted by virtue of—

  (i) the Afghan Relocations and Assistance Policy; or

  (ii) the previous scheme for locally-employed staff in Afghanistan (sometimes referred to as the ex-gratia scheme);

(zzb) a person in Great Britain not coming within sub-paragraph (zza) or [¹⁸ (h)] who left Afghanistan in connection with the collapse of the Afghan government that took place on 15th August 2021;]

[¹⁸ (zzc) a person in Great Britain who was residing in Ukraine immediately before 1st January 2022, left Ukraine in connection with the Russian invasion which took place on 24th February 2022 and—

  (i) has been granted leave in accordance with immigration rules made under section 3(2) of the Immigration Act 1971; [¹⁹ . . .]

  (ii) has a right of abode in the United Kingdom within the meaning given in section 2 of that Act;] [¹⁹ or

  (iii) does not require leave to enter or remain in the United Kingdom in accordance with section 3ZA of that Act;]

[¹⁰ (za) a qualified person for the purposes of [¹⁶ regulation 6 of the Immigration (European Economic Area) Regulations 2016] as a worker or a self-employed person;

(zb) a family member of a person referred to in sub-paragraph (za) [¹³ . . .];

(zc) a person who has a right to reside permanently in the United Kingdom by virtue of regulation 15(1)(c), (d) or (e) of those Regulations;]

[¹³ (zd) a family member of a relevant person of Northern Ireland, with a right to reside which falls within paragraph (3A)(a), provided that the relevant person of Northern Ireland falls within sub-paragraph (za), or would do so but for the fact that they are not an EEA national;]

[¹⁴ (ze) a frontier worker within the meaning of regulation 3 of the Citizens' Rights (Frontier Workers) (EU Exit) Regulations 2020;

(zf) a family member, of a person referred to in sub-paragraph (ze), who has been granted limited leave to enter, or remain in, the United Kingdom by virtue of Appendix EU to the immigration rules made under section 3(2) of the Immigration Act 1971;]

(g) a refugee within the definition in Article 1 of the Convention relating to the Status of Refugees done at Geneva on 28th July 1951, as extended by Article 1(2) of the Protocol relating to the Status of Refugees done at New York on 31st January 1967;

[³ [⁹ (h) a person who has been granted leave or who is deemed to have been granted leave outside the rules made under section 3(2) of the Immigration Act 1971 [¹⁸ . . .];

(hh) a person who has humanitarian protection granted under those rules;] [⁹ or]

(i) a person who is not a person subject to immigration control within the meaning of section 115(9) of the Immigration and Asylum Act and who is in the United Kingdom as a result of his deportation, expulsion or other removal by compulsion of law from another country to the United Kingdom; [⁵ . . .] [⁹ . . .]

[¹³ (5) In this regulation—

"EEA national" has the meaning given in regulation 2(1) of the Immigration (European Economic Area) Regulations 2016;

"family member" has the meaning given in regulation 7(1)(a), (b) or (c) of the Immigration (European Economic Area) Regulations 2016 except that regulation 7(4) of those Regulations does not apply for the purposes of paragraphs (3B) and (4)(zd);

"relevant person of Northern Ireland" has the meaning given in Annex 1 of Appendix EU to the immigration rules made under section 3(2) of the Immigration Act 1971.]

[¹⁴ (6) In this regulation references to the Immigration (European Economic Area) Regulations 2016 are to be read with Schedule 4 to the Immigration and Social Security Co-ordination (EU Withdrawal) Act 2020 (Consequential, Saving, Transitional and Transitory Provisions) Regulations 2020.]"

AMENDMENTS

1. Social Security (Persons from Abroad) Amendment Regulations 2006 (SI 1026/2006) reg.6(3) (April 30, 2006).
2. Social Security (Lebanon) Amendment Regulations 2006 (SI 2006/1981) reg.2 (July 25, 2006). The amendment ceased to have effect from January 31, 2007.

3. Social Security (Persons from Abroad) Amendment (No. 2) Regulations 2006 (SI 2006/2528) reg.2 (October 9, 2006).
4. Social Security (Bulgaria and Romania) Amendment Regulations 2006 (SI 2006/3341) reg.2 (January 1, 2007).
5. Social Security (Habitual Residence) (Amendment) Regulations 2009 (SI 2009/362) reg.2 (March 18, 2009).
6. Social Security (Miscellaneous Amendments) (No. 3) Regulations 2011 (SI 2011/2425) reg.7(1) and (3) (October 31, 2011).
7. Social Security (Habitual Residence) (Amendment) Regulations 2012 (SI 2012/2587) reg.2 (November 8, 2012).
8. Social Security (Croatia) Amendment Regulations 2013 (SI 2013/1474) reg.2 (July 1, 2013).
9. Social Security (Miscellaneous Amendments) (No. 3) Regulations 2013 (SI 2013/2536) reg.4(1) and (5) (October 29, 2013).
10. Social Security (Habitual Residence) (Amendment) Regulations 2014 (SI 2014/902) reg.2(1) (May 31, 2014).
11. Social Security (Updating of EU References) (Amendment) Regulations 2018 (SI 2018/1084) reg.4 and Sch. para.6 (November 15, 2018).
12. Social Security (Income-related Benefits) (Updating and Amendment) (EU Exit) Regulations 2019 (SI 2019/872) reg.2 (May 7, 2019).
13. Social Security (Income-Related Benefits) (Persons of Northern Ireland —Family Members) (Amendment) Regulations 2020 (SI 2020/683) reg.2 (August 24, 2020).
14. Immigration and Social Security Co-ordination (EU Withdrawal) Act 2020 (Consequential, Saving, Transitional and Transitory Provisions) (EU Exit) Regulations 2020 (SI 2020/1309) reg.53 (December 31, 2020 at 11.00pm).
15. Immigration (Citizens' Rights etc.) (EU Exit) Regulations 2020 (SI 2020/1372) reg.8 (December 31, 2020 at 11.00 pm).
16. Social Security (Income-related Benefits) (Updating and Amendment) (EU Exit) Regulations (SI 2019/872) reg.2 (May 7, 2019).
17. Social Security (Habitual Residence and Past Presence) (Amendment) Regulations 2021 (SI 2021/1034) reg.2 (September 15, 2021).
18. Social Security (Habitual Residence and Past Presence) (Amendment) Regulations 2022 (SI 2022/344) reg.2 (March 22, 2022).
19. Social Security (Habitual Residence and Past Presence) (Amendment) (No. 2) Regulations 2022 (SI 2022/990) reg.2 (October 18, 2022).

p.355, *annotation to the Income Support (General) Regulations 1987 (SI 1987/1967) reg.23 (Calculation of the income and capital of members of claimant's family and of a polygamous marriage)*

6.010　In line 4 of p.355, for "on the exclusion of", substitute "so as to exclude" and in line 5 for "s.11", substitute "ss.11 and 12".

p.421, *amendment to the Income Support (General) Regulations 1987 (SI 1987/1967) reg.42(4ZB) (Notional income—exceptions)*

6.011　With effect from January 1, 2022, reg.2(3) of the Social Security (Income and Capital Disregards) (Amendment) Regulations 2021 (SI 2021/1405) amended para.(4ZB) by substituting the following for "a payment of income which is a Grenfell Tower payment":

"any of the following payments of income—
    (a) a Grenfell Tower payment;
    (b) a child abuse payment;
    (c) a Windrush payment."

All of those payments are defined in reg.2(1). See the entry for p.684 for discussion of the nature of child abuse and Windrush payments.

p.438, *annotation to the Income Support (General) Regulations 1987 (SI 1987/967) reg.45 (Capital limit)*

In the Institute for Government and the Social Security Advisory   6.012
Committee's 2021 joint report *Jobs and benefits: The Covid-19 challenge* it was noted that if the capital limit of £16,000 had risen in line with prices since 2006 it would be close to £23,500 (or £25,000: different figures are given) and recommended that the limit should be increased to £25,000 and subsequently automatically indexed to maintain its real value (pp.22 and 31). That recommendation was summarily rejected in the Government's response of March 22, 2022.

p.439, *annotation to the Income Support (General) Regulations 1987 (SI 1987/1967) reg.46 (Calculation of capital)*

At some point, the valuation of digital assets, such as non-fungible   6.013
tokens, cryptocurrency etc., may have to be addressed, including how they fit into the notions of capital and of personal possessions. There is extensive discussion of the existing legal framework in the Law Commission's *Digital Assets: Consultation Paper* (Law Com. No.256, July 28, 2022).

p.443, *annotation to the Income Support (General) Regulations 1987 (SI 1987/967) reg.46 (Calculation of capital—claimant holding as trustee)*

In line 10 of the paragraph starting "One particular", insert the   6.014
following between "return it" and the full stop:

"(a result most recently confirmed by the decision of the Privy Council in the *Prickly Bay* case)"

p.446, *annotation to the Income Support (General) Regulations 1987 (SI 1987/967) reg.46 (Calculation of capital—claimant holding as trustee)*

Note, in relation to the discussion of cases in which the *Quistclose*   6.015
principle has or has not been applied, that the Privy Council in *Prickly Bay Waterside Ltd v British American Insurance Co Ltd* [2022] UKPC 8; [2022] 1 W.L.R. 2087, while accepting the value of summaries of principles, in particular of those established by the judgment of Lord Millett in *Twinsectra Ltd v Yardley* [2002] 2 A.C. 164, warned against not going back to the "core analysis" in that judgment. It was emphasised again that it is not enough that money is provided for a particular purpose. The question is whether the parties intended that the money should be at the

free disposition of the recipient. An intention that it should not be need not be mutual, in the sense of being shared or reciprocated, but could be imposed by one party and acquiesced in by the other. A *Quistclose* trust is a default trust, so can be excluded or moulded by the terms of the parties' express agreements. In the particular case, involving complex commercial transactions in which a sum was loaned to a bank that contracted to guarantee payment of the purchase price of a property on future completion, it was significant to the outcome that a *Quistclose* trust had not been established that there had been no requirement that the sum be segregated by the bank from its other funds. It is submitted that in other contexts, such as family or other relatively informal arrangements more likely to be encountered in the social security context, a lack of segregation, say into a separate account, would not carry nearly such weight.

p.451, *annotation to the Income Support (General) Regulations 1987 (SI 1987/1967) reg.46 (Calculation of capital—claimant holding as trustee)*

6.016   Note the decision of the Supreme Court, by a majority of three to two, in *Guest v Guest* [2022] UKSC 27; [2022] 3 W.L.R. 911 on proprietary estoppel and the nature of the remedies available in equity. Lord Briggs, giving the majority judgment, conducted an exhaustive survey of the English and Australian case law, as well as academic debate, and rejected the theory that the aim of the remedy was to compensate the person given a promise or assurance about the acquisition of property for the detriment suffered in reliance on the promise or assurance, rather than primarily to hold the person who had given the promise or assurance to the promise or assurance, which would usually prevent the unconscionability inherent in the repudiation of the promise or assurance that had been detrimentally relied on (paras 71 and 61). However, the remedy was a flexible one dependent on the circumstances. Lord Briggs summarised the principles as follows:

> "74. I consider that, in principle, the court's normal approach should be as follows. The first stage (which is not in issue in this case) is to determine whether the promisor's repudiation of his promise is, in the light of the promisee's detrimental reliance upon it, unconscionable at all. It usually will be, but there may be circumstances (such as the promisor falling on hard times and needing to sell the property to pay his creditors, or to pay for expensive medical treatment or social care for himself or his wife) when it may not be. Or the promisor may have announced or carried out only a partial repudiation of the promise, which may or may not have been unconscionable, depending on the circumstances.
> 75. The second (remedy) stage will normally start with the assumption (not presumption) that the simplest way to remedy the unconscionability constituted by the repudiation is to hold the promisor to the promise. The promisee cannot (and probably would not) complain, for example, that his detrimental reliance had cost him more than the value of the promise, were it to be fully performed. But the court may have to listen to many other reasons from the promisor (or

his executors) why something less than full performance will negate the unconscionability and therefore satisfy the equity. They may be based on one or more of the real-life problems already outlined. The court may be invited by the promisor to consider one or more proxies for performance of the promise, such as the transfer of less property than promised or the provision of a monetary equivalent in place of it, or a combination of the two.

76. If the promisor asserts and proves, the burden being on him for this purpose, that specific enforcement of the full promise, or monetary equivalent, would be out of all proportion to the cost of the detriment to the promisee, then the court may be constrained to limit the extent of the remedy. This does not mean that the court will be seeking precisely to compensate for the detriment as its primary task, but simply to put right a disproportionality which is so large as to stand in the way of a full specific enforcement doing justice between the parties. It will be a very rare case where the detriment is equivalent in value to the expectation, and there is nothing in principle unjust in a full enforcement of the promise being worth more than the cost of the detriment, any more than there is in giving specific performance of a contract for the sale of land merely because it is worth more than the price paid for it. An example of a remedy out of all proportion to the detriment would be the full enforcement of a promise by an elderly lady to leave her carer a particular piece of jewellery if she stayed on at very low wages, which turned out on valuation by her executors to be a Faberge worth millions. Another would be a promise to leave a generous inheritance if the promisee cared for the promisor for the rest of her life, but where she unexpectedly died two months later."

Thus, in circumstances where proprietary estoppel might be in play (as would probably now be the case on similar facts to *R(SB) 23/85* and *R(SB) 7/87*), great care would be needed in establishing the primary facts and, outside the clearest cases, in a deeper investigation of the principles of law governing the nature of any remedy available. And would a repudiation of a promise when the promisor would otherwise be forced to rely on a means-tested benefit be unconscionable? However, even if it were to be concluded that the claimant did not hold the property in question on trust for someone else, the possibility of a claim in equity, e.g. for some monetary compensation, may well affect the valuation of the property.

p.457, *amendment to the Income Support (General) Regulations 1987 (SI 1987/1967) reg.48(10) (Income treated as capital—exceptions)*

With effect from January 1, 2022, reg.2(4) of the Social Security **6.017** (Income and Capital Disregards) (Amendment) Regulations 2021 (SI 2021/1405) amended para.(10) by inserting the following after sub-para.(ab):

"(ac) which is a child abuse payment;
(ad) which is a Windrush payment; or"

Both of those payments are defined in reg.2(1). See the entry for p.684 for discussion of their nature. The "or" following sub-para.(ab), omitted in error in the main volume, has also been removed.

p.467, *amendment to the Income Support (General) Regulations 1987 (SI 1987/1967) reg.51(3B) (Notional capital—exceptions)*

6.018   With effect from January 1, 2022, reg.2(5) of the Social Security (Income and Capital Disregards) (Amendment) Regulations 2021 (SI 2021/1405) amended para.(3B) by substituting the following for "a payment of capital which is a Grenfell Tower payment":

"any of the following payments of capital—
  (a) a Grenfell Tower payment;
  (b) a child abuse payment;
  (c) a Windrush payment."

All of those payments are defined in reg.2(1). See the entry for p.684 for discussion of the nature of child abuse and Windrush payments.

pp.520–523, *annotations to the Income Support (General) Regulations 1987 (SI 1987/1967) reg.61 (Interpretation—students—meaning of "Full-time course")*

6.019   The principles derived from the case law, taking into account Court of Appeal decisions not all of which are discussed in the main volume, have recently very helpfully been summarised by Judge Rowley in para.19 of *BK v SSWP (UC)* [2022] UKUT 73 (AAC) (some references added by annotator):

"a. Whether or not a person is undertaking a full-time course is a question of fact for the tribunal having regard to the circumstances in each particular case (*R/SB 40/83* at [13]; *R(SB) 41/83* at [12]). Parameters have been set, as appear below:
  b. The words 'full-time' relate to the course and not to the student. Specifically, they do not permit the matter to be determined by reference to the amount of time which the student happens to dedicate to their studies (*R/SB 40/83* at [14], [15]; *R(SB) 2/91* at [7]; *R(SB) 41/83* at [11]).
  c. Evidence from the educational establishment as to whether or not the course is full-time is not necessarily conclusive, but it ought to be accepted as such unless it is inconclusive on its face, or is challenged by relevant evidence which at least raises the possibility that it ought to be rejected (*R/SB 40/83* at [18]), and any evidence adduced in rebuttal should be weighty in content (*R/SB 41/83* at [12]). See also *Flemming v Secretary of State for Work and Pensions* [2002] EWCA Civ 641; [2002] 1 W.L.R. 2322 [also reported as *R(G) 2/02* at [21]–[22] and [38]; and *Deane v Secretary of State for Work and Pensions* [2010] EWCA Civ 699; [2011] 1 W.L.R.

743 [also reported at [2010] AACR 42] where the Court of Appeal repeated an earlier statement in *Flemming* that:

'38 . . . A tribunal of fact should, I think be very slow to accept that a person expects or intends to devote—or does, in fact, devote—significantly less time to the course than those who have conduct of the course expect of him, and very slow to hold that a person who is attending a course considered by the educational establishment to be a part-time course is to be treated as receiving full-time education because he devotes significantly more time than that which is expected of him . . . "

d. If the course is offered as a full-time course, the presumption is that the recipient is in full-time education. There may be exceptions to the rule, such where a student is granted exemptions from part of the course: *Deane* [51]."

In *BK* itself, the claimant was on a one-year MA course at Goldsmiths, University of London, described by that institution as full-time and involving more than 24 hours of study per week. Letters from the Department concerned confirmed six contact hours of teaching in two terms, with an expectation of at least six hours per week in independent study. A dissertation was to be written in the third term. The First-tier Tribunal rejected the claimant's argument that those letters, and the fact that he could arrange his time to be available for work, showed that the course was not full-time. Judge Rowley held that it did not err in law in doing so and that in saying that Goldsmiths' description was "determinative" of the nature of the course it had not strayed into regarding the description as conclusive, but had applied the test in [19(c)] above.

p.550, *amendments to the Income Support (General) Regulations 1987 (SI 1987/1967) Sch.1B (Prescribed categories of persons)*

With effect from July 26, 2021, Sch.1 para.4 of the Social Security   6.020
(Scotland) Act 2018 (Disability Assistance for Children and Young People) (Consequential Modifications) Order 2021 (SI 2021/786) makes the following amendments:

- In para.4(a) of Sch.1B (persons caring for another person):
  - in para.(i), after "Contributions and Benefits Act" insert ", the care component of child disability payment at the highest or middle rate in accordance with the DACYP Regulations (see regulation 11(5) of those Regulations),";
  - in para.(iii), after "disability living allowance", insert ", child disability payment";
  - after para.(iiia), insert "(iiib) the person being cared for ("P") has claimed entitlement to the care component of child disability payment in accordance with regulation 24 (when an application is to be treated as made and beginning of entitlement to assistance) of the DACYP Regulations, an award at the highest or middle rate has been made in respect of P's claim, and where the period for which the award is payable has begun, P is in receipt of that payment;".

With effect from March 21, 2022, art.2(4)–(5) of the Social Security (Disability Assistance for Working Age People) (Consequential Amendments) Order 2022 (SI 2022/177) makes the following amendments:

- In para.4(a) (persons caring for another person) of Sch.1B (prescribed categories of person):
  - in sub-para.(i):
    - for "or" after "(see regulation 11(5) of those Regulations)," substitute ",";
    - after "2012 Act" insert "or the daily living component of adult disability payment at the standard or enhanced rate in accordance with regulation 5 of the Disability Assistance for Working Age People (Scotland) Regulations 2022";
  - in sub-para.(iii):
    - for "or" after "armed forces independence payment" substitute ",";
    - after "personal independence payment" insert "or adult disability payment";
  - after sub-para.(iv) insert "(v)the person being cared for has claimed entitlement to the daily living component of adult disability payment in accordance with regulation 35 (when an application is to be treated as made and beginning of entitlement to assistance) of the Disability Assistance for Working Age People (Scotland) Regulations 2022, an award at the standard or enhanced rate has been made in respect of that claim and, where the period for which the award is payable has begun, that person is in receipt of the payment;".
- In para.7A (certain persons in receipt of the daily living component of personal independence payment) of Sch.1B:
  - in the heading, after "personal independence payment" insert "or adult disability payment";
  - after "at the enhanced rate" insert "or the daily living component of adult disability payment at the enhanced rate".

pp.571–572, *amendments to the Income Support (General) Regulations 1987 (SI 1987/1967) Sch.2 (Applicable amounts)*

6.021 The text in the main volume at paras 2.606–2.626 should be replaced with the following:

"SCHEDULE 2

Regulations 17 [³ (1)] and 18

APPLICABLE AMOUNTS

[³⁵ PART I

PERSONAL ALLOWANCES

2.606 1.—The weekly amounts specified in column (2) below in respect of each person or couple specified in column (1) shall be the weekly amounts specified for the purposes of regulations 17(1) and 18(1) (applicable amounts and polygamous marriages).

Column (1) *Person or Couple*	Column (2) *Amount*

(1) Single claimant aged—
  (a) except where head (b) or (c) of this sub-paragraph applies, less than 18;
  [²⁸(b) less than 18 who falls within any of the circumstances specified in paragraph 1A;]
  (c) less than 18 who satisfies the condition in [⁶⁵ paragraph 11(1)(a)]
  (d) not less than 18 but less than 25;
  (e) not less than 25.
	(1)
	  (a) [⁸⁴ £61.05];
	
	  (b) [⁸⁴ £61.05];
	
	  (c) [⁸⁴ £61.05];
	
	  (d) [⁸⁴ £61.05];
	  (e) [⁸⁴ £77.00].

(2) Lone parent aged—
  (a) except where head (b) or (c) of this sub-paragraph applies, less than 18;
  [²⁸(b) less than 18 who falls within any of the circumstances specified in paragraph 1A;]
  (c) less than 18 who satisfies the condition in [⁶⁵ paragraph 11(1)(a)]
  (d) not less than 18.
	(2)
	  (a) [⁸⁴ £61.05];
	
	  (b) [⁸⁴ £61.05];
	
	  (c) [⁸⁴ £61.05];
	
	  (d) [⁸⁴ £77.00].

[²⁸(3) Couple—
  (a) where both members are aged less than 18 and—
    (i) at least one of them is treated as responsible fora child; or
    (ii) had they not been members of a couple, each would have qualified for income support under regulation 4ZA [⁷¹ or income-related employment and support allowance]; or
    (iii) the claimant's partner satisfies the requirement of section 3(1)(f)(iii) of the Jobseekers Act 1995 (prescribed circumstances for persons aged 16 but less than 18); or
    (iv) there is in force in respect of the claimant's partner a direction under section 16 of the Jobseekers Act 1995 (persons under 18: severe hardship);
  (b) where both members are aged less than 18 and head (a) does not apply but one member of the couple falls within any of the circumstances specified in paragraph 1A;
  (c) where both members are aged less than 18 and heads (a) and (b) do not apply;
  (d) where both members are aged not less than 18;
  (e) where one member is aged not less than 18 and the other member is a person under 18 who—(2)
    (i) qualifies for income support under regulation 4ZA [⁷¹ or income-related employment and support allowance], or who would so qualify if he were not a member of a couple; or
    (ii) satisfies the requirements of section 3(1)(f)(iii) of the Jobseekers Act 1995 (prescribed circumstances for persons aged 16 but less than 18); or
    (iii) is the subject of a direction under section 16 of the Jobseekers Act 1995 (persons under 18: severe hardship);
  (f) where the claimant is aged not less than 18 but less than 25 and his partner is a person under 18 who—
	(3)
	  (a) [⁸⁴ £92.20];
	
	  (b) [⁸⁴ £61.05];
	
	  (c) [⁸⁴ £61.05];
	
	  (d) [⁸⁴ £121.05];
	  (e) [⁸⁴ £121.05];
	
	  (f) [⁸⁴ £61.05];

Column (1)	Column (2)
Person or Couple	Amount

(i) would not qualify for income support under regulation 4ZA [⁷¹ or income-related employment and support allowance] if he were not a member of a couple; and
     (ii) does not satisfy the requirements of section 3(1)(f)(iii) of the Jobseekers Act 1995 (prescribed circumstances for persons aged 16 but less than 18); and
     (iii) is not the subject of a direction under section 16 of the Jobseekers Act 1995 (persons under 18: severe hardship);
 (g) where the claimant is aged not less than 25 and his (g) partner is a person under 18 who—
     (i) would not qualify for income support under regulation 4ZA [⁷¹ or income-related employment and support allowance] if he were not a member of a couple; and
     (ii) does not satisfy the requirements of section 3(1)(f)(iii) of the Jobseekers Act 1995 (prescribed circumstances for persons aged 16 but less than 18); and
     (iii) is not the subject of a direction under section 16 of the Jobseekers Act 1995 (persons under 18: severe hardship).]]
	(g) [⁸⁴ £77.00].

2.607   [²⁸ **1A.**—(1) The circumstances referred to in paragraph 1 are that—

(a) the person has no parents nor any person acting in the place of his parents;

(b) the person—

    (i) is not living with his parents nor any person acting in the place of his parents; and

    (ii) in England and Wales, was being looked after by a local authority pursuant to a relevant enactment who placed him with some person other than a close relative of his; or in Scotland, was in the care of a local authority under a relevant enactment and whilst in that care was not living with his parents or any close relative, or was in custody in any institution to which the Prison Act 1952 or the Prisons (Scotland) Act 1989 applied immediately before he attained the age of 16;

(c) the person is in accommodation which is other than his parental home, and which is other than the home of a person acting in the place of his parents, who entered that accommodation—

    (i) as part of a programme of rehabilitation or resettlement, that programme being under the supervision of the probation service or a local authority; or

    (ii) in order to avoid physical or sexual abuse; or

    (iii) because of a mental or physical handicap or illness and needs such accommodation because of his handicap or illness;

(d) the person is living away from his parents and any person who is acting in the place of his parents in a case where his parents are or, as the case may be, that person is, unable financially to support him and his parents are, or that person is—

    (i) chronically sick or mentally or physically disabled; or

    (ii) detained in custody pending trial or sentence upon conviction or under sentence imposed by a court; of

    (iii) prohibited from entering or re-entering Great Britain; or

(e) the person of necessity has to live away from his parents and any person acting in the place of his parents because—

    (i) he is estranged from his parents and that person; or

    (ii) he is in physical or moral danger; or

    (iii) there is a serious risk to his physical or mental health.

(2) In this paragraph—

  (a) "chronically sick or mentally or physically disabled" has the same meaning it has in regulation 13(3)(b) (circumstances in which persons in relevant education are to be entitled to income support);

  (b) in England and Wales, any reference to a person acting in place of a person's parents includes a reference to—

    (i) where the person is being looked after by a local authority or voluntary organisation who place him with a family, a relative of his, or some other suitable person, the person with whom the person is placed, whether or not any payment is made to him in connection with the placement; or

    (ii) in any other case, any person with parental responsibility for the child, and for this purpose "parental responsibility" has the meaning it has in the Children Act 1989 by virtue of section 3 of that Act;

  (c) in Scotland, any reference to a person acting in place of a person's parents includes a reference to a local authority or voluntary organisation where the person is in their care under a relevant enactment, or to a person with whom the person is boarded out by a local authority or voluntary organisation whether or not any payment is made by them.]

[^{35} **2.**—[^{59} . . .]]   **2.608**

[^{17} **2A.**—[^{55} . . .]]   **2.609**

PART II

Regulations 17[^{3} (1)](c) [^{3} and 18(1)](d)

FAMILY PREMIUM

3.—[^{59} . . .]   **2.610**

PART III

Regulations 17[^{3} (1)](d) [^{3} and 18(1)](e)

PREMIUMS

4.—Except as provided in paragraph 5, the weekly premiums specified in Part IV of this   **2.611** Schedule shall, for the purposes of regulations 17[^{3}(1)](d)[^{3} and 18(1)](e), be applicable to a claimant who satisfies the condition specified in [^{42} paragraphs 8A] [^{10} to 14ZA] in respect of that premium.

5.—Subject to paragraph 6, where a claimant satisfies the conditions in respect of more than one premium in this Part of this Schedule, only one premium shall be applicable to him and, if they are different amounts, the higher or highest amount shall apply.

[^{58} **6.**—(1) Subject to sub-paragraph (2), the following premiums, namely—

  (a) a severe disability to which paragraph 13 applies;

  (b) an enhanced disability premium to which paragraph 13A applies;

  (c) [^{59} . . .]; and

  (d) a carer premium to which paragraph 14ZA applies,

may be applicable in addition to any other premium that may apply under this Schedule.

(2) An enhanced disability premium in respect of a person shall not be applicable in addition

  to—

  (a) a pensioner premium under paragraph 9 or 9A; or

  (b) a higher pension premium under paragraph 10.]

7.—[^{10}(1) Subject to sub-paragraph (2)] for the purposes of this Part of this Schedule, once a premium is applicable to a claimant under this Part, a person shall be treated as being in receipt of any benefit—

(a) in the case of a benefit to which the Social Security (Overlapping Benefits) Regulations 1979 applies, for any period during which, apart from the provisions of those Regulations, he would be in receipt of that benefit; and

(b) for any period spent by a claimant in undertaking a course of training or instruction provided or approved by the [¹² Secretary of State [⁶⁸ . . .]] under section 2 of the Employment and Training Act 1973 [¹¹, or by [⁶⁹ Skills Development Scotland,] Scottish Enterprise or Highlands and Islands Enterprise under section 2 of the Enterprise and New Towns (Scotland) Act 1990,] [⁷ or for any period during which he is in receipt of a training allowance].

[¹⁰(2) For the purposes of the carer premium under paragraph 14ZA, a person shall be treated as being in receipt of [⁴⁹ carer's allowance] by virtue of sub-paragraph (1)(a) only if and for so long as the person in respect of whose care the allowance has been claimed remains in receipt of attendance allowance [¹⁵ , [⁷⁵ . . .] the care component of disability living allowance at the highest or middle rate prescribed in accordance with section 37ZB(3) of the Social Security Act [SSCBA, s.72(3)]] [⁸² , the care component of child disability payment at the highest or middle rate prescribed in accordance with the regulation 11(5) of the DACYP Regulations] [⁷⁵ or the daily living component of personal independence payment at the standard or enhanced rate in accordance with section 78(3) of the 2012 Act] [⁸³ , the daily living component of adult disability payment at the standard or enhanced rate in accordance with regulation 5 of the Disability Assistance for Working Age People (Scotland) Regulations 2022] [⁷⁶ or armed forces independence payment].]

Lone Parent Premium

2.612   **8.**—[²⁹ . . .].

[⁴² **Bereavement Premium**

2.613   **8A.**—[⁶⁷ . . .]]

[**Pensioner premium for persons under 75**

2.614   [⁵⁴ **9.**—The condition is that the claimant has a partner aged [⁷⁰ not less than the qualifying age for state pension credit] but less than 75.]

Pensioner premium for persons 75 and over

2.615   [⁵⁴ **9A.**—The condition is that the claimant has a partner aged not less than 75 but less than 80.]]

Higher Pensioner Premium

2.616   **10.**—[⁵⁴ (1) [⁶⁵ Subject to sub-paragraph (6), the] condition is that—

(a) the claimant's partner is aged not less than 80; or

(b) the claimant's partner is aged less than 80 but [⁷⁰ not less than the qualifying age for state pension credit] and either—

(i) the additional condition specified in [⁵⁸ paragraph 12(1)(a), (c) or (d)] is satisfied; or

(ii) the claimant was entitled to, or was treated as being in receipt of, income support and—

(aa) the disability premium was or, as the case may be, would have been, applicable to him in respect of a benefit week within eight weeks of [⁷⁰ the day his partner attained the qualifying age for state pension credit]; and

(bb) he has, subject to sub-paragraph (3), remained continuously entitled to income support since his partner attained [⁷⁰ the qualifying age for state pension credit].]

(2) [. . .]

(3) For the purposes of this paragraph and paragraph 12—

(a) once the higher pensioner premium is applicable to a claimant, if he then ceases, for a period of eight weeks or less, to be entitled to [⁴¹or treated as entitled to] income support, he shall, on becoming re-entitled to income support, thereafter be treated as having been continuously entitled thereto;

(b) in so far as [⁵⁴ sub-paragraph (1)(b)(ii) is] concerned, if a claimant ceases to be entitled to [⁴¹or treated as entitled to] income support for a period not exceeding eight weeks which includes [⁷⁰ the day his partner attained the qualifying age for state pension credit], he shall, on becoming re-entitled to income support, thereafter be treated as having been continuously entitled thereto.

[³³ (4) In the case of a claimant who is a welfare to work beneficiary, references in sub-paragraphs (1)(b)(ii) [⁶⁵ . . .] and (3)(b) to a period of 8 weeks shall be treated as references to a period of [⁶⁴ 104 weeks].]

[⁴¹ (5) For the purposes of this paragraph, a claimant shall be treated as having been entitled to and in receipt of income support throughout any period which comprises only days on which he was participating in an employment zone programme and was not entitled to income support because, as a consequence of his participation in that programme, he was engaged in remunerative work or had income in excess of his applicable amount as prescribed in Part IV.]

[⁶⁵ (6) The condition is not satisfied if the claimant's partner to whom sub-paragraph (1) refers is a long-term patient.]

Disability Premium

11.—[⁶⁵ (1) Subject to sub-paragraph (2), the] condition is that—   **2.617**
  (a) where the claimant is a single claimant or a lone parent, [⁵⁴ . . .] the additional condition specified in paragraph 12 is satisfied; or
  (b) where the claimant has a partner, either—
    [⁵⁴ (i) the claimant satisfies the additional condition specified in paragraph [⁵⁸ 12(1)(a), (b), (c) or (d)]; or]
    (ii) his partner [⁷⁰ has not attained the qualifying age for state pension credit] and the additional condition specified in [⁵⁸ paragraph 12(1)(a), (c) or (d)] is satisfied by his partner.

[⁶⁵ (2) The condition is not satisfied if—
  (a) the claimant is a single claimant or a lone parent and (in either case) is a long-term patient;
  (b) the claimant is a member of a couple or polygamous marriage and each member of the couple or polygamous marriage is a long-term patient; or
  (c) the claimant is a member of a couple or a polygamous marriage and a member of that couple or polygamous marriage is—
    (i) a long-term patient; and
    (ii) the only member of the couple or polygamous marriage to whom sub-paragraph (1)(b) refers.]

Additional condition for the Higher Pensioner and Disability Premiums

12.—(1) Subject to sub-paragraph (2) and paragraph 7 the additional condition referred   **2.618**
to in paragraphs 10 and 11 is that either—
  (a) the claimant or, as the case may be, his partner—
    (i) is in receipt of one or more of the following benefits: attendance allowance, [¹⁵ disability living allowance, [⁷⁶ armed forces independence payment,] [⁷⁵ personal independence payment,] [⁸³ adult disability payment,] [⁵⁰ the disability element or the severe disability element of working tax credit as specified in regulation 20(1)(b) and (f) of the Working Tax Credit (Entitlement and Maximum Rate) Regulations 2002]], mobility supplement, [²⁵ long-term incapacity benefit] under [²² Part II of the Contributions and Benefits Act or severe disablement allowance under Part III of that Act] [¹but, in the case of [²⁵ long-term incapacity benefit] or severe disablement allowance only where it is paid in respect of him]; or
    (ii) is provided by the Secretary of State with an invalid carriage or other vehicle under section 5(2) of the National Health Service Act 1977 (other services) or, in Scotland, under section 46 of the National Health Service (Scotland) Act 1978 (provision of vehicles) or receives payments by way of grant from the Secretary of State under paragraph 2 of Schedule 2 to that 1977 Act (additional provisions as to vehicles) or, in Scotland, under that section 46; or
    [⁷⁷ (iii) is certified as severely sight impaired or blind by a consultant ophthalmologist; or]
  [²⁶ (b) the claimant—
    (i) is entitled to statutory sick pay or [²⁷ is, or is treated as, incapable of work,] in accordance with the provisions of Part XIIA of the Contributions and Benefits Act and the regulations made thereunder (incapacity for work), and

      (ii) has been so entitled or so incapable [²⁷, or has been treated as so incapable,] for a continuous period of not less than—

        (aa) 196 days in the case of a claimant who is terminally ill within the meaning of section 30B(4) of the Contributions and Benefits Act; or

        (bb) [⁶³ subject to [⁶⁵ paragraph 2A] of Schedule 7] 364 days in any other case; and for these purposes any two or more periods of entitlement or incapacity separated by a break of not more than 56 days shall be treated as one continuous period; or]

[⁵⁴ (c) the claimant's partner was in receipt of long-term incapacity benefit under Part II of the Contributions and Benefits Act when entitlement to that benefit ceased on account of the payment of a retirement pension under that Act [⁸¹ or a state pension under Part 1 of the Pensions Act 2014] and—

      (i) the claimant has since remained continuously entitled to income support;

      (ii) the higher pensioner premium or disability premium has been applicable to the claimant; and

      (iii) the partner is still alive;

(d) except where paragraph [⁶³ 2A [⁶⁵ . . .]] of Schedule 7 (patients) applies, the claimant or, as the case may be, his partner was in receipt of attendance allowance [⁷⁵ , disability living allowance [⁸³ , personal independence payment or adult disability payment]]—

      (i) but payment of that benefit has been suspended under the [⁶⁰ Social Security (Attendance Allowance) Regulations 1991 [⁷⁵ , the Social Security (Disability Living Allowance) Regulations 1991 or regulations made under section 86(1) (hospital in-patients) of the 2012 Act]] or otherwise abated as a consequence of the claimant or his partner becoming a patient within the meaning of regulation 21(3); and

      (ii) a higher pensioner premium or disability premium has been applicable to the claimant.]

[³⁴(1A) In the case of a claimant who is a welfare to work beneficiary, the reference in sub-paragraph (1)(b) to a period of 56 days shall be treated as a reference to a period of [⁶⁴ 104 weeks].]

[⁷⁷ (2) For the purposes of sub-paragraph (1)(a)(iii), a person who has ceased to be certified as severely sight impaired or blind on regaining his eyesight shall nevertheless be treated as severely sight impaired or blind, as the case may be, and as satisfying the additional condition set out in that sub-paragraph for a period of 28 weeks following the date on which he ceased to be so certified.]

(3) [²⁶ . . .]

(4) For the purpose of [⁵⁸ sub-paragraph (1)(c) and (d)], once the higher pensioner premium is applicable to the claimant by virtue of his satisfying the condition specified in that provision, if he then ceases, for a period of eight weeks or less, to be entitled to income support, he shall on again becoming so entitled to income support, immediately thereafter be treated as satisfying the condition in [⁵⁸ sub-paragraph (1)(c) and (d)].

[⁴(5) For the purposes of sub-paragraph (1)(b), once the disability premium is applicable to a claimant by virtue of his satisfying the additional condition specified in that provision, he shall continue to be treated as satisfying that condition for any period spent by him in undertaking a course of training provided under section 2 of the Employment and Training Act 1973 [⁷ or for any period during which he is in receipt of a training allowance].]

[²⁵(6) For the purposes of [⁵⁸ sub-paragraph (1)(a)(i) and (c)], a reference to a person in receipt of long-term incapacity benefit includes a person in receipt of short-term incapacity benefit at a rate equal to the long-term rate by virtue of section 30B(4)(a) of the Contributions and Benefits Act (short-term incapacity benefit for a person who is terminally ill), or who would be or would have been in receipt of short-term incapacity benefit at such a rate but for the fact that the rate of short-term incapacity benefit already payable to him is or was equal to or greater than the long-term rate.]

[⁴⁰ [⁶¹ . . .]]

Severe Disability Premium

2.619   13.—(1) The condition is that the claimant is a severely disabled person.

(2) For the purposes of sub-paragraph (1), a claimant shall be treated as being a severely disabled person if, and only if—

(a) in the case of a single claimant[[19], a lone parent or a claimant who is treated as having no partner in consequence of sub-paragraph (2A)]—

    (i) he is in receipt of attendance allowance [[15] [[75] . . .] the care component of disability living allowance at the highest or middle rate prescribed in accordance with section 37ZB(3) of the Social Security Act [SSCBA, s.72(3)]] [[75] or the daily living component of personal independence payment at the standard or enhanced rate in accordance with section 78(3) of the 2012 Act] [[83] , the daily living component of adult disability payment at the standard or enhanced rate in accordance with regulation 5 of the Disability Assistance for Working Age People (Scotland) Regulations 2022] [[76] or armed forces independence payment], and

    (ii) subject to sub-paragraph (3), he has no non-dependants aged 18 or over [[23] normally residing with him or with whom he is normally residing,] and

    (iii) [[41] no person is entitled to, and in receipt of, [[49] a carer's allowance] under section 70 of the Contributions and Benefits Act [[80] or has an award of universal credit which includes the carer element] in respect of caring for him;]

(b) [[42] in the case of a claimant who] has a partner—

    (i) he is in receipt of attendance allowance [[15], [[75] . . .] the care component of disability living allowance at the highest or middle rate prescribed in accordance with section 37ZB(3) of the Social Security Act [SSCBA, s.72(3)]] [[75] or the daily living component of personal independence payment at the standard or enhanced rate in accordance with section 78(3) of the 2012 Act] [[83] , the daily living component of adult disability payment at the standard or enhanced rate in accordance with regulation 5 of the Disability Assistance for Working Age People (Scotland) Regulations 2022] [[76] or armed forces independence payment]; and

    (ii) his partner is also in receipt of such an allowance or, if he is a member of a polygamous marriage, all the partners of that marriage are in receipt thereof; and

    (iii) subject to sub-paragraph (3), he has no non-dependants aged 18 or over [[23] normally residing with him or with whom he is normally residing,]

and either [[41] a person is entitled to, and in receipt of, [[49] a carer's allowance] [[80] or has an award of universal credit which includes the carer element] in respect of caring for only one of the couple or, in the case of a polygamous marriage, for one or more but not all the partners of the marriage or, as the case may be, no person is entitled to, and in receipt of, such an allowance] [[80] or has such an award of universal credit] in respect of caring for either member of the couple or any partner of the polygamous marriage.

[[19] (2A) Where a claimant has a partner who does not satisfy the condition in sub-paragraph (2)(b)(ii), and that partner is [[77] severely sight impaired or blind or treated as severely sight impaired or blind] within the meaning of paragraph 12(1)(a)(iii) and (2), that partner shall be treated for the purposes of sub-paragraph (2) as if he were not a partner of the claimant.]

(3) For the purposes of sub-paragraph (2)(a)(ii) and (2)(b)(iii) no account shall be taken of—

(a) a person receiving attendance allowance [[15], [[75] . . .] the care component of disability living allowance at the highest or middle rate prescribed in accordance with section 37ZB(3) of the Social Security Act [SSCBA, s.72(3)]] [[75] or the daily living component of personal independence payment at the standard or enhanced rate in accordance with section 78(3) of the 2012 Act] [[83] , the daily living component of adult disability payment at the standard or enhanced rate in accordance with regulation 5 of the Disability Assistance for Working Age People (Scotland) Regulations 2022] [[76] or armed forces independence payment]; or

(b) [[21] . . .]

(c) subject to sub-paragraph (4), a person who joins the claimant's household for the first time in order to care for the claimant or his partner and immediately before so joining the claimant or his partner was treated as a severely disabled person; [[19] or (d) a person who is [[77] severely sight impaired or blind or treated as severely sight impaired or blind] within the meaning of paragraph 12(1)(a)(iii) and (2).]

[¹(3A) For the purposes of sub-paragraph (2)(b) a person shall be treated [⁴¹ . . .]

   (a) [⁴¹ as being in receipt of] attendance allowance [¹⁵, or the care component of disability living allowance at the highest or middle rate prescribed in accordance with section 37ZB(3) of the Social Security Act [SSCBA, s.72(3)]] if he would, but for his being a patient for a period exceeding 28 days, be so in receipt;

   (b) [⁴¹ as being entitled to and in receipt of [⁴⁹ a carer's allowance] [⁸⁰ or having an award of universal credit which includes the carer element] if he would, but for the person for whom he was caring being a patient in hospital for a period exceeding 28 days, be so entitled and in receipt [⁸⁰ of carer's allowance or have such an award of universal credit].]]

   [⁷⁵ (c) as being in receipt of the daily living component of personal independence payment at the standard or enhanced rate in accordance with section 78(3) of the 2012 Act if he would, but for a suspension of benefit in accordance with regulations under section 86(1) (hospital in-patients) of the 2012 Act, be so in receipt [⁸³ ;

   (d) as being in receipt of the daily living component of adult disability payment at the standard or enhanced rate in accordance with regulation 5 of the Disability for Working Age People (Scotland) Regulations 2022, if they would, but for regulation 28 (effect of admission to hospital on ongoing entitlement to Adult Disability Payment) of those Regulations, be so in receipt.]]

[²²(3ZA) For the purposes of sub-paragraph (2)(a)(iii) and (2)(b), no account shall be taken of an award of [⁴⁹ a carer's allowance] [⁸⁰ or universal credit which includes the carer element] to the extent that payment of such an award is back-dated for a period before [⁶⁶ the date on which the award is first paid].]

(4) Sub-paragraph (3)(c) shall apply only for the first 12 weeks following the date on which the person to whom that provision applies first joins the claimant's household.

[⁴⁵ (5) In sub-paragraph (2)(a)(iii) and (b), references to a person being in receipt of [⁴⁹ a carer's allowance] [⁸⁰ or as having an award of universal credit which includes the carer element] shall include references to a person who would have been in receipt of that allowance [⁸⁰ or had such an award] but for the application of a restriction under section [⁷² 6B or] 7 of the Social Security Fraud Act 2001 (loss of benefit provisions).]

[⁸⁰ (6) For the purposes of this paragraph, a person has an award of universal credit which includes the carer element if the person has an award of universal credit which includes an amount which is the carer element under regulation 29 of the Universal Credit Regulations 2013.]

[⁴³ **Enhanced disability premium**

13A.—[⁷⁵ ⁷⁶ (1) Subject to sub-paragraph (2), the condition is that—

(a)   the claimant; or

(b)   the claimant's partner, if any, who has not attained the qualifying age for state pension credit, is a person to whom sub-paragraph (1ZA) applies.

(1ZA) This sub-paragraph applies to the person mentioned in sub-paragraph (1) where—

(a)   armed forces independence payment is payable to that person;

(b)   the care component of disability living allowance is, or would, but for a suspension of benefit in accordance with regulations under section 113(2) of the Contributions and Benefits Act or but for an abatement as a consequence of hospitalization, be payable to that person at the highest rate prescribed under section 72(3) of that Act; [⁸² . . .

(ba) the care component of child disability payment is payable to that person at the highest rate in accordance with the DACYP Regulations (see regulation 11(5) of those Regulations); [⁸³ . . .]]

(c)   the daily living component of personal independence payment is, or would, but for regulations made under section 86(1) (hospital in-patients) of the 2012 Act, be payable to that person at the enhanced rate in accordance with section 78(2) of that Act [⁸³]; or

(d)   the daily living component of adult disability payment is, or would, but for regulation 28 (effect of admission to hospital on ongoing entitlement to Adult

2.620

Disability Payment) of the Disability for Working Age People (Scotland) Regulations 2022, be payable to that person at the enhanced rate in accordance with
regulation 5 of those Regulations.]]

[73 (1A) Where the condition in sub-paragraph (1) ceases to be satisfied because of the
death of a child or young person, the condition is that the claimant [74 or partner] is
entitled to child benefit in respect of that person under section 145A of the Contributions
and Benefits Act (entitlement after death of child or qualifying young person).]

[65 (2) The condition is not satisfied if the person to whom sub-paragraph (1) refers
is—

(a)   [50 . . .]

(b)   a single claimant or a lone parent and (in either case) is a long-term patient;

(c)   a member of a couple or polygamous marriage and each member of the couple or
polygamous marriage is a long-term patient; or

(d)   a member of a couple or polygamous marriage who—

    (i)   is a long-term patient; and

    (ii)   is the only member of the couple or polygamous marriage to whom sub-
paragraph (1) refers.]

Disabled Child Premium
  14.—[59 . . . 65]   **2.621**

[10 **Carer premium**
  14ZA.—(1) [13 Subject to sub-paragraphs (3) and (4),] the condition is that the claimant **2.622**
or his partner is, or both of them are, [41 entitled to [49 a carer's allowance] under section
70 of the Contributions and Benefits Act]

(2) [57 . . .]

[41 [48 (3) Where a carer premium is awarded but—

(a)   the person in respect of whose care the [49 carer's allowance] has been awarded dies;
or

(b)   in any other case the person in respect of whom a carer premium has been awarded
ceases to be entitled [57 . . .] to [49 a carer's allowance], the condition for the award
of the premium shall be treated as satisfied for a period of eight weeks from the
relevant date specified in sub-paragraph (3A) below.

(3A) The relevant date for the purposes of sub-paragraph (3) above shall be—

(a)   [57 where sub-paragraph (3)(a) applies,] the Sunday following the death of the
person in respect of whose care [49 a carer's allowance] has been awarded or the date
of death if the death occurred on a Sunday;

(b)   [57 . . .]

(c)   in any other case, the date on which the person who has been entitled to [46 a carer's
allowance] ceases to be entitled to that allowance.]

(4) Where a person who has been entitled to an invalid care allowance ceases to be
entitled to that allowance and makes a claim for income support, the condition for the
award of the carer premium shall be treated as satisfied for a period of eight weeks from the
date on which—

[48 (a) the person in respect of whose care the [49 carer's allowance] has been awarded
dies;

  (b)   [57 . . .]

[57 (c) in any other case, the person who has been entitled to a carer's allowance ceased
to be entitled to that allowance.]]]]

[3 **Persons in receipt of concessionary payments**
  14A.—For the purpose of determining whether a premium is applicable to a person **2.623**
[12 under paragraphs 12 to 14ZA], any concessionary payment made to compensate that
person for the non-payment of any benefit mentioned in those paragraphs shall be treated
as if it were a payment of that benefit.]

[8 **Person in receipt of benefit**
  14B.—For the purposes of this Part of this Schedule, a person shall be regarded as being **2.624**
in receipt of any benefit if, and only if, it is paid in respect of him and shall be so regarded
only for any period in respect of which that benefit is paid.]

Weekly Amounts of Premiums Specified in Part III

Column (1) Premium	Column (2) Amount
15.—(1) [²⁹ ...] [⁴²(1A) [⁶⁷ ...]] [⁵⁴(2) Pensioner premium for persons to whom paragraph 9 applies. (2A) Pensioner premium for persons to whom paragraph 9A applies. (3) Higher pensioner premium for persons to whom paragraph 10 applies.]	(1) [²⁹ ...]. [⁴² (1A) [⁶⁷ ...]] (2) [⁵⁴ ...] (2A) [⁵⁴ ...] (3) [⁵⁴ ...]

(4) Disability Premium—
  (a) where the claimant satisfies the condition in [⁶⁵ paragraph 11(1)(a)];
  (b) where the claimant satisfies the condition in [⁶⁵ paragraph 11(1)(b)].
(5) Severe Disability Premium—
  (a) where the claimant satisfies the condition in paragraph 13(2)(a);
  (b) where the claimant satisfies the condition in paragraph 13(2)(b).
    (i) if there is someone in receipt of [⁴⁹ a carer's allowance] or if he or any partner satisfies that condition only by virtue of paragraph 13(3A);
    (ii) if no-one is in receipt of such an allowance.
	(4)
	  (a) [⁸⁵ £36.20].
	
	  (b) [⁸⁵ £51.60].
	
	(5)
	  (a) [⁸⁵ £69.40];
	
	  (b)
	
	    (i) [⁸⁵ £69.40];
	
	    (ii) [⁸⁵ £138.80];

(6) [⁵⁹ ...]	(6) [⁵⁹ ...]
(7) Carer Premium—	(7) [⁸⁵ £38.85] in respect of each person who satisfied the condition specified in paragraph 14ZA.]

[⁴³ (8) Enhanced disability premium where the conditions in paragraph 13A are satisfied—	(8)
	  (a) [⁵⁹ ...]
	  (b) [⁸⁵ £17.75] in respect of each person who is neither—
	    (i) a child or young person; nor
	    (ii) a member of a couple or a polygamous marriage, in respect of whom the conditions specified in paragraph 13A are satisfied:
	  (c) [⁸⁵ £25.35] where the claimant is a member of a couple or a polygamous marriage and the conditions specified in paragraph 13A are satisfied in respect of a member of that couple or polygamous marriage.]

2.625

PART V

ROUNDING OF FRACTIONS

16. Where income support is awarded for a period which is not a complete benefit week **2.626** and the applicable amount in respect of that period results in an amount which includes a fraction of a penny that fraction shall be treated as a penny."

AMENDMENTS

1. Income Support (General) Amendment Regulations 1988 (SI 1988/663) reg.29 (April 11, 1988).
2. Income Support (General) Amendment No. 3 Regulations 1988 (SI 1988/1228) reg.9 (September 12, 1988).
3. Income Support (General) Amendment No. 4 Regulations 1988 (SI 1988/1445) reg.19 (September 12, 1988).
4. Income Support (General) Amendment No. 5 Regulations 1988 (SI 1988/2022) reg.17(*b*) (December 12, 1988).
5. Income Support (General) Amendment No. 5 Regulations 1988 (SI 1988/2022) reg.17(*a*) (April 10, 1989).
6. Income Support (General) Amendment Regulations 1989 (SI 1989/534) reg.5 (October 9, 1989).
7. Income Support (General) Amendment No. 3 Regulations 1989 (SI 1989/1678) reg.6 (October 9, 1989).
8. Income Support (General) Amendment Regulations 1990 (SI 1990/547) reg.17 (April 9, 1990).
9. Income Support (General) Amendment No. 2 Regulations 1990 (SI 1990/1168) reg.2 (July 2, 1990).
10. Income Support (General) Amendment No. 3 Regulations 1990 (SI 1990/1776) reg.8 (October 1, 1990).
11. Enterprise (Scotland) Consequential Amendments Order 1991 (SI 1991/3870) art.9 (April, 1991).
12. Income Support (General) Amendment Regulations 1991 (SI 1991/236) reg.2 (April 8, 1991).
13. Income Support (General) Amendment No. 4 Regulations 1991 (SI 1991/236) reg.15 (August 5, 1991).
14. Income Support (General) Amendment No. 4 Regulations 1991 (SI 1991/1559) reg.15 (October 7, 1991).
15. Disability Living Allowance and Disability Working Allowance (Consequential Provisions) Regulations 1991 (SI 1991/2742) reg.11(4) (April 6, 1992).
16. Income Support (General) Amendment Regulations 1992 (SI 1992/468) reg.6 (April 6, 1992).
17. Social Security Benefits (Amendments Consequential Upon the Introduction of community Care) Regulations 1992 (SI 1992/3147) reg.2 (April 1, 1993).
18. Social Security Benefits (Miscellaneous Amendments) Regulations 1993 (SI 1993/518) reg.5 (April 1, 1993).
19. Income-related Benefits Schemes (Miscellaneous Amendments) (No. 2) Regulations 1993 (SI 1993/1150) reg.3 (May 25, 1993).
[20.]
21. Income-related Benefits Schemes (Miscellaneous Amendments) (No. 4) Regulations 1993 (SI 1993/2119) reg.18 (October 4, 1993).
22. Income-related Benefits Schemes (Miscellaneous Amendments) (No. 5) Regulations 1994 (SI 1994/2139) reg.30 (October 3, 1994).
23. Income-related Benefits Schemes (Miscellaneous Amendments) (No. 6) Regulations 1994 (SI 1994/3061) reg.2(3) (December 2, 1994).
24. Income-related Benefits Schemes (Miscellaneous Amendments) Regulations 1995 (SI 1995/516) reg.24 (April 10, 1995).
25. Disability Working Allowance and Income Support (General) Amendment Regulations 1995 (SI 1995/482) reg.16 (April 13, 1995).
26. Disability Working Allowance and Income Support (General) Amendment Regulations 1995 (SI 1995/482) reg.17 (April 13, 1995).

241

27. Income-related Benefits Schemes and Social Security (Claims and Payments) (Miscellaneous Amendments) Regulations 1995 (SI 1995/2303) reg.6(8) (October 2, 1995).
28. Income Support (General) (Jobseeker's Allowance Consequential Amendments) Regulations 1996 (SI 1996/206) reg.23 and Sch.2 (October 7, 1996).
29. Child Benefit, Child Support and Social Security (Miscellaneous Amendments) Regulations 1996 (SI 1996/1803) reg.39 (April 7, 1997).
30. Income-related Benefits and Jobseeker's Allowance (Personal Allowances for Children and Young Persons) (Amendment) Regulations 1996 (SI 1996/2545) reg.2 (April 7, 1997).
31. Income-related Benefits and Jobseeker's Allowance (Amendment) (No. 2) Regulations 1997 (SI 1997/2197) regs 7(5) and (6)(a) (October 6, 1997).
32. Social Security Amendment (Lone Parents) Regulations 1998 (SI 1998/766) reg.12 (April 6, 1998).
33. Social Security (Welfare to Work) Regulations 1998 (SI 1998/2231) reg.13(3)(a) (October 5, 1998).
34. Social Security (Welfare to Work) Regulations 1998 (SI 1998/2231) reg.13(3)(b) (October 5, 1998).
35. Social Security Benefits Up-rating Order 1999 (SI 1999/264) art.18(3) and Sch.4 (April 12, 1999).
36. Social Security Benefits Up-rating Order 1999 (SI 1999/264) art.18(4)(b) (April 12, 1999).
37. Social Security Benefits Up-rating Order 1999 (SI 1999/264) art.18(5) and Sch.5 (April 12, 1999).
38. Social Security Amendment (Personal Allowances for Children and Young Persons) Regulations 1999 (SI 1999/2555) reg.2(1)(b) and (2)(April 10, 2000).
39. Social Security and Child Support (Tax Credits) Consequential Amendments Regulations 1999 (SI 1999/2566) reg.2(2) and Sch.2 Pt II (October 5, 1999).
40. Social Security (Miscellaneous Amendments) (No. 2) Regulations 1999 (SI 1999/2556) reg.2(8) (October 4, 1999).
41. Social Security (Miscellaneous Amendments) Regulations 2000 (SI 2000/681) reg.4 (April 3, 2000).
42. Social Security Amendment (Bereavement Benefits) Regulations 2000 (SI 2000/2239) reg.2(3) (April 9, 2001).
43. Social Security Amendment (Enhanced Disability Premium) Regulations 2000 (SI 2629) reg.2(c) (April 9, 2001).
44. Social Security Amendment (Residential Care and Nursing Homes) Regulations 2001 (SI 2001/3767) reg.2 and Sch. Pt I para.14 (April 8, 2002).
45. Social Security (Loss of Benefit) (Consequential Amendments) Regulations 2002 (SI 2002/490) reg.2 (April 1, 2002).
46. Social Security Amendment (Residential Care and Nursing Homes) Regulations 2001 (SI 2001/3767) reg.2 and Sch. Pt I para.14 (as amended by Social Security Amendment (Residential Care and Nursing Homes) Regulations 2002 (SI 2002/398) reg.4(2)) (April 8, 2002).
47. Social Security Amendment (Personal Allowances for Children and Young Persons) Regulations 2002 (SI 2002/2019) reg.2 (October 14, 2002).
48. Social Security Amendment (Carer Premium) Regulations 2002 (SI 2002/2020) reg.2 (October 28, 2002).
49. Social Security Amendment (Carer's allowance) Regulations 2002 (SI 2002/2497) reg.3 and Sch.2 (April 1, 2003).
50. Social Security (Working Tax Credit and Child Tax Credit) (Consequential Amendments) Regulations 2003 (SI 2003/455) regs 1(5) and 2 and Sch.1 para.20(b) (April 7, 2003).
51. Social Security Benefits Up-Rating Order 2003 (SI 2003/526) art.17(3) and Sch.2 (April 7, 2003).
52. Social Security Benefits Up-Rating Order 2003 (SI 2003/526) art.17(5) and Sch.3 (April 7, 2003).
53. Social Security Benefits Up-Rating Order 2003 (SI 2003/526) art.17(4) (April 7, 2003).
54. State Pension Credit (Consequential, Transitional and Miscellaneous Provisions) Regulations 2002 (SI 2002/3019) reg.29(5) (October 6, 2003).

242

55. Social Security (Removal of Residential Allowance and Miscellaneous Amendments) Regulations 2003 (SI 2003/1121) reg.2 and Sch.1 para.6 (October 6, 2003).
56. Social Security (Hospital In-Patients and Miscellaneous Amendments) Regulations 2003 (SI 2003/1195) reg.3 (May 21, 2003).
57. Social Security (Miscellaneous Amendments) (No. 2) Regulations 2003 (SI 2003/2279) reg.2(3) (October 1, 2003).
58. Income Support (General) Amendment Regulations 2003 (SI 2003/2379) reg.2 (October 6, 2003).
59. Social Security (Working Tax Credit and Child Tax Credit) (Consequential Amendments) Regulations 2003 (SI 2003/455) reg.2 and Sch.1 para.20 (April 6, 2004, except in "transitional cases" and see further the note to reg.17 of the Income Support Regulations).
60. Social Security (Miscellaneous Amendments) (No. 2) Regulations 2004 (SI 2004/1141) reg.6 (May 12, 2004).
61. Social Security (Back to Work Bonus and Lone Parent Run-on) (Amendment and Revocation) Regulations 2003 (SI 2003/1589) reg.2(d) (October 25, 2004).
62. Civil Partnership (Pensions, Social Security and Child Support) (Consequential, etc. Provisions) Order 2005 (SI 2005/2877) art.2(3) and Sch.3 para.13(3) (December 5, 2005).
63. Social Security (Hospital In-Patients) Regulations 2005 (SI 2005/3360) reg.4 (April 10, 2006).
64. Social Security (Miscellaneous Amendments) (No. 4) Regulations 2006 (SI 2006/2378) reg.5(7) (October 2, 2006).
65. Social Security (Miscellaneous Amendments) Regulations 2007 (SI 2007/719) reg.2(7) (April 9, 2007). As it relates to paras 13A(2)(a) and 14, the amendment only affects "transitional cases". See further the note to reg.17 of the Income Support Regulations and the commentary below.
66. Social Security (Miscellaneous Amendments) Regulations 2007 (SI 2007/719) reg.2(7)(e) (April 2, 2007).
67. Social Security (Miscellaneous Amendments) (No. 5) Regulations 2007 (SI 2007/2618) reg.2 and Sch. (October 1, 2007).
68. Social Security (Miscellaneous Amendments) Regulations 2008 (SI 2008/698) reg.2(12) (April 14, 2008).
69. Social Security (Miscellaneous Amendments) Regulations 2009 (SI 2009/583) reg.2(1) and (3) (April 6, 2009).
70. Social Security (Equalisation of State Pension Age) Regulations 2009 (SI 2009/1488) reg.3 (April 6, 2010).
71. Social Security (Miscellaneous Amendments) (No. 2) Regulations 2010 (SI 2010/641) reg.2(1) and (9) (April 13, 2010).
72. Social Security (Loss of Benefit) Amendment Regulations 2010 (SI 2010/1160) reg.10(1) and (3) (April 1, 2010).
73. Social Security (Miscellaneous Amendments) Regulations 2011 (SI 2011/674) reg.3(5) (April 11, 2011).
74. Social Security (Miscellaneous Amendments) (No. 3) Regulations 2011 (SI 2011/2425) reg.7(1) and (7) (October 31, 2011).
75. Personal Independence Payment (Supplementary Provisions and Consequential Amendments) Regulations 2013 (SI 2013/388) reg.8 and Sch. para.11(1) and (5) (April 8, 2013).
76. Armed Forces and Reserve Forces Compensation Scheme (Consequential Provisions: Subordinate Legislation) Order 2013 (SI 2013/591) art.7 and Sch. para.4(1) and (5) (April 8, 2013).
77. Universal Credit and Miscellaneous Amendments (No. 2) Regulations 2014 (SI 2014/2888) reg.3(2)(a) (November 26, 2014).
78. Welfare Benefits Up-rating Order 2015 (SI 2015/30) art.6 and Sch.1 (April 6, 2015).
79. Social Security Benefits Up-rating Order 2015 (SI 2015/457) art.14(5) and Sch.3 (April 6, 2015).
80. Universal Credit and Miscellaneous Amendments Regulations 2015 (SI 2015/1754) reg.14 (October 28, 2015).
81. Pensions Act 2014 (Consequential, Supplementary and Incidental Amendments) Order 2015 (SI 2015/1985) art.8(1) and (3) (April 6, 2016).

82. Social Security (Scotland) Act 2018 (Disability Assistance for Children and Young People) (Consequential Modifications) Order 2021 (SI 2021/786) Sch.1 para.5 (July 26, 2021).
83. Social Security (Disability Assistance for Working Age People) (Consequential Amendments) Order 2022 (SI 2022/177) art.2(6) (March 21, 2022).
84. Social Security Benefits Up-rating Order 2022 (SI 2022/292) art.21(1) and (3) and Sch.2 (April 11, 2022).
85. Social Security Benefits Up-rating Order 2022 (SI 2022/292) art.21(1) and (5) and Sch.3 (April 11, 2022).

DEFINITIONS

"adult disability payment"—see reg.2(1).
"attendance allowance"—*ibid.*
"benefit week"—*ibid.*
"child"—see SSCBA s.137(1).
"child disability payment"—see reg.2(1).
"claimant"—*ibid.*
"close relative"—*ibid.*
"couple"—*ibid.*
"the DACYP Regulations"—*ibid.*
"disability living allowance"—*ibid.*
"family"—see SSCBA s.137(1).
"invalid carriage or other vehicle"—see reg.2(1).
"lone parent"—*ibid.*
"mobility supplement"—*ibid.*
"non-dependent"—see reg.3.
"partner"—see reg.2(1).
"personal independence payment"—*ibid.*
"polygamous marriage"—*ibid.*
"preserved right"—see reg.2(1) and reg.19.
"single claimant"—see reg.2(1).
"Social Security Act"—*ibid.*
"welfare to work beneficiary"—*ibid.*
"young person"—*ibid.*, reg.14.
For the General Note to Sch.2, see Vol.V paras 2.627–2.650.

p.605, *amendments to the Income Support (General) Regulations 1987 (SI 1987/1967) Sch.3 para.18 (Housing costs—non-dependant deductions)*

6.022   With effect from April 11, 2022, art.21 of the Social Security Benefits Up-rating Order 2022 (SI 2022/292) makes the following amendments:

- in sub-para.(1)(a) for "£102.85" substitute "£106.05";
- in sub-para.(1)(b) for "£15.95" substitute "£16.45";
- in sub-para.(2)(a) for "£149.00" substitute "£154.00";
- in sub-para.(2)(b):
  - (i) for "£36.65" substitute "£37.80";
  - (ii) for "£149.00" substitute "£154.00"; and
  - (iii) for "£217.00" substitute "£224.00";
- in sub-para.(2)(c):
  - (i) for "£50.30" substitute "£51.85";
  - (ii) for "£217.00" substitute "£224.00"; and
  - (iii) for "£283.00" substitute "£292.00";

- in sub-para.(2)(d):
    (i) for "£82.30" substitute "£84.85";
    (ii) for "£283.00" substitute "£292.00"; and
    (iii) for "£377.00" substitute "£389.00"; and
- in sub-para.(2)(e):
    (i) for "£93.70" substitute "£96.60";
    (ii) for "£377.00" substitute "£389.00"; and
    (iii) for "£469.00" substitute "£484.00".

p.606, *amendments to the Income Support (General) Regulations 1987 (SI 1987/1967) Sch.3 para.18 (Housing costs—non-dependant deductions)*

With effect from January 1, 2022, reg.2(6) of the Social Security   6.023
(Income and Capital Disregards) (Amendment) Regulations 2021 (SI 2021/1405) inserts into para.18(8)(b), after "Grenfell Tower payment", ", child abuse payment or Windrush payment".

p.642, *amendments to the Income Support (General) Regulations 1987 (SI 1987/1967) Sch.9 paras 6 and 9 (Sums to be disregarded in the calculation of income other than earnings—mobility component and AA, care component and daily living component)*

With effect from March 21, 2022, art.2(8)(a) of the Social Security   6.024
(Disability Assistance for Working Age People) (Consequential Amendments) Order 2022 (SI 2022/177) amended para.6 to read as follows (square brackets indicate only the present amendment, those indicating previous amendments having been omitted):

"**6.**—The mobility component of disability living allowance[,] the mobility component of personal independence payment [or the mobility component of adult disability payment]."

With effect from March 21, 2022, art.2(8)(b) of the same Order amended para.9 to read as follows (square brackets indicate only the present amendment, those indicating previous amendments having been omitted):

"**9.**—Any attendance allowance, the care component of disability living allowance[,] the daily living component of personal independence payment [or the daily living component of adult disability payment]."

"Adult disability payment" is defined in reg.2(1) by reference to reg.2 of the Disability Assistance for Working Age People (Scotland) Regulations 2022 (SSI 2022/54) (see Vol.IV of this series).

p.644, *amendment to the Income Support (General) Regulations 1987 (SI 1987/1967) Sch.9 para.21(2) (Sums to be disregarded in the calculation of income other than earnings—income in kind)*

With effect from January 1, 2022, reg.2(7)(a) of the Social Security   6.025
(Income and Capital Disregards) (Amendment) Regulations 2021 (SI

2021/1405) amended sub-para.(2) by inserting ", a child abuse payment or a Windrush payment" after "Grenfell Tower payment". All of those payments are defined in reg.2(1). See the entry for p.684 for discussion of the nature of child abuse and Windrush payments.

p.646, *amendment to the Income Support (General) Regulations 1987 (SI 1987/1967) Sch.9 para.27(da) (Sums to be disregarded in the calculation of income other than earnings—payments for persons temporarily in care of claimant)*

6.026   With effect from July 1, 2022, reg.99 of and Sch. to the Health and Care Act 2022 (Consequential and Related Amendments and Transitional Provisions) Regulations 2022 (SI 2022/634) amended para.27(da) by substituting the following for the text after "(da)":

"an integrated care board established under Chapter A3 of Part 2 of the National Health Service Act 2006;"

p.648, *amendment to the Income Support (General) Regulations 1987 (SI 1987/1967) Sch.9 para.39(1A) (Sums to be disregarded in the calculation of income other than earnings)*

6.027   With effect from January 1, 2022, reg.2(7)(b) of the Social Security (Income and Capital Disregards) (Amendment) Regulations 2021 (SI 2021/1405) amended para.39 by substituting the following for sub-para.(1A):

"(1A) Any—
    (a) Grenfell Tower payment;
    (b) child abuse payment;
    (c) Windrush payment."

In addition, reg.2(7)(c) amended sub-paras (2) to (6) by inserting ", a child abuse payment or a Windrush payment" after "Grenfell Tower payment" in each place where those words occur. All of those payments are defined in reg.2(1).

See the entry for p.684 (Sch.10 (Capital to be disregarded) para.22) for some technical problems arising from the date of effect of these amendments. Because all the payments so far made from the approved historic institutional child abuse schemes and from the Windrush Compensation Scheme have been in the nature of capital, the question of disregarding income has not yet arisen.

p.665, *annotations to the Income Support (General) Regulations 1987 (SI 1987/1967) Sch.9 paras 6 and 9 (Sums to be disregarded in the calculation of income other than earnings—mobility component and AA, care component and daily living component)*

6.028   Note the amendments to paras 6 and 9 on p.642 to take account of the introduction of Scottish adult disability payment (see Vol.IV of this series).

p.676, *annotation to the Income Support (General) Regulations 1987 (SI 1987/1967) Sch.9 para.34 (Sums to be disregarded in the calculation of income other than earnings—payments by trade unions during trade disputes)*

The relevant sum was increased to £42.50 with effect from April 11, 2022 (see the entries for pp.15 and 18).

6.029

p.684, *amendment to the Income Support (General) Regulations 1987 (SI 1987/1967) Sch.10 para.22 (Capital to be disregarded)*

With effect from January 1, 2022, reg.2(8)(a) of the Social Security (Income and Capital Disregards) (Amendment) Regulations 2021 (SI 2021/1405) amended sub-para.(1A) by inserting ", child abuse payment, Windrush payment" after "Grenfell Tower payment" and amended sub-paras (2) to (6) by inserting ", a child abuse payment or a Windrush payment" after "Grenfell Tower payment" in each place where those words occur. All of those payments are defined in reg.2(1).

6.030

There are some technical problems with the addition only with effect from January 1, 2022 of the disregards of payments from approved schemes providing compensation in respect of historic institutional child abuse in the UK (para.(1)(a)(vii)) and from the Windrush Compensation Scheme. All the schemes so far in existence provide payments in the nature of capital.

The Explanatory Memorandum to the amending regulations reveals that four child abuse compensation schemes had been approved by the Secretary of State as at January 1, 2022: under the Historical Institutional Abuse (Northern Ireland) Act 2019; under the Redress for Survivors (Historical Child Abuse in Care) (Scotland) Act 2021; the London Borough of Lambeth Redress Scheme and the London Borough of Islington's proposed support payment scheme. All provide one-off capital payments. The Memorandum also reveals that payments under the Northern Ireland and Lambeth schemes could have been made prior to January 1, 2022. The application of the disregards provided under SI 2021/1405 to such pre-January 2022 payments has been authorised by a ministerial direction from the Secretary of State, acting under "common law powers" (see the letters of December 3, 2021 between the Permanent Secretary and the Secretary of State, published on the internet). The Windrush Compensation Scheme has also been making payments for some time. The correspondence above states that extra-statutory arrangements agreed with HM Treasury provided for the disregard in practice of such payments in means-tested benefits from the outset. It might be thought that the delay in putting that outcome on a proper statutory basis is symptomatic of the way in which the victims of that scandal have been treated.

Those arrangements raise questions as to what a tribunal on appeal should do if it has evidence of receipt prior to January 1, 2022 of a payment that would have been disregarded under the amendments if it had been received on or after that date. The legislation that a tribunal is bound to apply would not allow a disregard of such a payment unless it fell within an existing "personal injury" disregard in para.12 or 12A (possible for some historic institutional child abuse payments, though not for payments to next of kin or those who had merely been in "harm's way" or for Windrush Compensation Scheme payments). However, if an express submission from the DWP recorded the practical result of the application of the disregard either on the basis of a ministerial direction or an extra-statutory arrangement, it would appear that the issue of the treatment of the payment would not arise on the appeal (see SSA 1998 s.12(8)(a)) and it is submitted that it would then be irrational for the tribunal to exercise its discretion to consider the issue nonetheless. If evidence of a payment that had not been taken into account as capital emerged in the course of an appeal, but there was no express DWP submission to explain that outcome, it is submitted that a tribunal with knowledge of the matters mentioned above could still legitimately conclude that the issue did not arise on the appeal and decline to exercise its discretion under s.12(8)(a). Memo DMG 15/21 on the effect of the amendment to Sch.10 says nothing about these questions, although it does name the currently approved historic institutional child abuse schemes and give the date of approval (December 10, 2021).

p.685, *amendment to the Income Support (General) Regulations 1987 (SI 1987/1967) Sch.10 para.29 (Capital to be disregarded—payments in kind)*

6.031   With effect from January 1, 2022, reg.2(8)(b) of the Social Security (Income and Capital Disregards) (Amendment) Regulations 2021 (SI 2021/1405) amended para.29 by inserting ", child abuse payment or Windrush payment" after "Grenfell Tower payment". All of those payments are defined in reg.2(1). See also the entry for p.684.

p.697, *annotation to the Income Support (General) Regulations 1987 (SI 1987/1967) Sch.10 (Capital to be disregarded)*

6.032   With effect from June 28, 2022 "Cost of living payments" under the Social Security (Additional Payments) Act 2022 (see Part I of this Supplement), both those to recipients of specified means-tested benefits and "disability" payments, are not to be taken into account for any income support purposes by virtue of s.8(b) of the Act.

p.714, *annotation to the Income Support (General) Regulations 1987 (SI 1987/1967) Sch.10 para.18A (Capital to be disregarded—local welfare provision)*

6.033   There has been no specific provision made under Sch.10 (or the equivalent old style ESA or JSA provisions) to disregard 2022 Energy Rebate Scheme payments as capital, as has been done for universal credit in the Universal Credit (Energy Rebate Scheme Disregard) Regulations 2022 (SI 2022/257) (see Pt II of this volume). That is because the payments to be administered by local authorities (the £150 council tax rebate for properties in bands A–D and under the discretionary scheme for the vulnerable) are considered already to be covered by para.18A.

p.742, *amendment to the Fines (Deductions from Income Support) Regulations 1992 (SI 1992/2182) reg.4 (Deductions from offender's income support, universal credit, state pension credit or jobseeker's allowance)*

With effect from October 29, 2021, reg.2 of the Fines (Deductions   6.034 from Income Support) (Miscellaneous Amendments) Regulations 2021 (SI 2021/1077) substitutes a new reg.4(1B):

"(1B) The amount that may be deducted under paragraph (1A) is 5 per cent. of the appropriate universal credit standard allowance for the offender for the assessment period in question, as specified under regulation 36 of the UC Regulations."

This amendment follows the decision of Kerr J in *R. (Blundell) v SSWP* [2021] EWHC 608 (Admin); [2021] P.T.S.R. 1342, where the Secretary of State's policy on deductions was found to be unlawfully fettering her discretion about the amount to deduct under reg.4(1B). The new regulation removes that discretion, by limiting deductions to the smallest amount which could previously have been deducted.

PART III

OLD STYLE JOBSEEKER'S ALLOWANCE REGULATIONS

p.787, *amendments to the Jobseeker's Allowance Regulations 1996 (SI 1996/207), reg.1 (Citation, commencement, interpretation and application)*

With effect from July 26, 2021, Sch.3 para.2 of the Social Security   6.035 (Scotland) Act 2018 (Disability Assistance for Children and Young People) (Consequential Modifications) Order 2021 (SI 2021/786) inserts the following definitions:

"child disability payment" has the meaning given in regulation 2 of the DACYP Regulations;
   "DACYP Regulations" means the Disability Assistance for Children and Young People (Scotland) Regulations 2021;

With effect from January 1, 2022, reg.3(2) of the Social Security (Income and Capital Disregards) (Amendment) Regulations 2021 (SI 2021/1405) inserts the following definitions:

"child abuse payment" means a payment from a scheme established or approved by the Secretary of State for the purpose of providing compensation in respect of historic institutional child abuse in the United Kingdom;"
   "Windrush payment" means a payment made under the Windrush Compensation Scheme (Expenditure) Act 2020;"

With effect from January 1, 2022, reg.3(2) of the Social Security (Income and Capital Disregards) (Amendment) Regulations 2021 (SI 2021/1405) inserts ", a child abuse payment or a Windrush payment" into the definition of "qualifying person", after "Grenfell Tower payment".

In the definition of "qualifying person", after "Grenfell Tower payment" inserts ", a child abuse payment or a Windrush payment".

With effect from March 21, 2022, art.5 of the Social Security (Disability Assistance for Working Age People) (Consequential Amendments) Order 2022 (SI 2022/177) inserts the following definition:

"adult disability payment" has the meaning given in regulation 2 of the Disability Assistance for Working Age People (Scotland) Regulations 2022;

pp.851–852, *Jobseeker's Allowance Regulations 1996 (SI 1996/207) reg.16 (Further circumstances in which a person is to be treated as available: permitted period)*

6.036   Note that there has been no amendment to reg.16, equivalent to that made for universal credit and new style JSA purposes by SI 2022/108 (see the notes to reg.97(4) and (5) of the Universal Credit Regulations 2013 in Pt II of Vol.II of this series and to reg.14(3) of the JSA Regulations 2013 in Vol.I of this series), to reduce the maximum length of a "permitted period" from 13 weeks to four.

pp.872–873, *Jobseeker's Allowance Regulations 1996 (SI 1996/207) reg.20 (Further circumstances in which a person is to be treated as actively seeking employment: permitted period)*

6.037   Note that there has been no amendment to reg.20, equivalent to that made for universal credit and new style JSA purposes by SI 2022/108 (see the notes to reg.97(4) and (5) of the Universal Credit Regulations 2013 in Pt II of Vol.II of this series and to reg.14(3) of the JSA Regulations 2013 in Vol.I of this series), to reduce the maximum length of a "permitted period" from 13 weeks to four.

pp.910–912, *amendments to the Jobseeker's Allowance Regulations 1996 (SI 1996/207) reg.51 (Remunerative work)*

6.038   The text in the main volume at para.3.166 should be replaced with the following:

"Remunerative work

51.—(1) For the purposes of the Act "remunerative work" means—
  (a) in the case of [5 a claimant], work in which he is engaged or, where his hours of work fluctuate, is engaged on average, for not less than 16 hours per week; and
  (b) in the case of any partner of the claimant, work in which he is engaged or, where his hours of work fluctuate, is engaged on average, for not less than 24 hours per week; [1 and

(c) in the case of a non-dependant, or of a child or young person to whom paragraph 18 of Schedule 6 refers, work in which he is engaged or, where his hours of work fluctuate, is engaged on average, for not less than 16 hours per week,]

and for those purposes, [3 "work" is work] for which payment is made or which is done in expectation of payment.

(2) For the purposes of paragraph (1), the number of hours in which [5 a claimant] or his partner is engaged in work shall be determined—

(a) where no recognisable cycle has been established in respect of a person's work, by reference to the number of hours or, where those hours are likely to fluctuate, the average of the hours, which he is expected to work in a week;

(b) where the number of hours for which he is engaged fluctuate, by reference to the average of hours worked over—

    (i) if there is a recognisable cycle of work, and sub-paragraph (c) does not apply, the period of one complete cycle (including, where the cycle involves periods in which the person does not work, those periods but disregarding any other absences);

    (ii) in any other case, the period of five weeks immediately before the date of claim or the date of [4 supersession], or such other length of time as may, in the particular case, enable the person's average hours of work to be determined more accurately;

(c) [7 ...]

(3) In determining in accordance with this regulation the number of hours for which a person is engaged in remunerative work—

(a) that number shall include any time allowed to that person by his employer for a meal or for refreshments, but only where the person is, or expects to be, paid earnings in respect of that time;

(b) no account shall be taken of any hours in which the person is engaged in an employment or scheme to which any one of paragraphs (a) to (h) of regulation 53 (person treated as not engaged in remunerative work) applies;

(c) no account shall be taken of any hours in which the person is engaged otherwise than in an employment as an earner in caring for—

    (i) a person who is in receipt of attendance allowance [1 ...] [9, the care component of disability living allowance at the highest or middle rate [11 the care component of child disability payment at the highest or middle rate in accordance with regulation 11(5) of the DACYP Regulations] [10 , armed forces independence payment] [12 ...] the daily living component of personal independence payment at the standard or enhanced rate] [12 , or the daily living component of adult disability payment at the standard or enhanced rate]; or

    (ii) a person who has claimed an attendance allowance [1 ...] [9, disability living allowance [11 child disability payment] [10 , armed forces independence payment] [12 ...] personal independence payment] [12 or adult disability payment], but only for the period beginning with the date of claim and ending on the date the claim is determined or, if earlier, on the expiration of the period of 26 weeks from the date of claim; or

(iii) another person [² and] is in receipt of [⁶ carer's allowance] under Section 70 of the [¹ Benefits Act; or

(iv) a person who has claimed either attendance allowance or disability living allowance and has an award of attendance allowance or the care component of disability living allowance at one of the two higher rates prescribed under section 72(4) of the Benefits Act for a period commencing after the date on which that claim was made] [⁹ ; or

[¹¹ (iva) a person who has claimed child disability payment and has an award of the care component of child disability payment at the highest or middle rate in accordance with regulation 11(5) of the DACYP Regulations for a period commencing after the date on which the claim was made;] or

(v) a person who has claimed personal independence payment and has an award of the daily living component at the standard or enhanced rate under section 78 of the 2012 Act for a period commencing after the date on which that claim was made] [¹⁰ ; or

[¹² (va) a person who has claimed adult disability payment and has an award of the daily living component at the standard or enhanced rate under regulation 5 of the Disability Assistance for Working Age People (Scotland) Regulations 2022 for a period commencing after the date on which that claim was made;] or

(vi) a person who has claimed and has an award of armed forces independence payment for a period commencing after the date on which that claim was made.]

[⁸ . . .]"

AMENDMENTS

1. Jobseeker's Allowance (Amendment) Regulations 1996 (SI 1996/15160) reg.9 (October 7, 1996).
2. Jobseeker's Allowance (Amendment) Regulations 1996 (SI 1996/1516) reg.20 and Sch. (October 7, 1996).
3. Social Security (Miscellaneous Amendments) Regulations 1997 (SI 1997/454) reg.2(5) (April 7, 1997).
4. Social Security Act 1998 (Commencement No. 11, and Savings and Consequential and Transitional Provisions) Order 1999 (SI 1999/2860 (C.75)) art.3(1) and (12) and Sch.12 para.5 (October 18, 1999)
5. Jobseeker's Allowance (Joint Claims) Regulations 2000 (SI 2000/1978) reg.2(5) and Sch.2 para.14 (March 19, 2001).
6. Social Security (Miscellaneous Amendments) Regulations 2003 (SI 2003/511) reg.3(4) and (5) (April 1, 2003).
7. Social Security (Miscellaneous Amendments) Regulations 2009 (SI 2009/583) reg.4(1) and (4) (April 6, 2009).
8. Social Security (Miscellaneous Amendments) (No. 3) Regulations 2011 (SI 2011/2425) reg.10(1) and (3) (October 31, 2011).

9. Personal Independence Payment (Supplementary Provisions and Consequential Amendments) Regulations 2013 (SI 2013/388) reg.8 and Sch. para.16(1) and (3) (April 8, 2013).
10. Armed Forces and Reserve Forces Compensation Scheme (Consequential Provisions: Subordinate Legislation) Order 2013 (SI 2013/591) art.7 and Sch. para.10(1) and (3) (April 8, 2013).
11. Social Security (Scotland) Act 2018 (Disability Assistance for Children and Young People) (Consequential Modifications) Order 2021 (SI 2021/786) Sch.3 para.3 (July 26, 2021).
12. Social Security (Disability Assistance for Working Age People) (Consequential Amendments) Order 2022 (SI 2022/177) art.5(3) (March 21, 2022).

DEFINITIONS

"the Act"—see reg.1(3).
"adult disability payment"—*ibid.*
"attendance allowance"—*ibid.*
"the Benefits Act"—see Jobseekers Act s.35(1).
"child"—*ibid.*
"child disability payment"—see reg.1(3).
"claimant"—see Jobseekers Act s.35(1).
"date of claim"—see reg.1(3).
"DACYP Regulations"—*ibid.*
"disability living allowance"—*ibid.*
"earnings"—*ibid.*
"employment"—see reg.3.
"partner"—see reg.1(3).
"payment"—*ibid.*
"personal independence payment"—*ibid.*
"week"—*ibid.*
"young person"—*ibid.*, reg.76.
For the General Note to reg.51, see Vol.V paras 3.167–3.169.

p.923, *amendment to the Jobseeker's Allowance Regulations 1996 (SI 1996/207) reg.55ZA(2)(a) (Extended period of sickness)*

With effect from July 1, 2022, reg.4(1) of the Social Security (Medical Evidence) and Statutory Sick Pay (Medical Evidence) (Amendment) (No. 2) Regulations 2022 (SI 2022/630) omitted the words "a doctor's" between "form of" and "statement". 6.039

pp.974–977, *amendments to the Jobseeker's Allowance Regulations 1996 (SI 1996/207) reg.85A (Special cases: supplemental—persons from abroad)*

The text in the main volume at para.3.278 should be replaced with the following: 6.040

"**85A.**—(1) "Person from abroad" means, subject to the following provisions of this regulation, a claimant who is not habitually resident in the United Kingdom, the Channel Islands, the Isle of Man or the Republic of Ireland.

[¹⁰ (2) No claimant shall be treated as habitually resident in the United Kingdom, the Channel Islands, the Isle of Man or the Republic of Ireland unless—

  (a) [¹² subject to the exceptions in paragraph (2A),] the claimant has been living in any of those places for the past three months; and

  (b) the claimant has a right to reside in any of those places, other than a right to reside which falls within paragraph (3) [¹³ or (3A)].]

[¹² (2A) The exceptions are where the claimant has at any time during the period referred to in paragraph (2)(a)—

  (a) paid either Class 1 or Class 2 contributions by virtue of regulation 114, 118, 146 or 147 of the Social Security (Contributions) Regulations 2001 or by virtue of an Order in Council having effect under section 179 of the Social Security Administration Act 1992; or

  (b) been a Crown servant posted to perform overseas the duties of a Crown servant; or

  (c) been a member of Her Majesty's forces posted to perform overseas the duties of a member of Her Majesty's forces.]

(3) A right to reside falls within this paragraph if it is one which exists by virtue of, or in accordance with, one or more of the following—

  (a) regulation 13 of the [¹³ Immigration (European Economic Area) Regulations 2016]; [¹⁵ or]

[⁷ [¹³ (aa) regulation 16 of those Regulations, but only in a case where the right exists under that regulation because the claimant satisfies the criteria in paragraph (5) of that regulation;]]

  (b) [¹⁵ . . .]

  (c) [¹⁵ . . .]

[¹³ (3A) A right to reside falls within this paragraph if it exists by virtue of a claimant having been granted limited leave to enter, or remain in, the United Kingdom under the Immigration Act 1971 by virtue of—

  (a) Appendix EU to the immigration rules made under section 3(2) of that Act; [¹⁶ . . .]

  (b) being a person with a Zambrano right to reside as defined in Annex 1 of Appendix EU to the immigration rules made under section 3(2) of that Act.] [¹⁶; or

  (c) having arrived in the United Kingdom with an entry clearance that was granted under Appendix EU (Family Permit) to the immigration rules made under section 3(2) of that Act.]

[¹⁴ (3B) Paragraph (3A)(a) does not apply to a person who—

  (a) has a right to reside granted by virtue of being a family member of a relevant person of Northern Ireland; and

  (b) would have a right to reside under the Immigration (European Economic Area) Regulations 2016 if the relevant person of Northern Ireland were an EEA national, provided that the right to reside does not fall within paragraph (3A).]

(4) A claimant is not a person from abroad if he is—

[¹⁶(zza) a person granted leave in accordance with the immigration rules made under section 3(2) of the Immigration Act 1971, where such leave is granted by virtue of—

   (i) the Afghan Relocations and Assistance Policy; or

   (ii) the previous scheme for locally-employed staff in Afghanistan (sometimes referred to as the ex-gratia scheme);

(zzb) a person in Great Britain not coming within sub-paragraph (zza) or [¹⁷ (h)] who left Afghanistan in connection with the collapse of the Afghan government that took place on 15th August 2021;]

[¹⁷(zzc) a person in Great Britain who was residing in Ukraine immediately before 1st January 2022, left Ukraine in connection with the Russian invasion which took place on 24th February 2022 and—

  (i) has been granted leave in accordance with immigration rules made under section 3(2) of the Immigration Act 1971; [¹⁸ . . .]

  (ii) has a right of abode in the United Kingdom within the meaning given in section 2 of that Act;] [¹⁸ or

  (iii) does not require leave to enter or remain in the United Kingdom in accordance with section 3ZA of that Act;]

[¹¹(za) a qualified person for the purposes of regulation 6 of the [¹³ Immigration (European Economic Area) Regulations 2016] as a worker or a self-employed person;

(zb) a family member of a person referred to in sub-paragraph (za) [¹⁴ . . .];

(zc) a person who has a right to reside permanently in the United Kingdom by virtue of regulation 15(1)(c), (d) or I of those Regulations;]

[¹⁴(zd) a family member of a relevant person of Northern Ireland, with a right to reside which falls within paragraph (3A)(a), provided that the relevant person of Northern Ireland falls within sub-paragraph (za), or would do so but for the fact that they are not an EEA national;]

[¹⁵(ze) a frontier worker within the meaning of regulation 3 of the Citizens' Rights (Frontier Workers) (EU Exit) Regulations 2020;

(zf) a family member, of a person referred to in sub-paragraph (ze), who has been granted limited leave to enter, or remain in, the United Kingdom by virtue of Appendix EU to the immigration rules made under section 3(2) of the Immigration Act 1971;]

(g) a refugee within the definition in Article 1 of the Convention relating to the Status of Refugees done at Geneva on 28th July 1951, as extended by Article 1(2) of the Protocol relating to the Status of Refugees done at New York on 31st January 1967;

[³ [⁹(h) a person who has been granted leave or who is deemed to have been granted leave outside the rules made under section 3(2) of the Immigration Act 1971 [¹⁷ . . .]]

(hh) a person who has humanitarian protection granted under those rules;] [⁹ or]

(i) a person who is not a person subject to immigration control within the meaning of section 115(9) of the Immigration and Asylum Act and who is in the United Kingdom as a result of his deportation, expulsion or other removal by compulsion of law from another country to the United Kingdom; [⁵ . . .]

[⁹ . . .]

[¹⁴ (5) In this regulation—

"EEA national" has the meaning given in regulation 2(1) of the Immigration (European Economic Area) Regulations 2016;

"family member" has the meaning given in regulation 7(1)(a), (b) or (c) of the Immigration (European Economic Area) Regulations 2016 except that regulation 7(4) of those Regulations does not apply for the purposes of paragraphs (3B) and (4)(zd);

"relevant person of Northern Ireland" has the meaning given in Annex 1 of Appendix EU to the immigration rules made under section 3(2) of the Immigration Act 1971.]

[¹⁵ (6) In this regulation references to the Immigration (European Economic Area) Regulations 2016 are to be read with Schedule 4 to the Immigration and Social Security Co-ordination (EU Withdrawal) Act 2020 (Consequential, Saving, Transitional and Transitory Provisions) Regulations 2020.]"

AMENDMENTS

1. Social Security (Persons from Abroad) Amendment Regulations 2006 (SI 1026/2006) reg.7(3) (April 30, 2006).
2. Social Security (Lebanon) Amendment Regulations 2006 (SI 2006/1981) reg.3 (July 25, 2006). The amendment ceased to have effect from January 31, 2007.
3. Social Security (Persons from Abroad) Amendment (No. 2) Regulations 2006 (SI 2006/2528) reg.3 (October 9, 2006).
4. Social Security (Bulgaria and Romania) Amendment Regulations 2006 (SI 2006/3341) reg.3 (January 1, 2007).
5. Social Security (Habitual Residence) (Amendment) Regulations 2009 (SI 2009/362) reg.3 (March 18, 2009).
6. Social Security (Miscellaneous Amendments) (No. 3) Regulations 2011 (SI 2011/2425) reg.10(1) and (7) (October 31, 2011).
7. Social Security (Habitual Residence) (Amendment) Regulations 2012 (SI 2012/2587) reg.3 (November 8, 2012).
8. Social Security (Croatia) Amendment Regulations 2013 (SI 2013/1474) reg.3 (July 1, 2013).
9. Social Security (Miscellaneous Amendments) (No. 3) Regulations 2013 (SI 2013/2536) reg.6(1) and (8) (October 29,2013).
10. Jobseeker's Allowance (Habitual Residence) Amendment Regulations 2013 (SI 3196/2013) reg.2 (January 1, 2014).
11. Social Security (Habitual Residence) (Amendment) Regulations 2014 (SI 2014/902) reg.3 (May 31, 2014).
12. Jobseeker's Allowance (Habitual Residence) Amendment Regulations 2014 (SI 2014/2735) reg.3 (November 9, 2014).
13. Social Security (Income-related Benefits) (Updating and Amendment) (EU Exit) Regulations 2019 (SI 2019/872) reg.3 (May 7, 2019).
14. Social Security (Income-Related Benefits) (Persons of Northern Ireland —Family Members) (Amendment) Regulations 2020 (SI 2020/683) reg.3 (August 24, 2020).
15. Immigration and Social Security Co-ordination (EU Withdrawal) Act 2020 (Consequential, Saving, Transitional and Transitory Provisions)

(EU Exit) Regulations 2020 (SI 2020/1309) reg.55 (December 31, 2020 at 11.00 pm).

16. Social Security (Habitual Residence and Past Presence) (Amendment) Regulations 2021 (SI 2021/1034), reg.2 (September 15, 2021).
17. Social Security (Habitual Residence and Past Presence) (Amendment) Regulations 2022 (SI 2022/344) reg.2 (March 22, 2022).
18. Social Security (Habitual Residence and Past Presence) (Amendment) (No. 2) Regulations 2022 (SI 2022/990) reg.2 (October 18, 2022).

p.1014, *amendment to the Jobseeker's Allowance Regulations 1996 (SI 1996/207) reg.105(10A) (Notional income—exceptions)*

With effect from January 1, 2022, reg.3(3) of the Social Security   6.041
(Income and Capital Disregards) (Amendment) Regulations 2021 (SI 2021/1405) amended para.(10A) by inserting the following after sub-para.(ab):

"(ac) a child abuse payment;
(ad) a Windrush payment;"

Those payments are defined in reg.1(3). See the entry for p.684 for discussion of the nature of those payments.

p.1021, *annotation to the Jobseeker's Allowance Regulations 1996 (SI 1996/207) reg.107 (Capital limit)*

In the Institute for Government and the Social Security Advisory   6.042
Committee's 2021 joint report *Jobs and benefits: The Covid-19 challenge* it was noted that if the capital limit of £16,000 had risen in line with prices since 2006 it would be close to £23,500 (or £25,000: different figures are given) and recommended that the limit should be increased to £25,000 and subsequently automatically indexed to maintain its real value (pp.22 and 31). That recommendation was summarily rejected in the Government's response of March 22, 2022.

p.1023, *amendment to the Jobseeker's Allowance Regulations 1996 (SI 1996/207) reg.110(10) (Income treated as capital—exceptions)*

With effect from January 1, 2022, reg.3(4) of the Social Security   6.043
(Income and Capital Disregards) (Amendment) Regulations 2021 (SI 2021/1405) amended para.(10) by inserting the following after sub-para.(ab):

"(ac) which is a child abuse payment;
(ad) which is a Windrush payment; or"

Those payments are defined in reg.1(3). See the entry for p.684 for discussion of the nature of those payments. The "or" following sub-para.(ab), omitted in error in the main volume, has also been removed.

p.1027, *amendment to the Jobseeker's Allowance Regulations 1996 (SI 1996/207) reg.113(3B) (Notional capital—exceptions)*

6.044   With effect from January 1, 2022, reg.3(5) of the Social Security (Income and Capital Disregards) (Amendment) Regulations 2021 (SI 2021/1405) amended para.(3B) by substituting the following for "a payment of capital which is a Grenfell Tower payment":

"any of the following payments of capital—
   (a) a Grenfell Tower payment;
   (b) a child abuse payment;
   (c) a Windrush payment."

All of those payments are defined in reg.1(3). See the entry of p.684 for discussion of the nature of child abuse and Windrush payments.

pp.1059–1060, *amendments to the Jobseeker's Allowance Regulations 1996 (SI 1996/207) reg.140 (Hardship payments)*

6.045   With effect from July 26, 2021, Sch.3 para.4 of the Social Security (Scotland) Act 2018 (Disability Assistance for Children and Young People) (Consequential Modifications) Order 2021 (SI 2021/786) makes the following amendments to reg.140(1)(h):

- in para.(i), after "Benefits Act", insert ", the care component of child disability payment at the highest or middle rate in accordance with regulation 11(5) of the DACYP Regulations";
- in para.(ii), after "disability living allowance", insert ", child disability payment";
- after para.(iii), insert "(iiia) has claimed child disability payment and has an award of the care component of child disability payment at the highest or middle rate in accordance with regulation 11(5) of the DACYP Regulations for a period commencing after the date on which the claim was made; or".

With effect from March 21, 2022, art.5 of the Social Security (Disability Assistance for Working Age People) (Consequential Amendments) Order 2022 (SI 2022/177) makes the following amendments to reg.140(1)(h):

- in para.(i):
  - after "DACYP Regulations" for "or" substitute ",";
  - after "the 2012 Act" insert ", the daily living component of adult disability payment at the standard or enhanced rate in accordance with regulation 5 of the Disability Assistance for Working Age People (Scotland) Regulations 2022";
- in para.(ii):
  - after "armed forces independence payment" for "or" substitute ",";
  - after "personal independence payment" insert "or adult disability payment";
- after para.(iv) insert "(iva) has claimed adult disability payment and has an award of the daily living component of adult disability

payment at the standard or enhanced rate in accordance with regulation 5 of the Disability Assistance for Working Age People (Scotland) Regulations 2022 for a period commencing after the date on which that claim was made; or".

pp.1071–1072, *amendments to the Jobseeker's Allowance Regulations 1996 (SI 1996/207) reg.146A (Meaning of "couple in hardship")*

With effect from July 26, 2021, Sch.3 para.5 of the Social Security **6.046** (Scotland) Act 2018 (Disability Assistance for Children and Young People) (Consequential Modifications) Order 2021 (SI 2021/786) makes the following amendments to reg.146A(1)(e):

- in para.(i), after "Benefits Act", insert ", the care component of child disability payment at the highest or middle rate in accordance with regulation 11(5) of the DACYP Regulations";
- in para.(ii), after "disability living allowance", insert ", child disability payment";
- after para.(iii), insert "(iiia) has claimed child disability payment and has an award of the care component of child disability payment at the highest or middle rate in accordance with regulation 11(5) of the DACYP Regulations for a period commencing after the date on which the claim was made; or".

With effect from March 21, 2022, art.5(5) of the Social Security (Disability Assistance for Working Age People) (Consequential Amendments) Order 2022 (SI 2022/177) makes the following amendments to reg.146A(1)(e):

- in para.(i):
  - after "armed forces independence payment", for "or" substitute ", ";
  - after "the 2012 Act" insert ", or the daily living component of adult disability payment at the standard or enhanced rate in accordance with regulation 5 of the Disability Assistance for Working Age People (Scotland) Regulations 2022";
- in para.(ii):
  - after "armed forces independence payment", for "or" substitute ", ";
  - after "personal independence payment" insert "or adult disability payment";
- after para.(iv) insert "(iva) has claimed adult disability payment and has an award of the daily living component at the standard or enhanced rate in accordance with regulation 5 of the Disability Assistance for Working Age People (Scotland) Regulations 2022 for a period commencing after the date on which that claim was made; or".

p.1086, *amendment to the Jobseeker's Allowance Regulations 1996 (SI 1996/207) reg.172 (Trade disputes: prescribed sum)*

With effect from April 11, 2022, art.28 of the Social Security Benefits **6.047** Uprating Order 2022 (SI 2022/292) substituted "£42.50" for "£41".

pp.1087–1088, *amendments to the Jobseeker's Allowance Regulations 1996 (SI 1996/207) Sch.A1 (Categories of members of a joint-claim couple who are not required to satisfy the conditions in section 1(2B)(b))*

6.048 With effect from July 26, 2021, Sch.3 para.6 of the Social Security (Scotland) Act 2018 (Disability Assistance for Children and Young People) (Consequential Modifications) Order 2021 (SI 2021/786) makes the following amendments to para.3(a) (member caring for another person):

- in para.(i), after "Benefits Act", insert ", the care component of child disability payment at the highest or middle rate in accordance with regulation 11(5) of the DACYP Regulations";
- in para.(iv), after "disability living allowance", insert ", child disability payment";
- after para.(v), insert "(va) the person being cared for ("P") has claimed entitlement to the care component of child disability payment in accordance with regulation 24 (when an application is to be treated as made and beginning of entitlement to assistance) of the DACYP Regulations, an award at the highest or middle rate has been made in respect of P's claim, and where the period for which the award is payable has begun, P is in receipt of that payment;"

With effect from March 21, 2022, art.5(6) of the Social Security (Disability Assistance for Working Age People) (Consequential Amendments) Order 2022 (SI 2022/177) makes the following amendments to para.3(a) (member caring for another person):

- in para.3(a)(i) (member caring for another person):
  - after "armed forces independence payment" for "or" substitute ", ";
  - after "the 2012 Act" insert "or the daily living component of adult disability payment at the standard or enhanced rate in accordance with regulation 5 of the Disability Assistance for Working Age People (Scotland) Regulations 2022";
- in para.3(a)(iv):
  - after "armed forces independence payment" for "or" substitute ", ";
  - after "personal independence payment" insert "or adult disability payment";
- in para.3(a)(vi) omit "or" at the end; and
- after para.3(a)(vi) insert "(via) the person being cared for has claimed entitlement to the daily living component of adult disability payment in accordance with regulation 35 (when an application is to be treated as made and beginning of entitlement to assistance) of the Disability Assistance for Working Age People (Scotland) Regulations 2022, an award of the standard or enhanced rate of the daily living component has been made in respect of that claim and, where the period for which the award is payable has begun, that person is in receipt of that payment; or"

p.1091, *amendments to the Jobseeker's Allowance Regulations 1996 (SI 1996/207) Sch.1 (Applicable amounts)*

Substitute the following for paras 3.479–3.508   **6.049**

"SCHEDULE 1

Regulations 83 and 84(1)

APPLICABLE AMOUNTS

[⁹ PART I

PERSONAL ALLOWANCES

1.—The weekly amounts specified in column (2) below in respect of each person or   **3.479**
couple specified in column (1) shall be the weekly amounts specified for the purposes of
regulations 83 [²⁸ 84(1), 86A and 86B] (applicable amounts and polygamous marriages).

Column (1) Person or Couple	Column (2) Amount

(1) Single claimant aged—
(a) except where head (b) or (c) of this sub-paragraph applies, less than 18;
(b) less than 18 who falls within paragraph (2) of regulation 57 and who—
  (i) is a person to whom regulation 59, 60 or 61 applies [¹ . . .]; or
  (ii) is the subject of a direction under section 16;
(c) less than 18 who satisfies the condition in [³³ paragraph 13(1)(a)] of Part 3;
(d) not less than 18 but less than 25;
(e) not less than 25.
	1.
	(a) [⁵⁴ £61.05];
	
	(b) [⁵⁴ £61.05];
	
	(c) [⁵⁴ £61.05];
	
	(d) [⁵⁴ £61.05];
	(e) [⁵⁴ £74.70];

(2) Lone parent aged—
(a) except where head (b) or (c) of this sub-paragraph applies, less than 18;
(b) less than 18 who falls within paragraph (2) of regulation 57 and who—
  (i) is a person to whom regulation 59, 60 or 61 applies [¹ . . .]; or
  (ii) is the subject of a direction under section 16;
(c) less than 18 who satisfies the condition in [³³ paragraph 13(1)(a)] [² of Part 3];
(d) not less than 18.
	2.
	(a) [⁵⁴ £61.05];
	
	(b) [⁵⁴ £61.05];
	
	(c) [⁵⁴ £61.05];
	
	(d) [⁵⁴ £77.00].

(3) Couple—
(a) where both members are aged less than 18 and—
  (i) at least one of them is treated as responsible for a child; or
  (ii) had they not been members of a couple, each would have been a person to whom regulation 59, 60 or 61 (circumstances in which a person aged 16 or 17 is eligible for a jobseeker's allowance) applied or
  (iii) had they not been members of a couple, the claimant would have been a person to whom regulation 59, 60 or 61 (circumstances in which a person aged 16 or 17 is eligible for a
	3.
	(a) [⁵⁴ £92.20];

Column (1) Person or Couple	Column (2) Amount
jobseeker's allowance) applied and his partner satisfies the requirements for entitlement to income support [³⁶ or an income-related employment and support allowance] other than the requirement to make a claim for it; or	
[¹(iv) they are married [³¹ or civil partners]and one member a of the couple is person to whom regulation 59, 60 or 61 applies and the other member is registered in accordance with regulation 62; or	
(iva) they are married [³¹ or civil partners] and each member of the couple is a person to whom regulation 59, 60 or 61 applies; or]	
(v) there is a direction under section 16 (jobseeker's allowance in cases of severe hardship) in respect of each member; or	
(vi) there is a direction under section 16 in respect of one of them and the other is a person to whom regulation 59, 60 or 61 applies [¹ . . .], or	
(vii) there is a direction under section 16 in respect of one of them and the other satisfies requirements for entitlement to income support [³⁶ or an income-related employment and support allowance] other than the requirement to make a claim for it;	
(b) where both members are aged less than 18 and sub-paragraph (3)(a) does not apply but one member of the couple falls within paragraph (2) of regulation 57 and either—	(b) [⁵⁴ £61.05];
(i) is a person to whom regulation 59, 60 or 61 applies [¹ . . .]; or	
(ii) is the subject of a direction under section 16 of the Act;	
(c) where both members are aged less than 18 and neither head (a) nor (b) of sub-paragraph (3) applies but one member of the couple—	(c) [⁵⁴ £61.05];
(i) is a person to whom regulation 59, 60 or 61 applies [¹ . . .]; or	
(ii) is the subject of a direction under section 16;	
(d) where both members are aged less than 18 and none of heads (a), (b) or (c) of sub-paragraph (3) apply but one member of the couple is a person who satisfies the requirements of [³³ paragraph 13(1)(a)];	(d) [⁵⁴ £61.05];
[³⁵ (e) where—	(e) [⁵⁴ £121.05];
(i) both members are aged not less than 18; or	
(ii) one member is aged not less than 18 and the other member is a person who is—	
(aa) under 18, and	
(bb) treated as responsible for a child;]	
(f) where [³⁵ paragraph (e) does not apply and] one member is aged not less than 18 and the other member is a person under 18 who—	(f) [⁵⁴ £121.05];
(i) is a person to whom regulation 59, 60 or 61 applies [¹ . . .]; or	

Column (1) *Person or Couple*	Column (2) *Amount*
(ii) is the subject of a direction under section 16; [³⁸ or (iii) satisfies requirements for entitlement to income support or who would do so if he were not a member of a couple, other than the requirement to make a claim for it; or (iv) satisfies requirements for entitlement to an income-related employment and support allowance other than the requirement to make a claim for it;] (g) where one member is aged not less than 18 but less than 25 and the other member is a person under 18— (i) to whom none of the regulations 59 to 61 applies; or (ii) who is not the subject of a direction under section 16; and (iii) does not satisfy requirements for entitlement to income support [³⁶ or an income-related employment and support allowance] disregarding the requirement to make a claim for it; (h) where one member is aged not less than 25 and the other member is a person under 18— (i) to whom none of the regulations 59 to 61 applies; or (ii) is not the subject of a direction under section 16; and (iii) does not satisfy requirements for entitlement to income support [³⁶ or an income-related employment and support allowance] disregarding the requirement to make a claim for it.	(g) [⁵⁴ £61.05]; (h) [⁵⁴ £77.00].
2.—[³⁰ . . .]	
3.—[²⁹ . . .]	

Part II

Family Premium

4.—[³⁰ . . .] **3.480**

Part III

Premiums

5.—Except as provided in paragraph 6, the weekly premiums specified in Part IV of this **3.481** Schedule shall for the purposes of regulations 83(e) and 84(1)(f), be applicable to a claimant who satisfies the condition specified in [⁴ ¹⁵ paragraphs 9A] to 17 in respect of that premium.

6.—Subject to paragraph 7, where a claimant satisfies the conditions in respect of more than one premium in this Part of this Schedule, only one premium shall be applicable to him and, if they are different amounts, the higher or highest amount shall apply.

[¹⁶ 7.—(1) Subject to sub-paragraph (2), the following premiums, namely—

(a) a severe disability premium to which paragraph 15 applies;

(b) an enhanced disability premium to which paragraph 15A applies;

(c) [³⁰ . . .]; and

(d) a carer premium in which paragraph 17 applies,

may be applicable in addition to any other premium which may apply under this Part of this Schedule.

(2) An enhanced disability premium in respect of a person shall not be applicable in addition to—

(a) a pensioner premium under paragraph 10 or 11; or

(b) a higher pensioner premium under paragraph 12.]

8.—(1) Subject to sub-paragraph (2) for the purposes of this Part of this Schedule, once a premium is applicable to a claimant under this Part, a person shall be treated as being in receipt of any benefit—

(a) in the case of a benefit to which the Social Security (Overlapping Benefits) Regulations 1979 applies, for any period during which, apart from the provisions of those Regulations, he would be in receipt of that benefit; and

[³(b) for any period spent by a claimant in undertaking a course of training or instruction provided or approved by the Secretary of State [³⁵ . . .] under section 2 of the Employment and Training Act 1973, or by [³⁷ Skills Development Scotland,] Scottish Enterprise or Highlands and Islands Enterprise under section 2 of the Enterprise and New Towns (Scotland) Act 1990 or for any period during which he is in receipt of a training allowance.]

(2) For the purposes of the carer premium under paragraph 17, a person shall be treated as being in receipt of [²⁴ carer's allowance] by virtue of sub-paragraph (1)(a) only if and for so long as the person in respect of whose care the allowance has been claimed remains in receipt of attendance allowance, [⁴⁶ the care component of disability living allowance at the highest or middle rate prescribed in accordance with section 72(3) of the Benefits Act [⁵², the care component of child disability payment at the highest or middle rate prescribed in accordance with regulation 11(5) of the DACYP Regulations] [⁴⁷ , armed forces independence payment] [⁵³ ,] the daily living component of personal independence payment at the standard or enhanced rate prescribed in accordance with section 78(3) of the 2012 Act] [⁵³ , or the daily living component of adult disability payment at the standard or enhanced rate prescribed in accordance with regulation 5 of the Disability Assistance for Working Age People (Scotland) Regulations 2022].

Lone Parent Premium

3.482   **9.**—[⁴ . . .]

[¹⁵ **Bereavement Premium**

3.483   **9A.**—[³⁴ . . .]]

Pensioner premium for persons [⁴⁰ over the qualifying age for state pension credit]

3.484   **10.**—The condition is that the claimant—

(a) is a single claimant or lone parent who has attained [⁴⁰ the qualifying age for state pension credit]; or

(b) has attained [⁴⁰ the qualifying age for state pension credit] and has a partner; or

(c) has a partner and the partner has attained [⁴⁰ the qualifying age for state pension credit] but not the age of 75.

Pensioner premium where claimant's partner has attained the age of 75

3.485   **11.**—The condition is that the claimant has a partner who has attained the age of 75 but not the age of 80.

Higher Pensioner Premium

3.486   **12.**—(1) [³³ Subject to sub-paragraph (5), the] condition is that—

(a) the claimant is a single claimant or lone parent who has attained [⁴⁰ the qualifying age for state pension credit] and either—

(i) satisfies one of the additional conditions specified in paragraph 14(1)(a), (c), [⁵¹ (ca), (cb),] (e), (f) [⁵¹, (fa)] or (h); or

(ii) was entitled to either income support or income-based jobseeker's allowance [¹², or was treated as being entitled to either of those benefits and the disability premium was or, as the case may be, would have been,] applicable to him in respect of a benefit week within 8 weeks of [⁴⁰ the date he attained the qualifying age for state pension credit] and he has, subject to sub-paragraph (2), remained continuously entitled to one of those benefits since attaining that age; or

(b) the claimant has a partner and—
    (i) the partner has attained the age of 80; or
    (ii) the partner has attained [⁴⁰ the qualifying age for state pension credit] but not the age of 80, and the additional conditions specified in paragraph 14 are satisfied in respect of him; or

(c) the claimant—
    (i) has attained [⁴⁰ the qualifying age for state pension credit];
    [³(ii) satisfies the requirements of either sub-head (i) or (ii) of paragraph 12(1)(a); and]
    (iii) has a partner.

(2) For the purposes of this paragraph and paragraph 14—

(a) once the higher pensioner premium is applicable to a claimant, if he then ceases, for a period of eight weeks or less, to be entitled to either income support or income-based jobseeker's allowance [¹² or ceases to be treated as entitled to either of those benefits], he shall, on becoming re-entitled to either of those benefits, thereafter be treated as having been continuously entitled thereto;

(b) in so far as sub-paragraphs (1)(a)(ii) and (1)(c)(ii) are concerned, if a claimant ceases to be entitled to either income support or an income-based jobseeker's allowance [¹² or ceases to be treated as entitled to either of those benefits] for a period not exceeding eight weeks which includes [⁴⁰ the date he attained the qualifying age for state pension credit], he shall, on becoming re-entitled to either of those benefits, thereafter be treated as having been continuously entitled thereto.

[⁸(3) In this paragraph where a claimant's partner is a welfare to work beneficiary, sub-paragraphs (1)(a)(ii) and (2)(b) shall apply to him as if for the words "8 weeks" there were substituted the words "[³² 104 weeks]".]

[¹² (4) For the purposes of this paragraph, a claimant shall be treated as having been entitled to income support or to an income-based jobseeker's allowance throughout any period which comprises only days on which he was participating in an employment zone programme and was not entitled to—

(a) income support because, as a consequence of his participation in that programme, he was engaged in remunerative work or had income in excess of the claimant's applicable amount as prescribed in Part IV of the Income Support Regulations; or

(b) a jobseeker's allowance because, as a consequence of his participation in that programme, he was engaged in remunerative work or failed to satisfy the condition specified in section 2(1)(c) or in section 3(1)(a).]

[³³ (5) The condition is not satisfied if—

(a) the claimant is a single claimant or a lone parent and (in either case) is a long-term patient;

(b) the claimant is a member of a couple or polygamous marriage and each member of the couple or polygamous marriage is a long-term patient; or

(c) the claimant is a member of a couple or a polygamous marriage and a member of that couple or polygamous marriage is—
    (i) a long-term patient; and
    (ii) the only member of the couple or polygamous marriage to whom sub-paragraph (1)(b) or (c) refers.]

Disability Premium

13. [³³ —(1) Subject to sub-paragraph (2), the] condition is that the claimant—   **3.487**

(a) is a single claimant or lone parent who has not attained [⁴⁰ the qualifying age for state pension credit] and satisfies any one of the additional conditions specified in paragraph 14(1)(a), (c), [⁵¹ (ca), (cb),] (e), (f) [⁵¹, (fa)] or (h); or

(b) has not attained [⁴⁰ the qualifying age for state pension credit], has a partner and the claimant satisfies any one of the additional conditions specified in paragraph 14(1)(a), (c), [⁵¹ (ca), (cb),] (e), (f) [⁵¹, (fa)] or (h); or

(c) has a partner and the partner has not attained [⁴⁰ the qualifying age for state pension credit] and also satisfies any one of the additional conditions specified in paragraph 14.

[³³ (2) The condition is not satisfied if—

(a) the claimant is a single claimant or a lone parent and (in either case) is a long-term patient;

(b) the claimant is a member of a couple or polygamous marriage and each member of the couple or polygamous marriage is a long-term patient; or

(c) the claimant is a member of a couple or polygamous marriage and a member of that couple or polygamous marriage—

    (i) is a long-term patient; and

    (ii) is the only member of the couple or polygamous marriage to whom the condition in sub-paragraph (1)(b) or (c) refers.]

Additional conditions for Higher Pensioner and Disability Premium

3.488
14.—(1) The additional conditions specified in this paragraph are that—

(a) the claimant or, as the case may be, his partner, is in receipt [²⁵ the disability element or the severe disability element of working tax credit as specified in regulation 20(1)(b) and (f) of the Working Tax Credit (Entitlement and Maximum Rate) Regulations 2002] or mobility supplement;

(b) the claimant's partner is in receipt of severe disablement allowance;

(c) the claimant or, as the case may be, his partner, is in receipt of attendance allowance or disability living allowance or is a person whose disability living allowance is payable, in whole or in part, to another in accordance with regulation 44 of the Claims and Payments Regulations (payment of disability living allowance on behalf of third party);

[⁴⁶ (ca) the claimant or, as the case may be, his partner, is in receipt of personal independence payment or is a person whose personal independence payment is payable, in whole or in part, to another in accordance with regulation 58(2) of the Universal Credit etc. Claims and Payments Regulations (payment to another person on the claimant's behalf);]

[⁵³ (caa) the claimant or, as the case may be, the claimant's partner, is in receipt of adult disability payment or is a person whose adult disability payment is payable, in whole or in part, to another in accordance with regulation 33 of the Disability Assistance for Working Age People (Scotland) Regulations 2022 (making payments);]

[⁴⁷ (cb) the claimant or, as the case may be, the claimant's partner, is in receipt of armed forces independence payment or is a person whose armed forces independence payment is payable, in whole or in part, to another in accordance with article 24D of the Armed Forces and Reserve Forces (Compensation Scheme) Order 2011;]

(d) the claimant's partner is in receipt of long-term incapacity benefit or is a person to whom section 30B(4) of the Benefits Act (long term rate of incapacity benefit payable to those who are terminally ill) applies;

(e) the claimant or, as the case may be, his partner, has an invalid carriage or other vehicle provided to him by the Secretary of State under section 5(2)(a) of and Schedule 2 to the National Health Service Act 1977 or under section 46 of the National Health Service (Scotland) Act 1978 or provided by the Department of Health and Social Services for Northern Ireland under article 30(1) of the Health and Personal Social Services (Northern Ireland) Order 1972, or receives payments by way of grant from the Secretary of State under paragraph 2 of Schedule 2 to the Act of 1977 (additional provisions as to vehicles) or, in Scotland, under section 46 of the Act of 1978;

(f) the claimant or, as the case may be, his partner, is a person who is entitled to the mobility component of disability living allowance but to whom the component is not payable in accordance with regulation 42 of the Claims and Payments Regulations (cases where disability living allowance not payable);

[⁴⁶ (fa) the claimant or, as the case may be, his partner, is a person who is entitled to the mobility component of personal independence payment but to whom the component is not payable in accordance with regulation 61 of the Universal Credit etc. Claims and Payments Regulations (cases where mobility component of personal independence payment not payable);]

[⁵³ (fb) the claimant or, as the case may be, the claimant's partner, is a person who is entitled to the mobility component of adult disability payment but to whom the component is not payable in accordance with regulation 34(6) of the Disability Assistance for Working Age People (Scotland) Regulations 2022 (amount and form of adult disability payment);]

(g) the claimant's partner was either—

(i) in receipt of long term incapacity benefit under section 30A(5) of the Benefits Act immediately before attaining pensionable age and he is still alive;

(ii) entitled to attendance allowance or disability living allowance but payment of that benefit was suspended in accordance with regulations under section 113(2) of the Benefits Act or otherwise abated as a consequence of [² the partner] becoming a patient within the meaning of regulation 85(4) (special cases), [⁵³ ; . . .]

(iii) entitled to personal independence payment but no amount is payable in accordance with regulations made under section 86(1) (hospital in-patients) of the 2012 Act] [⁵³ ; or

(iv) entitled to adult disability payment but no amount is payable in accordance with regulation 28 (effect of admission to hospital on ongoing entitlement to Adult Disability Payment) of the Disability Assistance for Working Age People (Scotland) Regulations 2022;]

and [⁵³ in any of the cases described in sub-paragraphs (i) to (iv),]the higher pensioner premium or disability premium had been applicable to the claimant or his partner;

[⁴⁸ (h) the claimant or, as the case may be, his partner, is certified as severely sight impaired or blind by a consultant ophthalmologist.]

[⁴⁸ (2) For the purposes of sub-paragraph (1)(h), a person who has ceased to be certified as severely sight impaired or blind on regaining his eyesight shall nevertheless be treated as severely sight impaired or blind, as the case may be, and as satisfying the additional condition set out in that sub-paragraph for a period of 28 weeks following the date on which he ceased to be so certified.]

Severe Disability Premium
15.—(1) In the case of a single claimant, a lone parent or a claimant who is treated as **3.489** having no partner in consequence of sub-paragraph (3), the condition is that—

(a) he is in receipt of attendance allowance [⁴⁶ , the care component of disability living allowance at the highest or middle rate prescribed in accordance with section 72(3) of the Benefits Act [⁴⁷ , armed forces independence payment] [⁵³ ,] the daily living component of personal independence payment at the standard or enhanced rate in accordance with section 78(3) of the 2012 Act] [⁵³ , or the daily living component of adult disability payment at the standard or enhanced rate in accordance with regulation 5 of the Disability Assistance for Working Age People (Scotland) Regulations 2022]; and

(b) subject to sub-paragraph (4), there are no non-dependants aged 18 or over normally residing with him or with whom he is normally residing; and

[¹¹(c) no person is entitled to, and in receipt of, [²⁴ a carer's allowance] under section 70 of the Benefits Act [⁵⁰ or has an award of universal credit which includes the carer element] in respect of caring for him;]

(2) Where the claimant has a partner, the condition is that—

(a) the claimant is in receipt of attendance allowance [⁴⁶ , the care component of disability living allowance at the highest or middle rate prescribed in accordance with section 72(3) of the Benefits Act [⁴⁷ , armed forces independence payment] [⁵³ ,] the daily living component of personal independence payment at the standard or enhanced rate in accordance with section 78(3) of the 2012 Act] [⁵³ , or the daily living component of adult disability payment at the standard or enhanced rate in accordance with regulation 5 of the Disability Assistance for Working Age People (Scotland) Regulations 2022]; and

 (b) the partner is also in receipt of a qualifying benefit, or if he is a member of a polygamous marriage, all the partners of that marriage are in receipt of a qualifying benefit; and

 (c) subject to sub-paragraph (4), there is no non-dependant aged 18 or over normally residing with him or with whom he is normally residing; and (d) either—

  (i) [¹¹ no person is entitled to, and in receipt of, [²⁴ a carer's allowance] under section 70 of the Benefits Act [⁵⁰ or has an award of universal credit which includes the carer element] in respect of] caring for either member of the couple or all the members of the polygamous marriage; or

  (ii) a person is engaged in caring for one member (but not both members) of the couple, or one or more but not all members of the polygamous marriage, and in consequence is [¹¹ entitled to] [²⁴ a carer's allowance] under section 70 of the Benefits Act [⁵⁰ or has an award of universal credit which includes the carer element].

(3) Where the claimant has a partner who does not satisfy the condition in sub-paragraph (2)(b), and that partner is [⁴⁸ severely sight impaired or blind or treated as severely sight impaired or blind] within the meaning of paragraph 14(1)(h) and (2), that partner shall be treated for the purposes of sub-paragraph (2) as if he were not a partner of the claimant.

(4) The following persons shall not be regarded as a non-dependant for the purposes of sub-paragraphs (1)(b) and (2)(c)—

 (a) a person in receipt of attendance allowance [⁴⁶ , the care component of disability living allowance at the highest or middle rate prescribed in accordance with section 72(3) of the Benefits Act [⁴⁷ , armed forces independence payment] [⁵³ ,] the daily living component of personal independence payment at the standard or enhanced rate in accordance with section 78(3) of the 2012 Act] [⁵³ , or the daily living component of adult disability payment at the standard or enhanced rate in accordance with regulation 5 of the Disability Assistance for Working Age People (Scotland) Regulations 2022];

 (b) subject to sub-paragraph (6), a person who joins the claimant's household for the first time in order to care for the claimant or his partner and immediately before so joining the claimant or his partner satisfied the condition in sub-paragraph (1) or, as the case may be, (2);

 (c) a person who is [⁴⁸ severely sight impaired or blind or treated as severely sight impaired or blind] within the meaning of paragraph 14(1)(h) and (2).

(5) For the purposes of sub-paragraph (2), a person shall be treated [¹¹ . . .] (a) [¹¹ as being in receipt of] attendance allowance, or the care component of disability living allowance at the highest or middle rate prescribed in accordance with section 72(3) of the Benefits Act if he would, but for his being a patient for a period exceeding 28 days, be so in receipt;

[⁴⁶ (aa) as being in receipt of the daily living component of personal independence payment at the standard or enhanced rate in accordance with section 78 of the 2012 Act if he would, but for regulations made under section 86(1) (hospital in-patients) of the 2012 Act, be so in receipt;]

[⁵³ (ab) as being in receipt of the daily living component of adult disability payment at the standard or enhanced rate in accordance with regulation 5 of the Disability Assistance for Working Age People (Scotland) Regulations 2022 if they would, but for regulation 28 (effect of admission to hospital on ongoing entitlement to Adult Disability Payment) of those Regulations be so in receipt;]

[¹¹(b) as being entitled to and in receipt of [²⁴ a carer's allowance] [⁵⁰ or having an award of universal credit which includes the carer element] if he would, but for the person for whom he was caring being a patient in hospital for a period exceeding 28 days, be so entitled and in receipt [⁵⁰ of carer's allowance or have such an award of universal credit].]

(6) Sub-paragraph (4)(b) shall apply only for the first 12 weeks following the date on which the person to whom that provision applies first joins the claimant's household.

(7) For the purposes of sub-paragraph (1)(c) and (2)(d), no account shall be taken of an award of [²⁴ carer's allowance] [⁵⁰ or universal credit which includes the carer element] to the extent that payment of such an award is backdated for a period before [³⁴ the date on which the award is first paid].

(8) A person shall be treated as satisfying this condition if he would have satisfied the condition specified for a severe disability premium in income support in paragraph 13 of Schedule 2 to the Income Support Regulations by virtue only of regulations 4 to 6 of the Income Support (General) Amendment (No. 6) Regulations 1991 (savings provisions in relation to severe disability premium) and for the purposes of determining whether in the particular case regulation 4 of those Regulations had ceased to apply in accordance with regulation 5(2)(a) of those Regulations, a person who is entitled to an income-based jobseeker's allowance shall be treated as entitled to income support.

[²⁰ (9) In sub-paragraphs (1)(c) and (2)(d), references to a person being in receipt of [²⁴ a carer's allowance] [⁵⁰ or as having an award of universal credit which includes the carer element] shall include references to a person who would have been in receipt of that allowance [⁵⁰ or had such an award] but for the application of a restriction under section [³⁹ 6B or] 7 of the Social Security Fraud Act 2001 (loss of benefit provisions).]

[⁵⁰ (10) For the purposes of this paragraph, a person has an award of universal credit which includes the carer element if the person has an award of universal credit which includes an amount which is the carer element under regulation 29 of the Universal Credit Regulations 2013.]

[¹⁶ **Enhanced disability premium**

15A.—[⁴⁶ (1) Subject to sub-paragraph (2), the condition is that—   **3.490**

    (a) the claimant; or

    (b) the claimant's partner (if any), is a person who has not attained the qualifying age for state pension credit and is a person to whom sub-paragraph (1ZA) applies.

(1ZA) This sub-paragraph applies to the person mentioned in sub-paragraph (1) where—

    (a) the care component of disability living allowance is, or would, but for a suspension of benefit in accordance with regulations under section 113(2) of the Benefits Act or but for an abatement as a consequence of hospitalisation, be payable to that person at the highest rate prescribed under section 72(3) of the Benefits Act; or

    [⁵² (aa) the care component of child disability payment is payable to that person at the highest rate in accordance with regulation 11(5) of the DACYP Regulations; or]

    (b) the daily living component of personal independence payment is, or would, but for a suspension of benefits in accordance with regulations under section 86(1) (hospital in-patients) of the 2012 Act, be payable to that person at the enhanced rate in accordance with section 78(2) of the 2012 Act] [⁴⁷ ; or

    [⁵³ (ba) the daily living component of adult disability payment is, or would, but regulation 28 (effect of admission to hospital on ongoing entitlement to Adult Disability Payment) of the Disability Assistance for Working Age People (Scotland) Regulations 2022, be payable to that person at the enhanced rate in accordance with regulation 5 of those Regulations]

    (c) armed forces independence payment is payable to that person.]

[⁴² (1A) Where the condition in sub-paragraph (1) ceases to be satisfied because of the death of a child or young person, the condition is that the claimant is entitled to child benefit in respect of that person under section 145A of the Benefits Act (entitlement after death of child or qualifying young person).]

[³³ (2) The condition is not satisfied where the person to whom sub-paragraph (1) refers is—

    (a) a child or young person—

        (i) whose capital if calculated in accordance with Part 8 of these Regulations in like manner as for the claimant, except as provided in regulation 106(1), would exceed £3,000; or

        (ii) who is a long-term patient;

    (b) a single claimant or a lone parent and (in either case) is a long-term patient;

    (c) a member of a couple or polygamous marriage and each member of the couple or polygamous marriage is a long-term patient; or

    (d) a member of a couple or polygamous marriage who is—

        (i) a long-term patient; and

        (ii) the only member of the couple or polygamous marriage to whom sub-paragraph (1) refers.]]

Disabled Child Premium

3.491 **16.**—[³⁰ . . . ³³]

Carer Premium

3.492 **17.**—(1) Subject to sub-paragraphs (3) and (4), the condition is that the claimant or his partner is, or both of them are, [¹¹ entitled to] [²⁴ a carer's allowance] under section 70 of the Benefits Act.

(2) [²⁸ . . .]

[²³ (3) Where a carer premium is awarded but—

    (a) the person in respect of whose care the [²⁴ carer's allowance] has been awarded dies; or

    (b) in any other case the person in respect of whom a carer premium has been awarded ceases to be entitled [²⁸ . . .] to [²⁴ a carer's allowance], the condition for the award of the premium shall be treated as satisfied for a period of eight weeks from the relevant date specified in sub-paragraph (3A) below.

(3A) The relevant date for the purposes of sub-paragraph (3) above shall be—

    (a) [²⁸ where sub-paragraph (3)(a) applies,] the Sunday following the death of the person in respect of whose care [²⁴ a carer's allowance] has been awarded or the date of death if the death occurred on a Sunday;

    (b) [²⁸ . . .]

    (c) in any other case, the date of which the person who has been entitled to [²⁴ a carer's allowance] ceases to be entitled to that allowance.]

(4) Where a person who has been entitled to an invalid care allowance ceases to be entitled to that allowance and makes a claim for a jobseeker's allowance, the condition for the award of the carer premium shall be treated as satisfied for a period of eight weeks from the date on which—

    [²³(a) the person in respect of whose care the [²⁴ carer's allowance] has been awarded dies;

    (b) [²⁸ . . .]

    [²⁸ (c) in any other case, the person who has been entitled to a carer's allowance ceased to be entitled to that allowance.]]

Persons in receipt of concessionary payments

3.493 **18.**—For the purpose of determining whether a premium is applicable to a person under paragraphs 14 to 17, any concessionary payment made to compensate that person for the non-payment of any benefit mentioned in those paragraphs shall be treated as if it were a payment of that benefit.

Person in receipt of benefit

3.494 **19.**—For the purposes of this Part of this Schedule, a person shall be regarded as being in receipt of any benefit if, and only if, it is paid in respect of him and shall be so regarded only for any period in respect of which that benefit is paid.

PART IV

WEEKLY AMOUNTS OF PREMIUMS SPECIFIED IN PART III

Premium	Amount
20.—(1) [⁴ . . .]	(1) [⁴ . . .]
(1A) [³⁴ . . .]	(1A) [³⁴ . . .];

(2) Pensioner premium for persons [⁴⁰ who have attained the qualifying age for state pension credit]—
    (a) where the claimant satisfies the condition in paragraph 10(a);
    (b) where the claimant satisfies the condition in paragraph 10(b).
    (c) where the claimant satisfies the condition in paragraph 10(c).
	(2)
	
	(a) [⁵⁵ £105.60];
	
	(b) [⁵⁵ £157.65];
	
	(c) [⁵⁵ £157.65];

Premium	Amount
(3) Pensioner premium for claimants whose partner has attained the age of 75 where the claimant satisfies the condition in paragraph 11;	(3) [⁵⁵ £157.65];
(4) Higher Pensioner Premium— (a) where the claimant satisfies the condition in paragraph 12(1)(a); (b) where the claimant satisfies the condition in paragraph 12(1)(b) or (c).	(4) (a) [⁵⁵ £105.60]; (b) [⁵⁵ £157.65];
(5) Disability Premium— (a) where the claimant satisfies the condition in [³³ paragraph 13(1)(a)]; (b) where the claimant satisfies the condition in [³³ paragraph 13(1)(b) or (c)].	(5) (a) [⁵⁵ £36.20]; (b) [⁵⁵ £51.60].
(6) Severe Disability Premium— (a) where the claimant satisfies the condition in paragraph 15(1); (b) where the claimant satisfies the condition in paragraph 15(2)— (i) if there is someone in receipt of [²⁴ a carer's allowance] or [² if any partner of the claimant] satisfies that condition by virtue of paragraph 15(5); (ii) if no-one is in receipt of such an allowance.	(6) (a) [⁵⁵ £69.40]; (b) (i) [⁵⁵ £69.40] [⁵⁵ £138.80]
(7) [³⁰ ...]	(7) [³⁰ ...]
(8) Carer Premium.	(8) [⁵⁵ £38.85] in respect of each person who satisfied the condition specified in paragraph 17.
[¹⁶ (9) Enhanced disability premium where the conditions in paragraph 15A are satisfied.]	[¹⁶ (9) (a)[³⁰ ...] (b) [⁵⁵ £17.75] in respect of each person who is neither— (i) a child or young person; nor (ii) a member of a couple or a polygamous marriage, respect of whom the in conditions specified in paragraph 15A are satisfied; (c) [⁵⁵ £25.35] where the claimant is a member of a couple or a polygamous marriage and the conditions specified in paragraph 15A are satisfied in respect of a member of that couple or polygamous marriage.]

[¹⁴ Part IVA

Premiums for Joint-claim Couples

3.497   **20A.**—Except as provided in paragraph 20B, the weekly premium specified in Part IVB of this Schedule shall, for the purposes of regulations 86A(c) and 86B(d), be applicable to a joint-claim couple where either or both members of a joint-claim couple satisfy the condition specified in paragraphs 20E to 20J in respect of that premium.

20B.—Subject to paragraph 20C, where a member of a joint-claim couple satisfies the conditions in respect of more than one premium in this Part of this Schedule, only one premium shall be applicable to the joint-claim couple in respect of that member and, if they are different amounts, the higher or highest amount shall apply.

[¹⁶ **20C.**—(1) Subject to sub-paragraph (2), the following premiums, namely—

(a) a severe disability premium to which paragraph 20I applies;

(b) an enhanced disability premium to which paragraph 20IA applies; and

(c) a carer premium to which paragraph 20J applies,

may be applicable in addition to any other premium which may apply under this Part of this Schedule.

(2) An enhanced disability premium in respect of a person shall not be applicable in addition to—

(a) a pensioner premium under paragraph 20E; or

(b) a higher pensioner premium under paragraph 20F.]

20D.—(1) Subject to sub-paragraph (2) for the purposes of this Part of this Schedule, once a premium is applicable to a joint-claim couple under this Part, a person shall be treated as being in receipt of any benefit—

(a) in the case of a benefit to which the Social Security (Overlapping Benefits) Regulations 1979 applies, for any period during which, apart from the provisions of those Regulations, he would be in receipt of that benefit; and

(b) for any period spent by a person in undertaking a course of training or instruction provided or approved by the Secretary of State under section 2 of the Employment and Training Act 1973, or by [³⁷ Skills Development Scotland,] Scottish Enterprise or Highlands and Islands Enterprise under section 2 of the Enterprise and New Towns (Scotland) Act 1990, or for any period during which he is in receipt of a training allowance.

(2) For the purposes of the carer premium under paragraph 20J, a person shall be treated as being in receipt of [²⁴ carer's allowance] by virtue of sub-paragraph (1)(a) only if and for so long as the person in respect of whose care the allowance has been claimed remains in receipt of attendance allowance, [⁴⁶ the care component of disability living allowance at the highest or middle rate prescribed in accordance with section 72(3) of the Benefits Act [⁵² or the care component of child disability payment at the highest or middle rate in accordance with regulation 11(5) of the DACYP Regulations]or the daily living component of personal independence payment at the standard or enhanced rate in accordance with section 78(3) of the 2012 Act [⁵³ , the daily living component of adult disability payment at the standard or enhanced rate in accordance with regulation 5 of the Disability Assistance for Working Age People (Scotland) Regulations 2022] [⁴⁷ or armed forces independence payment]].

Pensioner premium where one member of a joint-claim couple has attained [⁴⁰ the qualifying age for state pension credit]

3.498   **20E.**—The condition is that one member of a joint-claim couple has attained [⁴⁰ the qualifying age for state pension credit]but not the age of 75.

Higher Pensioner Premium

3.499   **20F.**—(1) [³³ Subject to sub-paragraph (5), the] condition is that one member of a joint claim couple—

(a) has attained [⁴⁰ the qualifying age for state pension credit] but not the age of 80, and either the additional conditions specified in paragraph 20H are satisfied in respect of him; or

(b) has attained [⁴⁰ the qualifying age for state pension credit] and—

(i) was entitled to or was treated as entitled to either income support or an income-based jobseeker's allowance and the disability premium was or, as the case may be, would have been applicable to him in respect of a benefit week within 8 weeks of [⁴⁰ the date he attained the qualifying age for state pension credit] and he has, subject to sub-paragraph (2), remained continuously entitled to one of those benefits since attaining that age; or

 (ii) was a member of a joint-claim couple who had been entitled to, or who had been treated as entitled to, a joint-claim jobseeker's allowance and the disability premium was or, as the case may be, would have been applicable to that couple in respect of a benefit week within 8 weeks of [⁴⁰ the date either member of that couple attained the qualifying age for state pension credit] and the couple have, subject to that sub-paragraph (2), remained continuously entitled to a joint claim jobseeker's allowance since that member attained that age.

(2) For the purpose of this paragraph and paragraph 20H—

 (a) once the higher pensioner premium is applicable to a joint-claim couple, if that member then ceases, for a period of 8 weeks or less, to be entitled or treated as entitled to either income support or income-based jobseeker's allowance or that couple cease to be entitled to or treated as entitled to a joint-claim jobseeker's allowance, he shall or, as the case may be, that couple shall, on becoming re-entitled to any of those benefits, thereafter be treated as having been continuously entitled thereto;

 (b) in so far as sub-paragraph (1)(b)(i) or (ii) is concerned, if a member of a joint-claim couple ceases to be entitled or treated as entitled to either income support or an income-based jobseeker's allowance or that couple cease to be entitled to or treated as entitled to a joint-claim jobseeker's allowance for a period not exceeding 8 weeks which includes [⁴⁰ the date either member of that couple attained the qualifying age for state pension credit], he shall or, as the case may be, the couple shall, on becoming re-entitled to either of those benefits, thereafter be treated as having been continuously entitled thereto.

(3) In this paragraph, where a member of a joint-claim couple is a welfare to work beneficiary, sub-paragraphs (1)(b)(i) and (2)(b) shall apply to him as if for the words "8 weeks" there were substituted the words "[³²104 weeks]".

(4) For the purposes of this paragraph, a member of a joint-claim couple shall be treated as having been entitled to income support or to an income-based jobseeker's allowance or the couple of which he is a member shall be treated as having been entitled to a joint-claim jobseeker's allowance throughout any period which comprises only days on which a member was participating in an employment zone scheme and was not entitled to—

 (a) income support because, as a consequence of his participation in that scheme, he was engaged in remunerative work or had income in excess of the claimant's applicable amount as prescribed in Part IV of the Income Support Regulations; or

 (b) a jobseeker's allowance because, as a consequence of his participation in that scheme, he was engaged in remunerative work or failed to satisfy the condition specified in section 2(1)(c) or the couple of which he was a member failed to satisfy the condition in section 3A(1)(a).

[³³ (5) The condition is not satisfied if the member of the joint-claim couple to whom sub-paragraph (1) refers is a long-term patient.]

[³³ Disability Premium

20G.—(1) Subject to sub-paragraph (2), the condition is that a member of a joint-claim **3.500** couple has not attained [⁴⁰ the qualifying age for state pension credit] and satisfies any one of the additional conditions specified in paragraph 20H.

(2) The condition is not satisfied if—

 (a) paragraph (1) only refers to one member of a joint-claim couple and that member is a long-term patient; or

 (b) paragraph (1) refers to both members of a joint-claim couple and both members of the couple are long-term patients.]

Additional conditions for Higher Pensioner and Disability Premium

20H.—(1) The additional conditions specified in this paragraph are that a member of a **3.501** joint-claim couple—

 (a) is in receipt of [²⁶ the disability element or the severe disability element of working tax credit as specified in regulation 20(1)(b) and (f) of the Working Tax Credit (Entitlement and Maximum Rate) Regulations 2002] or mobility supplement;

   (b) is in receipt of severe disablement allowance;

   (c) is in receipt of attendance allowance or disability living allowance or is a person whose disability living allowance is payable, in whole or in part, to another in accordance with regulation 44 of the Claims and Payments Regulations (payment of disability living allowance on behalf of third party);

[⁴⁶ (ca) is in receipt of personal independence payment or is a person whose personal independence payment is payable, in whole or in part, to another in accordance with regulation 58(2) of the Universal Credit etc. Claims and Payments Regulations (payment to another person on the claimant's behalf);]

[⁵³ (caa) is in receipt of adult disability payment or is a person whose adult disability payment is payable, in whole or in part, to another in accordance with regulation 33 of the Disability Assistance for Working Age People (Scotland) Regulations 2022 (making payments);]

[⁴⁷ (cb) is in receipt of armed forces independence payment or is a person whose armed forces independence payment is payable, in whole or in part, to another in accordance with article 24D of the Armed Forces and Reserve Forces (Compensation Scheme) Order 2011;]

   (d) is in receipt of long-term incapacity benefit or is a person to whom section 30B(4) of the Benefits Act (long-term rate of incapacity benefit payable to those who are terminally ill) applies;

   (e) has been entitled to statutory sick pay, has been incapable of work or has been treated as incapable of work for a continuous period of not less than—
     (i) 196 days in the case of a member of a joint-claim couple who is terminally ill within the meaning of section 30B(4) of the Benefits Act; or
     (ii) 364 days in any other case,
and for these purposes, any two or more periods of entitlement or incapacity separated by a break of not more than 56 days shall be treated as one continuous period;

[³⁶ (ee) has had limited capability for work or has been treated as having limited capability for work for a continuous period of not less than—
     (i) 196 days in the case of a member of a joint-claim couple who is terminally ill within the meaning of regulation 2(1) of the Employment and Support Allowance Regulations; or
     (ii) 364 days in any other case,
and for these purposes any two or more periods of limited capability for work separated by a break of not more than 12 weeks is to be treated as one continuous period;]

   (f) has an invalid carriage or other vehicle provided to him by the Secretary of State under section 5(2)(a) of, and Schedule 2 to, the National Health Service Act 1977 or under section 46 of the National Health Service (Scotland) Act 1978 or provided by the Department of Health and Social Services for Northern Ireland under article 30(1) of the Health and Personal Social Services (Northern Ireland) Order 1972, or receives payments by way of grant from the Secretary of State under paragraph 2 of Schedule 2 to the Act of 1977 (additional provisions as to vehicles) or, in Scotland, under section 46 of the Act of 1978;

   (g) is a person who is entitled to the mobility component of disability living allowance but to whom the component is not payable in accordance with regulation 42 of the Claims and Payments Regulations (cases where disability living allowance not payable);

[⁴⁶ (ga) is a person who is entitled to the mobility component of personal independence payment but to whom the component is not payable in accordance with regulation 61 of the Universal Credit etc. Claims and Payments Regulations (cases where mobility component of personal independence payment not payable);]

[⁵³ (gb) is a person who is entitled to the mobility component of adult disability payment but to whom the component is not payable in accordance with regulation 34(6) of the Disability Assistance for Working Age People (Scotland) Regulations 2022 (amount and form of adult disability payment);]

   (h) was either—
     (i) in receipt of long-term incapacity benefit under section 30A(5) of the Benefits Act immediately before attaining pensionable age and he is still alive; or

      (ii) entitled to attendance allowance or disability living allowance but payment of that benefit was suspended in accordance with regulations under section 113(2) of the Benefits Act or otherwise abated as a consequence of either member of the joint-claim couple becoming a patient within the meaning of regulation 85(4) (special cases), [⁴⁶ [⁵³ . . .]

      (iii) entitled to personal independence payment but no amount is payable in accordance with regulations under section 86(1) (hospital in-patients) of the 2012 Act,] [⁵³ or

      (iv) entitled to adult disability payment but no amount is payable in accordance with regulation 28 (effect of admission to hospital on ongoing entitlement to Adult Disability Payment) of the Disability Assistance for Working Age People (Scotland) Regulations 2022,]

and [⁵³ in any of the cases described in paragraphs (i) to (iv)], the higher pensioner premium or disability premium had been applicable to the joint-claim couple; or

  [⁴⁸ (l) is certified as severely sight impaired or blind by a consultant ophthalmologist.]

(2) [⁴¹ . . . [³² . . .]]

[⁴⁸ (3) For the purposes of sub-paragraph (1)(i), a person who has ceased to be certified as severely sight impaired or blind on regaining his eyesight shall nevertheless be treated as severely sight impaired or blind, as the case may be, and as satisfying the additional condition set out in that sub-paragraph for a period of 28 weeks following the date on which he ceased to be so certified.]

Severe Disability Premium

20I.—(1) The condition is that—   3.502

    (a) a member of a joint-claim couple is in receipt of attendance allowance [⁴⁶ , the care component of disability living allowance at the highest or middle rate prescribed in accordance with section 72(3) of the Benefits Act [⁴⁷ , armed forces independence payment] [⁵³ ,] the daily living component of personal independence payment at the standard or enhanced rate in accordance with section 78(3) of the 2012 Act] [⁵³ , or the daily living component of adult disability payment at the standard or enhanced rate in accordance with regulation 5 of the Disability Assistance for Working Age People (Scotland) Regulations 2022]; and

    (b) the other member is also in receipt of such an allowance, or if he is a member of a polygamous marriage, all the partners of that marriage are in receipt of a qualifying benefit; and

    (c) subject to sub-paragraph (3), there is no non-dependant aged 18 or over normally residing with the joint-claim couple or with whom they are normally residing; and

    (d) either—

      (i) no person is entitled to, and in receipt of, [²⁴ a carer's allowance] under section 70 of the Benefits Act [⁵⁰ or has an award of universal credit which includes the carer element] in respect of caring for either member or the couple or all the members of the polygamous marriage; or

      (ii) a person is engaged in caring for one member (but not both members) of the couple, or one or more but not all members of the polygamous marriage, and in consequence is entitled to [²⁴ a carer's allowance] under section 70 of the Benefits Act [⁵⁰ or has an award of universal credit which includes the carer element].

(2) Where the other member does not satisfy the condition in sub-paragraph (1)(b), and that member is [⁴⁸ severely sight impaired or blind or treated as severely sight impaired or blind] within the meaning of paragraph 20H(1)(i) and (2), that member shall be treated for the purposes of sub-paragraph (1) as if he were not a member of the couple.

(3) The following persons shall not be regarded as non-dependant for the purposes of sub-paragraph (1)(c)—

    (a) a person in receipt of attendance allowance [⁴⁶ , the care component of disability living allowance at the highest or middle rate prescribed in accordance with section 72(3) of the Benefits Act [⁴⁷ , armed forces independence payment] [⁵³ ,] the daily living component of personal independence payment at the standard or enhanced rate in accordance with section 78(3) of the 2012 Act] [⁵³ , or the daily living component of adult disability payment at the standard or enhanced rate in accordance with regulation 5 of the Disability Assistance for Working Age People (Scotland) Regulations 2022];

(b) subject to sub-paragraph (5), a person who joins the joint-claim couple's household for the first time in order to care for a member of a joint claim couple and immediately before so joining, that member satisfied the condition in sub-paragraph (1);

(c) a person who is [⁴⁸ severely sight impaired or blind or treated as severely sight impaired or blind] within the meaning of paragraph 20H(1)(i) and (2).

(4) For the purposes of sub-paragraph (1), a member of a joint-claim couple shall be treated—

(a) as being in receipt of attendance allowance, or the care component of disability living allowance at the highest or middle rate prescribed in accordance with section 72(3) of the Benefits Act if he would, but for his being a patient for a period exceeding 28 days, be so in receipt;

(b) as being entitled to and in receipt of [²⁴ a carer's allowance] [⁵⁰ or having an award of universal credit which includes the carer element] if he would, but for the person for whom he was caring being a patient in hospital for a period exceeding 28 days, be so entitled and in receipt [⁵⁰ of carer's allowance or have such an award of universal credit].

[⁴⁶ (c) as being in receipt of the daily living component of personal independence payment at the standard or enhanced rate in accordance with section 78 of the 2012 Act if he would, but for regulations made under section 86(1) (hospital in-patients) of the 2012 Act, be so in receipt.]

[⁵³ (d) as being in receipt of the daily living component of adult disability payment at the standard or enhanced rate in accordance with regulation 5 of the Disability for Working Age People (Scotland) Regulations 2022, if he would, but for regulation 28 (effect of admission to hospital on ongoing entitlement to Adult Disability Payment) of those Regulations, be so in receipt]

(5) Sub-paragraph (3)(b) shall apply only for the first 12 weeks following the date on which the person to whom that provision applies first joins the joint-claim couple's household.

(6) For the purposes of sub-paragraph (1)(d), no account shall be taken of an award of [²⁴ carer's allowance] [⁵⁰ or universal credit which includes the carer element] to the extent that payment of such an award is back-dated for a period before [³⁴ the date on which the award is first paid].

[²⁰ (7) In sub-paragraph (1)(d), the reference to a person being in receipt of [²⁴ a carer's allowance] [⁵⁰ or as having an award of universal credit which includes the carer element] shall include a reference to a person who would have been in receipt of that allowance [⁵⁰ or had such an award] but for the application of a restriction under section [³⁹ 6B or] 7 of the Social Security Fraud Act 2001 (loss of benefit provisions).]

[⁵⁰ (8) For the purposes of this paragraph, a person has an award of universal credit which includes the carer element if the person has an award of universal credit which includes an amount which is the carer element under regulation 29 of the Universal Credit Regulations 2013.]

[¹⁶ **Enhanced disability premium**

3.503   **20IA.**—[⁴⁶ (1) Subject to sub-paragraph (2), the condition is that in respect of a member of a joint-claim couple who has not attained the qualifying age for state pension credit—

(a) the care component of disability living allowance is, or would, but for a suspension of benefit in accordance with regulations under section 113(2) of the Benefits Act or but for an abatement as a consequence of hospitalisation, be payable at the highest rate prescribed under section 72(3) of the Benefits Act; or

(b) the daily living component of personal independence payment is, or would, but for regulations made under section 86(1) (hospital in-patients) of the 2012 Act, be payable at the enhanced rate in accordance with section 78(2) of the 2012 Act [⁵³ , the daily living component of adult disability payment is, or would, but for regulation 28 (effect of admission to hospital on ongoing entitlement to Adult Disability Payment) of the Disability for Working Age People (Scotland) Regulations 2022, be payable at the enhanced rate under those Regulations,] [⁴⁷ or armed forces independence payment is payable].]

[³³ (2) The condition is not satisfied if—

(a) paragraph (1) only refers to one member of a joint-claim couple and that member is a long-term patient; or

(b) paragraph (1) refers to both members of a joint-claim couple and both members of the couple are long-term patients.]]

Carer Premium

20J.—(1) Subject to sub-paragraphs (3) and (4), the condition is that either or both members of a joint-claim couple are entitled to [²⁸ . . .] [²⁴ a carer's allowance] under section 70 of the Benefits Act.

(2) [²⁸ . . .]

[²³ (3) Where a carer premium is awarded but—

(a) the person in respect of whose care the [²⁴ carer's allowance] has been awarded dies; or

(b) in any other case the member of the joint-claim couple in respect of whom a carer premium has been awarded ceases to be entitled [²⁸ . . .] to [²⁴ a carer's allowance], the condition for the award of the premium shall be treated as satisfied for a period of eight weeks from the relevant date specified in sub-paragraph (3A) below.

(3A) The relevant date for the purposes of sub-paragraph (3) above shall be—

(a) [²⁸ where sub-paragraph (3)(a) applies,] the Sunday following the death of the person in respect of whose care [²⁴ a carer's allowance] has been awarded or beginning with the date of death if the death occurred on a Sunday;

(b) [²⁸ . . .]

(c) in any other case, the date on which that member ceased to be entitled to [²⁴ a carer's allowance].]

(4) Where a member of a joint-claim couple who has been entitled to an invalid care allowance ceases to be entitled to that allowance and makes a claim for a jobseeker's allowance jointly with the other member of that couple, the condition for the award of the carer premium shall be treated as satisfied for a period of eight weeks from the date on which—

[²³(a) the person in respect of whose care the [²⁴ carer's allowance] has been awarded dies;

(b) [²⁸ . . .]

(c) [²⁸ in any other case, the person who has been entitled to a carer's allowance ceased to be entitled to that allowance.]]

Member of a joint-claim couple in receipt of concessionary payments

20K.—For the purpose of determining whether a premium is applicable to a joint-claim couple under paragraphs 20H to 20J, any concessionary payment made to compensate a person for the non-payment of any benefit mentioned in those paragraphs shall be treated as if it were a payment of that benefit.

Person in receipt of benefit

20L.—For the purposes of this Part of this Schedule, a member of a joint-claim couple shall be regarded as being in receipt of any benefit if, and only if, it is paid in respect of him and shall be so regarded only for any period in respect of which that benefit is paid.

3.504

3.505

3.506

PART IVB

Premium	Amount
20M.— (1) Pensioner premium where one member of a joint-claim couple [⁴⁰ has attained the qualifying age for state pension credit] and the condition in paragraph 20E is satisfied.	(1) [⁵⁶ £157.65].
(2) Higher Pensioner Premium where one member of a joint-claim couple satisfies the condition in paragraph 20F.	(2) [⁵⁶ £157.65].

Premium	Amount
(3) Disability Premium where one member of a joint-claim couple satisfies the condition in paragraph [³³ 20G(1)].	(3) [⁵⁶ £51.60].
(4) Severe Disability Premium where one member of a joint-claim couple satisfies the condition in paragraph 20I(1)— (i) if there is someone in receipt of [²⁴ a carer's allowance] or if either member satisfies that condition only by virtue of paragraph [¹⁶ 20I(4)]; (ii) if no-one is in receipt of such an allowance.	(4) (i) [⁵⁶ £69.40]; (ii) [⁵⁶ £157.65].
(5) Carer Premium.	(5) [⁵⁶ £38.85] in respect of each person who satisfied the condition specified in paragraph 20J.]
[¹⁶ (6) Enhanced disability premium where the conditions specified in paragraph 20IA are satisfied.	(6) [⁵⁶ £25.35] where the conditions in paragraph 20IA are satisfied in respect of a member of a joint-claim couple.]

PART V

ROUNDING OF FRACTIONS

3.508   **21.**—Where an income-based jobseeker's allowance is awarded for a period which is not a complete benefit week and the applicable amount in respect of that period results in an amount which includes a fraction of one penny that fraction shall be treated as one penny."

AMENDMENTS

1. Jobseeker's Allowance (Amendment) Regulations 1996 (SI 1996/1516) reg.18 (October 7, 1996).
2. Jobseeker's Allowance (Amendment) Regulations 1996 (SI 1996/1516) reg.20 and Sch. (October 7, 1996).
3. Social Security and Child Support (Jobseeker's Allowance) (Miscellaneous Amendments) Regulations 1996 (SI 1996/2538) reg.2(11) (October 28, 1996).
4. Child Benefit, Child Support and Social Security (Miscellaneous Amendments) Regulations 1996 (SI 1996/1803) reg.44 (April 7, 1997).
5. Income-related Benefits and Jobseeker's Allowance (Personal Allowances for Children and Young Persons) (Amendment) Regulations 1996 (SI 1996/2545) reg.2 (April 7, 1997).
6. Income-related Benefits and Jobseeker's Allowance (Amendment) (No. 2) Regulations 1997 (SI 1997/2197) reg.7(5) and (6)(b) (October 6, 1997).
7. Social Security Amendment (Lone Parents) Regulations 1998 (SI 1998/766) reg.14 (April 6, 1998).
8. Social Security (Welfare to Work) Regulations 1998 (SI 1998/2231) reg.14(3) (October 5, 1998).
9. Social Security Amendment (Personal Allowances for Children and Young Persons) Regulations 1999 (SI 1999/2555) reg.2(1)(b) and (2) (April 10, 2000).

278

10. Social Security and Child Support (Tax Credits) Consequential Amendments Regulations 1999 (SI 1999/2566) reg.2(2) and Sch.2 Pt III (October 5, 1999).
11. Social Security (Miscellaneous Amendments) Regulations 2000 (SI 2000/681) reg.4(3) (April 3, 2000).
12. Social Security Amendment (Employment Zones) Regulations 2000 (SI 2000/724) reg.4 (April 3, 2000).
13. Social Security Amendment (Personal Allowances for Children) Regulations 2000 (SI 2000/1993) reg.2 (October 23, 2000).
14. Jobseeker's Allowance (Joint Claims) Regulations 2000 (SI 2000/1978) reg.2(5) and Sch.2 para.53 (March 19, 2001).
15. Social Security Amendment (Bereavement Benefits) Regulations 2000 (SI 2000/2239) reg.3(2) (April 9, 2001).
16. Social Security Amendment (Enhanced Disability Premium) Regulations 2000 (SI 2629) reg.5(c) (April 9, 2001).
17. Social Security Amendment (Joint Claims) Regulations 2001 (SI 2001/518) reg.2(7) (March 19, 2001).
18. Social Security Amendment (Bereavement Benefits) Regulations 2000 (SI 2000/2239) reg.3(2)(c) (April 9, 2001).
19. Social Security Amendment (Residential Care and Nursing Homes) Regulations 2001 (SI 2001/3767) reg.2 and Sch. Pt II para.18 (April 8, 2002).
20. Social Security (Loss of Benefit) (Consequential Amendments) Regulations 2002 (SI 2002/490) reg.2 (April 1, 2002).
21. Social Security Amendment (Residential Care and Nursing Homes) Regulations 2001 (SI 2001/3767) reg.2 and Sch. Pt II para.18 (as amended by Social Security Amendment (Residential Care and Nursing Homes) Regulations 2002 (SI 2002/398) reg.4(3)) (April 8, 2002).
22. Social Security Amendment (Personal Allowances for Children and Young Persons) Regulations 2002 (SI 2002/2019) reg.2 (October 14, 2002).
23. Social Security Amendment (Carer Premium) Regulations 2002 (SI 2002/2020) reg.3 (October 28, 2002).
24. Social Security (Miscellaneous Amendments) Regulations 2003 (SI 2003/511) reg.3(4) and (5) (April 1, 2003).
25. Social Security (Working Tax Credit and Child Tax Credit) (Consequential Amendments) Regulations 2003 (SI 2003/455) regs 1(9), 3 and Sch.2 para.20(b) (April 7, 2003).
26. Social Security (Working Tax Credit and Child Tax Credit) (Consequential Amendments) Regulations 2003 (SI 2003/455) regs 1(9), 3 and Sch.2 para.20(e) (April 7, 2003).
27. Social Security (Hospital In-Patients and Miscellaneous Amendments) Regulations 2003 (SI 2003/1195) reg.6 (May 21, 2003).
28. Social Security (Miscellaneous Amendments) (No. 2) Regulations 2003 (SI 2003/2279) reg.3(3) (October 1, 2003).
29. Social Security (Removal of Residential Allowance and Miscellaneous Amendments) Regulations 2003 (SI 2003/1121) reg.4 and Sch.2 para.9 (October 6, 2003).
30. Social Security (Working Tax Credit and Child Tax Credit) (Consequential Amendments) Regulations 2003 (SI 2003/455) reg.3 and Sch.2 para.20 (April 6, 2004, except in "transitional cases" and see further the note to regs 83 and to 17 of the Income Support Regulations).
31. Civil Partnership (Pensions, Social Security and Child Support) (Consequential, etc. Provisions) Order 2005 (SI 2005/2877) art.2(3) and Sch.3 para.26(11) (December 5, 2005).

32. Social Security (Miscellaneous Amendments) (No. 4) Regulations 2006 (SI 2006/2378) reg.13(10) (October 1, 2006).
33. Social Security (Miscellaneous Amendments) Regulations 2007 (SI 2007/719) reg.3(8) (April 9, 2007). As it relates to paras 15(2)(a) and 16, the amendment only affects "transitional cases". See further the note to reg.17 of the Income Support Regulations and the commentary below.
34. Social Security (Miscellaneous Amendments) (No. 5) Regulations 2007 (SI 2007/2618) reg.2 and Sch. (October 1, 2007).
35. Social Security (Miscellaneous Amendments) Regulations 2008 (SI 2008/698) reg.4(14) (April 14, 2008).
36. Employment and Support Allowance (Consequential Provisions) (No. 2) Regulations 2008 (SI 2008/1554) reg.3(1) and (24) (October 27, 2008).
37. Social Security (Miscellaneous Amendments) Regulations 2009 (SI 2009/583) reg.4(1) and (3) (April 6, 2009).
38. Social Security (Students and Miscellaneous Amendments) Regulations 2009 (SI 2009/1575) reg.3 (August 1, 2009).
39. Social Security (Loss of Benefit) Amendment Regulations 2010 (SI 2010/1160) reg.11(1) and (3) (April 1, 2010).
40. Social Security (Equalisation of State Pension Age) Regulations 2009 (SI 2009/1488) reg.13 (April 6, 2010).
41. Employment and Support Allowance (Transitional Provisions, Housing Benefit and Council Tax Benefit) (Existing Awards) (No. 2) Regulations 2010 (SI 2010/1907) reg.26(1) and Sch.4 para.1A(3) (as amended by the Employment and Support Allowance (Transitional Provisions, Housing Benefit and Council Tax Benefit) (Existing Awards) (No. 2) (Amendment) Regulations 2010 (SI 2010/2430) reg.15) (November 1, 2010).
42. Social Security (Miscellaneous Amendments) Regulations 2011 (SI 2011/674) reg.7(7) (April 11, 2011).
43. Social Security Benefits Up-rating Order 2012 (SI 2012/780) art.25(3) and Sch.13 (April 9, 2012).
44. Social Security Benefits Up-rating Order 2012 (SI 2012/780) art.25(5) and Sch.14 (April 9, 2012).
45. Social Security Benefits Up-rating Order 2012 (SI 2012/780) art.25(6) and Sch.15 (April 9, 2012).
46. Personal Independence Payment (Supplementary Provisions and Consequential Amendments) Regulations 2013 (SI 2013/388) reg.8 and Sch. para.16(1) and (7) (April 8, 2013).
47. Armed Forces and Reserve Forces Compensation Scheme (Consequential Provisions: Subordinate Legislation) Order 2013 (SI 2013/591) art.7 and Sch. para.10(1) and (7) (April 8, 2013).
48. Universal Credit and Miscellaneous Amendments (No. 2) Regulations 2014 (SI 2014/2888) reg.3(3) (November 26, 2014).
49. Welfare Benefits Up-rating Order 2015 (SI 2015/30) art.9 and Sch.3 (April 6, 2015).
50. Universal Credit and Miscellaneous Amendments Regulations 2015 (SI 2015/1754) reg.15 (October 28, 2015).
51. Universal Credit and Jobseeker's Allowance (Miscellaneous Amendments) Regulations 2018 (SI 2018/1129) reg.2 (November 28, 2018).
52. Social Security (Scotland) Act 2018 (Disability Assistance for Children and Young People) (Consequential Modifications) Order 2021 (SI 2021/786) Sch.3 paras 7–8 (July 26, 2021).
53. Social Security (Disability Assistance for Working Age People) (Consequential Amendments) Order 2022 (SI 2022/177) art.7 (March 21, 2022).

54. Social Security Benefits Up-rating Order 2022 (SI 2022/292) art.27(1) and (3)(a), and Sch.8 (April 11, 2022).
55. Social Security Benefits Up-rating Order 2022 (SI 2022/292) art.27(1) and (5), and Sch.9 (April 11, 2022).
56. Social Security Benefits Up-rating Order 2022 (SI 2022/292) art.27(1) and (6), and Sch.10 (April 11, 2022).

DEFINITIONS

"adult disability payment"—see reg.1(3).
"attendance allowance"—*ibid.*
"the Benefits Act"—see Jobseekers Act s.35(1).
"child"—*ibid.*
"child disability payment"—*ibid.*
"claimant"—*ibid.*
"couple"—see reg.1(3).
"DACYP Regulations"—*ibid.*
"disability living allowance"—*ibid.*
"family"—see Jobseekers Act s.35(1).
"invalid carriage or other vehicle"—see reg.1(3).
"lone parent"—*ibid.*
"mobility supplement"—*ibid.*
"non-dependent"—see reg.2.
"partner"—see reg.1(3).
"personal independence payment"—*ibid.*
"polygamous marriage"—*ibid.*
"preserved right"—*ibid.*
"single claimant"—*ibid.*
"welfare to work beneficiary"—*ibid.*
"young person"—see reg.76.
For the General Note to Sch.1, see Vol.V paras 3.509–3.518.

p.1120, *amendments to the Jobseeker's Allowance Regulations 1996 (SI 1996/207) Sch.2 para.17 (Non-dependant deductions)*

With effect from April 11, 2022, art.27 of the Social Security Benefits Up-rating Order 2022 (SI 2022/292) makes the following amendments to para.17 of Sch.2:
6.050
- in sub-para.(1)(a) for "£102.85" substitute "£106.05";
- in sub-para.(1)(b) for "£15.95" substitute "£16.45";
- in sub-para.(2)(a) for "£149.00" substitute "£154.00";
- in sub-para.(2)(b):
    (i) for "£36.65" substitute "£37.80";
    (ii) for "£149.00" substitute "£154.00"; and
    (iii) for "£217.00" substitute "£224.00";
- in sub-para.(2)(c):
    (i) for "£50.30" substitute "£51.85";
    (ii) for "£217.00" substitute "£224.00"; and
    (iii) for "£283.00" substitute "£292.00";
- in sub-para.(2)(d):
    (i) for "£82.30" substitute "£84.85";
    (ii) for "£283.00" substitute "£292.00"; and
    (iii) for "£377.00" substitute "£389.00"; and

- in sub-para.(2)(e):
  - (i) for "£93.70" substitute "£96.60";
  - (ii) for "£377.00" substitute "£389.00"; and
  - (iii) for "£469.00" substitute "£484.00".

pp.1120–1122, *amendments to the Jobseeker's Allowance Regulations 1996 (SI 1996/207) Sch.2 para.17 (Housing costs—non-dependant deductions)*

6.051 With effect from July 26, 2021, Sch.3 para.9 of the Social Security (Scotland) Act 2018 (Disability Assistance for Children and Young People) (Consequential Modifications) Order 2021 (SI 2021/786) makes the following amendments to Sch.2 para.17:

- in sub-para.(6)(b), at the end of para.(ii), insert "or (iia) the care component of child disability payment;"
- in sub-para.(8)(a), after "disability living allowance", insert ", child disability payment".

With effect from January 1, 2022, reg.3(6) of the Social Security (Income and Capital Disregards) (Amendment) Regulations 2021 (SI 2021/1405) inserts into para.17(8)(b), after "Grenfell Tower payment", ", child abuse payment or Windrush payment".

With effect from March 21, 2022, art.5(8) of the Social Security (Disability Assistance for Working Age People) (Consequential Amendments) Order 2022 (SI 2022/177) makes the following amendments to Sch.2 para.17:

- after para.17(6)(b)(iii) (non-dependant deductions), insert "(iiia) the daily living component of adult disability payment;";
- in para.17(8)(a):
  - after "armed forces independence payment" for "or" substitute ", ";
  - after "personal independence payment" insert "or adult disability payment".

p.1146, *amendment to the Jobseeker's Allowance Regulations 1996 (SI 1996/207) Sch.7 para.7 (Sums to be disregarded in the calculation of income other than earnings—mobility component)*

6.052 With effect from March 21, 2022, art.5(9)(a) of the Social Security (Disability Assistance for Working Age People) (Consequential Amendments) Order 2022 (SI 2022/177) amended para.7 to read as follows (square brackets indicate only the present amendment, those indicating previous amendments having been omitted):

"7.—The mobility component of disability living allowance[,] the mobility component of personal independence payment [or the mobility component of adult disability payment]."

"Adult disability payment" is defined in reg.1(3) by reference to reg.2 of the Disability Assistance for Working Age People (Scotland) Regulations 2022 (SSI 2022/54) (see Vol.IV of this series).

p.1147, *amendment to the Jobseeker's Allowance Regulations 1996 (SI 1996/207) Sch.7 para.10 (Sums to be disregarded in the calculation of income other than earnings—attendance allowance, care component of DLA or daily living component)*

With effect from March 21, 2022, art.5(9)(b) of the Social Security 6.053
(Disability Assistance for Working Age People) (Consequential Amendments) Order 2022 (SI 2022/177) amended para.10 to read as follows (square brackets indicate only the present amendment, those indicating previous amendments having been omitted):

"**10.**—Any attendance allowance, the care component of disability living allowance[,] the daily living component of personal independence payment [or the daily living component of adult disability payment]."

"Adult disability payment" is defined in reg.1(3) by reference to reg.2 of the Disability Assistance for Working Age People (Scotland) Regulations 2022 (SSI 2022/54) (see Vol.IV of this series).

p.1149, *amendment to the Jobseeker's Allowance Regulations 1996 (SI 1996/207) Sch.7 para.22(2) (Sums to be disregarded in the calculation of income other than earnings—income in kind)*

With effect from January 1, 2022, reg.3(7)(a) of the Social Security 6.054
(Income and Capital Disregards) (Amendment) Regulations 2021 (SI 2021/1405) amended sub-para.(2) by inserting ", a child abuse payment or a Windrush payment" after "Grenfell Tower payment". All of those payments are defined in reg.1(3). See the entry for p.684 for discussion of the nature of child abuse and Windrush payments.

p.1151, *amendment to the Jobseeker's Allowance Regulations 1996 (SI 1996/207) Sch.7 para.28(da) (Sums to be disregarded in the calculation of income other than earnings—payments for persons temporarily in care of claimant)*

With effect from July 1, 2022, reg.10 of the Health and Care Act 2022 6.055
(Consequential and Related Amendments and Transitional Provisions) Regulations 2022 (SI 2022/634) amended para.28 by substituting the following for sub-para.(da):

"(da) an integrated care board established under Chapter A3 of Part 2 of the National Health Service Act 2006;"

Note that sub-para.(dzb) seems to be out of the proper order in the 2021/22 main volume.

p.1153, *amendments to the Jobseeker's Allowance Regulations 1996 (SI 1996/207) Sch.7 para.41 (Sums to be disregarded in the calculation of income other than earnings)*

With effect from January 1, 2022, reg.3(7)(b) of the Social Security 6.056
(Income and Capital Disregards) (Amendment) Regulations 2021 (SI

2021/1405) amended para.41 by substituting the following for sub-para.(1A):

"(1A) Any—
  (a) Grenfell Tower payment;
  (b) child abuse payment;
  (c) Windrush payment."

In addition, reg.3(7)(c) amended sub-paras (2) to (6) by inserting ", a child abuse payment or a Windrush payment" after "Grenfell Tower payment" in each place where those words occur. All of those payments are defined in reg.1(3).

See the entry for p.684 (Income Support Regulations, Sch.10 (capital to be disregarded) para.22) for some technical problems arising from the date of effect of these amendments. Because all the payments so far made from the approved historic institutional child abuse compensation schemes and from the Windrush Compensation Scheme have been in the nature of capital, the question of disregarding income has not yet arisen.

pp.1167–1168, *amendments to the Jobseeker's Allowance Regulations 1996 (SI 1996/207) Sch.8 para.27 (Capital to be disregarded)*

6.057   With effect from January 1, 2022, reg.3(8)(a) of the Social Security (Income and Capital Disregards) (Amendment) Regulations 2021 (SI 2021/1405) amended sub-para.(1A) by inserting ", child abuse payment, Windrush payment" after "Grenfell Tower payment" and amended sub-paras (2) to (6) by inserting ", a child abuse payment or a Windrush payment" after "Grenfell Tower payment" in each place where those words occur. All of those payments are defined in reg.1(3).

See the entry for p.684 (Income Support Regulations Sch.10 (Capital to be disregarded) para.22) for some technical problems with the addition only with effect from January 1, 2022 of the disregards of payments from approved schemes providing compensation in respect of historic institutional child abuse in the UK and from the Windrush Compensation Scheme. All the schemes so far in existence provide payments in the nature of capital. That entry also contains information about the nature of the schemes involved, including the child abuse compensation schemes so far approved.

p.1168, *amendment to the Jobseeker's Allowance Regulations 1996 (SI 1996/207) Sch.8 para.31 (Capital to be disregarded—payments in kind)*

6.058   With effect from January 1, 2022, reg.3(8)(b) of the Social Security (Income and Capital Disregards) (Amendment) Regulations 2021 (SI 2021/1405) amended para.31 by inserting ", a child abuse payment or a Windrush payment" after "Grenfell Tower payment". All of those payments are defined in reg.1(3). See also the entry for p.684.

p.1177, *annotation to the Jobseeker's Allowance Regulations 1996 (SI 1996/207) Sch.8 (Capital to be disregarded)*

With effect from June 28, 2022 "Cost of living payments" under the   6.059
Social Security (Additional Payments) Act 2022 (see Part I of this
Supplement), both those to recipients of specified means-tested benefits
and "disability" payments are not to be taken into account for any old
style JSA purposes by virtue of s.8(b) of the Act.

p.1184, *annotation to the Jobseeker's Allowance (Schemes for Assisting Persons to Obtain Employment) Regulations 2013 (SI 2013/276)*

Note the doubts expressed in the note to reg.3 in the 2021/22 main   6.060
volume about the validity of the prescription of the Work and Health
Programme in reg.3(8C) and in the entry below for p.1187 about the
validity of the prescription of the Restart Scheme in reg.3(8D).

p.1187, *amendment to the Jobseeker's Allowance (Schemes for Assisting Persons to Obtain Employment) Regulations 2013 (SI 2013/276) reg.3 (Schemes for assisting persons to obtain employment)*

With effect from March 14, 2022, reg.2(3) of the Jobseeker's Allow-   6.061
ance (Schemes for Assisting Persons to Obtain Employment) (Amendment) Regulations 2022 (SI 2022/154) amended reg.3 by omitting
para.(8) and by inserting the following after para.(8C):

"(8D) The Restart Scheme is a scheme which provides support for a
period of up to 12 months for claimants who have been unemployed
for 9 months or more and reside in England and Wales."

The Explanatory Memorandum to SI 2022/154 (note that a revised
Memorandum, not labelled as such in its heading but with an additional
"001" in the version online, was issued on April 13, 2022) explains that
the Work Programme no longer exists. There is therefore no controversy
about the removal of para.(8), which described that scheme.

However, the introduction of the new para.(8D) is of very doubtful
validity. That is because s.17A(1) of the old style Jobseekers Act 1995
only allows claimants to be required to participate in schemes designed
to assist them to obtain employment that are of a "prescribed description". The Supreme Court in *R. (Reilly and Wilson) v SSWP* [2013]
UKSC 68; [2014] 1 A.C. 453 held that the Jobseeker's Allowance
(Employment, Skills and Enterprise Scheme) Regulations 2011 (SI
2011/917) reg.2 did not satisfy that test because it did not add anything
to the description of the schemes in the Act itself, which was necessary
for the requirement for a prescribed description to have any point.
Regulation 2 had provided that the Employment, Skills and Enterprise
Scheme (ESES) meant a scheme of that name within s.17A and provided pursuant to arrangements by the Secretary of State that was
designed to assist claimants to obtain employment or self-employment
and which might include for any individual work-related activity, including work experience or job search. The Supreme Court must therefore

have regarded the reference to the possible inclusion of work-related activity as too vague to constitute any kind of description of what the scheme involved. The Court agreed that it was not necessary in the case of the ESES to explore how much detail needed to be included in the regulations to comply with s.17A(1), as no description at all was given.

The amendment contained in SI 2022/154 may therefore not be on all fours with the ESES Regulations reg.2, because the new para.(8D) could be said to contain *some* description of the Restart Scheme, in identifying the categories of claimants who could be directed to the Restart Scheme, the maximum length of the scheme and that it would provide support (although arguably that word, in conjunction with the other specified elements, is also so vague as not to constitute any meaningful description at all). If it is accepted that there is *some* description, the question then, as in *R. (Smith) v SSWP* [2015] EWCA Civ 229 on the Jobseeker's Allowance (Mandatory Work Activity Scheme) Regulations 2011 (SI 2021/688), would be whether there is sufficient description for the purposes of s.17A(1). In *Smith*, Underhill LJ suggested at para.25 that the natural reading of "prescribed description" connoted "no more than an indication of the character of the scheme provided for, such as a scheme in which the claimant was required to undergo training or education or to work with a mentor, or—as here—to do work or work-related activity". So the CA held that the mention of work or work-related activity, with the specification of maximum weekly hours and length of participation, was enough for the MWAS Regulations to be valid. Although the present amendment specifies which claimants fall into the scope of the Restart Scheme and the maximum length, it says nothing worthwhile about the nature of the scheme. All it says is that it "provides support", nothing about what kind of support or who it will be provided by. Equally, if not more, important, it says nothing about what a claimant is to be expected to do by way of participation. What does it mean to have "support" thrust on a claimant? The argument that the new para.(8D) provides an insufficient description seems very strong. It might be thought that the Explanatory Memorandum betrays the faulty approach in paras 7.8 and 7.9, where it is said that the current legislation "lists" the employment schemes claimants can be required to participate in and that the amendment adds the Restart Scheme to the list. To be valid, and to carry the requirement to participate backed by sanctions, a regulation must not merely "list" a scheme, but must describe it.

The Explanatory Memorandum records that the Restart Scheme was already in existence through 12 providers in England and Wales, initially for universal credit claimants who had spent 12 to 18 months uninterrupted time in the Intensive Work Search Regime (i.e. subject to all work-related requirements), but now with the time reduced to nine months. Because of improved labour market conditions the opportunity arose to widen the eligibility criteria to provide intensive employment support for old style JSA claimants that had previously only been available to limited groups. The Scheme is still only available in England and Wales. The emphasis is said to be on positive engagement with the claimant to encourage participation, with the requirement to participate being "used as a backstop where reasonable attempts at engagement fail without good reason" (para.6.7). However, it is stated that claimants who fail to comply with the requirement to participate in compulsory activities may be issued with a low-level sanction (para.6.6). It is far from clear that "compulsory activities" are adequately described by the term "support" in para.(8D).

The policy paper *How the Restart Scheme will work* (January 18, 2022, updated April 26, 2022, available on the gov.uk website) states:

> "Through regular contact with all participants, providers will develop a strong understanding of individuals' employment history, skills, aspirations and support needs to develop the right package of support to help each participant succeed.
>
> For some this might be bespoke training to take advantage of opportunities in a growth sector or to succeed in a major recruitment exercise, for others it might be support to get the right certificate to take up a job in a different industry such as construction or transport or to update skills such as IT."

That document thus gets to a description of the scheme, but as there is no reference to it in para.(8D) there can be no reliance on its description merely by use of the label "Restart Scheme".

Providers will be given letters of empowerment under reg.17 authorising them to exercise the functions of the Secretary of State to issue notices requiring participation (reg.5) or that that requirement has ceased (reg.6(3)(a)) (Explanatory Memorandum, para.6.3). It is understood that providers and employees will not be designated as "employment officers" under s.35 of the old style Jobseekers Act 1995, so that they will have no power to issue jobseeker's directions under s.19A(2)(c).

p.1188, *annotation to the Jobseeker's Allowance (Schemes for Assisting Persons to Obtain Employment) Regulations 2013 (SI 2013/276) reg.3 (Schemes for assisting persons to obtain employment)*

Note, in addition to the points made in the entry for p.1187, that in the last paragraph of the existing note the reference to s.19(2)(c) should be to s.19A(2)(c).   6.062

PART IV

OLD STYLE EMPLOYMENT AND SUPPORT ALLOWANCE REGULATIONS

p.1209, *amendments to the Employment and Support Allowance Regulations 2008 (SI 2008/794) reg.2 (Interpretation)*

With effect from January 1, 2022, reg.7(2) of the Social Security (Income and Capital Disregards) (Amendment) Regulations 2021 (SI 2021/1405) inserts the following definitions: 6.063

"child abuse payment" means a payment from a scheme established or approved by the Secretary of State for the purpose of providing compensation in respect of historic institutional child abuse in the United Kingdom;"
"Windrush payment" means a payment made under the Windrush Compensation Scheme (Expenditure) Act 2020;"

With effect from January 1, 2022, reg.7(2) of the Social Security (Income and Capital Disregards) (Amendment) Regulations 2021 (SI 2021/1405) inserts ", a child abuse payment or a Windrush payment" into the definition of "qualifying person", after "Grenfell Tower payment".

p.1209, *amendments to the Employment and Support Allowance Regulations 2008 (SI 2008/794) reg.2 (Interpretation)*

6.064   With effect from July 26, 2021, Sch.9 para.2 of the Social Security (Scotland) Act 2018 (Disability Assistance for Children and Young People) (Consequential Modifications) Order 2021 (SI 2021/786) adds the following definitions:

"child disability payment" has the meaning given in regulation 2 of the DACYP Regulations;
"the DACYP Regulations" means the Disability Assistance for Children and Young People (Scotland) Regulations 2021;

With effect from March 21, 2022, art.11 of the Social Security (Disability Assistance for Working Age People) (Consequential Amendments) Order 2022 (SI 2022/177) adds the following definition:

"adult disability payment" has the meaning given in regulation 2 of the Disability Assistance for Working Age People (Scotland) Regulations 2022;

With effect from April 4, 2022, reg.2(1) of the Universal Credit and Employment and Support Allowance (Terminal Illness) (Amendment) Regulations 2022 (SI 2022/260) amends the definition of "terminally ill" by substituting for "6 months", "12 months".

p.1220, *amendment to the Employment and Support Allowance Regulations 2008 (SI 2008/794) reg.2 (Interpretation)*

6.065   With effect from April 4, 2022, reg.2(1) of the Universal Credit and Employment and Support Allowance (Terminal Illness) (Amendment) Regulations 2022 (SI 2022/260) substituted "12 months" for "6 months" in the definition of "terminally ill".

p.1230, *revocation of the Employment and Support Allowance Regulations 2008 (SI 2008/794) reg.6 (The assessment phase—a claimants appealing against a decision)*

6.066   Strictly speaking, reg.6 was *revoked* by reg.9(5) of the Social Security (Miscellaneous Amendments) (No. 3) Regulations 2010/840 (rather than *omitted* by the annotator).

pp.1238–1239, *amendment of the Employment and Support Allowance Regulations 2008 (SI 2008/794) reg.18 (Circumstances in which the condition that the claimant is not receiving education does not apply)*

Regulation 18 now reads, as amended, as follows: 6.067

"Paragraph 6(1)(g) of Schedule 1 to the Act does not apply where the claimant is entitled to a disability living allowance [3, child disability payment] [2, armed forces independence payment] [4,] [1 personal independence payment] [4 or adult disability payment]."

In addition, the following notes should be added to the list of AMENDMENTS:

3. Social Security (Scotland) Act 2018 (Disability Assistance for Children and Young People) (Consequential Modifications) Order 2021 (SI 2021/786) Sch.9 para.3 (July 26, 2021).
4. Social Security (Disability Assistance for Working Age People) (Consequential Amendments) Order 2022 (SI 2022/177) art.11(3) (March 21, 2022).

p.1250, *amendment to the Employment and Support Allowance Regulations 2008 (SI 2008/794) reg.21 (Information required for determining capability for work)*

With effect from July 1, 2022, reg.4(2) of the Social Security (Medical   6.068 Evidence) and Statutory Sick Pay (Medical Evidence) (Amendment) (No. 2) Regulations 2022 (SI 2022/630) omitted the words "a doctor's" between "form of" and "statement".

p.1260, *annotation to the Employment and Support Allowance Regulations 2008 (SI 2008/794) reg.24 (Matters to be taken into account in determining good cause in relation to regs 22 or 23)*

See also the unsuccessful application for a new inquest in *Dove v HM*   6.069 *Assistant Coroner for Teesside and Hartlepool, Rahman and SSWP* [2021] EWHC 2511 (Admin), Mrs Dove's daughter, Ms W, had died of an overdose shortly after her ESA award had been stopped. Mrs Dove applied to the High Court under the Coroners Act 1988 s.13, (a) to quash the coroner's suicide verdict; and (b) to order a new inquest covering the circumstances surrounding her daughter's death. Ms W had a history of mental health problems, suicidal ideation and overdoses, as well as physical ill-health. She had been in receipt of ESA for several years. In 2016, on a periodic review, she asked for a home visit. The DWP neglected to deal with that request and required her to attend an HCP assessment, which she failed to attend. The DWP decided that Ms W had shown neither good cause for the failure to attend nor that she had limited capability for work. Ms W's ESA was duly stopped on February 7, 2017, and she died a fortnight later. Mrs Dove believed that the withdrawal of benefit had created extra stress and contributed to her daughter's death. The coroner ruled that questioning the DWP's decisions was beyond her remit under the Coroners and Justice Act 2009.

Mrs Dove submitted that (1) the coroner's inquiry was insufficient in scope and should have covered the DWP's failings; (2) those failings meant that the state was in breach of ECHR art.2, so requiring a wider inquiry; (3) fresh evidence (in the form of an ICE report on a complaint about the DWP's handling of Ms W's claim and a psychiatrist's report) showed that a new inquest was necessary. A strong Administrative Court (Warbey LJ, Farbey J and HH Judge Teague QC) dismissed the application on the following grounds:

(1) *Scope of inquiry*—The coroner's inquiry was sufficient. Her function was to conduct an inquest in accordance with the Coroners and Justice Act 2009, and her rulings involved no *Wednesbury* or other public law error. She was not required by the public interest to undertake a wider inquiry about the DWP's handling of Ms W's case. Coroners had no specialism in social security issues and were not well-equipped to undertake such an inquiry. Other forms of scrutiny existed (e.g. via the DWP's complaints procedure, which was subject to judicial review, and via the statutory appeals process to a tribunal against substantive ESA decisions). It would be contrary to the administration of justice for coroners to stand in the shoes of specialist tribunal judges, who were best placed to balance the rights of vulnerable social security claimants with the fair and proportionate allocation of public resources (see [71]–[75] of the judgment).

(2) *ECHR art.2*—In protecting a person's right to life, art.2 imposed an operational duty on the state to take reasonable steps to prevent real and immediate risk to life (including the risk of suicide), and a systems duty to establish a framework of laws, procedures and means of enforcement to protect life. Where art.2 was engaged, the scope of an inquest could expand to include the wider circumstances of death. However, it was not engaged in the present case. So far as any operational duty was concerned the DWP, in providing funds by way of welfare benefits, had not assumed responsibility for preventing the suicide of those who received such funds. Further, although Ms W undoubtedly had both mental and physical and health problems that made her particularly vulnerable, she was not under the control or care of the state. There was no general obligation on the state to prevent suicide in the absence of the assumption of responsibility. So far as any systems duty was concerned, the DWP's undoubted errors constituted individual failings attributable to errors or poor judgement and were not systemic in nature.

(3) *Fresh evidence*—It was not in the interests of justice to order a new inquest in light of the fresh evidence. The ICE report certainly concluded that there had been significant failings on the part of DWP staff in dealing with Ms W's case, in breach of departmental guidance on safeguarding vulnerable claimants. But this did not mean that an inquest needed to hear further evidence about such

matters. The psychiatrist's report drew a causal link between the DWP's failings and Ms W's state of mind, rather than her death. It did not say in terms that the DWP's decision to stop her ESA had caused Ms W to take her own life, and did not rule out other causative stress factors. It would be very difficult for a new inquest to conclude that the DWP caused her death ([91]–[94]).

p.1302, *annotation to the Employment and Support Allowance Regulations 2008 (SI 2008/794) reg.35 (Certain claimants to be treated as having limited capability for work-related activity)*

For further examples of the need for sufficient fact-finding and ade-   6.070
quate reasons in appeals where reg.35 is in issue, see *MH v SSWP (ESA)* [2021] UKUT 90 (AAC) and *CT v SSWP (ESA)* [2021] UKUT 131 (AAC). On the importance of tribunals in universal credit appeals (that turn on the equivalent provision to reg.35 in Sch.9 para.4) ensuring they have been provided with an accurate list of work-related activities, see *KS v SSWP (UC)* [2021] UKUT 132 (AAC). Secretary of State appeal responses on such appeals may not have included accurate lists of work-related activities until after July 2020.

pp.1334–1335, *amendment of the Employment and Support Allowance Regulations 2008 (SI 2008/794) reg.64D (The amount of a hardship payment)*

The text in the main volume at para.4.174 should be replaced with   6.071
the following:

"[1 The amount of a hardship payment

64D.—[2 (1) A hardship payment is either—
(a) 80% of the prescribed amount for a single claimant as set out in paragraph (1)(a) of Part 1 of Schedule 4 where—
  (i) the claimant has an award of employment and support allowance which does not include entitlement to a work-related activity component under section 4(2)(b) of the Welfare Reform Act 2007 as in force immediately before 3rd April 2017; and
  (ii) the claimant or any other member of their family is either pregnant or seriously ill; or
(b) 60% of the prescribed amount for a single claimant as set out in paragraph (1)(a) of Part 1 of Schedule 4 in any other case.]
(2) A payment calculated in accordance with paragraph (1) shall, if it is not a multiple of 5p, be rounded to the nearest such multiple or, if it is a multiple of 2.5p but not of 5p, to the next lower multiple of 5p.]"

AMENDMENTS

1. Employment and Support Allowance (Sanctions) (Amendment) Regulations 2012 (SI 2012/2756) reg.6 (December 3, 2012).
2. Employment and Support Allowance (Exempt Work Hardship Amounts) (Amendment) Regulations 2017 (SI 2017/205) reg.5 (April 3, 2017).

pp.1341–1342, *amendment to the Employment and Support Allowance Regulations 2008 (SI 2008/794) reg.70 (Special cases: supplemental—persons from abroad)*

6.072   The text in the main volume at para.4.187 should be replaced with the following:

"Special cases: supplemental—persons from abroad

70.—(1) "Person from abroad" means, subject to the following provisions of this regulation, a claimant who is not habitually resident in the United Kingdom, the Channel Islands, the Isle of Man or the Republic of Ireland.

(2) A claimant must not be treated as habitually resident in the United Kingdom, the Channel Islands, the Isle of Man or the Republic of Ireland unless the claimant has a right to reside in (as the case may be) the United Kingdom, the Channel Islands, the Isle of Man or the Republic of Ireland other than a right to reside which falls within paragraph (3) [8 or (3A)].

(3) A right to reside falls within this paragraph if it is one which exists by virtue of, or in accordance with, one or more of the following—

    (a) regulation 13 of the [8 Immigration (European Economic Area) Regulations 2016];

    (b) regulation 14 of those Regulations, but only in a case where the right exists under that regulation because the claimant is—

        (i) a jobseeker for the purpose of the definition of "qualified person" in regulation 6(1) of those Regulations; or

        (ii) a family member (within the meaning of regulation 7 of those Regulations) of such a jobseeker; [10 or]

[4 [8 (bb) regulation 16 of those Regulations, but only in a case where the right exists under that regulation because the claimant satisfies the criteria in paragraph (5) of that regulation;]]

    (c) [10 . . .]

    (d) [10 . . .]

    (e) [10 . . .]

[8 (3A) A right to reside falls within this paragraph if it exists by virtue of a claimant having been granted limited leave to enter, or remain in, the United Kingdom under the Immigration Act 1971 by virtue of—

    (a) Appendix EU to the immigration rules made under section 3(2) of that Act; [11 . . .];

    (b) being a person with a Zambrano right to reside as defined in Annex 1 of Appendix EU to the immigration rules made under section 3(2) of that Act.] [11; or

    (c) having arrived in the United Kingdom with an entry clearance that was granted under Appendix EU (Family Permit) to the immigration rules made under section 3(2) of that Act.]

[9 (3B) Paragraph (3A)(a) does not apply to a person who—

   (a) has a right to reside granted by virtue of being a family member of a relevant person of Northern Ireland; and

   (b) would have a right to reside under the Immigration (European Economic Area) Regulations 2016 if the relevant person of Northern Ireland were an EEA national, provided that the right to reside does not fall within paragraph (3).]

(4) A claimant is not a person from abroad if the claimant is—

[¹² (zza) a person granted leave in accordance with the immigration rules made under section 3(2) of the Immigration Act 1971, where such leave is granted by virtue of—

     (i) the Afghan Relocations and Assistance Policy; or

     (ii) the previous scheme for locally-employed staff in Afghanistan (sometimes referred to as the ex-gratia scheme);

  (zzb) a person in Great Britain not coming within sub-paragraph (zza) or [¹³ (h)] who left Afghanistan in connection with the collapse of the Afghan government that took place on 15th August 2021;]

[¹³ (zzc) a person in Great Britain who was residing in Ukraine immediately before 1st January 2022, left Ukraine in connection with the Russian invasion which took place on 24th February 2022 and—

     (i) has been granted leave in accordance with immigration rules made under section 3(2) of the Immigration Act 1971; [¹⁴ . . .]

     (ii) has a right of abode in the United Kingdom within the meaning given in section 2 of that Act;] [¹⁴ or

     (iii) does not require leave to enter or remain in the United Kingdom in accordance with section 3ZA of that Act;]

[⁷ (za) a qualified person for the purposes of regulation 6 of the [⁸ Immigration (European Economic Area) Regulations 2016] as a worker or a self-employed person;

  (zb) a family member of a person referred to in sub-paragraph (za) [⁹ . . .];

  (zc) a person who has a right to reside permanently in the United Kingdom by virtue of regulation 15(1)(c), (d) or (e) of those Regulations;]

[⁹ (zd) a family member of a relevant person of Northern Ireland, with a right to reside which falls within paragraph (3A)(a), provided that the relevant person of Northern Ireland falls within sub-paragraph (za), or would do so but for the fact that they are not an EEA national;]

[¹⁰ (ze) a frontier worker within the meaning of regulation 3 of the Citizens' Rights (Frontier Workers) (EU Exit) Regulations 2020;

  (zf) a family member of a person referred to in sub-paragraph (ze), who has been granted limited leave to enter, or remain in, the United Kingdom by virtue of Appendix EU to the immigration rules made under section 3(2) of the Immigration Act 1971;]

   (g) a refugee within the definition in Article 1 of the Convention relating to the Status of Refugees done at Geneva on 28th July 1951, as extended by Article 1(2) of the Protocol relating to the Status of Refugees done at New York on 31st January 1967;

[⁶ (h) a person who has been granted leave or who is deemed to have been granted leave outside the rules made under section 3(2) of the Immigration Act 1971 [¹³ . . .]

   (i) a person who has humanitarian protection granted under those rules; [⁶ or]

   (j) a person who is not a person subject to immigration control within the meaning of section 115(9) of the Immigration and Asylum Act and who is in the United Kingdom as a result of deportation, expulsion or other removal by compulsion of law from another country to the United Kingdom; [¹ . . .]

   (k) [⁶ . . .]

   (l) [¹ [⁶ . . .]]]

[⁹ (5) In this regulation—

"EEA national" has the meaning given in regulation 2(1) of the Immigration (European Economic Area) Regulations 2016;

"family member" has the meaning given in regulation 7(1)(a), (b) or (c) of the Immigration (European Economic Area) Regulations 2016 except that regulation 7(4) of those Regulations does not apply for the purposes of paragraphs (3B) and (4)(zd);

"relevant person of Northern Ireland" has the meaning given in Annex 1 of Appendix EU to the immigration rules made under section 3(2) of the Immigration Act 1971.]

[¹⁰ (6) References in this regulation to the Immigration (European Economic Area) Regulations 2016 are to be read with Schedule 4 to the Immigration and Social Security Co-ordination (EU Withdrawal) Act 2020(Consequential, Saving, Transitional and Transitory Provisions) Regulations 2020.]"

AMENDMENTS

1. Social Security (Habitual Residence) (Amendment) Regulations 2009 (SI 2009/362) reg.9 (March 18, 2009).
2. Social Security (Miscellaneous Amendments) (No. 3) Regulations 2011 (SI 2011/2425) reg.23(1) and (7) (October 31, 2011).
3. Treaty of Lisbon (Changes in Terminology or Numbering) Order 2012 (SI 2012/1809) art.3(1) and Sch.1 Pt.2 (August 1, 2012).
4. Social Security (Habitual Residence) (Amendment) Regulations 2012 (SI 2012/2587) reg.2 (November 8, 2012).
5. Social Security (Croatia) Amendment Regulations 2013 (SI 2013/1474) reg.7 (July 1, 2013).
6. Social Security (Miscellaneous Amendments) (No. 3) Regulations 2013 (SI 2013/2536) reg.13(1) and (24) (October 29, 2013).

7. Social Security (Habitual Residence) (Amendment) Regulations 2014 (SI 2014/902) reg.7 (May 31, 2014).
8. Social Security (Income-related Benefits) (Updating and Amendment) (EU Exit) Regulations 2019 (SI 2019/872) reg.7 (May 7, 2019).
9. Social Security (Income-Related Benefits) (Persons of Northern Ireland –Family Members) (Amendment) Regulations 2020 (SI 2020/638) reg.7 (August 24, 2020).
10. Immigration and Social Security Co-ordination (EU Withdrawal) Act 2020 (Consequential, Saving, Transitional and Transitory Provisions) (EU Exit) Regulations 2020 (SI 2020/1309) reg 73 (December 31, 2020 at 11.00 pm).
11. Immigration (Citizens' Rights etc.) (EU Exit) Regulations 2020 (SI 2020/1372) reg.23 (December 31, 2020 at 11.00 pm).
12. Social Security (Habitual Residence and Past Presence) (Amendment) Regulations 2021 (SI 2021/1034) reg.2 (September 15, 2021).
13. Social Security (Habitual Residence and Past Presence) (Amendment) Regulations 2022 (SI 2022/344) reg.2 (March 22, 2022).
14. Social Security (Habitual Residence and Past Presence) (Amendment) (No. 2) Regulations 2022 (SI 2022/990) reg.2 (October 18, 2022).

MODIFICATION

Regulation 70 is modified by Sch.1 para.10A of the Employment and Support Allowance (Transitional Provisions, Housing Benefit and Council Tax Benefit) (Existing Awards) (No. 2) Regulations 2010 (SI 2010/1907) as amended for the purposes specified in reg.6(1) of those Regulations. For the details of the modification, pp.1410–1452 of Vol.I of the 2020/21 edition.

DEFINITION

"Immigration and Asylum Act"—reg.2(1).

p.1373, *amendment to the Employment and Support Allowance Regulations 2008 (SI 2008/794) reg.107(10A) (Notional income—exceptions)*

With effect from January 1, 2022, reg.7(3) of the Social Security 6.073 (Income and Capital Disregards) (Amendment) Regulations 2021 (SI 2021/1405) amended para.(10A) by substituting the following for "a payment of income which is a Grenfell Tower payment":

"any of the following payments of income—
    (a) a Grenfell Tower payment;
    (b) a child abuse payment;
    (c) a Windrush payment."

All of those payments are defined in reg.2(1). See the entry for p.684 for discussion of the nature of child abuse and Windrush payments.

p.1377, *annotation to the Employment and Support Allowance Regulations 2008 (SI 2008/794) reg.110 (Capital limit)*

In the Institute for Government and the Social Security Advisory 6.074 Committee's 2021 joint report *Jobs and benefits: The Covid-19 challenge* it was noted that if the capital limit of £16,000 had risen in line with prices since 2006 it would be close to £23,500 (or £25,000: different figures are given) and recommended that the limit should be increased to £25,000 and subsequently automatically indexed to maintain its real value (pp.22 and 31). That recommendation was summarily rejected in the Government's response of March 22, 2022.

p.1378, *amendment to the Employment and Support Allowance Regulations 2008 (SI 2008/794) reg.112(8) (Income treated as capital—exceptions)*

6.075   With effect from January 1, 2022, reg.7(4) of the Social Security (Income and Capital Disregards) (Amendment) Regulations 2021 (SI 2021/1405) amended para.(8) by substituting the following for sub-para.(b):

"any—
  (a) Grenfell Tower payment;
  (b) child abuse payment;
  (c) Windrush payment."

All of those payments are defined in reg.2(1). See the entry for p.684 for discussion of the nature of child abuse and Windrush payments.

p.1382, *amendment to the Employment and Support Allowance Regulations 2008 (SI 2008/794) reg.115(5A) (Notional capital—exceptions)*

6.076   With effect from January 1, 2022, reg.7(5) of the Social Security (Income and Capital Disregards) (Amendment) Regulations 2021 (SI 2021/1405) amended para.(5A) by substituting the following for "a payment of capital which is a Grenfell Tower payment":

"any of the following payments of capital—
  (a) a Grenfell Tower payment;
  (b) a child abuse payment;
  (c) a Windrush payment."

All of those payments are defined in reg.2(1). See the entry for p.684 for discussion of the nature of child abuse and Windrush payments.

p.1413, *annotation to the Employment and Support Allowance Regulations 2008 (SI 2008/794) reg.145 (Linking rules)*

6.077   For more detailed analysis see the commentary on SSCBA 1992 s.30C(1)(c) in Vol.I of the 2011/12 edition of this work (at paras 1.67–1.77).

pp.1431–1432, *amendments to the Employment and Support Allowance Regulations 2008 (SI 2008/794) reg.158 (Meaning of "person in hardship")*

6.078   With effect from July 26, 2021, Sch.9 para.4 of the Social Security (Scotland) Act 2018 (Disability Assistance for Children and Young

People) (Consequential Modifications) Order 2021 (SI 2021/786) makes the following amendments to reg.158:

- In para.(3):
  - in sub-para.(c), after "disability living allowance", insert ", child disability payment";
  - in sub-para.(d)(ii), after "disability living allowance", insert ", child disability payment".
- For para.(7), substitute:
  "(7) In this regulation, "care component" means—
  (a) the care component of disability living allowance at the highest or middle rate prescribed under section 72(3) of the Contributions and Benefits Act; or
  (b) the care component of child disability payment at the highest or middle rate provided for in regulation 11(5) of the DACYP Regulations.".

With effect from March 21, 2022, art.11(4) of the Social Security (Disability Assistance for Working Age People) (Consequential Amendments) Order 2022 (SI 2022/177) makes the following amendments to reg.158(3):

- in sub-para.(b):
  - after "armed forces independence payment" for "or" substitute ", ";
  - after "daily living component" insert "or the daily living component of adult disability payment";
- in sub-para.(c):
  - after "armed forces independence payment" for "or" substitute ", ";
  - after "personal independence payment", insert "or adult disability payment";
- in sub-para.(d):
  - in para.(i):
    - after "armed forces independence payment" for "or" substitute ", ";
    - after "daily living component" insert "or the daily living component of adult disability payment";
  - in para.(ii):
    - after "armed forces independence payment" for "or" substitute ", ";
    - after "personal independence payment", insert "or adult disability payment".

pp.1494–1496, *annotation to the Employment and Support Allowance Regulations 2008 (SI 2008/794) Sch.2 Activity 17 (Appropriateness of behaviour with other people, due to cognitive impairment or mental disorder)*

Consideration of Activity 17 may require the disclosure of Unacceptable Customer Behaviour (UCB) forms as provided in confidence by the DWP to HMCTS: *MH v SSWP (ESA)* [2021] UKUT 90 (AAC).   6.079

pp.1507–1514, *amendments to the Employment and Support Allowance Regulations 2008 (SI 2008/794) Sch.4 (Amounts)*

6.080   Substitute the following for paras 4.420–4.429

"SCHEDULE 4

Regulations 67(1)(a) and (2) and 68(1)(a) and (b)

AMOUNTS

PART 1

PRESCRIBED AMOUNTS

4.420   **1.** The weekly amounts specified in column (2) in respect of each person or couple specified in column (1) are the weekly amounts specified for the purposes of regulations 67(1) and 68 (prescribed amounts and polygamous marriages).

(1) *Person or Couple*	*(2)* *Amount*

(1) *Single claimant*—
    (a) who satisfies the conditions set out in section 2(2) [¹² . . .] or 4(4) [¹² . . .] of the Act [¹³ or who is a member of the work-related activity group];
    (b) aged not less than 25
    (c) aged less than 25.
	(1)
	
	(a) [¹⁵ £77.00];
	
	(b) [¹⁵ £77.00];
	(c) [¹⁵ £61.05];

(2) Lone parent [⁶ or a person who has no partner and who is responsible for and a member of the same household as a young person]—
    (a) who satisfies the conditions set out in section 4(4) [¹² . . .] of the Act [¹³ or who is a member of the work-related activity group and satisfies
    (b) the conditions set out in Part 2 of
    (c) Schedule 1 to the Act];
	(2)
	
	(a) [¹⁵ £77.00];
	
	(c) [¹⁵ £61.05];

(3) aged not less than 18;
    (a) aged less than 18.
Couple—
    (b) where both members are aged not less than 18; where one member is aged not less than 18 and the other member is a person under 18 who—
        (i) [³ if that other member had not been a member] of a couple, would satisfy the requirements for entitlement to income support other than the requirement to make a claim for it; or
        (ii) [³ if that other member had not been a member] of a couple, would satisfy the requirements for entitlement to an income-related allowance; or
        (iii) satisfies the requirements of section 3(1)(f)(iii) of the Jobseekers Act (prescribed circumstances for persons aged 16 but less than 18); or
        (iv) is the subject of a direction under section 16 of that Act (persons under 18: severe hardship);
    (c) where the claimant satisfies the conditions set out in section 4(4) [¹² . . .] of the Act [¹³ or the claimant is a member of the work-related activity group and satisfies the conditions set out in Part 2 of Schedule 1 to the Act] and both members are aged less than 18 and—
	(3)
	(a) [¹⁵ £121.05];
	
	(b) [¹⁵ £121.05];
	
	(c) [¹⁵ £121.05];

Column (1) *Person or Couple*	Column (2) *Amount*
(i) at least one of them is treated as responsible for a child; or	
(ii) had they not been members of a couple, each would have qualified for an income-related allowance; or	
(iii) had they not been members of a couple the claimant's partner would satisfy the requirements for entitlement to income support other than the requirement to make a claim for it; or	
(iv) the claimant's partner satisfies the requirements of section 3(1)(f)(iii) of the Jobseekers Act (prescribed circumstances for persons aged 16 but less than 18); or	
(v) there is in force in respect of the claimant's partner a direction under section 16 of that Act (persons under 18: severe hardship);	
(d) where both members are aged less than 18 and—	(d) [¹⁵ £92.20];
(i) at least one of them is treated as responsible for a child; or	
(ii) had they not been members of a couple, each would have qualified for an income-related allowance; or	
(iii) had they not been members of a couple the claimant's partner satisfies the requirements for entitlement to income support other than a requirement to make a claim for it; or	
(iv) the claimant's partner satisfies the requirements of section 3(1)(f)(iii) of the Jobseekers Act (prescribed circumstances for persons aged 16 but less than 18); or	
(v) there is in force in respect of the claimant's partner a direction under section 16 of that Act (persons under 18: severe hardship);	
(e) where the claimant is aged not less than 25 and the claimant's partner is a person under 18 who—	(e) [¹⁵ £77.00];
(i) would not qualify for an income-related allowance if the person were not a member of a couple;	
(ii) would not qualify for income support if the person were not a member of a couple;	
(iii) does not satisfy the requirements of section 3(1)(f)(iii) of the Jobseekers Act (prescribed circumstances for persons aged 16 but less than 18); and	
(iv) is not the subject of a direction under section 16 of that Act (persons under 18: severe hardship);	
(f) where the claimant satisfies the conditions set out in section 4(4) [¹² . . .] of the Act [¹³ or the claimant is a member of the work-related activity group and satisfies the conditions set out in Part 2 of Schedule 1 to the Act] and the claimant's partner is a person under 18 who—	(f) [¹⁵ £77.00];
(i) would not qualify for an income-related allowance if the person were not a member of a couple;	

Column (1) *Person or Couple*	Column (2) *Amount*

(ii) would not qualify for income support if the person [¹ were] not a member of a couple;
   (iii) does not satisfy the requirements of section 3(1)(f)(iii) of the Jobseekers Act (prescribed circumstances for persons aged 16 but less than 18); and
   (iv) is not the subject of a direction under section 16 of that Act (persons under 18: severe hardship);	

(g) where the claimant satisfies the conditions set out in section 4(4) [¹² . . .] of the Act [¹³ or the claimant is a member of the work-related activity group and satisfies the conditions set out in Part 2 of Schedule 1 to the Act] and both members are aged less than 18 and paragraph (c) does not apply;	(g) [¹⁵ £77.00];

(h) where the claimant is aged not less than 18 but less than 25 and the claimant's partner is a person under 18 who—
   (i) would not qualify for an income-related allowance if the person were not a member of a couple;
   (ii) would not qualify for income support if the person were not a member of a couple;
   (iii) does not satisfy the requirements of section 3(1)(f)(iii) of the Jobseekers Act (prescribed circumstances for persons aged 16 but less than 18); and
   (iv) is not the subject of a direction under section 16 of that Act (persons under 18: severe hardship);
	(h) [¹⁵ £61.05];

(i) where both members are aged less than 18 and paragraph (d) does not apply.	(i) [¹⁵ £61.05].

Regulations 67(1)(b) and 68(1)(c)

PART 2

PREMIUMS

4.421   **2.** Except as provided in paragraph 4, the weekly premiums specified in Part 3 of this Schedule are, for the purposes of regulation 67(1)(b) and 68(1)(c), to be applicable to a claimant who satisfies the condition specified in paragraphs 5 to 8 in respect of that premium.

3. An enhanced disability premium in respect of a person is not applicable in addition to a pensioner premium.

4.—(1) For the purposes of this Part of this Schedule, once a premium is applicable to a claimant under this Part, a person is to be treated as being in receipt of any benefit—

   (a) in the case of a benefit to which the Social Security (Overlapping Benefits) Regulations 1979 applies, for any period during which, apart from the provisions of those Regulations, the person would be in receipt of that benefit; and

   (b) for any period spent by a person in undertaking a course of training or instruction provided or approved by the Secretary of State under section 2 of the Employment and Training Act 1973, or by [³ Skills Development Scotland] or Highlands and Islands Enterprise under section 2 of the Enterprise and New Towns (Scotland) Act 1990, or for any period during which the person is in receipt of a training allowance.

[⁷ (2) For the purposes of the carer premium under paragraph 8, a claimant is to be treated as being in receipt of a carer's allowance by virtue of sub-paragraph (1)(a) only if and for so long as the person in respect of whose care the allowance has been claimed remains in receipt of—

(a) attendance allowance;

(b) the care component of disability living allowance at the highest or middle rate prescribed in accordance with section 72(3) of the Contributions and Benefits Act; [⁸ . . .]

(c) the daily living component of personal independence payment at the standard or enhanced rate in accordance with section 78(3) of the 2012 Act [⁸ [¹⁴ . . .

(ca) the daily living component of adult disability payment at the standard or enhanced rate in accordance with regulation 5 of the Disability Assistance for Working Age People (Scotland) Regulations 2022; or]

(d) armed forces independence payment.]]

Pensioner premium

5. The condition is that the claimant or the claimant's partner has attained the qualifying age for state pension credit.   4.422

Severe disability premium

6.—(1) The condition is that the claimant is a severely disabled person.   4.423

(2) For the purposes of sub-paragraph (1), a claimant is to be treated as being a severely disabled person if, and only if—

(a) in the case of a single claimant, a lone parent [⁶ , a person who has no partner and who is responsible for and a member of the same household as a young person] or a claimant who is treated as having no partner in consequence of sub-paragraph (3)—

    (i) the claimant is in receipt of the care component [⁷ , the daily living component] [¹⁴ , the daily living component of adult disability payment] [⁸ , armed forces independence payment] [⁵ or attendance allowance];

    (ii) subject to sub-paragraph (4), the claimant has no non-dependants aged 18 or over normally residing with the claimant or with whom the claimant is normally residing; and

    (iii) no person is entitled to, and in receipt of, [¹¹ a carer's allowance or has an award of universal credit which includes the carer element] in respect of caring for the claimant;

(b) in the case of a claimant who has a partner—

    (i) the claimant is in receipt of the care component [⁷ , the daily living component] [¹⁴ , the daily living component of adult disability payment] [⁸ , armed forces independence payment] [⁵ or attendance allowance];

    (ii) the claimant's partner is also in receipt of the care component [⁷ , the daily living component] [¹⁴ , the daily living component of adult disability payment] [⁸ , armed forces independence payment] or attendance allowance or, if the claimant is a member of a polygamous marriage, all the partners of that marriage are in receipt of the care component [⁷ , the daily living component] [¹⁴ , the daily living component of adult disability payment] [⁸ , armed forces independence payment] or attendance allowance; and

    (iii) subject to sub-paragraph (4), the claimant has no non-dependants aged 18 or over normally residing with the claimant or with whom the claimant is normally residing, and,

either a person is entitled to, and in receipt of, a carer's allowance [¹¹ or has an award of universal credit which includes the carer element] in respect of caring for only one of the couple or, in the case of a polygamous marriage, for one or more but not all the partners of the marriage or, as the case may be, no person is entitled to, and in receipt of, such an allowance [¹¹ or has such an award of universal credit] in respect of caring for either member of the couple or any partner of the polygamous marriage.

(3) Where a claimant has a partner who does not satisfy the condition in sub-paragraph (2)(b)(ii) and that partner is blind or severely sight impaired or is treated as blind or severely sight impaired that partner is to be treated for the purposes of sub-paragraph (2) as if the partner were not a partner of the claimant.

(4) For the purposes of sub-paragraph (2)(a)(ii) and (b)(iii) no account is to be taken of—

    (a) a person receiving attendance allowance, [⁷ the daily living component] [¹⁴ , the daily living component of adult disability payment] [⁸ , armed forces independence payment] or the care component;

    (b) subject to sub-paragraph (7), a person who joins the claimant's household for the first time in order to care for the claimant or the claimant's partner and immediately before so joining the claimant or the claimant's partner was treated as a severely disabled person; or

    (c) a person who is blind or severely sight impaired or is treated as blind or severely sight impaired.

(5) For the purposes of sub-paragraph (2)(b) a person is to be treated—

    (a) as being in receipt of attendance allowance or the care component if the person would, but for the person being a patient for a period exceeding 28 days, be so in receipt;

    (b) as being entitled to, and in receipt of, a carer's allowance [¹¹ or having an award of universal credit which includes the carer element] if the person would, but for the person for whom the person was caring being a patient in hospital for a period exceeding 28 days, be so entitled and in receipt [¹¹ of carer's allowance or have such an award of universal credit] .

    [⁷(c) as being in entitled to, and in receipt of, the daily living component if the person would, but for regulations under section 86(1) (hospital in-patients) of the 2012 Act, be so entitled and in receipt.]

    [¹⁴ (d) as being in entitled to, and in receipt of, the daily living component of adult disability payment if the person would, but for regulation 28 (effect of admission to hospital on ongoing entitlement to Adult Disability Payment) of the Disability Assistance for Working Age People (Scotland) Regulations 2022, be so in receipt.]

(6) For the purposes of sub-paragraph (2)(a)(iii) and (b), no account is to be taken of an award of carer's allowance [¹¹ or universal credit which includes the carer element] to the extent that payment of such an award is backdated for a period before the date on which the award is first paid.

(7) Sub-paragraph (4)(b) is to apply only for the first 12 weeks following the date on which the person to whom that provision applies first joins the claimant's household.

(8) In sub-paragraph (2)(a)(iii) and (b), references to a person being in receipt of a carer's allowance [¹¹ or as having an award of universal credit which includes the carer element] are to include references to a person who would have been in receipt of that allowance [¹¹ or had such an award] but for the application of a restriction under section [⁴ 6B or] 7 of the Social Security Fraud Act 2001 (loss of benefit provisions).

(9) [¹¹ (a)] In this paragraph—

[⁹ "blind or severely sight impaired" means certified as blind or severely sight impaired by a consultant ophthalmologist and a person who has ceased to be certified as blind or severely sight impaired where that person's eyesight has been regained is, nevertheless, to be treated as blind or severely sight impaired for a period of 28 weeks following the date on which the person ceased to be so certified;]

"the care component" means the care component of disability living allowance at the highest or middle rate prescribed in accordance with section 72(3) of the Contributions and Benefits Act.

[¹¹ (b) A person has an award of universal credit which includes the carer element if the person has an award of universal credit which includes an amount which is the carer element under regulation 29 of the Universal Credit Regulations 2013.]

Enhanced disability premium

4.424   7.—(1) Subject to sub-paragraph (2), the condition is that—

    (a) the claimant's applicable amount includes the support component; [⁷ . . .]

    (b) the care component of disability living allowance is, or would, but for a suspension of benefit in accordance with regulations under section 113(2) of the Contributions and Benefits Act or, but for an abatement as a consequence of hospitalisation, be payable at the highest rate prescribed under section 72(3) of that Act in respect of—

      (i) the claimant; or

      (ii) the claimant's partner (if any) who is aged less than the qualifying age for state pension credit [⁷ ; [⁸ . . .]

  (c) the daily living component is, or would, but for regulations made under section 86(1) (hospital in-patients) of the 2012 Act, be payable at the enhanced rate under section 78(2) of that Act in respect of—

      (i) the claimant; or

      (ii) the claimant's partner (if any) who is aged less than the qualifying age for state pension credit"]; [¹⁴ . . .

 (ca) the daily living component of adult disability payment is, or would, but for regulation 28 (effect of admission to hospital on ongoing entitlement to Adult Disability Payment) of the Disability Assistance for Working Age People (Scotland) Regulations 2022, be payable at the enhanced rate under section 78(2) of those Regulations in respect of—

      (i) the claimant; or

      (ii) the claimant's partner (if any) who is aged less than the qualifying age for state pension credit; or]

  (d) armed forces independence payment is payable in respect of—

      (i) the claimant; or

      (ii) the claimant's partner (if any) who is aged less than the qualifying age for state pension credit.]

(2) An enhanced disability premium is not applicable in respect of—

  (a) a claimant who—

      (i) is not a member of a couple or a polygamous marriage; and

      (ii) is a patient within the meaning of regulation 69(2) and has been for a period of more than 52 weeks; or

  (b) a member of a couple or a polygamous marriage where each member is a patient within the meaning of regulation 69(2) and has been for a period of more than 52 weeks.

Carer premium

8.—(1) Subject to sub-paragraphs (2) and (4), the condition is that the claimant or the   **4.425** claimant's partner is, or both of them are, entitled to a carer's allowance under section 70 of the Contributions and Benefits Act.

(2) Where a carer premium is awarded but—

  (a) the person in respect of whose care the carer's allowance has been awarded dies; or

  (b) in any other case the person in respect of whom a carer premium has been awarded ceases to be entitled to a carer's allowance, the condition for the award of the premium is to be treated as satisfied for a period of 8 weeks from the relevant date specified in sub-paragraph (3).

(3) The relevant date for the purposes of sub-paragraph (2) is—

  (a) where sub-paragraph (2)(a) applies, the Sunday following the death of the person in respect of whose care a carer's allowance has been awarded or the date of death if the death occurred on a Sunday; or

  (b) in any other case, the date on which the person who has been entitled to a carer's allowance ceases to be entitled to that allowance.

(4) Where a person who has been entitled to a carer's allowance ceases to be entitled to that allowance and makes a claim for an income-related allowance, the condition for the award of the carer premium is to be treated as satisfied for a period of 8 weeks from the date on which—

  (a) the person in respect of whose care the carer's allowance has been awarded dies; or

  (b) in any other case, the person who has been entitled to a carer's allowance ceased to be entitled to that allowance.

Persons in receipt of concessionary payments

9. For the purpose of determining whether a premium is applicable to a person under   **4.426** paragraphs 6, 7 and 8, any concessionary payment made to compensate that person for the non-payment of any benefit mentioned in those paragraphs is to be treated as if it were a payment of that benefit.

Persons in receipt of benefit

4.427   **10.** For the purposes of this Part of this Schedule, a person is to be regarded as being in receipt of any benefit if, and only if, it is paid in respect of the person and is to be so regarded only for any period in respect of which that benefit is paid.

PART 3

WEEKLY AMOUNT OF PREMIUMS SPECIFIED IN PART 2

4.428   **11.**—

Premium	*Amount*

(1) Pension premium for a person to whom paragraph 5 applies who—
  (a) is a single claimant and—
    (i) [¹² ...];
    (ii) is entitled to the support component; or
    [¹²(iii) is not entitled to the support component;]
  (b) is a member of a couple and—
    (i) [¹² ...]
    (ii) is entitled to the support component; or
    [¹² (iii) is not entitled to the support component;]
	(1)
	
	  (a)
	    (i) [¹² ...];
	    (ii) [¹⁶ £65.00];
	    (iii) [¹⁶ £105.60];
	  (b)
	    (i) [¹²];
	    (ii) [¹⁶ £117.05];
	    (iii) [¹⁶ £157.65];

(2) Severe disability premium—
  (a) where the claimant satisfies the condition in paragraph 6(2)(a);
  (b) where the claimant satisfies the condition in paragraph 6(2)(b)—
    (i) if there is someone in receipt of a carer's allowance or if the person or any partner satisfies that condition only by virtue of paragraph 6(5);
    (ii) if no-one is in receipt of such an allowance.
	(2)
	  (a) [¹⁶ £69.40];
	
	  (b)
	
	    (i) [¹⁶ £69.40];
	
	    (ii) [¹⁶ £138.80].

(3) Carer premium.	(3) [¹⁶ £38.85]; in respect of each person who satisfies the condition specified in [¹ paragraph 8(1)].

(4) Enhanced disability premium where the conditions in paragraph 7 are satisfied.	(4)(a) [¹⁶ £17.75]; in respect of each person who is neither—
	    (i) a child or young person; nor
	    (ii) a member of a couple or a polygamous marriage, in respect of whom the conditions specified in paragraph 7 are satisfied;
	  (b) [¹⁶ £25.35]; where the claimant is a member of a couple or a polygamous marriage and the conditions specified in [¹ paragraph 7] are satisfied in respect of a member of that couple or polygamous marriage.

Regulation 67(3)

PART 4

[¹² THE COMPONENT]

12. [¹² . . .].   **4.429**

13. The amount of the support component is [¹⁷ £40.60]."

AMENDMENTS

1. Employment and Support Allowance (Miscellaneous Amendments) Regulations 2008 (SI 2008/2428) reg.14 (October 27, 2008).
2. Social Security (Miscellaneous Amendments) Regulations 2009 (SI 2009/583) reg.10(2) (April 6, 2009).
3. Social Security (Miscellaneous Amendments) (No. 4) Regulations 2009 (SI 2009/2655) reg.11(1) and (16) (October 26, 2009).
4. Social Security (Loss of Benefit) Amendment Regulations 2010 (SI 2010/1160) reg.12(1) and (3) (April 1, 2010).
5. Social Security (Miscellaneous Amendments) (No. 3) Regulations 2011 (SI 2011/2425) reg.23(14) (October 30, 2011).
6. Social Security (Work-focused Interviews for Lone Parents and Partners) (Amendment) Regulations 2011 (SI 2011/2428) reg.5(5) (October 30, 2011).
7. Personal Independence Payment (Supplementary Provisions and Consequential Amendments) Regulations 2013 (SI 2013/388) reg.8 and Sch. para.40(1) and (5) (April 8, 2013).
8. Armed Forces and Reserve Forces Compensation Scheme (Consequential Provisions: Subordinate Legislation) Order 2013 (SI 2013/591) art.7 and Sch. para.37(1) and (5) (April 8, 2013).
9. Universal Credit and Miscellaneous Amendments (No. 2) Regulations 2014 (SI 2014/2888) reg.3(7)(a) (November 26, 2014).
10. Welfare Benefits Up-rating Order 2015 (SI 2015/30) art.11(1) and Sch.4 (April 6, 2015).
11. Universal Credit and Miscellaneous Amendments Regulations 2015 (SI 2015/1754) reg.19 (November 4, 2015).
12. Employment and Support Allowance and Universal Credit (Miscellaneous Amendments and Transitional and Savings Provisions) Regulations 2017 (SI 2017/204) reg.2(1) and (4) (April 3, 2017).
13. Employment and Support Allowance (Miscellaneous Amendments and Transitional and Savings Provision) Regulations 2017 (SI 2017/581) reg.7(1) and (4) (June 23, 2017, subject to the transitional and savings provision in reg.10).
14. Social Security (Disability Assistance for Working Age People) (Consequential Amendments) Order 2022 (SI 2022/177) art.11(5) (March 21 2022).
15. Social Security Benefits Up-rating Order 2022 (SI 2022/292) art.31(1) and (2) and Sch.11 (April 11, 2022).
16. Social Security Benefits Up-rating Order 2022 (SI 2022/292) art.31(1) and (4) and Sch.12 (April 11, 2022).
17. Social Security Benefits Up-rating Order 2022 (SI 2022/292) art.21(6)(b) (April 11, 2022).

For the General Note to Sch.4, see Vol.V para.4.430.

pp.1525–1532, *amendments to the Employment and Support Allowance Regulations 2008 (SI 2008/794) Sch.6 (Housing costs)*

6.081   With effect from July 26, 2021, Sch.9 para.5 of the Social Security (Scotland) Act 2018 (Disability Assistance for Children and Young People) (Consequential Modifications) Order 2021 (SI 2021/786) makes the following amendments to Sch.6:

- In para.15(11)(b) (linking rule), after "disability living allowance", insert ", child disability payment".
- In para.19(6)(b) (non-dependent deductions), after sub-para.(ii), insert "(iia) the care component of child disability payment;".

With effect from January 1, 2022, reg.7(6) of the Social Security (Income and Capital Disregards) (Amendment) Regulations 2021 (SI 2021/1405) inserts into para.19(8)(b), after "Grenfell Tower payment", ", child abuse payment or Windrush payment".

With effect from March 21, 2022, art.11(5) of the Social Security (Disability Assistance for Working Age People) (Consequential Amendments) Order 2022 (SI 2022/177) makes the following amendments to Sch.6:

- in para.15(11)(b) (linking rule):
  - after "armed forces independence payment" for "or" substitute ", ";
  - after "personal independence payment", insert "or adult disability payment";
- in para.19(8)(a) (non-dependent deductions):
  - after "armed forces independence payment" for "or" substitute ", ";
  - after "personal independence payment", insert "or adult disability payment";
- at the end of para.19(6)(b)(iii) omit "or";
- after para.19(6)(b)(iii) insert "(iiia) the daily living component of adult disability payment; or".

With effect from April 11, 2022, art.31 of the Social Security Benefits Up-rating Order 2022 (SI 2022/292) makes the following amendments to para.19 of Sch.6:

- in sub-para.(1)(a) for "£102.85" substitute "£106.05";
- in sub-par.(1)(b) for "£15.95" substitute "£16.45";
- in sub-para.(2)(a) for "£149.00" substitute "£154.00";
- in sub-para.(2)(b):
  - (i)   for "£36.65" substitute "£37.80";
  - (ii) for "£149.00" substitute "£154.00"; and
  - (iii) for "£217.00" substitute "£224.00";
- in sub-para.(2)(c):
  - (i)   for "£50.30" substitute "£51.85";
  - (ii) for "£217.00" substitute "£224.00"; and
  - (iii) for "£283.00" substitute "£292.00";

- in sub-para.(2)(d):
    - (i) for "£82.30" substitute "£84.85";
    - (ii) for "£283.00" substitute "£292.00"; and
    - (iii) for "£377.00" substitute "£389.00"; and
- in sub-para.(2)(e):
    - (i) for "£93.70" substitute "£96.60";
    - (ii) for "£377.00" substitute "£389.00"; and
    - (iii) for "£469.00" substitute "£484.00".

p.1540, *amendments to the Employment and Support Allowance Regulations 2008 (SI 2008/794) Sch.8 paras 8 and 11 (Sums to be disregarded in the calculation of income other than earnings—mobility component and AA, care component and daily living component)*

With effect from March 21, 2022, art.11(7)(a) of the Social Security (Disability Assistance for Working Age People) (Consequential Amendments) Order 2022 (SI 2022/177) amended para.8 to read as follows (square brackets indicate only the present amendment, those indicating previous amendments having been omitted): **6.082**

"**8.**—The mobility component of disability living allowance[,] the mobility component of personal independence payment [or the mobility component of adult disability payment]."

With effect from March 21, 2022, art.11(7)(b) of the same Order amended para.11 to read as follows (square brackets indicate only the present amendment, those indicating previous amendments having been omitted):

"**9.**—Any attendance allowance, the care component of disability living allowance[,] the daily living component of personal independence payment [or the daily living component of adult disability payment]."

"Adult disability payment" is defined in reg.2(1) by reference to reg.2 of the Disability Assistance for Working Age People (Scotland) Regulations 2022 (SSI 2022/54) (see Vol.IV of this series).

p.1542, *amendment to the Employment and Support Allowance Regulations 2008 (SI 2008/794) Sch.8 para.22(2) (Sums to be disregarded in the calculation of income other than earnings—income in kind)*

With effect from January 1, 2022, reg.7(7)(a) of the Social Security (Income and Capital Disregards) (Amendment) Regulations 2021 (SI 2021/1405) amended sub-para.(2) by inserting ", a child abuse payment or a Windrush payment" after "Grenfell Tower payment". All of those payments are defined in reg.2(1). See the entry for p.684 for discussion of the nature of child abuse and Windrush payments. **6.083**

p.1544, *amendment to the Employment and Support Allowance Regulations 2008 (SI 2008/794) Sch.8 para.29(da) (Sums to be disregarded in the calculation of income other than earnings—payments for persons temporarily in care of claimant)*

6.084 With effect from July 1, 2022, reg.99 of and Sch. to the Health and Care Act 2022 (Consequential and Related Amendments and Transitional Provisions) Regulations 2022 (SI 2022/634) amended para.29(da) by substituting the following for the text after "(da)":

"an integrated care board established under Chapter A3 of Part 2 of the National Health Service Act 2006;"

p.1546, *amendments to the Employment and Support Allowance Regulations 2008 (SI 2008/794) Sch.8 para.41 (Sums to be disregarded in the calculation of income other than earnings)*

6.085 With effect from January 1, 2022, reg.7(7)(b) of the Social Security (Income and Capital Disregards) (Amendment) Regulations 2021 (SI 2021/1405) amended para.41 by substituting the following for sub-para.(1A):

"(1A) Any—
  (a) Grenfell Tower payment;
  (b) child abuse payment;
  (c) Windrush payment."

In addition, reg.7(7)(c) amended sub-paras (2) to (6) by inserting ", a child abuse payment or a Windrush payment" after "Grenfell Tower payment" in each place where those words occur. All of those payments are defined in reg.2(1).

See the entry for p.684 (Income Support Regulations Sch.10 (capital to be disregarded) para.22) for some technical problems arising from the date of effect of these amendments. Because all the payments so far made from the approved historic institutional child abuse compensation schemes and from the Windrush Compensation Scheme have been in the nature of capital, the question of disregarding income has not yet arisen.

pp.1558–1559, *amendments to the Employment and Support Allowance Regulations 2008 (SI 2008/794) Sch.9 para.27 (Capital to be disregarded)*

6.086 With effect from January 1, 2022, reg.7(8)(a) of the Social Security (Income and Capital Disregards) (Amendment) Regulations 2021 (SI 2021/1405) amended sub-para.(1A) by inserting ", child abuse payment, Windrush payment" after "Grenfell Tower payment" and amended sub-paras (2) to (6) by inserting ", a child abuse payment or a Windrush payment" after "Grenfell Tower payment" in each place where those words occur. All of those payments are defined in reg.2(1).

See the entry for p.684 (Income Support Regulations Sch.10 (Capital to be disregarded) para.22) for some technical problems with the addition only with effect from January 1, 2022 of the disregards of payments from approved schemes providing compensation in respect of historic institutional child abuse in the UK and from the Windrush Compensation Scheme. All the schemes so far in existence provide payments in the nature of capital. That entry also contains information about the nature of the schemes involved, including the child abuse compensation schemes so far approved.

p.1559, *amendment to the Employment and Support Allowance Regulations 2008 (SI 2008/794) Sch.9 para.31 (Capital to be disregarded—payments in kind)*

With effect from January 1, 2022, reg.7(8)(b) of the Social Security (Income and Capital Disregards) (Amendment) Regulations 2021 (SI 2021/1405) amended para.31 by inserting ", a child abuse payment or a Windrush payment" after "Grenfell Tower payment". All of those payments are defined in reg.2(1). See also the entry for p.684. **6.087**

pp.1565–1566, *annotation to the Employment and Support Allowance Regulations 2008 (SI 2008/794) Sch.9 (Capital to be disregarded)*

With effect from June 28, 2022 "Cost of living payments" under the Social Security (Additional Payments) Act 2022 (see Part I of this Supplement), both those to recipients of specified means-tested benefits and "disability" payments are not to be taken into account for any old style ESA purposes by virtue of s.8(b) of the Act. **6.088**

PART V

UNIVERSAL CREDIT COMMENCEMENT ORDERS

p.1613, *amendment of the Welfare Reform Act 2012 (Commencement No.9 and Transitional and Transitory Provisions and Commencement No.8 and Savings and Transitional Provisions (Amendment)) Order 2013 (SI 2013/983) art.5A (Transitional provision where Secretary of State determines that claims for universal credit may not be made: effect on claims for employment and support allowance and jobseeker's allowance)*

With effect from March 30, 2022, art.5 and Sch.1 para.1(2) of the Welfare Reform Act 2012 (Commencement No. 34 and Commencement No. 9, 21, 23, 31 and 32 and Transitional and Transitory Provisions (Amendment)) Order 2022 (SI 2022/302) omitted the phrase "or article 4(11) of the Welfare Reform Act 2012 (Commencement No. 32 and Savings and Transitional Provisions) Order 2019 (no claims for universal credit by frontier workers)" in art.5A(1). But note also the next entry. **6.089**

p.1613, *revocation of the Welfare Reform Act 2012 (Commencement No. 9 and Transitional and Transitory Provisions and Commencement No. 8 and Savings and Transitional Provisions (Amendment)) Order 2013 (SI 2013/983) art. 5A (Transitional provision where Secretary of State determines that claims for universal credit may not be made: effect on claims for employment and support allowance and jobseeker's allowance)*

6.090   With effect from July 25, 2022, reg. 11 of, and Sch. para. 2(2) to, the Universal Credit (Transitional Provisions) Amendment Regulations 2022 (SI 2022/752) revoked art. 5A.

p.1615, *amendments to the Welfare Reform Act 2012 (Commencement No. 9 and Transitional and Transitory Provisions and Commencement No. 8 and Savings and Transitional Provisions (Amendment)) Order 2013 (SI 2013/983) art. 6 (Transitional provision: where the abolition of income-related employment and support allowance and income-based jobseeker's allowance is treated as not applying)*

6.091   With effect from March 30, 2022, art. 5 and Sch. 1 para. 1(3) of the Welfare Reform Act 2012 (Commencement No. 34 and Commencement No. 9, 21, 23, 31 and 32 and Transitional and Transitory Provisions (Amendment)) Order 2022 (SI 2022/302) omitted the phrase "or article 4(11) of the Welfare Reform Act 2012 (Commencement No. 32 and Savings and Transitional Provisions) Order 2019 (no claims for universal credit by frontier workers)" in art. 6(1)(e)(ii).
    With effect from July 25, 2022, reg. 11 of, and Sch. para. 2(3) to, the Universal Credit (Transitional Provisions) Amendment Regulations 2022 (SI 2022/752) omitted para. (1)(e)(ii) in art. 6 and the "or" preceding it.

pp.1663–1664, *annotation to the Welfare Reform Act 2012 (Commencement No. 20 and Transitional and Transitory Provisions and Commencement No. 9 and Transitional and Transitory Provisions (Amendment)) Order 2014 (SI 2014/3094)*

6.092   Article 6 of SI 2014/3094 (Transitory provision: claims for housing benefit, income support or a tax credit) was revoked with effect from July 25, 2022, by reg. 11 of, and Sch. para. 5 to, the Universal Credit (Transitional Provisions) Amendment Regulations 2022 (SI 2022/752).

pp.1670–1672, *amendment of the Welfare Reform Act 2012 (Commencement No. 21 and Transitional and Transitory Provisions) Order 2015 (SI 2015/33) art. 6 (Transitional provision: claims for housing benefit, income support or a tax credit)*

6.093   With effect from March 30, 2022, art. 5 and Sch. 1 para. 2 of the Welfare Reform Act 2012 (Commencement No. 34 and Commencement No. 9, 21, 23, 31 and 32 and Transitional and Transitory Provisions (Amendment)) Order 2022 (SI 2022/302) omitted the phrase "or by virtue of article 4(11) of the Welfare Reform Act 2012 (Commencement No. 32 and Savings and Transitional Provisions) Order 2019" in art.6(11). But note also the next entry.

pp.1670–1672, *revocation of the Welfare Reform Act 2012 (Commencement No.21 and Transitional and Transitory Provisions) Order 2015 (SI 2015/33) art.6 (Transitional provision: claims for housing benefit, income support or a tax credit)*

With effect from July 25, 2022, reg.11 of, and Sch. para.3 to, the Universal Credit (Transitional Provisions) Amendment Regulations 2022 (SI 2022/752) revoked art.6.   6.094

p.1674, *annotation to the Welfare Reform Act 2012 (Commencement No.23 and Transitional and Transitory Provisions) Order 2015 (SI 2015/634) (General Note)*

Delete the letter "a" after "These" in line 3 of the General Note at para.5.116.   6.095

p.1681, *amendment of the Welfare Reform Act 2012 (Commencement No.23 and Transitional and Transitory Provisions) Order 2015 (SI 2015/634) art.7 (Transitional provision: claims for housing benefit, income support or a tax credit)*

With effect from March 30, 2022, art.5 and Sch.1 para.3 of the Welfare Reform Act 2012 (Commencement No. 34 and Commencement No. 9, 21, 23, 31 and 32 and Transitional and Transitory Provisions (Amendment)) Order 2022 (SI 2022/302) omitted the phrase "or by virtue of article 4(11) of the Welfare Reform Act 2012 (Commencement No. 32 and Savings and Transitional Provisions) Order 2019" in art.7(2). But note also the next entry.   6.096

pp.1681–1683, *revocation of the Welfare Reform Act 2012 (Commencement No.23 and Transitional and Transitory Provisions) Order 2015 (SI 2015/634) art.7 (Transitional provision: claims for housing benefit, income support or a tax credit)*

With effect from July 25, 2022, reg.11 of, and Sch. para.6 to, the Universal Credit (Transitional Provisions) Amendment Regulations 2022 (SI 2022/752) revoked art.7.   6.097

p.1732, *amendment to the Welfare Reform Act 2012 (Commencement No. 31 and Savings and Transitional Provisions and Commencement No. 21 and 23 and Transitional and Transitory Provisions (Amendment)) Order 2019 (SI 2019/37) art.2 (Interpretation)*

With effect from July 25, 2022, reg.11 of, and Sch. para.4(2) to, the Universal Credit (Transitional Provisions) Amendment Regulations 2022 (SI 2022/752) omitted "and article 8(2)(b)" in art.2(3).   6.098

p.1734, *amendment to the Welfare Reform Act 2012 (Commencement No. 31 and Savings and Transitional Provisions and Commencement No. 21 and 23 and Transitional and Transitory Provisions (Amendment)) Order 2019 (SI 2019/37) art.6 (Transitional provision: termination of awards of housing benefit)*

6.099   With effect from July 25, 2022, reg.11 of, and Sch. para.4(3) to, the Universal Credit (Transitional Provisions) Amendment Regulations 2022 (SI 2022/752) substituted "in regulation 2 of the Universal Credit (Transitional Provisions) Regulations 2014" for "respectively in sub-paragraphs (h) and (l) of article 7(11) of the No.23 Order" in art.6(4).

p.1734, *amendment to the Welfare Reform Act 2012 (Commencement No. 31 and Savings and Transitional Provisions and Commencement No. 21 and 23 and Transitional and Transitory Provisions (Amendment)) Order 2019 (SI 2019/37) art.7 (Transitional provision: application to housing benefit of the rules in universal credit for treatment of couples and polygamous marriages)*

6.100   With effect from July 25, 2022, reg.11 of, and Sch. para.4(4) to, the Universal Credit (Transitional Provisions) Amendment Regulations 2022 (SI 2022/752) substituted "regulation 6A of the Universal Credit (Transitional Provisions) Regulations 2014" for "article 6 of the No. 21 Order or article 7 of the No. 23 Order" in art.7(1)(a)(i).

p.1735, *amendment of the Welfare Reform Act 2012 (Commencement No. 31 and Savings and Transitional Provisions and Commencement No. 21 and 23 and Transitional and Transitory Provisions (Amendment)) Order 2019 (SI 2019/37) art.8 (Transitional provision: where restrictions on claims for universal credit are in place)*

6.101   With effect from March 30, 2022, art.5 and Sch.1 para.4 of the Welfare Reform Act 2012 (Commencement No. 34 and Commencement No. 9, 21, 23, 31 and 32 and Transitional and Transitory Provisions (Amendment)) Order 2022 (SI 2022/302) inserted "or" at the end of art.8(1)(a) and omitted both art.8(1)(c) and the "or" preceding it. But note also the next entry.

pp.1735–1736, *revocation of the Welfare Reform Act 2012 (Commencement No. 31 and Savings and Transitional Provisions and Commencement No. 21 and 23 and Transitional and Transitory Provisions (Amendment)) Order 2019 (SI 2019/37) art.8 (Transitional provision: where restrictions on claims for universal credit are in place)*

6.102   With effect from July 25, 2022, reg.11 of, and Sch. para.4(5) to, the Universal Credit (Transitional Provisions) Amendment Regulations 2022 (SI 2022/752) revoked art.8.

p.1738, *amendment of the Welfare Reform Act 2012 (Commencement No. 32 and Savings and Transitional Provisions) Order 2019 (SI 2019/167) art.1 (Citation and interpretation)*

6.103   With effect from March 30, 2022, art.4(3) of the Welfare Reform Act 2012 (Commencement No. 34 and Commencement No. 9, 21, 23, 31

and 32 and Transitional and Transitory Provisions (Amendment))
Order 2022 (SI 2022/302) omitted art.1(3).

p.1742, *amendment of the Welfare Reform Act 2012 (Commencement No.
32 and Savings and Transitional Provisions) Order 2019 (SI 2019/167)
art.4 (Appointed day—coming into force of universal credit provisions and
abolition of income-related employment and support allowance and income-
based jobseeker's allowance: persons resident outside Great Britain)*

With effect from March 30, 2022, art.4(4) of the Welfare Reform Act   6.104
2012 (Commencement No. 34 and Commencement No. 9, 21, 23, 31
and 32 and Transitional and Transitory Provisions (Amendment))
Order 2022 (SI 2022/302) omitted art.4(11).

p.1745, *insertion of new Commencement Order at para.5.188 onwards.*

The Welfare Reform Act 2012 (Commencement No. 34 and Commencement No. 9, 21, 23, 31 and 32 and Transitional and Transitory Provisions (Amendment)) Order 2022

SI 2022/302 (c.12)

The Secretary of State makes the following Order in exercise of the powers conferred by section   6.105
150(3) and (4)(a), (b)(i) and (c) of the Welfare Reform Act 2012:

ARRANGEMENT OF ARTICLES

1. Citation
2. Interpretation
3. Full commencement of universal credit
4. Removal of restriction preventing frontier workers from claiming universal credit
5. Consequential amendments
Schedule: Consequential amendments

Citation

1. This Order may be cited as the Welfare Reform Act 2012 (Com-   5.188
mencement No. 34 and Commencement No. 9, 21, 23, 31 and 32 and
Transitional and Transitory Provisions (Amendment)) Order 2022.

Interpretation

2. In this Order—   5.189
"the No. 9 Order" means the Welfare Reform Act 2012 (Commencement No. 9 and Transitional and Transitory Provisions and Commencement No. 8 and Savings and Transitional Provisions
(Amendment)) Order 2013;

"the No. 32 Order" means the Welfare Reform Act 2012 (Commencement No. 32 and Savings and Transitional Provisions) Order 2019.

Full commencement of universal credit

5.190   **3.** 30th March 2022 ("the appointed day") is the appointed day for the coming into force of the provisions of the Welfare Reform Act 2012 listed in Schedule 2 (universal credit provisions coming into force in relation to certain claims and awards) to the No. 9 Order, in so far as they are not already in force.

Removal of restriction preventing frontier workers from claiming universal credit

5.191   **4.**—(1) The amendments of the No. 32 Order set out in paragraphs (3) and (4) have effect from the appointed day.

(2) The No. 32 Order is amended as follows.

(3) In article 1 (citation and interpretation), omit paragraph (3).

(4) In article 4 (appointed day—coming into force of universal credit provisions and abolition of income-related employment and support allowance and income-based jobseeker's allowance: persons resident outside Great Britain), omit paragraph (11).

Consequential amendments

5.192   **5.** The consequential amendments set out in the Schedule have effect from the appointed day.

SCHEDULE

Article 5

Consequential Amendments

5.193   **1.**—(1) The No. 9 Order is amended as follows.

(2) In article 5A (transitional provision where Secretary of State determines that claims for universal credit may not be made: effect on claims for employment and support allowance and jobseeker's allowance), in paragraph (1) omit "or article 4(11) of the Welfare Reform Act 2012 (Commencement No. 32 and Savings and Transitional Provisions) Order 2019 (no claims for universal credit by frontier workers)".

(3) In article 6 (transitional provision: where the abolition of income-related employment and support allowance and income-based jobseeker's allowance is treated as not applying), in paragraph (1)(e)(ii) omit "or article 4(11) of the Welfare Reform Act 2012 (Commencement No. 32 and Savings and Transitional Provisions) Order 2019 (no claims for universal credit by frontier workers)".

2.—(1) The Welfare Reform Act 2012 (Commencement No. 21 and Transitional and Transitory Provisions) Order 2015 is amended as follows.

(2) In article 6 (transitional provision: claims for housing benefit, income support or a tax credit), in paragraph (11) omit "or by virtue of article 4(11) of the Welfare Reform Act 2012 (Commencement No. 32 and Savings and Transitional Provisions) Order 2019".

3.—(1) The Welfare Reform Act 2012 (Commencement No. 23 and Transitional and Transitory Provisions) Order 2015 is amended as follows.

314

(2) In article 7 (transitional provision: claims for housing benefit, income support or a tax credit), in paragraph (2) omit "or by virtue of article 4(11) of the Welfare Reform Act 2012 (Commencement No. 32 and Savings and Transitional Provisions) Order 2019".

4.—(1) The Welfare Reform Act 2012 (Commencement No. 31 and Savings and Transitional Provisions and Commencement No. 21 and 23 and Transitional and Transitory Provisions (Amendment)) Order 2019 is amended as follows.

(2) In article 8 (transitional provision: where restrictions on claims for universal credit are in place)—
(a) at the end of paragraph (1)(a) insert "or"; and
(b) omit subparagraph (1)(c) and the "or" preceding it.

PART VI

TRANSITIONAL, SAVINGS AND MODIFICATIONS PROVISIONS

PART VII

IMMIGRATION STATUS AND THE RIGHT TO RESIDE

p.1793, *annotation to the Immigration (European Economic Area) Regulations 2016 (SI 2016/1052) (General Note—EEA nationals and their family members with pre-settled status)*

In *R. (Fratila) v SSWP* [2021] UKSC 53 the Supreme Court allowed the appeal by the Secretary of State against a decision of the Court of Appeal which had found reg.9(3)(c)(i) unlawfully discriminatory contrary to art.18 of the TFEU for treating EU nationals with pre-settled status differently to UK nationals. The judgment of the Court of Appeal had become unsustainable following the decision of the CJEU, in *CG v Department for Communities* (C-709/20) (July 15, 2021), that such a provision is not contrary to art.18 of the TFEU, or Directive 2004/38. 6.106

However, what the Supreme Court elected not to address (since it was a new point, which would have required new evidence) was the implications for the domestic Regulations of what had also been said in *CG* about the Charter of Fundamental Rights of the European Union (the Charter). The Court of Justice had stated:

"[93] . . . [Where] a Union citizen resides legally, on the basis of national law, in the territory of a Member State other than that of which he or she is a national, the national authorities empowered to grant social assistance are required to check that a refusal to grant such benefits based on that legislation does not expose that citizen, and the children for which he or she is responsible, to an actual and current risk of violation of their fundamental rights, as enshrined in Articles 1,

7 and 24 of the Charter. Where that citizen does not have any resources to provide for his or her own needs and those of his or her children and is isolated, those authorities must ensure that, in the event of a refusal to grant social assistance, that citizen may nevertheless live with his or her children in dignified conditions. In the context of that examination, those authorities may take into account all means of assistance provided for by national law, from which the citizen concerned and her children are actually entitled to benefit."

Important questions arising from *CG* are:

- whether the Charter has any ongoing application, since the end of the transition period in December 2020, for EU nationals resident in the UK on the basis of pre-settled status; and
- what if any substantive or procedural requirements are imposed on the Secretary of State by the obligation to 'check' that Charter rights will not be breached.

In *SSWP v AT (UC)* [2022] UKUT 330 (AAC) (December 12, 2022), a three-judge panel addressed those questions. It dismissed the Secretary of State's appeal against a decision that a destitute parent who was also a victim of domestic violence was entitled to UC. Though her only right of residence was on the basis of her pre-settled status, the refusal of UC would breach her Charter rights. The panel decided that by virtue of the Withdrawal Agreement, the Charter does indeed continue to apply following the end of the transition period where a person is residing in the UK with pre-settled status. It also decided that *CG* does indeed impose a requirement on the Secretary of State (and by extension the FTT) to check in individual cases that there is no breach of Charter rights. It gives guidance on how that check should be conducted. The Secretary of State has been given permission to appeal to the Court of Appeal.

p.1798, *annotation to the Immigration (European Economic Area) Regulations 2016 (SI 2016/1052) (General Note—Overview)*

6.107   In *FN v SSWP (UC)* [2022] UKUT 77 (AAC), Judge Ward records an example of the evidential problems which can arise for claimants seeking to demonstrate a right of residence under these Regulations:

"[4] . . . On the (erroneous) basis that it was necessary to demonstrate that the husband was a 'qualified person', the claimant, by her social worker, had informed the DWP that she and her daughter had fled the family home due to domestic violence and that the claimant had obtained a non-molestation order against her husband. His name, date of birth, national insurance number and details of his then current and previous employers were provided to the DWP, who were asked to contact them, as although the social worker had had some contact with the husband, he had been uncooperative in providing the information necessary.

[5] On mandatory reconsideration, the DWP upheld the original decision saying that the Data Protection Act prevented them from

providing the information relating to the husband that had been requested.

[6] On appeal, the DWP indicated they could provide information if in response to a tribunal or court order. The claimant's representatives emailed the FtT on 6 February 2020 explaining this and asking for an order to be made. The email did not on its face identify that the claimant and her husband were estranged due to domestic violence and that may have contributed to why the District Tribunal Judge (DTJ) refused the application, saying, put shortly, that the husband should get them and send them to the DWP and that the FtT would only become involved if the parties had exhausted their own efforts. This prompted a follow-up email on 16 March 2020 explaining the background of domestic abuse and providing a copy of the non-molestation order. The DTJ remained adamant, indicating that the order did not prevent the claimant from contacting her husband through solicitors and until there was evidence that an attempt had been made to do so and had been unsuccessful the decision remained unaltered. Subsequently, on 26 May 2020 a registrar did make an order for the evidence to be supplied by DWP but it was not, despite the representative sending a follow-up email. The case was then listed as a paper hearing, without further notification to the claimant or her representative, and decided [adversely to the claimant]."

As the facts of *FN* indicate, problems are particularly likely where a right of residence may derive from a family member from whom the claimant is estranged. A Tribunal's failure to exercise the FTT's inquisitorial duty to seek evidence of a right of residence, including by establishing details about a relative's identity and possible rights of residence, may constitute an error of law. See, e.g. *AS v SSWP (UC)* [2018] UKUT 260 (AAC); *ZB v SSWP* CIS/468/2017 unreported April 25, 2019 ([21]: "an award of benefit is not a prize rewarding only the most adept"), and *PM v SSWP (IS)* [2014] UKUT 474 (AAC). It is clear from those decisions that the Tribunal can direct the Secretary of State to provide information she holds about an estranged family member. Further, while the Secretary of State appears to consider that due to her data protection obligations she can provide information about such a third party only if ordered to do so by a court or tribunal, there is room for doubt about whether that view is in fact correct, as noted in *ZB* at [19].

pp.1826–1829, *annotation to the Immigration (European Economic Area) Regulations 2016 (SI 2016/1052) reg.4 ("Worker", "self-employed person", "self-sufficient person" and "student")*

Self-sufficient persons

In *VI v Commissioners for HMRC* (C–247/20 O) (September 30, 2021) **6.108** at [56]–[64], AG Hogan's opinion described a "fundamental question" in that case as "probably" being whether free access to the NHS satisfies the requirement to have CSI, and lamented that the UK Government had not made any submissions about that issue. However, the AG did not express an opinion on the answer, and advised the Court not to do so either.

Surprisingly, the court's judgment ([2022] EUECJ C-247/20 (March 10, 2022)) did give an answer, and the answer was that free access to the NHS does satisfy the CSI requirement:

> "[68] In the present case, it is apparent from the documents before the Court that VI and her son were affiliated during the period in question, namely from 1 May 2006 to 20 August 2006, to the United Kingdom's public sickness insurance system offered free of charge by the National Health Service.
>
> [69] In that regard, it must be recalled that, although the host Member State may, subject to compliance with the principle of proportionality, make affiliation to its public sickness insurance system of an economically inactive Union citizen, residing in its territory on the basis of Article 7(1)(b) of Directive 2004/38, subject to conditions intended to ensure that that citizen does not become an unreasonable burden on the public finances of that Member State, such as the conclusion or maintaining, by that citizen, of comprehensive private sickness insurance enabling the reimbursement to that Member State of the health expenses it has incurred for that citizen's benefit, or the payment, by that citizen, of a contribution to that Member State's public sickness insurance system (judgment of 15 July 2021, *A (Public health care)* (C–535/19) EU:C:2021:595 at [59]), the fact remains that, once a Union citizen is affiliated to such a public sickness insurance system in the host Member State, he or she has comprehensive sickness insurance within the meaning of Article 7(1)(b).
>
> [70] Furthermore, in a situation, such as that in the main proceedings, in which the economically inactive Union citizen at issue is a child, one of whose parents, a third-country national, has worked and was subject to tax in the host State during the period at issue, it would be disproportionate to deny that child and the parent who is his or her primary carer a right of residence, under Article 7(1)(b) of Directive 2004/38, on the sole ground that, during that period, they were affiliated free of charge to the public sickness insurance system of that State. It cannot be considered that that affiliation free of charge constitutes, in such circumstances, an unreasonable burden on the public finances of that State."

That decision is obviously inconsistent with a long line of domestic authority, cited in the main volume commentary: for example *Ahmad v Secretary of State for the Home Department* [2014] EWCA Civ 988; *FK (Kenya) v Secretary of State for the Home Department* [2010] EWCA Civ 1302; *W (China) and X (China) v Secretary of State for the Home Department* [2006] EWCA Civ 1494 and *VP v SSWP (JSA)* [2014] UKUT 32 (AAC) and *SSWP v GS (PC) (European Union law: free movement)* [2016] UKUT 394 (AAC); [2017] AACR 7.

VI falls within the scope of art.89 of the Withdrawal Agreement (as a CJEU reference made before the end of the Transition Period). As such, it so far appears to be uncontentious that *VI* is directly binding, in relation to periods before December 31, 2020, and that the old domestic authorities should no longer be followed. See *WH v Powys County Council and SSWP* [2022] UKUT 203 (AAC), para.3.

pp.1891–1892, *annotation to the Immigration (European Economic Area) Regulations 2016 (SI 2016/1052) reg.16 (Derivative right to reside)*

Primary carers of self-sufficient children

The main volume General Note discusses a pending reference to the CJEU in *Bajratari v Secretary of State for the Home Department* [2017] NICA 74. The Court's judgment (C-93/18) was delivered on October 2, 2019. It agreed with AG Szpunar and held (at [53]), that a Union citizen minor can meet the requirement to have sufficient resources not to become an unreasonable burden on the social assistance system of the host Member State during his period of residence, "despite his resources being derived from income obtained from the unlawful employment of his parent, a third-country national without a residence card and work permit". 6.109

pp.1892–1893, *annotation to the Immigration (European Economic Area) Regulations 2016 (SI 2016/1052) reg.16 (Derivative right to reside)*

Primary carer of children of migrant workers in education

The main volume General Note asserts: "Where primary carers are also jobseekers (in the EU sense of that term), they cannot be denied social assistance on the basis of the derogation in art.24(2) of the Citizenship Directive". There is now domestic authority for that proposition: *Sandwell MBC v KK and SSWP (HB)* [2022] UKUT 123 (AAC). 6.110

p.1893, *annotation to the Immigration (European Economic Area) Regulations 2016 reg.16 (SI 2016/1052) (Derivative right to reside)*

Primary carers of previously self-sufficient children with a right of permanent residence

Regulation 16(2) and reg.16(5) address the position of carers of *Chen* children and of *Zambrano* children respectively (*Zhu and Chen v Home Secretary* (C-200/02); *Zambrano v Office national de l'emploi (ONEm)* (C-34/09)). It might be thought that both groups are in essentially the same position, insofar as the carer's right of residence does not generate a right to reside triggering social security entitlement. However, the difference is that the *Chen* child may eventually acquire a right of permanent residence under Directive 2004/38 art.16. The situation of primary carers of *previously* self-sufficient children who *now* have a right of permanent residence is not recognised in domestic law. But in *FE v HMRC (CHB)* [2022] UKUT 4 (AAC) the Upper Tribunal decides that it is necessary to treat that category differently, and recognise their right of access to social assistance. 6.111

PART VII

FORTHCOMING CHANGES AND UP-RATING OF BENEFITS

FORTHCOMING CHANGES

Bereavement benefits

7.001
The Bereavement Benefits (Remedial) Order 2023 (SI 2023/134) came into force on February 9, 2023, although most of its provisions have effect from August 30, 2018. It represents the Government's response to *Re McLaughlin's Application for Judicial Review (Northern Ireland)* [2018] UKSC 48 and *R. (on the application of Jackson) v SSWP* [2020] EWHC 183 (Admin). The Order amends the Social Security Contributions and Benefits (Northern Ireland) Act 1992 and the Pensions Act 2014 in order to remove the incompatibilities with human rights. It also amends the Social Security Contributions and Benefits Act 1992 and the Pensions Act (Northern Ireland) 2015 to make the equivalent amendments to the legislation of Great Britain (in the case of widowed parent's allowance) and Northern Ireland (in the case of bereavement support payment) and, in relation to bereavement support payment, amends the Bereavement Support Payment Regulations 2017 (SI 2017/410) and the Bereavement Support Payment (No. 2) Regulations (Northern Ireland) 2019 (SR 2019/181).

Universal credit—administrative earnings threshold (AET)

7.002
The Universal Credit (Administrative Earnings Threshold) (Amendment) Regulations 2023 (SI 2023/7) came into force on January 30, 2023, and amended reg.99 of the Universal Credit Regulations 2013 (SI 2013/376), which sets out the circumstances in which work search and work availability requirements may not be imposed on a universal credit claimant (see further para.3.023 above). Regulation 99(6) is amended so that work search and work availability requirements may not be imposed where a single claimant has monthly earnings from employment that are equal to, or more than, 15 hours per week at the national minimum wage rate (as set out in reg.4 of the National Minimum Wage Regulations 2015). Where the claimant is a member of a couple, the threshold is where their combined earnings from employment are equal to, or more than, 24 hours per week at the national living wage rate. In both cases earnings are converted to a monthly amount by multiplying by 52 and dividing by 12.

Pilot scheme testing universal credit in-work conditionality extended for further 12 months

7.003
With effect from February 19, 2023, the Universal Credit (Work-Related Requirements) In Work Pilot Scheme (Extension) Order 2023

(SI 2023/157) extends the period for which the pilot scheme established under the Universal Credit (Work-Related Requirements) In Work Pilot Scheme and Amendment Regulations 2015 (SI 2015/89) takes effect for a further period of 12 months. The pilot scheme tests the imposition of work-related requirements on universal credit claimants in paid work where those requirements would otherwise be suspended by virtue of reg.99(6) of the Universal Credit Regulations 2013 (SI 2013/376)—see further Vol.II para.2.363. The provisions to enable the pilot scheme were originally due to end in February 2018, but have remained in place following a series of extensions each for 12 months.

Additional payments and tax credits

7.004   The Tax Credits Act 2002 (Additional Payments Modification and Disapplication) Regulations 2022 (SI 2022/1208) came into force on December 22, 2022, but regs 2–6 have effect from June 28, 2022. They modify the Tax Credits Act 2002 to create a distinct recovery mechanism for HMRC to recover additional payments made under ss.1(2) or 4(1) or (2) of the Social Security (Additional Payments) Act 2022 where it is determined that a person has received a payment of the additional payment to which they were not entitled

Winter heating payments in Scotland

7.005   Winter heating payments are being introduced in Scotland to replace Social Fund cold weather payments for those resident there. Whereas cold weather payments are payments of £25 in respect of each period of particularly cold weather during the winter, winter heating payments are payments of £50 (in 2022–23) payable each winter without needing to be triggered by any particularly cold weather. Otherwise, the conditions of entitlement are more-or-less the same.

People resident in Scotland ceased to be entitled to the Social Fund cold weather payments from November 1, 2022 (see paras 3.052 and 3.053, above).

With effect from January 25, 2023, the Winter Heating Assistance (Low Income) (Scotland) Regulations 2023 (SSI 2023/16) make provision for a winter heating payment to be made each winter to claimants entitled to specified benefits in the week commencing on the first Monday of November. The benefits specified are state pension credit and (subject to additional conditions aimed at targeting families that include a disabled adult or are responsible for a disabled child or young person or a child under the age of 5) universal credit, income support, income-based jobseeker's allowance, income-based employment and support allowance and "support for mortgage interest".

Generally, no claim is required for a winter heating payment because those entitled should be identified automatically.

NEW BENEFIT RATES FROM APRIL 2023

NEW BENEFIT RATES FROM APRIL 2023

(Benefits covered in Volume I)

	April 2022	April 2023
	£ pw	£ pw
Disability benefits		
Attendance allowance		
higher rate	92.40	101.75
lower rate	61.85	68.10
Disability living allowance		
care component		
highest rate	92.40	101.75
middle rate	61.85	68.10
lowest rate	24.45	26.90
mobility component		
higher rate	64.50	71.00
lower rate	24.45	26.90
Personal independence payment		
daily living component		
enhanced rate	92.40	101.75
standard rate	61.85	68.10
mobility component		
enhanced rate	64.50	71.00
standard rate	24.45	26.90
Carer's allowance	69.70	76.75
Maternity allowance		
standard rate	156.66	172.48

	April 2022 £ pw	April 2023 £ pw
Bereavement benefits and retirement pensions		
Widowed parent's allowance or widowed mother's allowance	126.35	139.10
Widow's pension *standard rate*	126.35	139.10
Retirement pension		
Category A or Category B (higher)	141.85	156.20
Category B (lower), Category C or Category D	85.00	93.60
New state pension	185.15	203.85
Dependency increase for child		
The only, elder or eldest child for whom child benefit is being paid	8.00	8.00
Any other child	11.35	11.35
Industrial injuries benefits		
Disablement benefit		
100%	188.60	207.60
90%	169.74	186.84
80%	150.88	166.08
70%	132.02	145.32
60%	113.16	124.56
50%	94.30	103.80
40%	75.44	83.04
30%	56.58	62.28
20%	37.72	41.52
unemployability supplement		
basic rate	116.60	128.40
increase for adult dependant	69.70	76.75
increase for child dependant	11.35	11.35
increase for early incapacity—higher rate	24.15	26.60
increase for early incapacity—middle rate	15.50	17.10
increase for early incapacity—lower rate	7.75	8.55
constant attendance allowance		
exceptional rate	151.00	166.20
intermediate rate	113.25	124.65
normal maximum rate	75.50	83.10
part-time rate	37.75	41.55

	April 2022	April 2023
	£ pw	£ pw
exceptionally severe disablement allowance	75.50	83.10
reduced earnings allowance—*maximum rate*	75.44	83.04
retirement allowance—*maximum rate*	18.86	20.76

Death benefit
widow's pension (higher rate) or widower's

	April 2022	April 2023
pension	141.85	156.20
widow's pension (lower rate)	42.56	46.86

"New-style" jobseeker's allowance

personal allowances

	April 2022	April 2023
aged under 25	61.05	67.20
aged 25 or over	77.00	84.80

"New style" employment and support allowance

personal allowances

	April 2022	April 2023
assessment phase—*aged under 25*	61.05	67.20
aged 25 or over	77.00	84.80
main phase	77.00	84.80
work-related activity component	30.60	33.70
support component	40.60	44.70

NEW BENEFIT RATES FROM APRIL 2023

(Benefits covered in Volume II)

Universal credit	April 2022	April 2023
	£ pm	£ pm
Standard allowances		
Single claimant—*aged under 25*	265.31	292.11
aged 25 or over	334.91	368.74
Joint claimants—*both aged under 25*	416.45	458.51
one or both aged 25 or over	525.72	578.82
Child element—*first child (if born before April 6, 2017)*	290.00	315.00
each other child	244.58	269.58
Disabled child addition—*lower rate*	132.89	146.31
higher rate	414.88	456.89
Limited Capability for Work element	132.89	146.31
Limited Capability for Work and Work-Related Activity element	354.28	390.06
Carer element	168.81	185.86
Childcare element—*maximum for one child*	646.35	646.35
maximum for two or more children	1,108.04	1,108.04
Non-dependants' housing cost contributions	77.87	85.73
Work allowances		
Higher work allowance (no housing element)		
one or more children	573.00	631.00
limited capability for work	573.00	631.00
Lower work allowance		
one or more children	344.00	379.00
limited capability for work	344.00	379.00
Pension credit		
Standard minimum guarantee		
single person	182.60	201.05
couple	278.70	306.85
Additional amount for child or qualifying young person		
first child (if born before April 6, 2017)	66.85	72.31
each other child	56.35	61.88

New Benefit Rates from April 2023

	April 2022 £ pm	April 2023 £ pm
Additional amount for severe disability		
single person	69.40	76.40
couple (one qualifies)	69.40	76.40
couple (both qualify)	138.80	152.80
Additional amount for carers	38.85	42.75
Additional amount for additional spouse in a polygamous marriage	96.10	105.80
Savings credit threshold		
single person	158.47	174.49
couple	251.70	277.12
Maximum savings credit		
single person	14.48	15.94
couple	16.20	17.84

NEW TAX CREDIT AND BENEFIT RATES 2023–2024

(Benefits covered in Volume IV)

HMRC-administered payments	2022–23	2023–24
	£ pw	£ pw
Benefits in respect of children		
Child benefit		
only, elder or eldest child (couple)	21.80	24.00
each subsequent child	14.45	15.90
Guardian's allowance	18.55	20.40
Employer-paid benefits		
Standard rates		
Statutory sick pay	99.35	109.40
Statutory maternity pay	156.66	172.48
Statutory paternity pay	156.66	172.48
Statutory shared parental pay	156.66	172.48
Statutory parental bereavement pay	156.66	172.48
Statutory adoption pay	156.66	172.48
Income threshold	123.00	123.00

Tax credits	2022–23	2023–24
	£ pa	£ pa
Working tax credit		
Basic element	2,070	2,280
Couple and lone parent element	2,125	2,340
30 hour element	860	950
Disabled worker element	3,345	3,685
Severe disability element	1,445	1,595
Child care element		
maximum eligible cost for one child	175 pw	175 pw
maximum eligible cost for two or more children	300 pw	300 pw
per cent of eligible costs covered	70%	70%
Child tax credit		
Family element	545	545
Child element	2,935	3,235
Disabled child element	3,545	3,905
Severely disabled child element	4,975	5,480

New Tax Credit and Benefit Rates 2023–2024

	April 2022	April 2023
	£ pw	£ pw
Tax credit income thresholds		
Income threshold	6,770	7,455
Income threshold for those entitled to child tax credit only	17,005	18,725
Scottish social security assistance		
Adult disability payment		
daily living component		
enhanced rate	92.40	101.75
standard rate	61.85	68.10
mobility component		
enhanced rate	64.50	71.00
standard rate	24.45	26.90
Child disability payment		
care component		
highest rate	92.40	101.75
middle rate	61.85	68.10
lowest rate	24.45	26.90
mobility component		
higher rate	64.50	71.00
lower rate	24.45	26.90
Scottish child payment	20.00[1]	25.00
	£	£
Best start grants		
Pregnancy and baby grant		
first child	642.35	707.25
subsequent child and additional payment for twins etc.	321.20	353.65
Early learning payment	267.65	294.70
School age payment	267.65	294.70

	April 2022	April 2023
	£ pw	£ pw
Funeral expense assistance		
standard rate	1,070.60	1,178.75
rate where the deceased has left in place a pre-paid funeral plan	130.65	143.85
maximum rate for removal of an implanted medical device by a person other than a registered medical practitioner	21.55	23.75
Young carer grant	326.65	359.65
Child winter heating assistance	214.10	235.70
Winter heating payment	50.00[2]	55.05
Carer's allowance supplement (bi-annual)	245.70	270.50

Notes: 1. Scottish child payment was increased to £25 pw from November 14, 2022.
2. Winter heating payments are introduced from January 25, 2023.

NEW BENEFIT RATES FROM APRIL 2023

(Benefits covered in Volume V)

	April 2022	April 2023
	£ pw	£ pw

Contribution-based jobseeker's allowance

Personal rates—*aged under 25*	61.05	67.20
aged 25 or over	77.00	84.80

Contributory employment and support allowance

Personal rates—assessment phase—*aged under 25*	61.05	67.20
aged 25 or over	77.00	84.80
main phase	77.00	84.80

Components		
work-related activity	30.60	33.70
support	40.60	44.70

Income support and income-based jobseeker's allowance

Personal allowances		
single person—aged under 25	61.05	67.20
aged 25 or over	77.00	84.80
lone parent—aged under 18	61.05	67.20
aged 18 or over	77.00	84.80
couple—both aged under 18	61.05	67.20
both aged under 18, with a child	92.20	101.50
one aged under 18, one aged under 25	61.05	67.20
one aged under 18, one aged 25 or over	77.00	84.80
both aged 18 or over	121.05	133.30
dependent child	70.80	77.78

Premiums		
family—ordinary	17.85	18.53
lone parent	17.85	18.53
pensioner—single person (JSA only)	105.60	116.25
couple	157.65	173.55
disability—single person	36.20	39.85
couple	51.60	56.80
enhanced disability—single person	17.75	19.55
couple	17.75	27.90
disabled child	27.74	30.17

	April 2022	April 2023
	£ pw	£ pw
severe disability—single person	69.40	76.40
couple (one qualifies)	69.40	76.40
couple (both qualify)	138.80	152.80
disabled child	68.04	74.69
carer	38.85	42.75

Income-related employment and support allowance

Personal allowances		
single person—aged under 25	61.05	67.20
aged 25 or over	77.00	84.80
lone parent—aged under 18	61.05	67.20
aged 18 or over	77.00	84.80
couple—both aged under 18	61.05	67.20
both aged under 18, with a child	92.20	101.50
both aged under 18, (main phase)	61.05	67.20
both aged under 18, with a child (main phase)	121.05	133.30
one aged under 18, one aged 18 or over	121.05	133.30
both aged 18 or over	121.05	133.30

Components		
work-related activity	30.60	33.70
support	40.60	44.70

Premiums		
pensioner—single person with no component	105.60	116.25
couple with no component	157.65	173.55
enhanced disability—single person	17.75	19.55
couple	25.35	27.90
severe disability—single person	69.40	76.40
couple (one qualifies)	69.40	76.40
couple (both qualifies)	138.80	152.80
carer	38.85	42.75